This book is about the formative years of the first field marshal in the Corps of Royal Engineers, John Burgoyne, and his service in the Napoleonic Wars. Burgoyne's early service was in the Mediterranean, followed by service in the Iberian Peninsula from 1808-1814. Having built up a good relationship with Wellington, Burgoyne was selected to command the engineers in the disastrous American campaign of 1814-15.

Burgoyne's father was also a well-known British general who, sadly, is remembered for his surrender of the British Army at Saratoga, rather than for more positive reasons. He died penniless, leaving his children, including John, to be cared for by family friends. Burgoyne seemed to spend the rest of his life working to obtain his independence. Like many engineers, Burgoyne kept detailed diaries, also writing comprehensive letters and analyses of his actions. These give contemporary knowledge of many notable events, particularly during the Peninsular War. His letters to fellow officers give an insight into the opinions and thoughts of an engineer officer, views which are often not visible in official communications.

The main theme of the book is to show the development of a young officer during the Napoleonic Wars from an inexperienced subaltern through to someone who advised Wellington and his generals directly on military matters. His involvement with the senior officers in the army was not restricted to 'engineering' matters and he was trusted to carry out staff roles on many occasions. Burgoyne was present at many of the sieges and commanded at some. There is a wealth of unpublished information in his journals and letters. Burgoyne was highly critical of some of the sieges, even those that were considered successful. He was also critical of those where he commanded, particularly, Burgos in 1812. When Burgoyne was advising Raglan in the Crimea at the siege of Sevastopol, the failures at Burgos were used to undermine his position.

The previous biography of Burgoyne by his son-in-law, George Wrottesley, was published nearly 150 years ago and is flawed in a number of ways. This new interpretation will help our understanding of this officer and present a different view on some of the key events during the Peninsular War.

Mark S. Thompson is an independent military historian specialising in the Peninsular War 1808-14. His first publication, *The Fatal Hill* covered the campaign culminating in the battle of Albuera in May 1811. In 2009, he completed a PhD focusing on the role of the Royal Engineers during this period. This was published as *Wellington's Engineers* in 2015. He has published several other books and journal articles on the period. He has presented at many conferences in the UK and abroad including the Wellington Congress and is a member of the British Commission for Military History, the Friends of the British Cemetery at Elvas, and the Friends of the Lines of Torres Vedras.

Wellington's Favourite Engineer

John Fox Burgoyne: Operations, Engineering, and the Making of a Field Marshal

Mark S. Thompson

Helion & Company Limited

Helion & Company Limited
Unit 8 Amherst Business Centre
Budbrooke Road
Warwick
CV34 5WE
England
Tel. 01926 499619
Email: info@helion.co.uk
Website: www.helion.co.uk
Twitter: @helionbooks
Visit our blog at http://blog.helion.co.uk/

Published by Helion & Company 2020
Designed and typeset by Mach 3 Solutions Ltd (www.mach3solutions.co.uk)
Cover designed by Paul Hewitt, Battlefield Design (www.battlefield-design.co.uk)

Cover: 'Storming of Ciudad Rodrigo, by the Light Division on the night of the 19th of January 1812…', colour aquatint by J.H. Clark and H. Merke (Anne S.K. Brown Collection).

ISBN 978-1-913118-93-8

British Library Cataloguing-in-Publication Data.
A catalogue record for this book is available from the British Library.

To Trish, my wife, for her constant support and for reminding me what is important in life

Contents

List of Maps and Illustrations

Preface

The first field marshal from the Corps of Royal Engineers was appointed to recognise the services to his country over a period of 71 years. John Fox Burgoyne's life was dedicated to his profession from entering the Royal Military Academy as a cadet in 1796 at the age of 14 until his retirement as field marshal in 1868 at the age of 86.

Although his illustrious father, Lieutenant General John Burgoyne, died penniless, Burgoyne could have had a life of luxury being taken into the household of Lord Derby (of horse racing fame) and treated like a member of his family. Burgoyne chose to make his own way, first enrolling at the Royal Military Academy and then pursuing a career in the military, never seeking to obtain patronage or wealth from his adopted family. By the Crimean War, Burgoyne's advice was eagerly sought by military and civilian leaders. The Burgoyne of Victorian England was forged in the furnaces of the Napoleonic Wars.

A junior engineer officer at the start of the 19th century had to learn fast, there was little peer support because there were so few officers in the field. For those chosen for field operations, there was only a journey in a ship from school field to battlefield.

Burgoyne from his first postings was recognised as a true professional by his peers and by the many senior army officers he came into contact with. He demonstrated characteristics that are as important today as they were 200 years ago and there is still much to learn from looking at his actions.

Throughout his military service he kept detailed diaries of his activities and the events in which he was involved and used this information to reflect and improve on his actions, learning from experience and from the experience of others. He readily shared his knowledge and challenged what he perceived as failures. He was not above directly criticising the actions and behaviour of his commanders, but this was often accompanied by explanations of why he thought differently.

In a number of his command positions, he faced the same challenges as an engineer officer often faces today, limited time and resources to achieve an objective where the consequences of failure could be severe. The mark of a good officer is one who can face these challenges and provide solutions that best meet the objective.

Burgoyne served with several well-known generals including Sir John Moore and the Duke of Wellington. They respected his competence and his opinions. It was said that Wellington tried hard to keep Burgoyne by his side in the later stages of the Peninsular War when other senior but less experienced engineer officers were available to command. It is almost certain that Wellington recommended Burgoyne to lead the engineers for the ill-fated American expedition of 1814.

What is certain is that the successes and failures of his service during the Napoleonic Wars formed the character and competence of an officer who would continue to serve his country for another fifty years.

This book takes a fresh look at the formative period in the life of one of the greatest officers ever to serve the Corps.

Lieutenant General Tyrone Urch CBE,
Chief Royal Engineer.

Foreword

In the late summer of 1813 Thomas Heaphy, an adventurous London artist, visited Wellington's headquarters in northern Spain with the idea of producing a grand work showing the victorious general and his staff on the field of battle. The painting took some years to finish and has since been lost, surviving only in a contemporary black and white engraving, but we still have the pencil and water-colour studies Heaphy made of individual officers. Among these is a young man with fair hair, pale blue eyes and a determined chin. This is Lieutenant Colonel John Fox Burgoyne, who by this time was the most experienced officer of the Royal Engineers attached to the army in the Peninsula, and Wellington's most trusted adviser on all matters concerning sieges and fortifications.

Although young – he was still only thirty-one years old when Heaphy made his study – Burgoyne had seen a great deal of action, including in both Malta and Egypt (1807), most of the Coruña campaign, and all of Wellington's operations from the spring of 1809 and the expulsion of the French from Oporto onwards. He was often employed, especially in the early part of the war, to survey the country through which the army might be operating, assessing the state of the roads, the difficulties of defiles and the capacity of bridges – essential information at a time when maps were few and unreliable. He was also present at many battles and other actions, often in the thick of the fighting if the three wounds suffered by his horse at Vitoria and the praise elicited from the French commander at El Bodón are any indication. But he deserves to be best remembered for the prominent part he played in the many sieges undertaken by the allied army. And in 1812, after the horrors of the storming of Badajoz, it was to Burgoyne that Wellington turned as the senior engineer officer to accompany his army in its advance to Salamanca, Madrid and, ultimately, Burgos.

Sieges were exceptionally dangerous for engineer officers, who were constantly in the trenches or guiding storming parties to the breach, and Burgoyne was exceptionally brave and cool under fire. He was also very lucky: wounded only once, at San Sebastian, when so many other engineers – including Richard Fletcher, his commander for most of the war – were killed in action or disabled for months by serious wounds.

As one of the central figures in shaping British tactics in a succession of sieges – not all of which proved successful, and none of them easy – Burgoyne's letters and journals give us important evidence into the conduct of some of Wellington's most controversial operations. However, until now historians have relied on the biography by Burgoyne published in 1873 by his son-in-law George Wrottesley. Like many biographers of his era, Wrottesley was anxious to protect his subject's reputation – Burgoyne had only died a couple of years before – and so he suppressed passages in the letters that did not reflect well on Burgoyne, or in which he thought that Burgoyne was too critical of Wellington's conduct of operations.

Now Mark Thompson, whose previous work has transformed our understanding of the role of the Engineers in the Peninsular War, has gone back to the original manuscripts and given us the real Burgoyne – the young, opinionated, forceful man in Heaphy's sketch – not Wrottesley's Victorian father-in-law. We see an unvarnished Wellington through the not always admiring eyes of an officer who worked closely with him, and come to appreciate the complexities of besieging fortresses that were so capably defended by the French. Anyone with a serious interest in the history of the British Army will turn to this book with eagerness and enthusiasm.

Rory Muir, July 2019

Acknowledgements

In my earlier research on the Peninsular War and the Royal Engineers, the name John Burgoyne kept appearing, often in unexpected places. This created an interest in knowing more about the man and the soldier. Reading Wrotteley's biography filled much of the detail, but, as I started discovering that it was not the full story, I wanted to retell his service in a different way as described by Rory Muir in his Foreword. To achieve this, I have had a great deal of help and would like to acknowledge this assistance.

I would like to thank Rory Muir for writing the foreword to this book and the many useful comments on the manuscript. More important is the constant help and advice over the last 15 years: he remains an inspiration to all modern Napoleonic authors. I would also like to thank Bob Burnham in a similar manner for his unstinting guidance over many years and for his management of the Napoleon Series website. It lives on in another form now but should not be forgotten. In this particular case I would also like to thank him for reviewing the draft manuscript and pointing out improvements. Any errors or omissions remain my responsibility.

Andrew Bamford, apart from being a scholar and author in his own right, is also my editor at Helion books. He had guided me through the process with quiet professionalism.

Since my first visit in 2004, I have returned many times to the Royal Engineers Museum to access their archives. Danielle Sellers and the rest of the team have been always very helpful in dealing with my incessant requests. I would especially like to thank Rebecca Nash, the Director of the Museum and Nigel Montagu, the Secretary of the Institution of Royal Engineers for allowing me to use images from their collection.

My interest in the Corps of Royal Engineers has brought me into contact with serving and retired officers and they have patiently listened to my enthusiasm. These include Major General (Ret'd) Mungo Melvin, Colonel (Ret'd) Gerald Napier, Lieutenant Colonel Séan Scullion, and Martin Stoneham, the Chairman of the Friends of the Royal Engineers Museum. I was very honoured to be the first speaker at the first conference of the Royal Engineers Historical Society in 2016 – talking about Burgoyne, of course.

There are several other people who have helped me on particular subjects. Colonel Nick Lipscombe and Dr Stephen Summerfield answered many questions about artillery; Marcus de la Poer Beresford and Moises Gaudencio about Beresford and the Portuguese army; Dr Janet MacDonald on the Corunna campaign; Carol Divall on Burgos particularly and Professor Bruce Collins on San Sebastian and sieges generally. Also, Gareth Glover who apart from answering many bizarre questions, like how heavy is 13-inch rope, gave me access to his images of the unpublished Clinton papers regarding the siege of the Salamanca forts.

There are many others who I have not mentioned by name. To all of you, I thank you for your support and sharing my passion for history.

Mark S. Thompson
www.marksthompson.co.uk

A Note on *Wellington's Despatches*

There are multiple editions of Gurwood's edited collection of *Wellington's Despatches* in circulation. As my primary source is the second (New and Enlarged edition), when citing from *Wellington's Despatches* I have included the details of the letter, including date, but not the volume and page number. This allows readers to use the first, 1837, 12 volume, edition to look up citations that were in the first edition (although obviously not those that were in the second edition only).

Introduction

> No two animals ever differed more completely ... than the British engineer and the British infantry soldier. The latter delights in an open field and a fair "stand-up fight" ... the engineer on the contrary, braves all the dangers of the siege with a cheerful countenance; he even courts them and no mole ever took greater delight in burrowing through a sandhill than an engineer does in mining a covered way, or blowing up a counterscarp. Not so the infantry soldier, who is obliged to stand to be shot at, with a pick axe or shovel in his hand instead of his firelock and bayonet.[1]

To Lieutenant William Grattan of the 88th Connaught Rangers, engineers were aliens. They were not understood and were to be feared. Dealing with them usually ended up with hard work and injury. His view was probably typical in the army and explains why it is difficult to get objective views on the major events where engineers were involved, usually sieges. It was simple: engineers organised sieges; soldiers got killed in large numbers in sieges; it must be the engineers' fault.

However, it was not that simple. Engineers played a much wider role in the operations of the army, even in the 19th Century. Today, the role of a Royal Engineer is threefold. First, they are soldiers, trained to fight; second, they are engineers to provide specialist military engineering services to the army; third, they are tradespeople, who are trained in a specific skill – joiners, electricians, and so forth. Two hundred years ago, the official role was to provide engineering services only, but they also informally took on many other tasks, as this book will demonstrate.

This book is about an engineer who learnt his trade in the field, commanded major engineering activities before he was 30, and, in later life, advised governments and the military on a wide range of civil and martial subjects. John Fox Burgoyne was the first officer from the Corps of Royal Engineers to attain the rank of field marshal in the British Army. In a military career that lasted 71 years, he attained the highest rank in the Corps as well as serving in numerous senior military and civil posts.

1 William Grattan, *Adventures with the Connaught Rangers* (London: Greenhill, 1989), p.105.

The typical image of John Fox Burgoyne is of the old man, a calm, experienced officer, and his role in the Crimean War is the most visible. However, there is a different side to this great man; the young officer looking to make his name. The young Burgoyne was proud, ambitious, full of energy, and had opinions on everything, from how to pack a mule to the faults of the great Duke of Wellington.

Burgoyne is best known through the biography, published in 1873, by his son-in-law, George Wrottesley who was also an officer in the Royal Engineers. Wrottesley served in the Crimean War and became Burgoyne's Aide-de-Camp until his retirement in 1868.

Wrottesley had the great advantage of being able to talk to Burgoyne as well as access his papers. One can see evidence of this as many of the papers in Royal Engineer archives have 'GW' written on them and on occasions his diaries are clearly marked with material which has or has not been used in his biography. Whilst some of his editing is understandable, other editing is a concern. The fact that Wrottesley gave no indication of when he had changed or omitted original material makes his biography a slightly unreliable source when writing on the life of Burgoyne.

Wrottesley removed much of the detail of the surveys and reconnaissances carried out by Burgoyne and this is understandable as it would be of limited interest to most readers. Yet, to students of logistics and Wellington's movements, this detailed information on routes shows a number of things including what Wellington faced when moving his troops and also the level of information on the roads, rivers and terrain that was available to Wellington. Wrottesley also removed much of the detail on the organisation and location of the army units. Again, much of this is available from other sources but the detail, sometimes, is relevant to students of Wellington's campaigns.

The most significant and worrying editing is where criticism of Wellington or Burgoyne are changed or omitted. Wrottesley completely ignored the occasion in late 1813 where Burgoyne was strongly criticised by Wellington for failing to move up the pontoon train. It feels like Wrottesley tried to change the public's perception of Burgoyne. The character portrayed by Wrottesley loses much of the passion, drive and ego that this future general had.

Finally, Wrottesley's biography tended not to comment on what Burgoyne wrote in his correspondence and the reader is left to form his own opinions and check facts himself. In many cases, what Burgoyne wrote was not always accurate. I will endeavour to point these out. Generally, throughout the book, I will be relying on my transcriptions from the original journals rather than Wrottesley's printed versions. However, there are some journals used by Wrottesley that are not in the Royal Engineers collection and Wrottesley had to be used on these occasions.

Burgoyne's military service can be split into three sections. The first covered his early career during the Napoleonic Wars including the War with America. The second covered his peacetime service between Waterloo and the Crimea. The third part was his service in the Crimea and after. This book will cover the first part of his service and will address some of the issues raised above. It will also introduce a great deal of information that was not available or accessed by Wrottesley. During this period, Burgoyne gained a lot of experience. However, his independent commands in Egypt, at Salamanca, Burgos and New Orleans, were difficult and success was limited, although his reputation did not seem to suffer at the time. Burgoyne's handling of the siege of Burgos in 1812 came back to haunt him in the Crimea when he was criticised over the advice he gave for the siege of Sevastopol.

This work on Burgoyne is also an opportunity to talk about some of the events that happened during the Peninsular War and analyse them in detail. So, on occasions I will dwell on points where there is a disagreement or confusion about an event which Burgoyne had some involvement in. For example, the decision on the routes taken by Moore's army in 1808 and the plan for the siege of Burgos in 1812.

This will also be an opportunity to evaluate Burgoyne's opinions on the events and the Royal Engineers. An undated document by Burgoyne, probably written soon after the end of the Napoleonic Wars, stated:

> The very despicable state of the engineer department in the field is too notorious to every officer of intelligence and experience in the British service. No general officer has served without having witness to the incapability of that department to execute the most common and necessary parts of their duties, but in the most dilatory and bungling manner.[2]

Why did Burgoyne feel so strongly about the capability and competence of the Royal Engineers? The short answer is, that he cared about the professionalism of the Corps which he served for his whole life. Some would say he was a 'moaner', but he was not just a moaner. He looked at events, analysed and critiqued them. On many occasions he offered improvements, often after discussing the issue with fellow engineers. Many of his papers of observations or evaluations found their way back to the School of Military Engineering where they are likely to have been included in the training of new engineers and sappers. This book will try and show that behind the criticism was usually someone trying to improve the systems.

At times it will appear that I am being critical of Burgoyne. Like all officers he had his own opinions. In his case, he wrote them down, so we can examine and critique them. We need to remember that Wellington thought highly of Burgoyne and trusted him, probably above all other engineer officers. It was almost certainly Wellington who pushed for Burgoyne being given command of the engineers for the American expedition in 1814 when there were many other engineer officers who were senior to him.

2 Royal Engineers Museum (REM), 4601-74, ff.120-125.

It is important that readers consider the purpose of letter writing in this period. As mentioned above, many of Burgoyne's letters appear highly critical. They were mostly written to close friends. Burgoyne will have had few peers who he could talk openly to. Other engineers were usually at some distance, so he had no-one to share his opinions and frustrations with. The analogy I would suggest is that many of these letters are the equivalent of talking with one's friends over a drink after work. Burgoyne's comments are sometimes outrageous, but the letters represent an opportunity for him to let off some steam. However, they do tell us a great deal about how he was thinking and feeling at the time.

As the war progressed, the number of correspondents decreased as his fellow officers were killed or invalided home. It is noticeable that, late in the war, many junior officers were writing to Burgoyne in confidence, sharing their concerns and experiences. Clearly Burgoyne was someone who could be trusted. Neither Richard Fletcher, the Commanding Engineer for most of the war, or his successor Howard Elphinstone generated that level of trust with their subordinates.

This book picks one of the officers out of my earlier work *Wellington's Engineers*[3] and allows us to dig a little deeper into the thoughts and services of someone who was, probably, Wellington's favourite engineer.

3 Mark S. Thompson, *Wellington's Engineers* (Barnsley: Pen & Sword, 2015).

1

Family and Early Life

John Fox Burgoyne's father was Lieutenant General John Burgoyne who commanded the British army that surrendered at Saratoga in 1777. As a young man, Burgoyne senior quickly gained a reputation as a gambler and womaniser, but he fell in love with Charlotte, the youngest daughter of Edward, 11th Earl of Derby. He first met her through his lifelong friendship with Lord Strange, Derby's eldest son. Derby was firmly against the relationship but Burgoyne eloped with Charlotte in 1751, marrying her the same year. They fled to the continent and Burgoyne sold his commission. Their only child, Charlotte-Elizabeth, who was born in 1754, sadly died at the age of 10.

John Burgoyne by Joshua Reynolds. (Public Domain)

Eventually, Burgoyne was reconciled with Lord Derby and they moved back to England. With Derby's support, Burgoyne re-joined the army in 1756, as a captain in the 11th Dragoons. Again with Derby's support, Burgoyne raised the 16th Light Dragoons in 1759, becoming the regiment's first colonel. Burgoyne also entered into politics and was a firm friend of Pitt the elder and Charles James Fox.

Burgoyne's wife died on 5 June 1776 while he was serving in North America. His subsequent campaign and his surrender of the British army at Saratoga were roundly condemned at the time although modern historians are more understanding of the circumstances.

In 1780, Burgoyne senior formed a long-term relationship with the actress Susan Caulfield. They never married but had four children. The eldest, John, was born in 1782 and when baptised, the statesman Charles James Fox was one of his godparents. In later life, Burgoyne senior became a successful playwright although he died penniless in 1792.[1] The four children from his relationship with Susan Caulfield were taken in and raised by Lord Derby.

Burgoyne junior, like many youngsters from wealthy families was privately educated, in his case in Cambridge until 1793. He was then sent to Eton for the next three years until October 1796, when he entered the Royal Military Academy at the minimum age of 14. The Royal Military Academy trained the artillery and engineer officers for the British military.

The decision for John to attend the Royal Military Academy is interesting. His father and grandfather both served in the Army, so a military career was not surprising. Burgoyne's financial position was weak. Although he and his siblings had been taken into the Stanley family, they had no independent wealth. John, as the eldest, probably felt great responsibility for his siblings.

Today, it is difficult to understand the maturity and responsibility required by a 14-year-old boy in the early 19th century. At this age, a young man might be leading soldiers or sailors into battle and would need a level of confidence that we would not expect today from someone that young. John, throughout his early career, was reluctant to accept money from Lord Derby to support his military life. This may have been part of the decision why the young man joined the Ordnance Corps rather than the army. One did not need to buy a commission in the Ordnance, which Burgoyne probably would have had to if he joined the army. Progression in the Ordnance Corps was based on seniority, not wealth. Based on the content of later letters, the present author entertains no doubts that Derby would have willingly bought a commission for John, but perhaps this was Burgoyne's first independent decision about his future and his desire to make his own way in the world.

However, to enter the Royal Military Academy required meeting two criteria. The first was the approval of the Master General of the Ordnance, who at this time was a member of the Cabinet in the British Government. This, of course, would not be a problem to someone with the connections that Lord Derby had. The second requirement was the passing of an entrance examination based on the 'The first four rules of arithmetic, with a competent knowledge of the rule of three and the elements of Latin grammar'.[2]

When Burgoyne arrived, the Academy at Woolwich housed 90 cadets. These cadets were being trained to serve primarily in the Royal Artillery with a small

1 His works included *The Maid of Oaks* (1774) and *The Heiress* (1776).

2 Francis Guggisberg, *The Shop* (London: Cassell, 1900), p.14.

number going to the Royal Engineers. Unlike the army, where there were no entry requirements outside of basic education, the Ordnance cadets had to pass final examinations before they were commissioned. If you failed the examinations, you were out. The training the cadets received was the same whether they wished to join the artillery or the engineers. The top cadets were given the choice on which corps they wanted to join and invariably opted for the Royal Engineers.

There was no fixed length for the training. Students, within reason, went at their own pace and sat the examinations when the masters felt they were ready. However, at this period, there was a huge demand for ordnance officers. The Academy doubled in size between 1793 and 1803. This demand for officers also led to some variation in the criteria to pass the examinations, with there being some relaxation in requirements when demand was highest. Burgoyne passed through the Academy during the period when the public examinations had been suspended, although that is not to say that he did not receive a thorough education. The fact he was commissioned in less than two years shows that Burgoyne was well versed in the requirements of the profession.

It is worth providing some detail on what a qualified Ordnance officer was expected to know. This is a summary of the Royal Military Academy Syllabus in 1792.

Fortifications
- The definitions and explanations of both regular and irregular Fortification,
- The construction of the 1st, 2nd and 3rd systems of M. De Vauban, described on paper. The same for Coehorn's and Cormontaigne's system
- The attack and defence of fortified places,
- The art of mining,
- The elements of field fortification,
- Tracing the ground; make plans with and without mathematical instruments,
- How to estimate the works of a fortification.

Artillery
- The definitions and explanations of the several parts of artillery; also, the general dimensions and construction of guns and mortars,
- The construction of brass and iron guns, mortars and howitzers,
- The construction of ship, garrison and travelling carriages, mortar beds,
- The same of the iron work for ship, garrison and travelling carriages,
- The different kinds of wood used for gun carriages and mortar beds,
- How to find the weight of guns, mortars and howitzers,
- To find the quantity of powder which a chamber contains,
- To find the diameter of shot and bores of guns,
- To find the weight of shot and shells,
- To find the number of shot and shells contained in a pile,
- To ascertain the number of horses necessary to draw the different guns,
- The number of men required to construct a battery in one night.

Mathematics

- Arithmetic, in all its parts,
- Logarithms, their nature, use and construction,
- Geometry, the theory from Euclid's elements four first books,
- Algebra, from the first elements, to the solution of cubic and higher equations,
- Trigonometry, with heights and distances,
- Mensuration, in superficies and solids, in theory and practice,
- Conic sections,
- Mechanics, including motions equable and variable, forces, constant, variable and percussive, gravity, sound and distances, inclined planes, projectiles, practical gunnery, pendulums, centres [sic] of gravity, percussion, oscillation and gyration, ballistic pendulum, etc,
- Fluxions,
- Hydrostatics and hydraulics, including the pressure, motion, and issuing of fluids, the filling and exhausting of vessels, specific gravities of bodies, syphons, pumps and diving bells,
- Pneumatics, the nature, properties, and effects of the air and the atmosphere,
- Resistance of fluids, as water, air, etc, with their action on bodies in motion,
- Gunnery, Robin's new principles of gunnery, experiments, particularly with the ballistic pendulum.

Drawing

- The human figure, perspective, light and shadows, aerial perspective; then to proceed to take views about Woolwich and other places.

The French Language

- Grammar and pronunciation, thoroughly learned, and the practical application of it. Translation, from English into French, and from French into English.

Chemistry

- A course of lectures in chemistry, the theory and practice of it, relative to artillery, as gun powder, the materials that compose it, metals, etc.

The Gentlemen Cadets are also taught Fencing and Dancing, the exercises of small arms, and light field pieces.[3]

The syllabus was designed to ensure that an Ordnance officer was capable of carrying out the duties of an artillery or an engineer officer. Burgoyne's time at Eton will have prepared him for the Academy both in terms of the requirement to study but also to survive in the 'boisterous' environment. Bullying and rowdy behaviour were both common at the Academy.

3 William D. Jones, *Records of the Royal Military Academy* (Woolwich: F.J. Cattermole, 1851), p.33.

Burgoyne was commissioned as Second Lieutenant in the Corps of Royal Engineers, on 29 August 1798. He was only 16 years old. Burgoyne's commission coincided with a change in the way that commissions were awarded. Until June 1798, all commissions were awarded into the Royal Artillery, with officers stating their preference to be transferred to the Royal Engineers. However:

> The Master-General … thinks it more advisable that a limited number of such cadets as may be found to have a turn for the [engineering] profession should (after being duly qualified at the Academy) be sent to some station where they may improve themselves … by acting as Assistant Engineers until vacancies occur for them in the Corps.[4]

The purpose of this change was to increase the practical experience that a new engineer officer had. The nature of the role meant that they would often serve with little peer support and required the confidence in their own abilities to convince a senior commander that they were competent to carry out the required tasks.

Burgoyne's first appointment to Dover met this new requirement.

4 Jones, *Records of the Royal Military Academy*, p.65.

2

Early Military Service to 1806

Burgoyne's first posting was to work on the defences around Dover. The Commanding Royal Engineer in the Southern Military District at this time was 53-year-old Lieutenant Colonel William Twiss. Twiss had seen much service in North America, he had been Commanding Royal Engineer under Burgoyne's father and was present at the surrender at Saratoga in 1777. Twiss subsequently spent some years improving the defences at Plymouth and Portsmouth before being tasked with improving the defences in Kent and specifically around Dover. Twiss went on to dig tunnels for the garrison barracks under the castle. No doubt he would have been very welcoming to the young and inexperienced Burgoyne, who was to spend the next 18 months under his command.

In March 1800, Burgoyne was appointed to the expedition heading for Egypt under Sir Ralph Abercromby.[1] There is no record, but based on his later behaviour, it seems likely that Burgoyne would have been actively seeking a field-based appointment. Burgoyne was one of a number of engineer officers who wanted to be field-based rather than garrison based. This same small group of officers would become Burgoyne's colleagues and friends for the next 20 years and more.

He initially embarked at Woolwich on 15 April 1800.[2] He joined the fleet transporting Abercromby's force at Spithead, leaving on 13 May 1800 and after some delays arrived at Lisbon on 13 June 1800. The fleet left the next day and after staying at Gibraltar for eight days, arrived at the British headquarters in the Mediterranean, at Minorca on 18 July 1800. The Lieutenant Governor at Minorca was Lieutenant General Henry Edward Fox, the younger brother of the politician Charles James Fox, Burgoyne's godfather.

The day after Burgoyne's arrival in Minorca, he noted in his journal that he 'was ordered to Malta in the *Cameleon*, sloop of war'.[3] Burgoyne, in later life, always

1 Wrottesley, *Life and Correspondence of Field Marshal Sir John Burgoyne* (London: Richard Bentley, 1873), Vol.I, p.6.

2 REM 4201-68, Memorandum, 15 April 1800.

3 REM 4201-68, Memorandum, 19 July 1800.

sought to be involved in active operations rather than the quieter life of a depot engineer and there is no reason to assume that he would have felt any different at the start of his career. The opportunity to be involved in the siege of Valetta (actually a blockade) was probably too good to miss for an inexperienced engineer. This would be Burgoyne's first experience of offensive engineering. Fox probably offered this opportunity to Burgoyne, and would continue to have a significant influence in Burgoyne's career for the next few years.

Certainly, the British forces on Malta were asking for such support. A recent modern thesis states 'When Brigadier General Thomas Graham landed in Malta in 1799 ... he had no engineers'. Graham initially resorted to employing a 'zealous and intelligent inhabitant' and his son as 'Assistant Engineers'.[4] Eventually, a number of Royal Engineer officers were sent to Malta during 1800, including Captains Samuel Dickens and William Gordon with Lieutenant James Arnold.[5]

Burgoyne arrived at Malta on 23 July 1800,[6] about six weeks before its surrender in September 1800. At this time, the British commander was Major General Henry Pigott who had arrived in May 1800 with reinforcements and had taken over command from Graham.[7] Burgoyne would serve with Graham a number of times in the coming years. A piece of good news also arrived soon after Burgoyne landed in Malta. He had been gazetted to first lieutenant on 1 July 1800, although the news would have taken several weeks to arrive.

Blockade of Malta 1799-1800

The near three-hundred-year rule of the Knights of Malta ended in June 1798 when Napoleon arrived on his way to Egypt and demanded access to the Maltese ports. When this was refused, he took the island and deposed the Knights. Initial Maltese civilian enthusiasm for the end of the rule of the Knights soon diminished as the French stripped the island of its wealth including looting the churches. Malta was a staunchly Catholic island. Following the destruction of the French Mediterranean Fleet at the Battle of the Nile on 1 August 1798, the French garrison on Malta found itself exposed and isolated.

The continued looting and destruction of church property eventually caused an insurrection in September 1798; the French retired to the forts at Valetta and

4 Andrew Phillipson, 'The Business of Engineers' (PhD Thesis, University of Portsmouth, 2007), p.45.

5 T.W.J. Connolly and R.F. Edwards, *List of Officers of the Corps of Royal Engineers* (Chatham: Royal Engineers Institute, 1898). See also T.W.J. Connolly, *History of the Corps of Royal Sappers and Miners* (London: Longman, Brown, Green and Longman, 1855), Vol.I, p.121.

6 REM 4201-68, Memorandum, 23 July 1800.

7 William James, *The Naval History of Great Britain, from the Declaration of War by France in 1793 to the Accession of George IV* (London: Richard Bentley, 1886), Vol.III, p.21; John Murray Graham, *Memoir of General Lord Lynedoch* (London: Blackwood, 1868), pp.28-29.

on the island of Gozo. The rebels appealed for help and received supplies from the Royal Navy who also blockaded the French ships in Valetta harbour. Rear Admiral Nelson saw the value of Malta as a secure harbour for the navy and wrote frequently to the commander of the British army in the Mediterranean, asking for forces to be sent to secure it.

This blockade and siege continued for two years until the French finally surrendered in September 1800. The initial attacking force primarily made up of Maltese citizens and a few Royal Navy sailors was increased by 800 when Graham arrived in December 1799. An additional force of Neapolitan troops also arrived in February 1800. Graham commanded for the next several months until superseded (at his own request) by Pigott, who received the French surrender on 4 September 1800.

Burgoyne's first experience of attacking a fortress lasted about six weeks. He was now about to spend six years on the island. He would have regretted his decision to go to Malta rather than wait for the fleet with Abercromby's army to sail to Egypt.

On being made Commander-in-Chief of the British forces in the Mediterranean in 1801, following the death of Abercromby in Egypt, Lieutenant General Fox moved to Malta from Minorca. It was a better location for the Mediterranean commander, having a central location and therefore in a better position to send and receive communications. It also meant that Burgoyne was again in contact with his patron.

On 18 February 1802, Burgoyne was appointed ADC to Fox. This was a slightly unusual step. Ordnance officers did not usually serve on a general's staff as they were, technically, not part of the Army. Such an appointment would be resented by Army officers who felt that their opportunities for advancement were being reduced by non-army officers taking prominent positions.

However, in the early 1800s there were almost no army officers trained to carry out staff roles. The Royal Military College, the brainchild of Colonel John Le Marchant, was not opened until May 1800, with the Senior Department not receiving its warrant until 1802. Royal Engineer officers were seen as a good alternative, if they could be spared. A small number of engineer officers held staff roles in the Mediterranean in the early 1800s but by the Peninsular War the practice was being actively discouraged.

In Burgoyne's case, this appointment was most likely due to the continued patronage of Lieutenant General Fox. However, Burgoyne's role as ADC was short lived. The war ended, temporarily, with the Peace of Amiens in March 1802 and Fox left Malta in July 1802, heading back to Britain, having been appointed to be Commander-in-Chief in Ireland. Burgoyne remained on Malta until 1806.

During his time in the Mediterranean, Burgoyne will have met several of the senior officers who would later serve in the Peninsula. These included John Moore, Thomas Graham, Rowland Hill, and Lowry Cole. Strong friendships were also formed with Royal Engineer officers such as Charles Lefebure, John Jones, Charles Pasley, Charles Boothby, John Squire and Edmund Mulcaster, Burgoyne would write and receive letters from these officers regularly throughout the war. There is little information on what Burgoyne did through this period but it is probable that he would have been involved in improving the defences on the island.

The end of the war in 1802 gave officers an opportunity to travel and Burgoyne embarked on a trip to the Eastern Mediterranean. The purpose of the journey is not clarified in his journal. Wrottesley wrote that Burgoyne, although taking leave, had been asked to visit the 'Turkish Pasha', present a plan of Cairo and seek further details on a request from the Pasha to produce a plan for a fortified camp for Cairo. The service 'was executed with so much judgement, that the Pasha presented him before leaving with a valuable Damascus scimitar'.[8]

Burgoyne's Journal noted that on 29 July 1802, he embarked on the appropriately named, *Adventure,* transport, with Major Alexander Bryce RE and Captain John Williamson RA. The party arrived at Alexandria on 6 August 1802 and then travelled down the Nile to Cairo. No further details are given on their activities in Cairo, but this is when Burgoyne would have visited the Pasha. Returning to Alexandria, Burgoyne headed into the Aegean, arriving at Stancho (Kos) on 15 September 1802, travelling past Samos island and arriving at Smyrna (Izmir) on 27 September 1802.[9] He was back in Malta in December 1802 where he reported to the Governor, Alexander Ball, some information he had collected on French activities in the Ionian Islands. Ball wrote to Burgoyne on 24 December 1802 asking him to provide further information and told him that he would be passing the information on to the British Government. Napoleon's activities in the Adriatic were of great interest and concern to the British government. If Napoleon controlled the Adriatic, then they were next to the crumbling Ottoman Empire which was seen as ripe for conquest and, with Egypt, a possible route to India. Burgoyne's trip to Egypt would prove useful to him in the future.

Following the Peace of Amiens, a sense of mutual distrust existed between the main parties. Napoleon continued to annex various states around Europe and Britain delayed handing back Malta to the Knights of St John. Britain was very concerned that Napoleon would fund the continuance of the Knights in exchange for use of the island. Also, the Maltese population did not want the Knights back and no-one was willing to force them. Britain's failure to return Malta to the Knights was given as one of the main reasons for the war restarting. In truth, no-one appeared to believe that war was not going to happen anyway. In May 1803, Britain and France were at war again.

The events of the last few years had shown Britain the importance of having a strong presence in the Mediterranean. The brief period in 1796-97 when Britain was forced out of the Mediterranean had shown how vulnerable the land routes to India would be if this happened again. Retention of Malta and the support of the Neapolitans in Sicily were now deemed as critical and both islands would be

8 Wrottesley, *Burgoyne*, p.10.

9 These travel details are taken from REM 4201-68, Memorandum.

substantial reinforced and fortified. Burgoyne would remain on Malta until summer 1806, missing both Lieutenant General James Craig's and Major General John Stuart's expeditions. It was probably even more galling when he received letters from his fellow engineer officers who were part of the operations.

Charles Boothby RE. (Author's collection)

Craig commanded a force which was to land at Naples and co-operate with a larger Russian force under General Lacy. In conjunction with this landing, the Austrian and Russian forces were to attack the French in central Europe. The Neapolitan defence was rendered impossible by the French victories at Ulm and Austerlitz. Craig's force disembarked at Naples around 26 November 1805 and remained there until 19 January 1806, when, despite protests from the Queen of Naples and the British Ambassador, Craig withdrew his forces to Sicily.[10]

Lieutenant Charles Boothby RE writing to Burgoyne from Naples Bay on 22 November 1805, reporting their arrival and giving news of the advance of the Russian forces. He also mentioned news of the victory at Trafalgar, although they did not know of Nelson's death at that time. Boothby's letter quickly moved on to other matters which concerned the young engineers such as the delay to their theatrical performance caused by being appointed to the expedition. This was a subject that Boothby mentioned in several of his letters and clearly was something that took up much of their leisure time.[11]

Captain Charles Pasley RE, wrote to Burgoyne on 27 January 1806, reporting his return from 'this ridiculous expedition':

> Yet, I do not regret having been in this affair. I have seen a country whose beauty, variety and fertility exceed every idea that could be formed from

10 Bunbury, *Narratives of some Passages of the Great War with France* (London: Richard Bentley, 1854), pp.211-12.

> description, I have had a hasty view of some of the many remains of antiquity and natural curiosities.[12]

Pasley finished his letter asking what Burgoyne thought about a model of a telegraph that he had built. Burgoyne responded on 19 February 1806:

> The telegraph is finished and … it appears to me to answer as well as you could possibly have expected … We have had an idea of revenging ourselves for being so laughed at by the expedition people for not being able to join the party to [?] Milan etc. etc. We were to have sent you a model of a medal cast in lead which was to have been presented to the officers of the army by the King of Naples after the manner of the Egyptian medals, on one side were to be seen the troops as embarking from Naples and the inscription (Naples A.D. 1806) on the other a man climbing over a fence to rob an orchard sees the owner of it on the other side the inscription (Sawney where are you ganging? Back Again). You recollect the story in Joe Miller of course. The Malta library has been taken by the gun boats at Gibraltar, but we expect to redeem them in which case we shall be gainers [sic], as we shall get the whole insurance and probably purchase them in at half price … Cricket is all the rage here at present; we play twice a week and our mess has challenged the garrison, but they are afraid of us. You have among your Clerks of Stores a man who was once the best player in England. His name is I believe, Ailward … You have been bridge building; prey let me have some particulars the next time you write.[13]

Pasley was one of the most forward-thinking of the engineer officers at this time. He is most well-known for his crusade to establish the School of Military Engineering, which opened in 1812. This materially improved the training of sappers and junior officers. Pasley was also fascinated with telegraphs and invented several different designs through this period. The model had been built to be sent to England to demonstrate the workings of his new design.

Burgoyne's teasing about the failure of the expedition will have disguised the frustration that many of the officers would have felt when they were not appointed to it. Joe Miller was a famous 18th Century actor, known for his seriousness. After his death, a joke book was published in his name which proved very popular. One of the stories in the book was the legend of Sawney Bean, a Scottish cannibal who allegedly killed and ate 1,000 people.

There is a theme in many letters from officers based in the Mediterranean at this time. They clearly had a lot of time on their hands. The threat of attacks on the

12 British Library (BL), ADD MS41961, Pasley Papers, Vol.I, f.313.
13 BL ADD MS41961, Pasley Papers, f.317.

various islands was real but there was little to do until the event happened. This explains both the desire to go on any expedition and also the leisure activities that most of them were involved in. There was only so much time that one could spend hunting. The Malta library was one example. The engineers at the main bases created libraries through membership and subscription. The subjects were general military so that there were opportunities for learning during the quieter periods. The theatre was another example of their activities and Boothby wrote a number of letters to report on him setting up a theatre at Messina and asking Burgoyne to visit Sicily due to the 'theatrical advantages resulting from your presence'. So, Burgoyne was clearly involved in the theatrical scene.[14] Of course, there was always sport as well. James Aylward was a famous English cricketer. His record score of 167 in 1777 stood for 43 years. By 1806 his 'professional' playing days were over, he was about 65 years old, but was probably still the best cricketer on the island.

Burgoyne's final point demonstrates the professional interest and knowledge-sharing that went on between the engineer officers. They were always looking to learn from other experiences. Pasley obviously provided details of his bridging activities and Burgoyne acknowledged them in a subsequent letter: 'Many thanks for … your ample account of the bridge over the Garigliano; I shall be very glad to hear an account of any professional operations you may happen to be witness to or employed in'.[15]

After a month's delay, approval was given by the Neapolitan government for Craig to land his troops in Sicily. The French arrived at the Strait of Messina a few weeks later, having taken Naples; only the fortress of Gaeta refusing to surrender. Ill health forced Craig to return to England in March 1806 leaving Stuart in command of the British Army.

Under intense pressure from the Neapolitan monarchy and the British Ambassador and not helped by the antics of Admiral Sir Sidney Smith, Stuart landed a force on the Calabrian mainland, his information being that Reynier's French troops were spread out and exposed. Arriving in the Bay of Santa Eufemia on the 30 June 1806, Stuart disembarked his troops over the next three days. With him were a number of engineer officers under the command of Captain Charles Lefebure. These included Captains Charles Pasley, John Jones, and William Nicholas, with Lieutenants Charles Boothby and George Hoste. Most of these officers corresponded with Burgoyne. Stuart immediately ordered the engineers to build a redoubt to protect the landing site but this was not fully complete when he moved forward on the morning of 4 July 1806. Boothby noted that as junior officer he was left to finish the task, his disappointment being 'childish and excessive'.[16] Stuart moved forward to meet Reynier in the vicinity of Maida and defeated him.

14 REM 4601-74, letters from Boothby dated 22 April 1806 and 11 May 1806.

15 BL ADD MS41961, f.319.

16 Boothby, *Under England's Flag* (London: A&C Black, 1900), p.71.

During the battle itself, Lefebure had a horse shot from under him and Nicholas wrote that his cloak was taken off the back of his horse by a cannon ball.[17]

Burgoyne, still stranded on Malta, kept in contact with the activities of his fellow officers. Lieutenant Thomas Dyneley RA, who was at the Royal Military Academy at the same time as Burgoyne, received a letter from him whilst still at St Eufemia and replied immediately:

> I have this instant received your letter and have sat down under a hedge to answer it. I suppose, before this reaches you, you will have heard of the dressing we have given Mr Reyney (I know not how his name is spelt) [Reynier]. All our lads are well, as yet, we have only three men wounded and two horses killed.[18]

Burgoyne must have also written at the same time to Pasley. He had heard that Pasley had been at Gaeta, which probably was a surprise as the Neapolitan Governor, Prince Louis of Hesse-Phillippsthal, had refused all assistance from Major General Stuart. Burgoyne asked for details of his visit and then went on to comment that he believed that it was unlikely that Fox would be re-appointed to command in the Mediterranean: 'his health from all accounts, is very bad and in point of emolument I should imagine he would be rather a loser giving up the immediate command of Gibraltar'.[19] Fox, had, in fact, been appointed to the command in April 1806 but did not set foot on Sicily for about three months. Also appointed as Fox's second in command was Lieutenant General John Moore. Pasley did not reply to Burgoyne until 19 August 1806, but he must have received the letter the same time as Dyneley:

> I received your letter of the [left blank] in camp at Sta Euphemia the day after the battle which I am sorry I neglected answering then ... I attached myself to the light infantry who were the first corps engaged and had the pleasure of witnessing the famous charge [of the 20th Regiment] in which they ran down the horses of Marengo like a flock of sheep ... Our duties as engineers, except at Scylla has been very trifling. An entrenchment at Sta Euphemia; reports on one or two positions.

Pasley went on to relate that Sir Sidney Smith 'has lost the good grace of the army' by interfering up and down the coast and failing to support the defenders at Gaeta as he had promised. His letter continued:

17 *Royal Military Chronicle*, First Series, (London: Davis, 1812), Vol.V, pp.253-4.

18 REM 4601-74, Dyneley to Burgoyne, St Eufemia, 6 July 1806.

19 BL ADD MS41961, f.330, Burgoyne to Pasley, 25 June 1806.

> You ask me the particulars of the operations at Gaeta. Whilst I was there, they were rather uninteresting. The great cause of the fall of that place was the Prince of Hesse, a man who without the smallest military knowledge or talents, believed he was a greater general than Caesar, who obstinately refused the assistance of the English army, of whom he was jealous and hateful and without the smallest foresight expended his powder shot and shells in an incessant fire, with little adequate effect, upon the enemy's trenches, ruining his guns before they almost returned a single shot … as soon as he was wounded things fell into the utmost confusion … A council of war was held, and the place was surrendered to the French … the English Navy who were cooperating were neither acquainted or included, so that some seamen and marines who were doing duty on shore might have fallen into the hands of the enemy. There were two breaches open but not practicable.

Pasley finished his very long letter to say that Lefebure had fallen out with Pasley and Stuart on account of Pasley having been ordered to Gaeta. Lefebure also argued with several other engineer officers before he went home. This quarrel soured relationships amongst the engineers for some years. Fortunately, Burgoyne managed to keep out of the disagreements.[20]

Charles William Pasley RE. (Royal Engineers Museum)

Burgoyne's reply of 4 September 1806, said Pasley's letter had 'afforded me much entertainment' although he did commiserate with the difficult position that Pasley was in. Of more importance was the news that Burgoyne had been given permission to leave Malta, either to go to Sicily or home to England. Having been away from home for six years, he was given the opportunity to spend some time in England. Burgoyne clarified that:

20 BL ADD MS41961, f.326, Pasley to Burgoyne, Messina, 19 August 1806.

> My desire is to join the army, but I fear if I do it immediately, General Fox will think I am sneaking for something, I shall therefore defer it for a short time after which I hope it will not have that appearance.[21]

Fox had arrived in Sicily in mid-July. Others, knowing that Fox was Burgoyne's patron, expected Burgoyne to go to Malta. Every officer in the Mediterranean wanted to be in Sicily as this was where the Commander-in-Chief was based and where officers would be selected for future expeditions. It is surprising that Burgoyne felt the need to delay his move to Sicily. The delay, however, was not that long, as he left Malta on 30 September, arriving at Messina on 4 October 1806.

Clearly, some officers were waiting for Burgoyne to arrive at headquarters. Captain Williamson wrote to Burgoyne asking for advice on writing directly to General Fox about his artillery company being employed on active service. Williamson had been at Malta on garrison duty for a number of years and felt that other artillery companies were getting the opportunities through favouritism and patronage. Burgoyne's advice included being as concise as possible as 'the general detests long letters' a point also made by John Moore.[22] Williamson also acknowledged in his letter that he was taking this action without the knowledge of his commanding officer and accepted that:

> Colonel Lemoine[23] would be hurt and feel piqued at my having taken this step without his knowledge. I have sent him a copy of my letter to the Commander in Chief.

It would probably take a lot more than sending a copy of his letter, to sooth the 'hurt' of his commanding officer. Williamson's motives for writing to Burgoyne were clearly explained in his letter:

> Knowing how much a young man is brought forward into notice by being near the person of the Commander in Chief, it was therefore with much satisfaction that I learnt of your being called over to Sicily, though from your acquaintance with General Fox, every reason was afforded and I certainly did expect, that such would be the case and notwithstanding that plea of more engineers being wanted was given as reason for your going, yet, I always thought it was the intention, and still think so, of the Commander in Chief to employ you on his staff.[24]

21 BL ADD MS41961, f.345.

22 Carola Oman, *Sir John Moore* (London: Hodder and Stoughton, 1953), p.377.

23 Lieutenant Colonel John Lemoine RA.

24 REM 4601-74, Williamson to Burgoyne, 23 October 1806. Williamson sent two more letters to Burgoyne asking him to speak on his behalf on 23 and 24 November 1806.

Burgoyne had clearly suggested to Williamson that he was considering a role on Fox's staff and away from the tedious garrison duty at Malta. His chance to get away from garrison duty would come sooner than he expected.

In the short term, Burgoyne settled into life on Sicily as an engineer officer, not as a member of Fox's staff. However, he would have spent some time with Fox and no doubt would have met his second-in-command, Moore, a man who would be very important to the next two years of Burgoyne's life. Burgoyne wrote a long letter to fellow engineer, Pasley on Christmas Day 1806. He commented on an idea that Pasley had been considering for some time; the publication of a book on the superiority of the British nation and soldier in times of war:

> I think you might make an excellent work, but I would not have it done through the medium of a newspaper, where it must necessarily be missed by all who do not happen to take that particular paper, but published as a distinct work with your name boldly prefixed to it. I think you might gain great credit if you could be induced to do something of this sort and such a subject would be admirable to begin upon as it must be popular.

It was four more years before Pasley completed the work. The *Essay on the Military Policy and institutions of the British Empire, Part 1,* was very well received in military circles and was reprinted three times over the next few years.[25] The significance of 'Part 1' was that Pasley said Part II would highlight the deficiencies in the Board of Ordnance, a brave move for a young captain in the Royal Engineers.

William Nicholas RE. (Author's collection)

Burgoyne finished his letter saying Lefebure had fallen out with another engineer officer, Nicholas, and was still trying to cause trouble for Pasley. Burgoyne's relationship with Lefebure remained good.

With the end of 1806, Burgoyne's period of relative inactivity in the Mediterranean came to an end and he would now serve in the field, almost without break for the next eight years.

25 Charles William Pasley, *Essay on the Military Policy and institutions of the British Empire, Part 1* (London: Edmund Lloyd, 1810).

3

1807 – Sicily, Egypt, and Moore's Portuguese and Swedish Expeditions

Burgoyne's year started quietly. He noted in his journal on 22 January 1807, 'Set out from Messina with Captain Lefebure; made a tour of Augusta, Catania and Syracuse and returned 4 February 1807'.[1] Burgoyne must have been unaware of plans for an expedition when he set off on his tour of Sicily as he sailed less than a month after his return. It is unlikely that he or Lefebure, his commander, would have gone on a two-week trip if they had known an expedition was imminent.

The reasons for mounting an expedition to Egypt in 1807 were very different from those for the attack in 1801. Previously, it was to support the Turks in ejecting the French forces under Bonaparte from the country. In 1807 it was to put pressure on the Turks, who, under French threats, had removed pro-Russian leaders from Moldavia and Wallachia and replaced them with pro-French leaders. The Tsar took exception to this action and invaded the provinces. England as a Russian ally was duty bound to support. The British response was in two parts. The first was to send a squadron under Vice Admiral Duckworth to blockade Constantinople and demand the surrender of the Turkish fleet. The second was an attack on Egypt, specifically Alexandria, as the British government were concerned that if the French gained possession of Egypt this could turn into a threat to India.

Duckworth arrived in the Dardanelles in February 1807. The Turks inflicted significant damage to the British ships on 3 March 1807 and Duckworth realised that even with the support of the Russian Fleet under Vice Admiral Dmitry Siniavin, he could not succeed as he had no troops to land to attack the Turkish batteries. Although Fox had known of his Government's intentions since November 1806, he waited until he had news from Constantinople before he sent the force to Egypt.

In February 1807, Fox appointed Burgoyne as Commanding Royal Engineer (CRE) under Major General Alexander Mackenzie Fraser, for the expedition

1 REM 4201-68, Memorandum, 22 January 1807.

to take Alexandria. Burgoyne had missed the Egyptian campaign of 1801, the Naples campaign of 1805-6, and the Maida campaign of 1806. It is highly likely that Burgoyne would have been seeking his patron's support to get appointed to the next expedition. This was why Burgoyne had moved from Malta to Sicily. Burgoyne, then aged 24, heard about his appointment on 10 February 1807 in a letter from his commanding officer, Lefebure:

> I am to inform you that his Excellency, General Fox has been pleased to appoint you Commanding Engineer to the expedition [to Egypt]. The officers who are to accompany you in this service are Captain Nicholas and Lieutenant Hoste, the former to continue in his situation on the staff [in the Quartermaster General's Department].[2]

Fraser's 6,000 troops were embarked in mid-February, but the fleet did not sail until 6 March 1807. The eternal problem of bad weather intervened and on 7 March, the fleet was dispersed with about 2,000 men arriving at Alexandria on the 16 March and the remainder on 22 March.

Throughout the expedition, poor information was provided to Fraser by the local British Consul, Major Ernest Misset, and this was a significant factor in the failure of the expedition and the significant casualties it suffered.[3]

Not waiting for the missing troops, the first landing was made to the west of Alexandria on the evening of 17 March 1807. Despite assurances that the local population was friendly, the gates to Alexandria were shut and the British were fired upon when they approached. Burgoyne writing home a few weeks later, described the early involvement of the engineers. The army's belief that there would be limited resistance minimised the call on the engineering services:

> At the taking of Alexandria, as it was proposed to do everything by storm, but little fell to our department; on the second night after the landing, I made the arrangements for conducting and fixing the scaling ladders to Fort Cretin [named after the French General Cretin], But the intention was defeated by the troops not being able to force the gate of the old wall.
>
> The defences of this place raised by the French, remain in very near as good a state as when I saw them in 1802; besides these, the Turks have executed (though very badly) a palisaded line of entrenchments to the westward, extending from the Fort des Bains to Lake Mareotis, this was the line stormed by the troops on 17th March.[4]

2 REM 4601-74, Lefebure to Burgoyne, 10 February 1807.

3 John Fortescue, *History of the British Army* (London: John Murray, 1910), Vol.VI, pp.5-15.

4 The National Archives (TNA) WO55/958, Burgoyne to Morse, 25 April 1807.

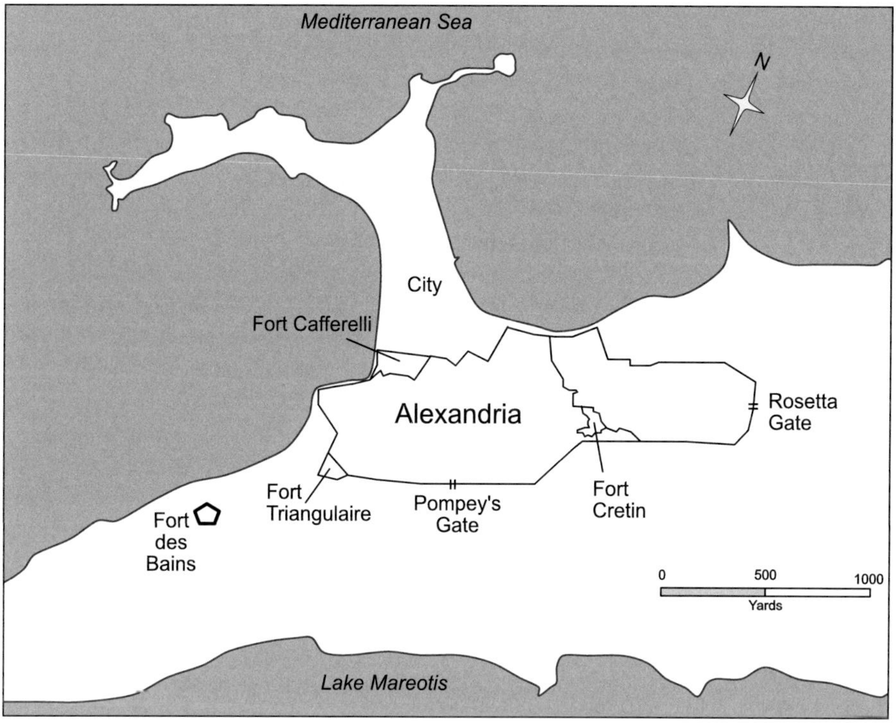

Alexandria 1807.

Burgoyne seems to have got his dates slightly wrong as there was no attack on the city until 18 March 1807. The plan of attack for the 18th was for a feint attack on the Turkish right (the seaward) and the main attack would be made on the left (southern) face of the city, attempting to take the Pompey Gate. Confusingly, Fort Cretin was further to the east of the Pompey Gate. The attack failed and Fraser moved his whole force to the east to block any force sent to relieve the place. Two days later, the Turks, seeing the arrival of reinforcements, surrendered. Burgoyne was mentioned in Fraser's despatch although not in a particularly positive way:

> It is but justice to Captain Pymm and to the officers and men of the detachment of the Royal Artillery that was with me, to mention the very great zeal and alacrity which they displayed on every occasion, which I am confident would have been equally conspicuous on the part of Captain Burgoyne and the officers of the engineers had circumstances permitted them to have acted.[5]

5 *London Gazette*, 9 May 1807, reporting Fraser's despatch of 25 March 1807.

Burgoyne's friend Pasley noted, future operations 'will entitle your services to be spoken of in stronger terms, than could be the case at Alexandria'.[6] Still from a young officer's perspective, being mentioned in despatches was still a very beneficial event.

Having taken Alexandria, Major General Fraser was now pressed by Misset to take Rosetta to ensure that food supplies would continue to reach the city. This was not part of Fraser's instructions and Rosetta was 30 miles north-east of Alexandria. With his small force, extending his operations was risky.

Burgoyne, having had an opportunity to review the situation, sent a letter to Lefebure in Sicily asking for more engineers to be sent. His view was that he needed more than three engineers to manage the defences of Alexandria and provide support for other operations, such as the attack on Rosetta.[7] Lefebure's reply was not sent until 30 April 1807 and said that despite his best efforts, Fox could not spare any other engineers but he would authorise any number of assistant engineers that Burgoyne required. Assistant engineers were officer volunteers from the army. Fox's consent was necessary as they received additional pay for their duties.

Eventually, due to the strong representations from Misset, on 29 March 1807, Fraser sent Major General Patrick Wauchope with about 1,600 men to take Rosetta. Burgoyne's description of the failure is short:

> The first expedition to Rosetta commanded by General Wauchope was attended by Captain Nicholas, but as that unfortunate affair ended in a fruitless attempt to take the place by a *coup de main*, no assistance was required from our department.[8]

The standard account of the attack on Rosetta has Wauchope approaching the town on 31 March. Finding no sign of life, he entered without carrying out any reconnaissance and was then ambushed in the narrow streets by the defenders.[9] More recent analysis suggests that Wauchope made a planned assault against determined defenders. Captain Nicholas, the engineer who accompanied the force, made his feelings clear on the poor information they had been provided: 'We were led to expect by those whom government had pointed out as the most able men … that this town had but few troops and would fall an easy prey into our hands; but the result was far otherwise'. He then went on the describe the

6 REM 5501-79, Pasley to Burgoyne, London, 27 May 1807.

7 REM 4601-74, Lefebure to Burgoyne, Messina, 30 April 1807, replying to Burgoyne's letter of 26 March 1807.

8 WO55/958, Burgoyne to Morse, Alexandria, 25 April 1807.

9 Primarily driven by Fraser's despatch, Bunbury (who was not present) and Misset who was possibly trying to shift the blame. See Bunbury, *Narratives*, pp.286-294; Alistair Nichols, *Wellington's Mongrel Regiment. A History of the Chasseurs Britanniques, 1801-1814* (Staplehurst: Spellmount, 2005), pp.36-40 and pp.231-3; Fortescue, *British Army*, Vol.VI, pp.15-17.

assault, with the attackers taking large casualties whilst they forced their way into the town. Nicholas was clearly involved in the attack:

> But the scene became more bloody and melancholy than before; every door, window and entrance was equally stopped and secured, and in breaking open the door of one house, they were knocked down from the windows of the next.[10]

By the time the attack failed, nearly 450 soldiers had been killed and wounded. Amongst the killed was Wauchope. Fraser now mounted a second expedition to take Rosetta. The force of 2,500 men under Major General William Stewart arrived in the area on 5 April 1807 and then brought up siege guns. Burgoyne described the engineer activities of this attack:

> At the second [attack on Rosetta], which was to be a siege, we all three attended until some days before the retreat when I was forced to return to Alexandria with ophthalmia; the command of the department then devolved upon Captain Nicholas ... As the object was to ruin the town, it is necessary to mention the particular situation of the batteries ... A battery for eight guns, one for three, one for two, and another for a howitzer, with four fleches to contain the pickets and three mortar platforms were the principal works done by the engineers.
>
> Each battery begun, was finished on the same night, Constant attention was paid to keeping them in repair and General Stuart who commanded, declared himself perfectly satisfied with the exertions of the Department ... Unfortunately, by the precipitate retreat of the army from before Rosetta, all our stores (consisting of more than one half of the small quantity we brought from Messina) have been lost, I have therefore requested General Frazer to apply to General Fox to have them replaced. I have likewise thought it necessary to apply for another officer at least, as our duties even in this garrison, exclusive of detachments to which we are liable, will be very heavy.[11]

Nichols' journal confirmed that the plan was to bombard the town. The British were very unhappy about the previous street fighting and at the barbaric beheading of soldiers during the last attack. They were not going to risk their troops in the streets of Rosetta again. The attack continued until 21 April 1807 but the difficulty in bringing up supplies meant the bombardment was sporadic and the defenders were not seriously affected. As the size of the Turkish forces, particularly

10 *Royal Military Chronicle* (London: Davis, 1812), Vol.V, pp.255-256.
11 TNA WO55/958. Burgoyne to Morse, Alexandria, 25 April 1807.

cavalry, grew, attacks on the British escalated. Part of the British detachment at El Hamed was cut off and destroyed on 20 April 1807. The following morning Stewart's troops started a withdrawal pursued by the Turks. Stewart lost over 100 men, but the whole of the detachment at El Hamed, over 800 men, was killed or captured. With little warning and no real opportunity to remove the siege guns, they were all spiked and the siege stores destroyed, Nicholas saying that the work was completed in two hours.

Due to his illness, Burgoyne had returned to Alexandria by this time and missed the precipitate retreat. Opthalmia was a contagious inflammation of the eyes. It was a common complaint amongst the locals as well as the invading armies. At its mildest (conjunctivitis) it would cause temporary blindness lasting several days. At its worst, it caused permanent blindness.[12]

Burgoyne handed command of the engineering services to Nichols and reported his incapacity to his commander in Messina. Lefebure wrote to him on 15 May 1807, reporting that:

> [Lieutenant Edward] Parker, with Captain [Frederick] Thackeray, are on the point of departure for Egypt ... I am extremely sorry you lose your command ... as it was not possible to guess the extent of your misfortunes, I considered it necessary to mention to General Moore that I ... would ... hold myself in readiness for any contingency.
>
> At one time, I had reason to suppose they would let me proceed to Egypt, upon the principle that if you had fallen, or met with any accident, my presence would be useful, but that if you were healthy and not disabled, I was to return.
>
> Thackeray's coming put all this out of the question, he being an officer who, from the earliest times of his existence, has enjoyed the patronage and countenance of General Fox, at least so I understand, and I believe it to be the fact.[13]

There is a certain irony in Lefebure sympathising with Burgoyne's loss of command to a favourite of Fox when most officers would have believed that Burgoyne originally got the position due to Fox's patronage. Thackeray arrived at Alexandria on 24 May 1807 to replace Burgoyne, although the latter remained there for another two months, until 26 July 1807, when he sailed for Sicily. On arriving at Messina on 9 August 1807, the ship was placed under quarantine and Burgoyne noted that he sailed for Malta 'to get Pratique',[14] returning to Syracuse on 5 September 1807.

12 Max Meyerhof, 'A Short History of Opthalmia during the Egyptian Campaigns of 1799 – 1807', *British Journal of Opthalmology*, (March 1932), pp.129-152.

13 REM 4601-74, Lefebure to Burgoyne, Messina, 15 May 1807.

14 REM 4201-68, Memorandum, 4 August 1807. Pratique: license that ship is free from contagion.

He then took a leisurely 11 days to return to Messina, calling at Mount Etna on the way.

Bryce, who had now replaced Lefebure as Commanding Engineer in Sicily, wrote to Burgoyne on 10 September 1807 appointing him to be the Commanding Engineer at Augusta. Bryce was concerned about the poor state of the defences on the east coast of Sicily, especially since the French now had control of the Ionian islands, including Corfu. This increased the risk of a French attack on Sicily. Bryce noted that Burgoyne's engineer friend, Charles Boothby was there and had recently completed a report on the present state of the defences.[15] Burgoyne arrived at Augusta on 21 August 1807 and remained there for the next month preparing proposals for the improvements in the defences. Bryce responded to two letters from Burgoyne on 1 October 1807. He expressed satisfaction about the proposals and approved the appointment of a local stone mason to carry out repairs on the castle. He asked Burgoyne to enquire into getting possession of the Dominican Convent to turn it into a strong point. Bryce, however, was concerned about getting a local valuer in to look at buildings and trees that were on the glacis of the defences, as this might generate an expectation that compensation would be paid when they were removed.

Whilst Burgoyne was busy at Augusta, priorities were changing for the British government. Napoleon's defeat of the Russians and Prussians meant that French strength in the Mediterranean had increased. There was no chance, with the forces available, of holding Egypt and even the security of Sicily was threatened. Moore was now in command in Sicily, Fox having been recalled. He gave ministers a frank view of the situation in Sicily and particularly the failures of the Neapolitan court. Somewhat unexpectedly, Moore now received orders to embark with a force from Sicily and to travel to Gibraltar where further instructions would be given. The force was to be prepared in strict secrecy. He could not leave until Fraser's force returned from Egypt, which did not happen until 16 October. Orders were issued for the new expedition as soon as Moore knew when these troops would arrive.[16]

Burgoyne had clearly made an impression on Moore. Bryce, the Commanding Engineer in Sicily, informed Burgoyne, on 15 October 1807, that he had been selected to be Commanding Engineer on Moore's expedition which was still secret. Bryce went on to say:

> Sir John Moore, in addition to the very good opinion he has of your qualifications for this situation, was guided in some considerable degree by the circumstance of your having been superseded by Captain Thackeray at Alexandria, which he thought unnecessary and probably unpleasant

15 REM 4601-74, Bryce to Burgoyne, Messina, 10 September 1807.
16 Oman, *Sir John Moore*, pp.434-440.

> to your feelings, although he was convinced that General Fox was very far from intending anything of this kind, but had overlooked the circumstances.[17]

Burgoyne makes no mention of his activities after Thackeray arrived in Alexandria, this would suggest that he continued to serve under the newly appointed Commanding Engineer. Although Thackeray was senior to Burgoyne, posting him to replace the latter could have been taken as criticism of Burgoyne. The same day, Mulcaster wrote to Burgoyne in great anxiety. He had also been selected to go on the expedition, but another engineer officer, Lieutenant George MacLeod had volunteered directly to Moore and Mulcaster had been replaced: 'For God's sake, write to him [Bryce] immediately and if you will do the same to [Moore], I think it will do a great deal for me. Mention your having before applied for me'.[18] Clearly, Mulcaster's arguments were accepted as he accompanied Moore's expedition and MacLeod did not.[19]

Although nobody knew at the time, this expedition was to land a force at Lisbon to support the Portuguese nation in their defence against an expected French invasion. Following Napoleon's successes in Europe, he introduced the Continental Blockade which forbade countries under his power to trade with Britain. Portugal was not under French control and Napoleon had threatened to invade and depose the Portuguese monarchy if they did not implement the Continental Blockade. Stuck between British and French threats, the Portuguese had nowhere to go and on 30 November 1807, a French force under *Général de Division* Jean-Andoche Junot reached Lisbon, the Portuguese king and government having sailed to Brazil.

Moore's force arrived at Gibraltar on 1 December 1807 only to find that it was too late to support Portugal. His troops were ordered back to England, arriving on 28 December 1807. Burgoyne lost no time in informing people he was back in England. His letter to Lord Derby caught the family by surprise as his previous letter from Gibraltar, written in December, had only just reached them. Before visiting his family, he went to London to report his arrival to the Ordnance Headquarters and then spent a few weeks at Derby's home where he saw his sister, Maria for the first time in eight years.

Burgoyne was soon on the move again, arriving at Chatham on 17 February 1808. He appeared to have no desire to be an officer who sat quietly in a garrison when there were other opportunities on offer. Pasley commented on his attitude in a letter to Burgoyne:

17 Quoted in Wrottesley, *Burgoyne*, p.16. The author has been unable to find the original letter at the Royal Engineers Museum.

18 REM 4601-74, Mulcaster to Burgoyne, Messina, 15 October 1807.

19 The Royal Engineer returns show that the officers with Moore were Burgoyne, Mulcaster, Boothby and Harding. Macleod remained in Sicily until October 1808.

> I trust you will continue to devote yourself to the military, not the garrison duty of our profession you will enrol yourself in the list of those engineers who make it their object to uphold the credit of the Corps in the field, which I know no-one of your standing more capable of doing. For my part, I have made up my mind always to go on service when I can, but I assure you I have often serious doubts whether I shall ever be able to do more than the common routine of duty. At all events, if one should never acquire any particular credit, yet, if no notorious blunder is made, the private character of an officer who has been much in the field must always be more respectable.[20]

Burgoyne had both a thirst for active service and a desire to make his own way in the world. A no point in his life did he stay long at the Derby residences. There is no evidence to suggest that Burgoyne was not on good terms with Derby and his family, but he clearly did not wish to be supported by them any more than was necessary. Nevertheless, Derby supported him unreservedly throughout his life.

The same day that Burgoyne arrived at Chatham, he received a letter from Boothby. In the letter, he explained that he had asked to be placed at Chatham so as to be close to Burgoyne and also because 'your being sent to Chatham; that is very much in favour of expeditioning [sic]'. Like Sicily in the Mediterranean, if one wished to be selected for field operations, it was necessary to be close to where the decisions were made, which in England was Chatham. Boothby reported that he had written to Sir John Moore, asking to be selected for his next expedition and had received a positive reply. He continued 'You said you would write to him; which I hope you have done'.[21] It looks like Boothby's question prompted a reaction and Burgoyne called on Moore in London a few days later. He did not see Moore who was involved in the Court Martial of Lieutenant General John Whitelocke, but received a reply stating, 'if I am to be employed, it will give me great pleasure to have you with me'.[22]

The next two months were spent at Chatham. Burgoyne continued to discuss with Pasley his views on the British army and the training of engineers. Pasley wrote:

> I have put off for some time my idea of publishing on the subject of military education … with regard to Morse[23] he certainly acted in this instance as my perceived enemy … I think he is unfit for his situation for want of views sufficiently enlarged to embrace [change] … I even had an

20 REM 5501-79, Pasley to Burgoyne, London, 27 May 1807.

21 REM 4601-74, Boothby to Burgoyne, Tipington, 17 February 1808.

22 Wrottesley, *Burgoyne*, pp.17-18.

23 General Robert Morse, Inspector General of Fortifications. The most senior Royal Engineer.

> idea of writing confidentially to him or Lord Chatham [Master General of the Ordnance] soon after I landed from Copenhagen, and would do it now if that would answer the end, viz., the improvement of the instruction at Woolwich … I find that Birch [Captain John Birch RE] … has concluded that I am red-hot raving with revengeful sentiments and likely to do something very rash … I trust no violence shall ever disgrace my printed opinions, tho' I cannot help it sometimes in conversation.[24]

Another opportunity was forming. Sweden was the only other country in Europe that was not part of Napoleon's Continental Blockade. England wanted to support the Swedes against the French pressure and also against the possibility that Russia would see an opportunity to annex Finland. On 8 February 1808, Britain and Sweden signed a treaty and soon after, news arrived that the Russians had invaded Finland. Moore met with the Duke of York and Lord Castlereagh on 19 April 1808, to discuss the despatch of a force to support the defence of Sweden.

Burgoyne and Boothby both received orders to prepare for foreign service, Burgoyne receiving his on 21 April 1808. The Commanding Engineer was Captain John Squire. It is possible that Moore met Squire in Egypt in 1801; it is certain he had met him at the trial of Whitelocke, as Squire was involved in the disastrous expedition to South America. On 4 May 1808, Squire wrote to the engineer headquarters asking if approval had been given to purchase maps of Sweden. Squire asked, if no decision had been made, then could the maps be purchased at his own expense![25]

Moore's force sailed on 10 May 1808, arriving at Gottenburg on the 17 May 1807. The plan to support the defence of Sweden rapidly collapsed with Moore being 'arrested' for refusing to put his troops under the direct command of the Swedish King who wished to use them to embark on offensive operations against Norway and Denmark. These options were outside of the orders Moore had received from the British government. Eventually, Moore had to escape from his arrest. He arrived back at the fleet on 29 June, and the fleet sailed for England on 3 July 1808.

Burgoyne wrote up his observations on Sweden and the Swedish expedition, an activity that would be very common in the coming years. These critiques often reflected his true opinions in ways that his official communications did not.[26]

The fleet carrying Burgoyne arrived back in England in 15 July 1808. Moore went to London to meet the Ministers and the transports including the engineer officers were ordered to sail straight to Portsmouth as they were destined for another operation. On 20 July 1808, Burgoyne wrote to Morse reporting their arrival at Spithead

24 BL ADD MS41962, Pasley Papers, Pasley to Burgoyne, Colchester, 9 April 1808.

25 TNA WO55/977, Squire to Rowley, 4 May 1808.

26 Burgoyne's notes on Sweden appear in Wrottesley, *Burgoyne*, pp.21-28. The author has been unable to locate the original papers.

and continued: 'The ships arrived with us are ordered to complete victualling and water immediately, and I take the liberty to express a hope that I may be allowed to continue with these troops on any service they may be ordered upon'.[27]

Burgoyne expected that the force would remain under Moore and despite the best efforts of the Government, Moore returned although now under the command of Sir Harry Burrard. Contrary winds, as often happened, delayed departure and the fleet did not sail until 31 July 1808; their destination, the Iberian Peninsula. With the fleet were several engineers including John Burgoyne and John Squire. A new Commanding Engineer had been appointed, Captain Richard Fletcher, and he also sailed with them. Fletcher would be Burgoyne's commanding officer for most of the Peninsular War.

27 TNA WO55/977, Burgoyne to Morse, Spithead, 20 July 1808.

4

1808 – The Peninsula and Moore's Campaign

Moore's troops were despatched to increase the size of the British force which had been ordered to the Iberian Peninsula, primarily to support the Spanish revolt against the French. The French invasion of Portugal in late 1807 was followed by the replacement of the Spanish King with Napoleon's brother, Joseph. The violent revolt by the Spanish population in Madrid and the brutal response from the French on the 2 May 1808 (*Dos de Mayo*), led to Spanish envoys traveling to England to ask for help. The British government and population were keen to support the revolt and through the summer of 1808 they first despatched agents to the northern coast of Spain and then followed this with troops.

The first force to arrive was under Lieutenant General Sir Arthur Wellesley, the future Duke of Wellington. His force had initially been put together for an invasion of South America; to interfere with Spanish trade; to look for new trading opportunities and to encourage the locals to seek independence. With the change of Spain from enemy to ally, this force was rapidly diverted to this new opportunity on the European mainland. Britain was determined to establish a foothold on the continent and prove their commitment to the defeat of Napoleon. Britain quickly realised that Wellesley's force was not sufficient, and further troops were despatched from England and the Mediterranean. Moore's force was also redirected. With strong suggestions that politics were at work, two officers senior to Moore were appointed as commander and second-in-command. Wellesley was one the most junior lieutenant generals in the British army and, even with the favour of the government, he could not be left in command of a force this size.

Wellesley arrived at La Coruña on 20 July 1808. The Spanish authorities, however, were reluctant to agree to the landing of the British troops and Wellesley sailed on to Portugal and started unloading the troops in Mondego Bay on 1 August 1808. The Spanish reluctance was understandable as technically, at this time, Spain and Britain were still at war. Also, Spanish confidence was high, following the surrender of the French forces at Bailén; they did not believe they needed British troops, although they were happy to accept arms and money.

In quick succession, Wellesley defeated the French at Roliça and Vimeiro in August 1808. Wellesley was now superseded, first by Lieutenant General Harry

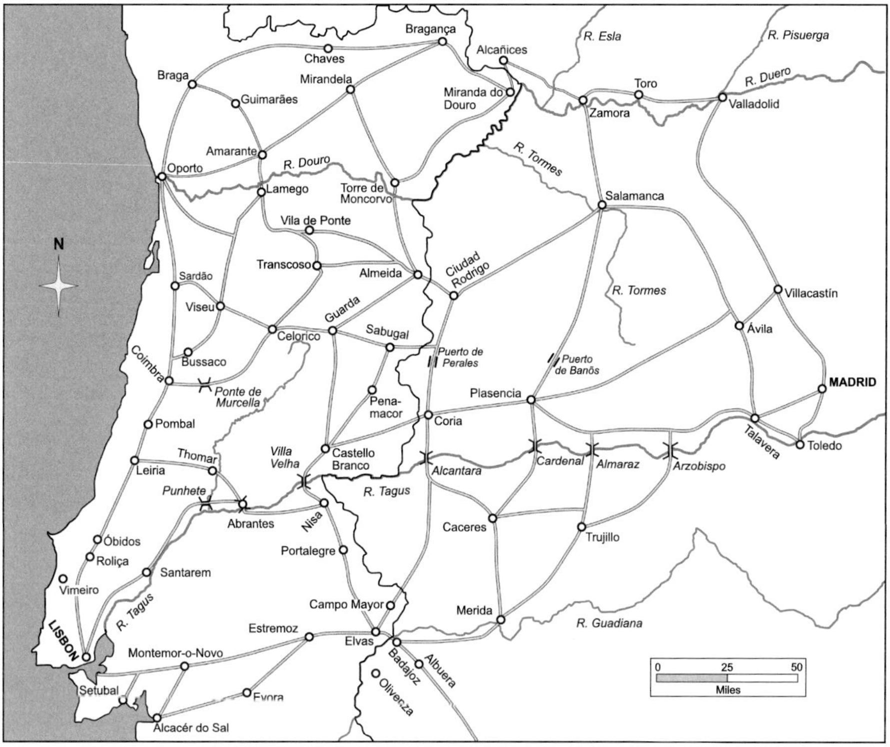

Central Portugal & Spain.

Burrard and then by Lieutenant General Hew Dalrymple. Although Wellesley was keen to push on against the disorganised French, his superiors urged caution and entered into negotiations with the French.

Moore arrived at Maceira Bay, about 40 miles north of Lisbon, on 24 August 1808. Arriving at the British headquarters at Torres Vedras the following day, he discovered that there was a suspension of hostilities whilst the French negotiated terms to evacuate Portugal. The terms of what became known as the Convention of Cintra caused great anger both in Portugal and at home. The Portuguese were incensed that they had not been consulted and felt that it gave the French the opportunity to keep their plunder.[1] In England, the decision to ship the French home in Royal Navy ships and not put any embargo on future service of the soldiers was met with dismay.

1 Marcus Beresford argues that there was a significant attempt to stop the French removing stolen goods. See Marcus Beresford, *William Carr Beresford The Ablest Man I have ever seen with the Army* (Newbridge: IAP, 2019), pp.35-40.

Dalrymple and Burrard were recalled home to face an inquiry. Wellesley had not waited for their recall, sailing home on 20 September 1808, having no confidence in these two generals. He also made his views on the Convention clear to Castlereagh. Whilst Wellesley got a poor reception when he landed in England, the view in Lisbon about who was to blame was clear. Boothby, who arrived in the Tagus on 1 September 1808, was told by his convoy commander: 'Junot was allowed to return to France with his troops and plunder … [and] that Sir J.M and Sir A.W. were raving at Sir H.D. and Sir H.B. on account of the terms allowed to General Junot'.[2]

Dalrymple left Lisbon on 4 October 1808. Two days later, Moore received a letter, dated 26 September 1808, appointing him to command the army in the Iberian Peninsula. Burrard would remain in Portugal as commandant at Lisbon.

Burgoyne had landed with Fletcher on 28 August 1808,[3] and waited in the British camp until the Convention was signed on 30 August. He would soon meet up again with senior officers he had served with in the Mediterranean including John Moore and Thomas Graham. Also, there were a number of engineer officers present who he had served with before. It was a small group and they knew each other well.

The army headquarters moved to Cintra on 5 September 1808 and the engineers moved to Fort St Julian on the Tagus estuary, the French having given up all positions outside of Lisbon.

The British army and its engineers arrived in the Peninsula with very little knowledge of the terrain in which they would be operating. Fletcher's urgent requests for maps had limited success and he needed to quickly develop information on the operating environment. Even two years later, engineers commented that:

> All the maps of Portugal, particularly in this part of the country are extremely incorrect. Faden's last map of January is as bad as any of them. The Carta Militar, published at Lisbon can never be depended upon. To form a good judgement, it is necessary to actually visit every part of the frontier.[4]

The first priority was to get information. Fletcher ordered Squire to accompany the first troops into Lisbon in the hope they could get possession of plans from the Portuguese military archives, although 'I feel he will not succeed, as the convention did not, I believe, mention anything of the kind'.[5] Other engineer officers

2 Boothby, *Under England's Flag*, p.141.
3 TNA WO55/977, Fletcher to Morse, 28 August 1808.
4 BL ADD MS63106, Letters from Squire to Bunbury, 10 September 1810., ff.9-10.
5 TNA WO55/977, Fletcher to Morse, 7 September 1808.

were making detailed plans of the defences on the Tagus at St Julian, Cascais, and Belem.

Prior to his recall, Dalrymple despatched troops to take possession of the border fortresses of Elvas and Almeida and engineers were attached to both forces. Boothby was given orders on 6 September 1808, to be ready to travel to Elvas, Burgoyne was sent to report on the northern fortress of Almeida. Fletcher writing home, said:

> It is ... one of the strongest places in Portugal, though doubts have been entertained as to its local importance in the defence of this kingdom. Captain Burgoyne is under orders to proceed thither and his sketches and reports, will enable me to give you further information.[6]

A few days later, Fletcher having had time to evaluate what information on the country was (or, more likely, was not) available, changed Burgoyne's orders from only collecting information on the fortresses themselves.

> In addition to your former instructions I have to request you will during your march [to Almeida] endeavour to ascertain the different places at which it would be practicable to obtain supplies of wood, water, provisions and forage for an army moving through the country; the possibility of procuring draft oxen and carts or such for the conveyance of stores and baggage, and the number of troops in different towns or villages capable of offering cantonments for troops. In general, whatever [?] might retard or prove useful to an army should be noted in your observations and reported to me by the first opportunity. It would be useful to mention as many as you can, the number of houses each town or village may contain.[7]

Oman was highly critical of Dalrymple and his Quartermaster-General (QMG), George Murray,[8] for their lack of activity in the period after the Convention was signed. He complained 'within a fortnight after the Convention was signed [30 August 1808], British officers ought to have explored every road to the frontier and to have reported on their facilities'.[9] Clearly, more was happening than Oman realised. The highly efficient QMG officers, Corps of Guides, and the Exploring Officers did not exist at this time, but officers were being despatched to carry out

6 TNA WO55/977, Fletcher to Morse, 7 September 1808.

7 TNA WO55/958, Fletcher to Burgoyne, 14 September 1808.

8 Unless otherwise specified, any reference to 'Murray' in the book is referring to George Murray. John Murray will be called 'John Murray'.

9 Charles Oman, *History of the Peninsular War* (Oxford: Clarendon Press, 1902-30), Vol.I, p.487. Oman wrote what is still considered to be the best account of the war, although there is much new information now.

this exact role. This included engineer officers who were sent out in September and the first reports on the routes to Almeida and Elvas were being written in the early days of October.[10] Moore's complaint to Castlereagh on 9 October 1808, that his army's movements 'depends on a knowledge of the country which I am still without',[11] was much wider than just the roads to the Portuguese border. Correspondence with the Spanish authorities had not resulted in any information on the intentions of the Spanish armies, the condition of the roads, or the supply situation in that country.

Moore, by this time, under intense pressure from the British and Spanish governments had decided on an advance into Spain, heading towards Salamanca where he could meet with British reinforcements under Lieutenant General David Baird who were to disembark at La Coruña. The major routes available to Moore were:

- North through Coimbra, Ponte de Murcella, Celorico, Almeida and Ciudad Rodrigo
- Along the Tagus through Abrantes, Villa Velha, Guarda, Almeida and Ciudad Rodrigo
- East through Elvas, Alcantara, Coria and Ciudad Rodrigo
- East through Elvas, Badajoz, Trujillo, Almaraz, Talavera and Villacastín (the longest route with the best roads).

Because of uncertainty on the quality of the roads, Moore sent most of his artillery, under Lieutenant General Sir John Hope, on the longest route which passed close to Madrid, whilst the bulk of his forces headed by more direct routes. According to Moore's biographer, Maurice, Moore and Hope originally intended to send the artillery via Alcantara until Hope reported that this route was impracticable.[12] Robert Ker Porter who travelled this route in November 1808, said north of Alcantara: 'The country over which we now travelled was highly dangerous for horses, on account of the rocky steepness of the road; and for carriages it was wholly impassable'.[13]

The decision was then made to send the artillery via the longer route on the high road to Madrid.[14] It must also be remembered that Moore's original intention was to concentrate his forces at Burgos or Valladolid behind a screen of Spanish troops and in that scenario, the route via Alcantara or Madrid was not appreciably

10 See TNA WO55/1561/9, Burgoyne's report on route to Almeida; TNA WO55/1561/4, Mulcaster's report on route to Abrantes; TNA WO55/1561/9, Squire's reports on route to Elvas.

11 Roger Parkinson, *Moore of Corunna* (Milton: PBS, 1976), p.175,

12 J.F. Maurice, *The Diary of Sir John Moore* (London: Arnold, 1904), Vol.II, p.321.

13 Robert Porter, *Letters from Portugal and Spain written During the March of the British Troops under Sir John Moore* (Cambridge: Ken Trotman, 1985), p.109.

14 Maurice, *John Moore*, Vol.II, p.321. See also Maurice's rejection of Oman's criticism, pp.319-322.

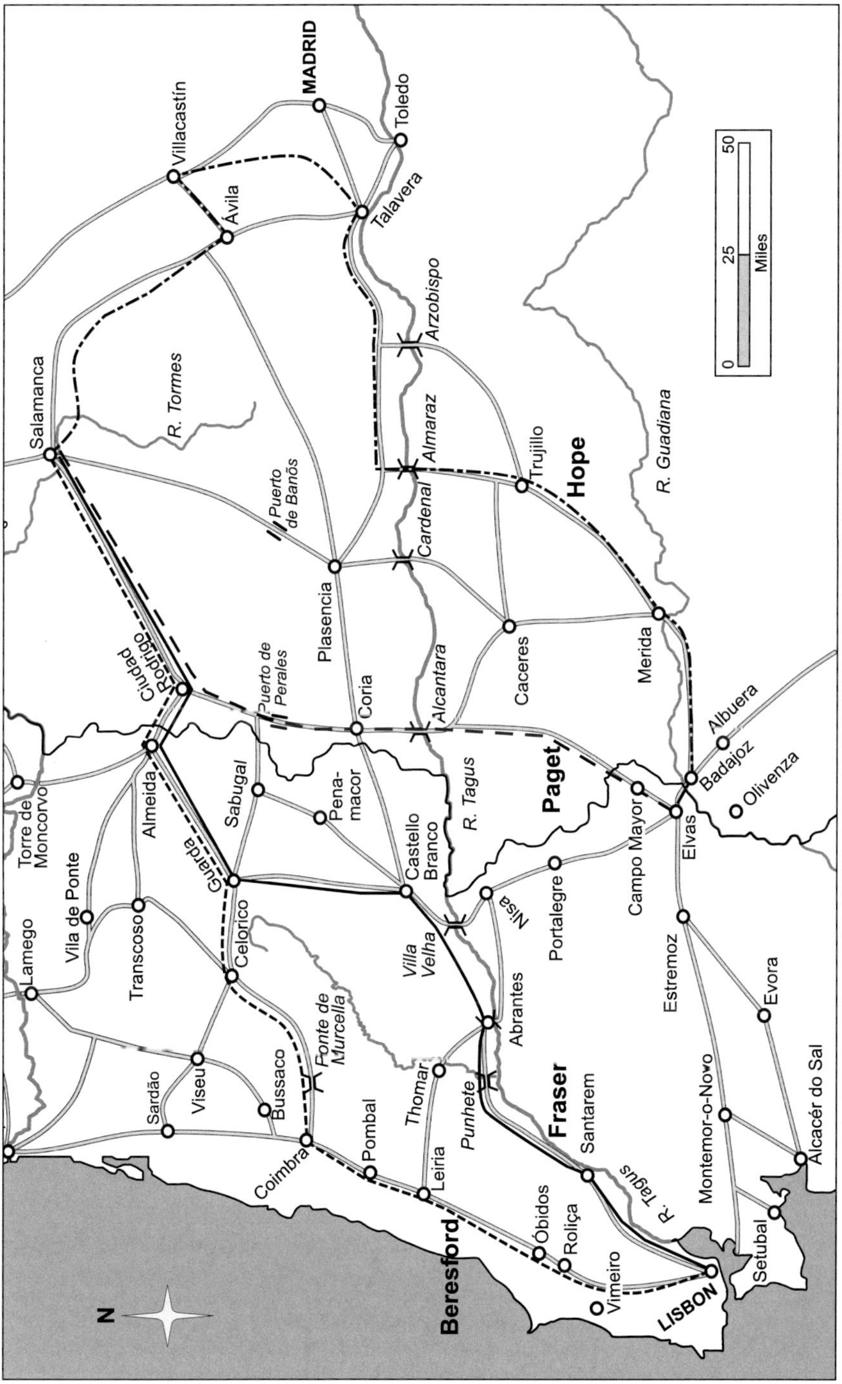

Moore's Advance into Spain, 1808.

longer. The defeat of the Spanish forces meant that Moore had to concentrate much further west and this led to the extended journey for Hope.

As there is still significant disagreement on whether Moore's decision to detach the artillery was justifiable, let us have a look at the information that was available to Moore. The issue was not whether the roads could be made passable for artillery; it was whether they were immediately ready for use by artillery. This was the sort of role that QMG, Royal Staff Corps (RSC) and Royal Engineer officers carried out throughout the war to give the best possible information to their commanders, to assist them in making their decisions. It is worth spending some time on this to understand the work that went on in the background.

Early histories, and even some recent ones, make the claim that one or more of the northern routes were passable.[15] However, much of the modern criticism of Moore's decision seems to be based upon the views of Charles Oman, who was strongly critical of the decision. As Oman saw it:

> Then followed an irreparable mistake: it was all important to find out which of the roads was most suitable for artillery and heavy baggage. Moore consulted the available officers of the old Portuguese army and received from them the almost incredibly erroneous information that neither [of the two northern roads] ... was practicable for artillery. It would also seem that he sought information from the officers whom Dalrymple had sent out into the province of Beira and that their answer tallied with those of the Portuguese.[16]

Oman heaped much of the blame on Brigadier General Robert Anstruther, who had been sent to Almeida, 'for he, more than anyone else had been given the chance of trying these roads':

> General Anstruther, then at Almeida, had warned Moore of the lamentable state of the Portuguese roads, hardly one of which did not have 'very bad steps; these are generally in or near villages, of which the streets are almost universally narrow, rocky and full of short turns impracticable for carriages of any sort', merely confirming what the Portuguese had admitted: 'that even in their own country they would be at a loss to indicate any road that was practical for artillery'.[17]

15 They include: John Jones, *Account of the War in Spain and Portugal* (London: Egerton, 1818), p.38. Also, George Landmann, *Historical, Military and Picturesque Observations on Portugal* (London: Cadell & Davis, 1818), Vol.I, p.503; James Moore, *Narrative of the Campaign of the British Army in Spain Commanded by His Excellency Sir John Moore* (London: Johnson, 1809), p.26.

16 Oman, *Peninsular War*, Vol.I, p.494. See also Vol.I, pp.598-599.

17 Ian Robertson, *A Commanding Presence* (Stroud: Spellmount, 2008), p.57.

Oman's criticism continued, stating that Moore's decision 'was not easily pardonable in any competent general … and in a fortnight, was bitterly regretting his credulity.' Oman quoted a letter from Moore to Hope dated Almeida, 8 November 1808:

> The road we are travelling is practicable for artillery; the brigade under [Captain Edward] Wilmott has already reached Guarda and as far as I have already seen, the road presents few obstacles and those easily surmounted.[18]

We will come back to this letter.

Moore ordered his first troops into movement on 11 October, five days after being given command. They were taking the northern route, by Coimbra, which Oman said was the best (we will also come back to this statement). Oman accepted that Moore, understandably, had limited knowledge of the routes, and that he was being pressured to move into Spain. All the officers around him were telling him that the routes were not practicable for artillery. Would it not have been 'incompetent' to ignore the advice he was being given and send his artillery by one of these shorter routes, when he did not know if they would be able to complete the journey? Having to retrace the route and go the longer route would then have lost much time.

It is not reasonable for Oman to say Moore was wrong and should have rejected all the advice he was getting from Portuguese and British officers. The present author has been unable to locate any source that says, in advance of travelling the route, that they were practicable. Hope commented in mid-November:

> [I have] made enquiries as to the best roads leading from here [Trujillo] … it seems beyond a doubt that the road from here to Plasencia is not practicable for artillery … I have no great hopes of being able to procure such decisive information as would warrant me to alter our route.[19]

So, what was said at the time about Oman's preferred northern route?

One officer sent to survey this particular route was John Burgoyne. Understanding the urgency of his orders from the Commanding Engineer, he submitted his report, dated Almeida, 1 October 1808. Burgoyne travelled the northern route via Coimbra. He reported the road was generally good all the way to Coimbra. Between Coimbra and Ponte de Murcella:

18 Oman, *Peninsular War*, Vol.I, p.495.

19 BL ADD MS57541, Hope to Moore, Truxillo dated 12 November 1808. The author is obliged to Dr Janet McDonald for this information.

> the road is very bad, steep and narrow and in its present state not practicable for artillery, the country carts do pass it, but with much difficulty, that they can scarcely get from Coimbra over this [sic] mountains, ten miles in a whole day; from the foot of the mountains the road is bad, but passable for carriages.[20]

He reported that there were several other points where the road was bad 'but passable for carriages,' He finished with the recommendation to 'repair the roads, which would not be attended with very great difficulty or labour'. Another description of parts of this northern route was 'goat tracks descending into ravines almost inaccessible'.[21] In February 1810, Wellington was complaining that the road from Ponte de Murcella to Thomar via Espinhal was impassable for artillery.[22]

The issue for Moore was whether the road was ready for immediate use by artillery. The answer was; it was not. There is another letter from Wellington in early 1810, ordering the repairs to be made to the route from Ponte Murcella 'for future operations'.[23] There were still issues with the roads around Coimbra a year after Moore needed to use them.

However, what about the other routes?

They were generally good to the main cities – Coimbra, Abrantes and Castelo Branco – then they deteriorated. However, even before the troops got to Castelo Branco, there were problems. The commissary Augustus Schaumann commented on the road from Nisa to Villa Velha:

> The road across the San Miguel range is very bad, and often quite perpendicular. Many of the carts containing ammunition were smashed to pieces, despite the fact that they are built expressly for that kind of road.[24]

A Portuguese ox cart was substantially sturdier than an artillery carriage. Robert Blakeney, described getting Wilmot's light 6-pounder battery across the Tagus at Villa Velha:

> The first gun conveyed across had two drag ropes attached and to resist its rapidity while being trailed downhill; these ropes were held by as many

20 TNA WO55/1561/9.

21 Maurice, *John Moore*, Vol.II, p.287.

22 Gurwood (ed.), *Dispatches of the Duke of Wellington*. 2nd New and Enlarged edition, 8 volumes, (London: John Murray, 1852). This is the edition referenced unless specifically stated otherwise. Wellington to Beresford, Viseu, 19 February 1810.

23 Gurwood (ed.), *Despatches*, Wellington to Baccelar, 26 January 1810. REM 4201-68, Journal, 17 February 1810, also mentioned repairing the route from Ponte de Murcella, but that was the route to Thomar via Espinhal not the route to Coimbra.

24 Augustus Schauman, *On the Road with Wellington* (London: Heinemann, 1924), p.59.

> soldiers as the short and frequent turning of this zig-zag descent would permit; yet their resistance was scarcely sufficient to preserve the guns from rolling over the precipice ... several men who could not get clear of the ropes on suddenly coming to the sharp turns were absolutely dragged through the walls ... there was not one soldier ... who had heels on his shoes after the drag.[25]

Eventually, Wilmot used several horse teams on each of the remaining guns and dragged them across the bed of the river. These were the lightest field artillery pieces with Moore's army! Each weighed about 650 kg; a 9-pounder weighing 1,300kg.[26]

Surgeon Adam Neale described the road to the north of Villa Velha:

> Here the road led by a narrow steep defile to the top of the mountain. The wrecks of ox-wains, broken wheels and disabled carriages marked the progress of our army. The whole of the road, indeed, to As Carnadas, is the very worst perhaps in Europe ... and the wheels of the carriages had cut it down, in most places in ruts at least three or four feet deep.[27]

Some commentaries suggest that Moore decided the roads were passable when he reached Atalaia, about 15 miles north of Castelo Branco: 'Next day, Sir John reached a small village called Atalaia, and found stage by stage, that the road, though bad, was practicable for artillery'.[28] Lieutenant William Forster RE reported on this route in November 1808, saying the route was good to Atalaia. However, a few miles north of Atalaia, when ascending a ridge:

> the road is extremely bad and steep, gaining the top of the hill the road continues over broken and uneven ground for two miles. About ten miles north of Atalaia the road is extremely bad the whole distance to Capinha.

He also reported that parts of the road east of Guarda were 'rocky and extremely bad'.[29] Moore, travelling from Castelo Branco to Guarda, was having second thoughts: 'Caria to Guarda; 7 November; 5 leagues, road good, 'though, it is

25 Robert Blakeney, *A Boy in the Peninsular War* (London: Greehill, 1989), pp.22-3.

26 These figures are approximated, for the gun only, from tables in Carl Franklin, *British Napoleonic Field Artillery* (Stroud: Spellmount, 2012), pp.286-288. A medium 12-pounder weighed nearly 1,600kg. The heavier guns were all left at Lisbon when Moore advanced.

27 Adam Neale, *Letters from Portugal and Spain, Comprising the Account of the Operation of the Armies under their excellencies Sir Arthur Wellesley and Sir John Moore* (London: Richard Phillips, 1809), p.176.

28 James Carrick Moore, *The Life of Sir John Moore* (London: John Murray, 1834), p.147.

29 TNA WO55/1561/9, Forster report dated 28 November 1808.

feared too narrow for our artillery, which … will have to take a worse road by the mountain'.[30]

Captain Alexander Tod, of the Royal Staff Corps, reported in early 1810 that some parts of the road from Atalaia to Capinha (north of Castelo Branco) were impassable in bad weather, the surface being clay. He went on to describe the construction of Portuguese roads:

> In a country like this where roads are seldom made, they are only better or worse as they are more or less travelled; when the bottom is hard, the more they are travelled the smoother the surface becomes and when it is soft it has exactly the reverse effect; in the few instances where they have attempted to make them, immediately close to the towns, they do it by paving them with large round stones; this is invariably calculated to destroy horses fast and shake carriages to pieces; add to this, if they are much used, these large stones become loose and the road is then quite impracticable.[31]

Mulcaster explored a slightly different route from Castelo Branco to Almeida through Idanha Nova. He reported that it was impassable in some places between Castelo Branco and Idanha Nova and between Penamacor and Sabugal.[32]

Having looked at the reports of several officers that were despatched to examine the roads, let us now look at what Moore's own staff said.

Captain William Gomm, who was on the QMG's staff, received orders on 12 October 1808 to look for the best roads along the Abrantes, Castelo Branco, Guarda, Almeida route. He wrote 'they are not at all satisfied with the accounts given them of this route'. Having scouted a number of possible alternatives, he was to return to Abrantes to provide information for the decision on which route to take.[33] Gomm's comments show that Moore did challenge the initial advice he was given. Although Gomm's biography does not report the results of his reconnaissance, no change in the route for the artillery was ordered.

Lieutenant Colonel John Colborne, Moore's Military Secretary, wrote on 26 November 1808, 'Owing to the badness of the roads, the cavalry and artillery were obliged to march by a different route'.[34] There is no mention here of this being an error and Colborne would have been with Moore during the advance.

30 Maurice, *Sir John Moore*, Vol.II, p.277.

31 REM 4601-72, Burgoyne Letters, Substance of a Report … of that part of the Province of Beira … between Guarda and Castello Branco … from a reconnaissance in January and February 1810.

32 TNA WO55/1561/9. Not dated but must have been October or November 1808.

33 F.C. Carr-Gomm (ed.), *Letters and Journals of Field-Marshal Sir William Maynard Gomm* (London: John Murray, 1881), pp.110-111.

34 GC Moore-Smith (ed.), *Life of John Colborne, Field Marshal Lord Seaton* (London: John Murray, 1903), p.95.

Finally, in late November the Commander of the Royal Artillery, Colonel William Robe despatched three officers to survey the main routes north.[35] One of these was Captain William Eliot who in 1810 published his *Treatise on the Defence of Portugal* which included comments on these routes. They were: Almeida to Guarda; 'road bad and mountainous'; Guarda to Caria, 'road is narrow and bad and might … be rendered passable for artillery'; Caria to Póvoa de Atalaya [Atalaia], 'road is for the most part mountainous, yet some, tolerably good'; Atalaia to Castelo Branco, 'the road as bad as before; The road from Caria, Alpedrinha to Castelo Branco is worse; in many instances an additional number of horses and the assistance of infantry would be required'; Villa del Rey [Vila de Rei] to Abrantes, 'this part of the road is the worst, being mountainous'; 'in many parts of this mountainous road, a six pounder would require a dozen horses and the assistance of 50 men to drag it up the steps and they would be frequently be unable to march more than one or two leagues a day'; Even between Abrantes and Santarem, Eliot commented on the road being, in places 'stony and rocky' and 'frequently inundated and impassable for carriages in the rainy season'.

Eliot also commented:

> There is a road on the left bank of the Tagus by which the armies of Sir John Moore and Wellington [later] advanced into Spain … this line of march was adopted in order to avoid the strong and difficult country in front of Abrantes.[36]

Charles Oman did not have a high opinion of Moore and it comes across in his writing. John Fortescue and Carola Oman amongst others were more sympathetic. Carola Oman noted that Moore passed Wilmot's artillery brigade around Atalaia on 6 November, when he felt that the roads were passable for artillery. However, she also noted that 'At Almeida, on the 13th, after seeing the condition to which the 6-pounders had been reduced by a week of rain on roads which were not much more than goat tracks in fine weather, he decided that … after all, the heavy artillery had gone by the only possible road'.[37] Fortescue was also clear, 'The artillery could not have travelled over any road except that which it actually took'.[38]

The final word on the choice of route should be left to Moore. Above, Oman's reference to the letter from Moore to Hope of 8 November was noted. Moore wrote

35 John Leslie. *The Services of the Royal Regiment of Artillery in the Peninsular War* (London: Hugh Rees, 1908), p.82.

36 William Granville Eliot, *Treatise on the Defence of Portugal* (London: Egerton, 1811), pp.76-86.

37 Oman, *Sir John Moore*, pp.525-527. This date must be wrong as Moore arrived in Salamanca on 13 November. It was clearly after Moore wrote to Hope on the 8 November but before he left Almeida for Salamanca. See also, Fortescue, *British Army*, Vol.VI, p.307.

38 Fortescue, *British Army*, Vol.VI, p.399.

again five days later and this time, he had a different opinion based on further information; an opinion that agreed with the advice he had been given:

> Yesterday, on my road to this place, I received your letter of the 8th and since my arrival this afternoon I have received that of the 10th from Almaraz. The first part of this last letter kept me upon the fidgets [Hope suggesting that he was looking for a direct route north from Almaraz], until I at last came to the part which states your decision to adhere to the route you were pursuing. Your decision in this is perfectly right. In the first place, I am now satisfied that no other practicable road exists in any other line, in the next, if there did, you would have lost more time in ascertaining it, and in providing the supplies, than you would have gained by shortening the distance.[39]

Based on the information Moore had in early October, he made the right decision on the routes. Based on the actual state of the roads, he still made the right decision.

The campaign which started in October 1808 was full of challenges, neatly summed up by Roger Parkinson:

> Sir John Moore walked to his horse to lead the stab into enemy territory; with too few men, too late in the year, along unfit roads, with his forces scattered, hampered by a lack of finance and heavy equipment, unable to rely on his Spanish ally; and against an experienced enemy far superior in numbers; "If we get over this march … nothing will appear difficult".[40]

Whilst Moore struggled with organising his army and deciding on the route of advance, Burgoyne was at Almeida. When he wrote his report on the route to Almeida on 1 October, he had clearly been there for some days already, as he also provided a very detailed return on the engineering stores in the fortress with the same date. This report, for example, included 1,463 spades of different types, 862 pickaxes, and then went on to detail many other items; hammers, chisels, trowels, nails and a large quantity of oak plank and other pieces of wood. He also noted that a proportion of the stores had been brought by the French from Fort Concepción when they abandoned and partially destroyed it.[41]

39 BL ADD MS57553, ff.47-48, Moore to Hope, Salamanca, 13 November 1808. Information kindly provided by Dr Janet McDonald.

40 Parkinson, *Moore of Corunna*, p.181.

41 TNA WO55/958, Burgoyne to Fletcher, Almeida, 1 October 1808. Fort Concepción was a substantial stand-alone fort on the border between Almeida and Ciudad Rodrigo. It will appear again later in the book.

Burgoyne's subsequently prepared a detailed report on the fortress of Almeida, dated 20 October 1808.[42] Some keys points from his report are included below:

> The works consist of an irregular hexagon of a low profile, with ravelins, ditch, covered way and glacis, the bastions are full and the flanks, large … The retrenchment is of a hard stone and the parapet of earth retained by sods…
>
> On the highest point of the hill and near one of the curtains is an old square castle with round towers and a ditch, of no service with regard to defence … In the bastion of St João de Deus, a tier of casemates have been built and on each side of the gateways are guard rooms and prisons, which include the whole of the bomb proof cover in the garrison for all purposes (except the magazines) and might be made to contain 1,000 men … The barracks in the town, exclusive of the bomb proofs might contain about 1,200 infantry and 300 cavalry, besides a very fine hospital, well provided … The only regular magazine is a large one in the castle containing 3,000 Portuguese barrels of powder of 62 pounds each [85,000kg in total] …
>
> The garrison may be abundantly supplied with spring water from two wells, one in the square before the gate of Cruz and the other in the castle … The works are generally speaking in a good state of repair except the counterscarp which is [bulged?] in several places, and the gorge of the Ravelin São Antonio has either fallen down or never been finished; the parapets of the ravelins are not complete, nor apparently has the glacis before the São Antonio and Nossa Señora das Brotas fronts been completed according to the original intention,
>
> There are at this time 142 serviceable guns almost all brass, mounted on the works of which 51 are heavy and the remainder 12-pounders and under; not including 15 mortars, 11 howitzers and 12 field pieces; with an abundant supply of ammunition of all sorts; of the carriages, not more than one third are good, but there is sufficient timber in the stores to re-establish the rest.

Burgoyne identified a number of defects, mainly in the design rather than the condition, which would make them 'extremely difficult to remedy'. He stated the biggest fault was the weakness of the defences on the side facing the River Côa, where the ground sloped away within 600 yards and provided cover for any attack. His recommendation was that the garrison should be around 2,000 troops, so there was insufficient bomb-proof cover for the troops.

His most prophetic recommendation was to prepare 'another magazine for 500 barrels of powder; as well as small expense magazines for the immediate service

42 Two copies are held in the National Archives, in TNA WO55/1561/6 and TNA WO55/1561/9.

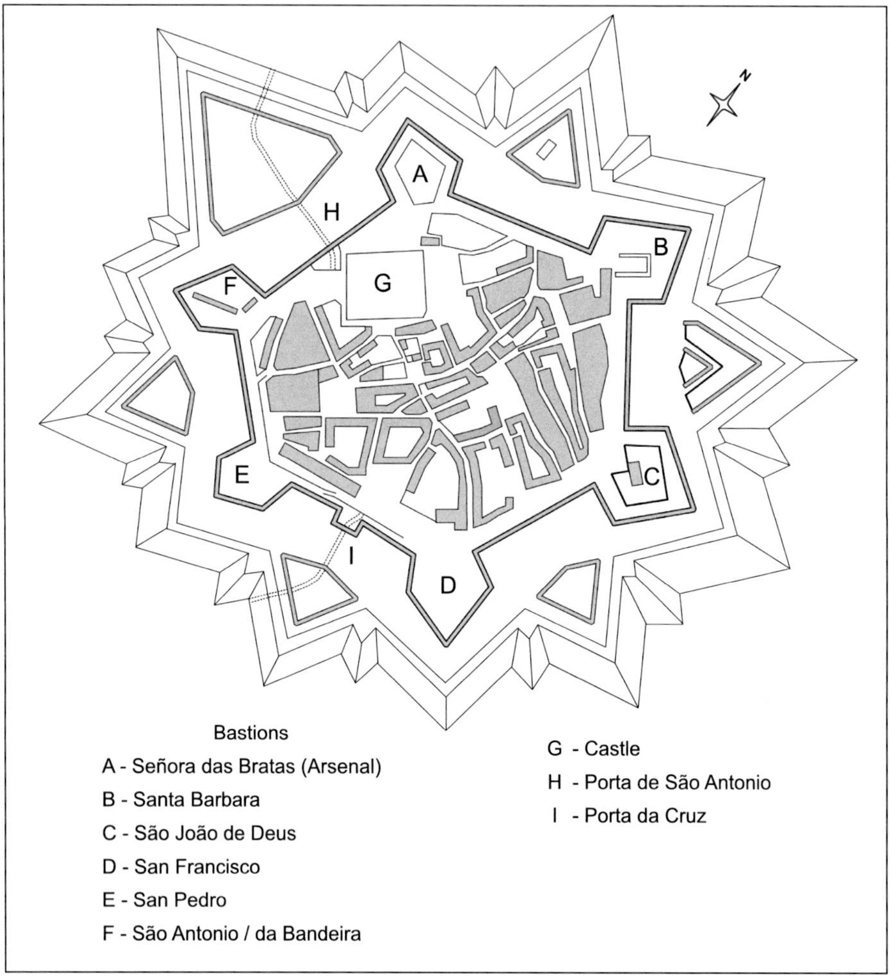

Almeida.

of the works, without having constantly to [recur?] to the great one'. From the disaster in August 1810, it would seem this recommendation was not followed.[43] It seems likely that Moore had seen this report. He commented, the fortress is 'defective in many parts of its construction and could not resist a serious attack for any time'.[44]

43 Two copies are held in TNA WO55/1561/9 and WO55/1561/6.

44 Maurice, *John Moore*, Vol.II, p.278.

Burgoyne remained at Almeida until his commander, Fletcher, arrived, probably around 10 November 1808. They then moved on to join Moore at Salamanca, arriving on 15 November. Boothby records meeting Fletcher and Burgoyne at Ciudad Rodrigo on 13 November 1808. Interestingly, Boothby also noted that Wilmot was still at Almeida on 16 November,[45] perhaps carrying out repairs to his damaged gun carriages?

The concern about topographical knowledge remained and every attempt was being made to build up information. Fletcher reported from Salamanca the duties he had assigned to his engineer officers:

> I have now sent Captain Burgoyne and Lieutenant [George] Meinecke, to reconnoitre the province of Ávila, its roads, rivers, bridges etc. and Lieutenant [Richard] Boteler is gone from hence to Zamora, and from thence will proceed up the Douro as far as he can, with safety, to examine that river and the roads leading to and from it. Lieutenant [John] Wells arrived this morning, from Elvas, by way of Badajoz, Merida, Trujillo, Almaraz and Plasencia, and he is going on towards Madrid, to meet the head of Lieutenant General Hope's column, and report on the country he has passed through.[46]

It was very clear that even if one could obtain a map, they were not to be relied on. Fletcher had ordered all his engineer officers to remedy that defect although he noted that 'objects more immediately professional have not as yet occurred'.[47] In a few weeks a substantial number of the key routes in Portugal and central Spain were surveyed.[48]

Burgoyne's subsequent movements, as told by his biographer, George Wrottesley, had Moore ordering Burgoyne to gallop the 140 miles from Salamanca to Madrid to order Lieutenant General Sir John Hope to join Moore at Salamanca. Burgoyne was also to lead Hope's force by the best route.[49] Burgoyne's letters tell a different story. His first task was to examine the route from Salamanca to Ávila, a possible route for Sir John Hope. His report dated 18 November 1808 stated that the road to Vinte [Aveinte] was generally good, then:

45 Boothby, *Under England's Flag*, p.188.

46 TNA WO55/977, Fletcher to Morse, Salamanca, 26 November 1808. George Meinecke was an officer in the King's German Legion engineers.

47 TNA WO55/977, Fletcher to Morse, Salamanca, 26 November 1808.

48 The map below shows routes where the present author has found evidence of surveys by Royal Engineers. There are likely to be more route surveys carried out by officers from the QMG department, Royal Staff Corps, and Royal Artillery.

49 Wrottesley, *Burgoyne*, p.29-30.

Routes surveyed by the Royal Engineers in October and November 1808.

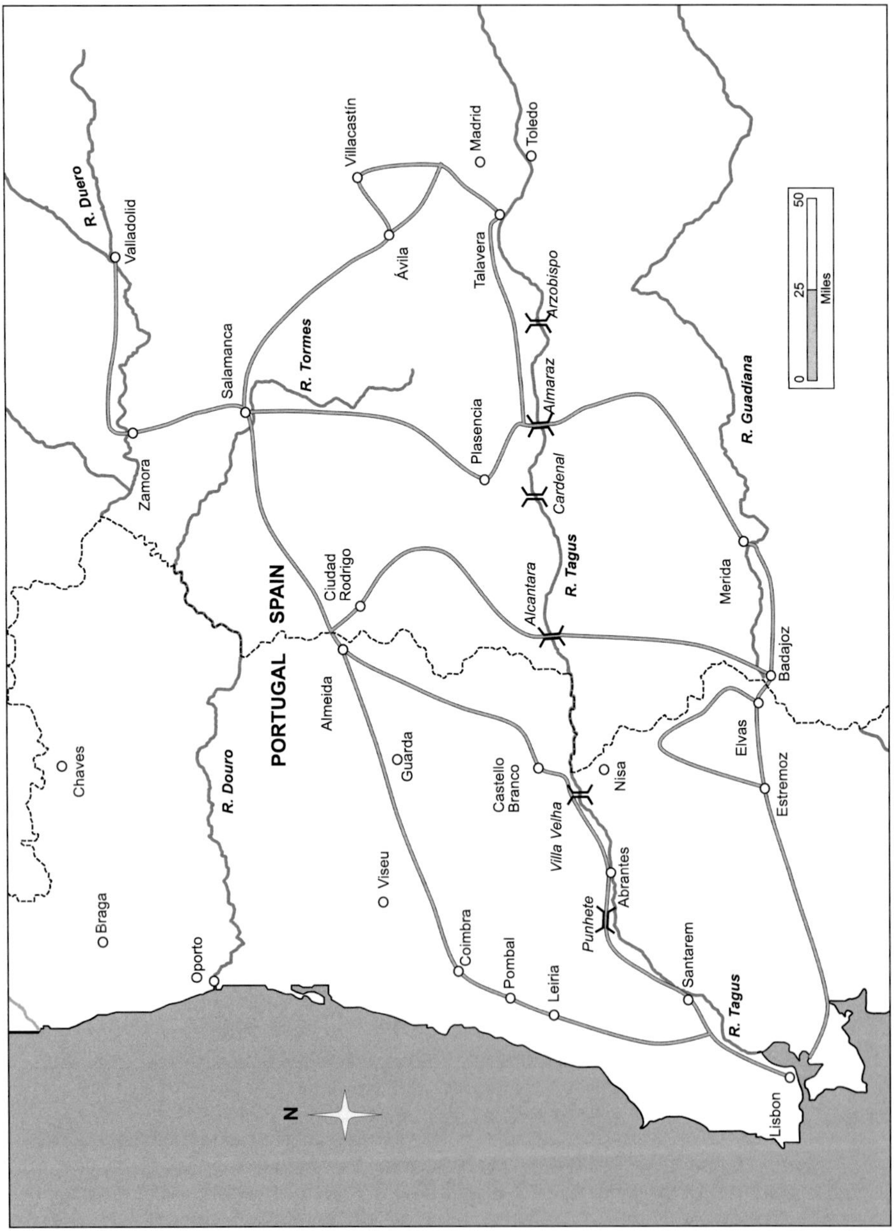

> [T]he road is over high rocky hills and so bad in parts as certainly not to be pronounced passable for artillery in its present state ... very little labour would render it practicable though it would always be a troublesome four leagues for carriages.[50]

Burgoyne now followed the road east to Villacastín, where on 19 November he heard that Hope was in Madrid. He rode there to update Hope on the situation and whilst he was there, Hope got the order to join Moore as quickly as possible. Burgoyne then advised him on the best route to take.[51] Burgoyne described the events:

> The morning after I wrote from Ávila, I came to this place [Villacastín] by Priolo Sana [Vicolozano], Dereja Lejo [Berrocalejo], Mediana [Mediana de Voltoyo] and Aldea Vieja, which is only a horse road and not passable for carriages. On my arrival, hearing General Hope was at Madrid (13 leagues from hence), I took post horses and with Lieutenant Meinecke arrived there next morning (21st inst.) having posted all night on [the] most miserable hacks, in order to communicate with the General.
>
> We remained there that day and the next morning accompanied the General to the Escorial where the 71st and [Major Percy] Drummond's Brigade of artillery arrived the same day, being the first that came up. General Hope, being directed to proceed to Salamanca, in consequence of the French being in the neighbourhood, seems determined to assemble all his force at Escorial previous to beginning his march across the Guadarrama, which will take some days; the cavalry will precede and will march between the infantry and the enemy with the accustomary [sic] precautions. At the Escorial, General Hope ordered me to join Colonel [William] De Lancey here and arrange with him the route etc. of his column to Salamanca and Meinecke has been sent to examine a road (the shortest) from Espinhar [El Espinar] to Ávila, of seven leagues, said to be practicable for carriages in fine weather.
>
> The French, from what I can collect [sic], appear to be in force about Valladolid and Aranda del Duero, but whether they are merely taking up a strong position between us and Castaños, to prevent the junction, which I rather am inclined to suspect, or whether (as is generally supposed) they mean to endeavour to cut off General Hope from joining you is doubtful; if the latter, Avila appears to me, of great consequence, being in a strong, hilly country and if we can find any decent roads about it, I think they will

50 TNA WO55/1561/9.

51 TNA WO55/1561/9, route from Salamanca to Avila; route to Villa Castin; WO55/958 & WO55/1561/9, Burgoyne to Fletcher, Villa Castin, 23 November 1808.

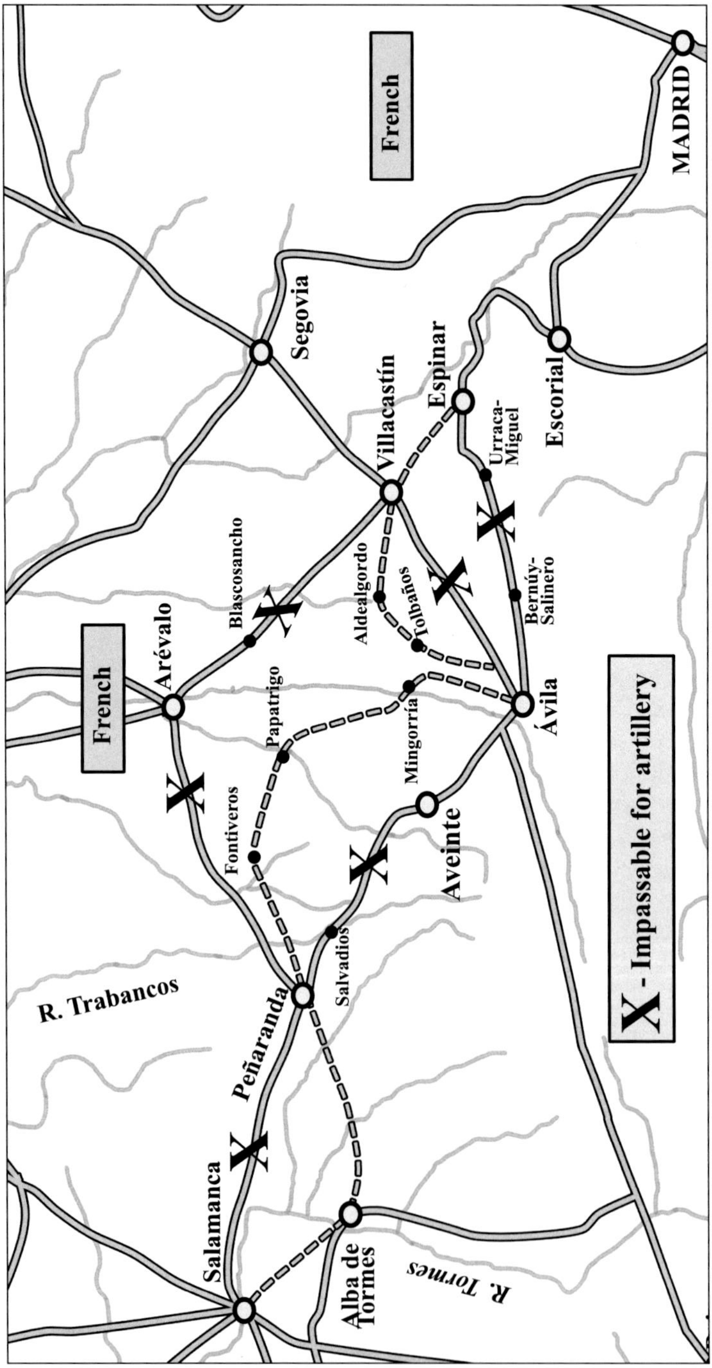

Route taken by Hope to join Moore.

> prove useful should the French come down in force; It will be an excellent center [sic] to work from and I think the only place in this part where any quantity of provisions should be deposited.
>
> The intention at present is, if the French keep at a distance, not to be able to come rapidly upon him, to march the cavalry by Arévalo and the infantry, artillery and park by Labajos, Blasco Sancho [Blascosancho] and Fontiveros.[52]

Hope was understandably concerned about his situation. He was close to Madrid. He knew there were significant French forces no more than a few days' march away, possibly much closer, and he knew from his trip into Madrid that there were no credible Spanish plans to resist them. He reported to Moore: 'It is perfectly evident that they [the Central Junta] are altogether without a plan as to their future military operations, either in case of success or misfortune'.[53]

Hope's original plan was to move north from Madrid on the good road to Arévalo, then turn west. He received reports that the French were at Valladolid and possibly in control of Arévalo and was forced to turn west earlier using smaller roads to Ávila. Burgoyne's and Meinecke's advice on the routes will have been vital to Hope in planning his forces movement.

Meinecke examined two routes. The first described the route from El Espinar to Ávila through Urruca [Urraca-Miguel] and Bernui [Bernúy-Salinero]

> The first league of the road from Espinhar is bad and cut up by the currents of rain from the mountains. The remaining part of the road to Ávila is good and practicable and though in several parts, rocky, may be used by any kind of carriage. The whole road is said to be difficult to pass after heavy rain.[54]

The second was a direct route on minor roads from Ávila to Salva Deos [Salvadios]. This report seems to stop in the middle of nowhere. As the roads were not practicable for artillery up to that point it is likely that Meinecke decided continuing was pointless.

Burgoyne also carried out a further reconnaissance; his report was dated 26 November 1808. His route used different roads from those he travelled and reported on previously on 18 and 23 November 1808. The new route went: Villacastín to Ávila through [Caserio de] Aldealgordo, Tolbaños and Venta de San Vicente. Then,

52 TNA WO55/1561/9, f.7, Burgoyne to Fletcher, Villacastín, 23 November 1808.

53 BL ADD MS57541, f.112, Hope to Moore, 20 November 1808. Quoted in Paul Reese, 'The Ablest Man in the British Army. The Life and Career of General Sir John Hope' (PhD Thesis, Florida State University, 2007), p.159.

54 TNA WO55/1561/9, Meinecke to Fletcher. Not dated.

Ávila to Salamanca through Mingorría, Papatrigo, Fontiveros, Peñaranda and Alba de Tormes. The key information was that this route was passable for artillery.[55]

Hope would have had access to these reports before he made his decision on the preferred route. The advantage of these routes, whilst not the best roads, apart from being passable for artillery, were that they would keep his forces away from the French who were near Arévalo on the best road. Hope had with him an officer who had ridden all these routes in the last two weeks and, more importantly, who could tell Hope that the most obvious routes from looking at a map were not practicable. Burgoyne's advice would have been invaluable. Whilst no detailed description of the route taken by Hope has been located, it seems reasonable that he would have followed the recommendations from Burgoyne.

Hope sent his artillery on ahead and then moved his infantry in a compact group screened by his cavalry. After an exhausting 48-mile march over 36 hours, they arrived at Peñaranda on 2 December and joined up with Moore on 4 December 1808. Burgoyne would have travelled with them.[56]

Whilst Burgoyne was working with Sir John Hope, other engineer officers were involved during the last two weeks of November carrying out several surveys to the north and east of Salamanca providing additional information to Moore.[57] This included Lieutenant Boteler reviewing the route from Salamanca to Zamora and the route of the Douro (Duero) from Zamora to Valladolid via Toro.

Moore, having arrived in Salamanca on 13 November, was faced with a difficult situation where he had little information on the movements or actions of either the Spanish or French armies. His instructions were to place himself under the orders of the Spanish Commander-in-Chief. Unfortunately, one had not been appointed. Moore also understood when he set off for Spain that there were substantial Spanish forces between his troops and the French armies, and that his role was to support the Spanish. Moore's original intention was for his forces to concentrate around Valladolid. However, before Moore arrived at Salamanca Blake had been defeated at Espinosa (north of Burgos) on 11 November and Castaños was defeated at Tudela (east of Burgos) on 23 November. There were now no Spanish forces between Moore and the French. He would have to concentrate his forces at Salamanca, extending Hope's route as the latter would have to travel west from Madrid to Salamanca rather than take the main road from Madrid to Valladolid.

55 TNA WO55/1561/9. Burgoyne to Fletcher, 26 November 1808. The way the report is written suggests that the two parts of the route went into Avila itself. Looking at the map one wonders if the route that Hope took went straight from the Tolbaños area to Mingorría, there being a road between them.

56 Reese, 'John Hope', pp.160-164.

57 Including: Route from Salamanca to Zamora, TNA WO55/1561/9, dated 18 November 1808; Report on River Douro from Zamora to Valladolid, TNA WO55/958, Boteler to Fletcher, 23 November 1808; Remarks on the River Tormes from Salamanca to Alba de Tormes, TNA WO55/1561/9, Mulcaster to Fletcher, 24 November 1808; Report on the River Tormes from Salamanca to Ledesma, Wedekind to Fletcher, 28 November 1808; Route from Zamora to Miranda, Boteler to Fletcher, 30 November 1808.

Moore, realising his precarious situation, wrote to Baird on 23 November, saying retreat was his only option in the face of overwhelming French forces. Moore continued to receive pressure from the British Ministers, John Hookham Frere and Stuart, to make some show of resistance and a delegation from the Spanish authorities also visited him to report that the Spanish forces and people were ready to defend their capital (they were not). With the arrival of Hope's force, Moore relented and decided to make an attempt to disrupt the French activities. His intention was to disturb any immediate French advance on Portugal. His small force could not hope to stop the French assault on Madrid. However, Moore still planned for the retreat that he knew would be coming.

One example of this planning was Burgoyne being sent back to the border, reporting directly to Moore on the state of the Spanish fortress of Ciudad Rodrigo. His report, dated 10 December 1808, stated:

> Ciudad Rodrigo in the common course of warfare would be deemed incapable of defence, but to the Spaniards fighting for the independence of their country, it would be difficult to point out the place [as] not susceptible of some defence. Its works though possessing nearly every fault a fortification can have, when vigorously and judiciously defended will delay an enemy some time and would protect the town from destruction till they were razed[sic] or lodgements made upon them. The town itself being built of stone and containing many capacious and strong buildings would be capable of considerable resistance when occupied by a determined body of men.
>
> On examining the place, there is no doubt but that the principal attack would be directed from the north where the ground affords cover from the town at 300 yards distance behind a small hill from the summit of which the works could be breached, the parapets having been ruined and the fire silenced from the previous batteries situated on the favourable hill above.
>
> This is a defect in its situation which cannot under present circumstances be remedied, the only thing therefore in our power is to render the approach of the enemy on that side as difficult as possible. For that purpose, the convents of San Francisco and Santa Cruz should be occupied and maintained as long as possible for these convents seeing the reverse of the hill should be removed as it forms a parapet against the place.
>
> In the Fausse Bray or lower line of works, platforms should be laid and embrasures pierced in the parapet to which guns might be brought from other parts of the works, in order to bring as much fire as possible on the situations of the enemy's first batteries. These guns might be removed when the enemy's batteries became too powerful.
>
> Two fleches might be constructed in a direction from a short distance, in front of the two salient angles of the counterscarp to the re-entering

> angles forming a sort of covered way to these two angles which would defend the hollows in the glacis, at present not seen from the place.
>
> On the main line the guns might be arranged in such manner by altering the platforms and making new embrasures that they might all be brought to bear on the dangerous ground, whereby the establishment of the enemy's batteries would be attended with great difficulty and loss and arranged in this manner there would be space for more guns; the mortar on that battery should be removed to some more distant spot where it would be more out of the way and its effect would be the same. The Cathedral and College forming two sides of a square within this battery would constitute an excellent retrenchment to it when breached. Traverses must then be made on the rampart to the right and left to prevent the enemy extending when on the breach; these traverses of course will be so constructed as to enable the garrison freely to communicate and even to convey guns or carriages along the ramparts.[58]

Burgoyne's evaluation of the defences and the best way to attack were confirmed by the later attacks on the town. The following day, Burgoyne wrote another 'private' letter on what he found there. It is not addressed but was likely to the Chief Engineer, Fletcher.

> I walked round the works this morning with the [Spanish] engineer here and Mr Ryan as an interpreter for what I could not myself make him understand and it was fortunate that I took the precaution, as it appeared to be the engineer's intention to beat about the bush and never come to the point. I was enabled to be assured of it. In short, it is evidently the intention of the people here to do nothing, nor do they wish anything to be done, even by us; They declare first, they have no money, second, there would not be more than 600 militia and half of them not serviceable to defend it and lastly, they have no order or permission from the Supreme Junta.
>
> To the first, I said perhaps that might be removed by our General but I could not say positively. To the second, I could not agree but that they could get plenty of people from the country, however they said the people of the country capable of carrying arms were all going to the armies; I told them that if there were not now many when the enemy were near many of course from the armies, at any rate there was no harm in being prepared and for the last, they agreed, that for trifling improvements the consent of the Supreme Junta would not be necessary. They, however, declare their intention of defending the place to the last with however few people may

58 BL ADD MS57544, f.184, Burgoyne to Moore, 10 December 1808.

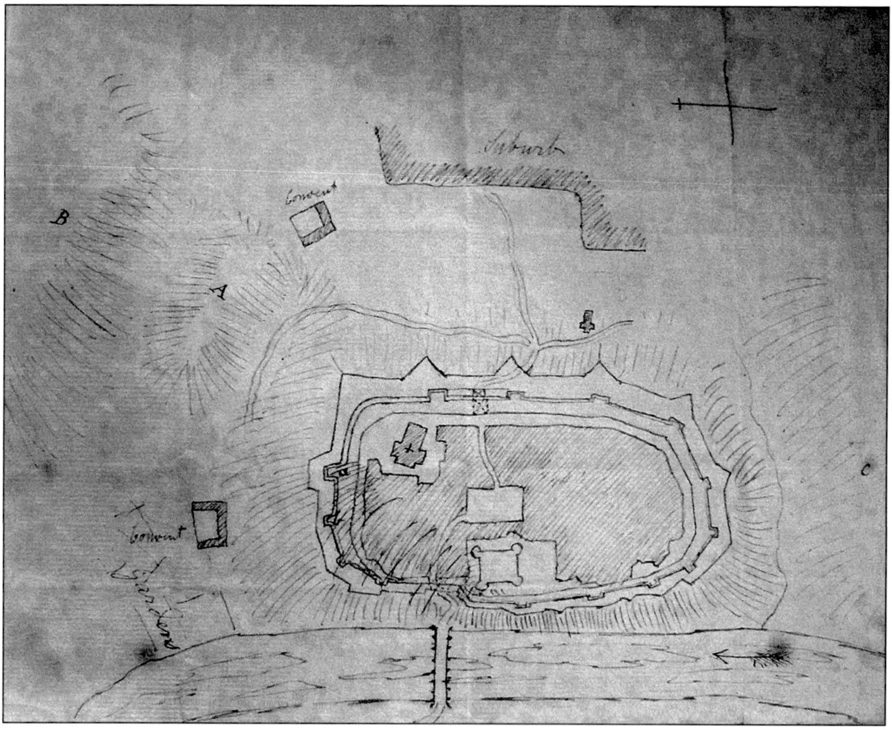

Ciudad Rodrigo, Burgoyne Papers. (Royal Engineers Museum)

be in it; Indeed, the Bishop attended this day on the Junta to administer some patriotic oath of conquering or dying, or something to a similar purpose. If the thing is thought of much consequence Mr Ryan will be at Salamanca with their letter, having been sent for by Colonel [George] Murray and will tell you the disposition of the Junta on the business as he has been present at all transactions I have had on the subject.

I told the engineer that at any rate it was my duty to examine what could be done in a trifling way and report to you and that if he would walk round with me, I should be happy to hear his ideas; this he consented to; but evidently during the whole course of our communication avoided coming to the point; I asked if he had any plans and he said no; he would constantly talk of considerable new works, nor could I get him to consider that as not our business; He said many proposals had been given in for the improvements of the works; I immediately asked to look at them and he declared that he did not know where they were to be found. In short, [he] would not communicate cordially in any way; [he] talked a great deal of nonsense, that it would be difficult to occupy the hill to the northward by works; that he found a great fault in the place, not having bombproofs and

> would expatiate upon the line toward the river, which is evidently the only one not requiring any consideration. To give you an idea of his abilities as engineer, it was him that placed the palisades on that line because the French were at Almeida.
>
> He told me there was plenty of water in the place as well as ammunition and artillery stores and a large quantity of entrenching tools and some artificers ditto, but no palisades or timber which it would take considerable time and expense to procure.
>
> You will perceive that I can in no way be of further use here. I shall therefore expect to be ordered to join the army immediately. Of course, I have not given them any paper.[59]

The tone of the last paragraph suggests that Burgoyne had been ordered to Ciudad Rodrigo to improve its defences and was he concerned he would miss the operations of Moore's army. By this time, Moore had decided on an advance, and it is likely that Burgoyne knew this.

Moore's forces began their advance from Salamanca towards Valladolid on 11 December 1808. First contact with the French was at Rueda on 13 December where a French cavalry picket was taken. On 16 December, Moore discovered from a captured French dispatch that *Maréchal* Jean-de-Dieu Soult was at Saldañha with no support nearby. He changed his plans to attack Soult, who was unaware that the British army was near. The leading elements of Moore's army reached Mayorga on 19 December: the weather was now bitterly cold and snowing. Another unsuspecting French cavalry advance guard of two regiments was ejected from Sahagun on 21 December and then Moore had to wait two days for the weather to clear and supplies to come up. The advance towards Soult at Saldañha continued on 23 December. During the day, Moore received the confirmation that the French had discovered his location and were advancing against him in overwhelming numbers. There was now no choice but to retreat. The soldiers and many officers openly showed their discontent with this decision, not understanding the danger they were facing. Moore's troops started the retreat on 24 December and his main body had passed the bridge of Castro Gonzalo at Benavente on 28 December 1808.

Burgoyne had been ordered to mine this bridge over the Esla at Benavente, a critical crossing point. With Burgoyne was Mulcaster, who noted in his diary: 'Last night cut away the woodwork and made a mine on the haunch of the arch which we lighted [sic] on the appearance of a French patrole among the burning ruins of the Posada and set [it] off'.[60] Leaving the destruction to the last minute to allow allied stragglers to cross, Burgoyne eventually blew an arch on 29 December,

59 NAM 1970-04-16, f.7, Ciudad Rodrigo, 10 December 1808.

60 Mark S. Thompson (ed.), *The Peninsular War Diary of Edmund Mulcaster RE*, 1808-10 (Sunderland: Amazon, 2015), p.13.

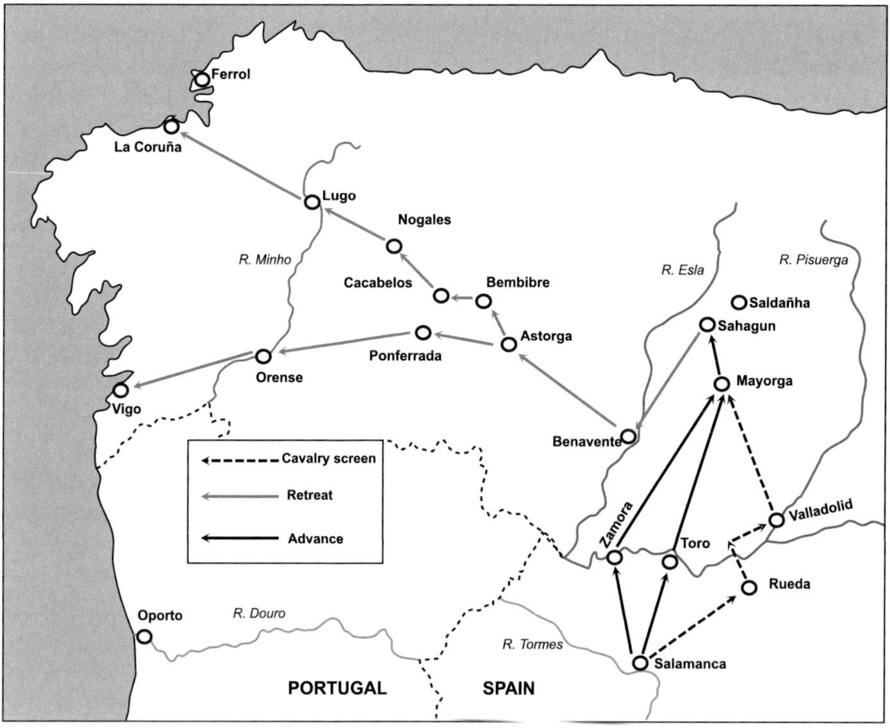

Moore's advance and retreat 1808-9.

in the face of the French advance guard. This gave the allied troops a valuable 24 hour respite from the French pursuit. Burgoyne believed that Napoleon was present in the large group of French officers who watched the proceedings.[61]

Leaving Benavente that day, Burgoyne travelled ahead of the troops with Fletcher and Mulcaster. They had been ordered to examine Vigo and La Coruña and make recommendations on the best place to embark the army. The original plan was to use Vigo, but Moore had a preference to use La Coruña. On 3 January 1809, at Lugo, Fletcher decided that there would not be time to examine both, so he sent Burgoyne to Vigo whilst he continued to La Coruña and Betanzos Bay.

Neither report seems to have survived, but Maurice says that Moore reviewed the 'reports from his engineers' on 5 January 1809 and decided to continue with the bulk of his troops to La Coruña.[62] Craufurd with five battalions of light infantry had already set off on the Vigo road on 31 December 1808. Moore was content that by using two ports and routes the retreat and embarkation would run smoother.

61 Wrottesley, *Burgoyne*, p.31.

62 Maurice, *Sir John Moore*, Vol.II, p.387.

Burgoyne wrote a detailed report on the town of Vigo, addressed to Fletcher, dated 18 January 1809. It seems unlikely that that this was the report that was sent to Moore as it goes into detail on the defences of the town rather than its suitability as an embarkation point.[63] Based on Fletcher's positive report, Moore retreated to La Coruña and fought the battle on 16 January 1809, that cost him his life but saved the British army. Burgoyne was spared the final days of the winter retreat and the battle, embarking from Vigo and arriving in England on 1 February 1809.

Burgoyne's action in destroying the bridge at Castro Gonzalo (Benavente) was one of the few successes during the retreat. A number of engineers were ordered to blow up bridges to delay the French. The results were very disappointing, with several failing, and this highlighted a concern amongst the field engineers about their limited training for field activities. We will come back to this issue later. At the time there was some concern in the army about how few bridges were being destroyed, but this was a decision made by Moore himself:

> There were some officers who criticised, occasionally, the operations that were adopted, in a manner injurious to the service; and this subject of blowing up bridges was one of those upon which they chiefly dwelt. General Paget at length mentioned this to Sir John Moore and pressed him to destroy more bridges. Sir John, in answer, requested him to look around and examine with him more particularly the nature of the rivers over which these bridges were thrown. He pointed out to him, that both infantry and cavalry could usually pass a little above or below the bridge; and that the obstruction to artillery would be quickly repaired by an army constituted like the French ... Whenever any important advantage could arise from blowing up a bridge, he thought it certainly should be done : but he was persuaded that General Paget would agree with him, that when the advantage was less, it was a cruel measure to do such lasting mischief to those allies we came to benefit, as to ruin, for a length of time, the communications of their country.
>
> This was the defence that Sir John Moore made, for what some have thought a neglect; but which increased General Paget's esteem for his friend and commander.[64]

63 REM 4601-74, f.68, Burgoyne to Fletcher, 18 January 1809.

64 James Moore, *A Narrative of the Campaign of the British Army in Spain* (London: Johnson, 1809), pp.312-3.

5

1809 – Ejection of the French from Portugal

Moore had left a small force of about 8,000 troops in Portugal when he advanced into Spain and this British presence remained through the winter of 1808/9 under the command of Lieutenant General Sir John Cradock. A small addition to the force, including some Royal Engineers, sailed from England on 14 January, arriving on 5 March 1809.

Less than three weeks after his arrival in England, Burgoyne was writing to the Ordnance Headquarters requesting further active service and he was immediately told to hold himself in readiness. Several other engineer officers received similar orders for Portugal and Burgoyne shared the common view: 'our prospect is only that of remaining quiet in a dull quarter and returning [to England] if the French approach'.[1] Much of the military and the public believed that the French were unstoppable. Despite that, the British government was committed to support the defence of Spain and Portugal and a convoy including Burgoyne sailed on 18 March 1809, arriving in Lisbon on 2 April 1809. Landing with Burgoyne were the Commanding Royal Engineer, Fletcher, and Lieutenants Boothby, George Hamilton and Mulcaster.[2]

Cradock was still in command of the British forces in Portugal. He was very concerned about the possibility of being attacked by the superior French forces, there being armies to the north (Soult) and east (Victor). The immediate threat came from the north, Napoleon having ordered Soult to invade and take the Portuguese capital. The timetable set by Napoleon was unrealistic. Soult entered Portugal from its northern border and met stiff resistance, not taking Oporto until 29 March. Cradock decided to move the bulk of his force north of Lisbon to counter the French invasion but was still wary of a second invasion from the east. Two days after his arrival, Burgoyne was on the south side of the Tagus looking at

1 Wrottesley, *Burgoyne*, p.34.

2 Unfortunately, the diary used by Wrottesley, covering the period from February to 24 May 1809 is not in the Royal Engineers collection.

'the position for securing Lisbon from bombardment'.[3] The allies were very aware of the risk of the French taking the southern bank and threatening the shipping in the Tagus estuary. Measures to prevent this were looked at several times through 1809 and 1810 but no work was started on improving the defences until late 1810.

On 6 April, Burgoyne noted being billeted on an English merchant in Rua da Emenda. This street, close to the waterfront, still exists. On the 8th, he hired an English servant, who had previously been the servant of another engineer officer, Captain Henry Goldfinch, who had been captured by the French at Oporto. The same day, he also received orders to join Major General John Randoll Mackenzie's brigade which he believed was at Castanheira although he learned after setting off that the brigade was actually at Sobral. Joining Mackenzie, he was then ordered to move north-west through Vila Verde and Bombarral to Óbidos.

Burgoyne's diary over these few days gives an insight into his character. He noted on 10 April, with sympathy, that he spoke with some muleteers who gave him 'a most miserable account of their sufferings'. They had been pressed into service, were not fed or paid and were guarded to ensure they did not leave; 'the mules, oxen etc., when once pressed into the service ... are frequently driven to death and always very much ill-used'.[4] The poor treatment of the locals pressed into service continued throughout the war although nothing like on the scale inflicted by the French. On arriving at Villa Verde, ahead of the troops, he obtained accommodation, 'had I not spoken a little of the language, been very mild and quiet and offered to pay for everything I got' he felt he would not have got a billet. He also noted that other allied troops were much more demanding and less willing to pay. Burgoyne seemed to have sympathy for the plight of the civilians who suffered at the hands of invading armies and allied armies. Burgoyne must have picked up some of the Portuguese language during the previous campaign.

At Óbidos, Burgoyne and fellow engineer Charles Boothby were ordered to join the right column of the army under Major General John Sherbrooke. Initially, the orders were to march to Santarem, but they were countermanded and the force moved north to Leiria. The convention throughout the war, was to assign engineer officers to the larger army units. The generals quickly came to appreciate this addition to their 'family' where the role was a mixture of staff, liaison, and engineer officer. Trained army staff officers were still a rarity as the Staff College had only recently been opened.

On 23 April 1809, Sir Arthur Wellesley arrived in Lisbon to take command of the allied forces. His most immediate threat were the forces of Soult in the north. Victor, whose troops were around Merida, was being watched by Cuesta's Spanish army.[5] Soult, having taken Oporto, worked to pacify the north-western corner of

3 Wrottesley, *Burgoyne*, p.35.
4 Wrottesley, *Burgoyne*, p.36.
5 See a detailed explanation in Oman, *Peninsular War*, Vol.II, pp.289-293.

the Iberian Peninsula which was still in a state of insurrection and threatened by Portuguese and Spanish forces. He was still there a month after he had taken the city. There is a suggestion that the reason for his delay was political, not military. We will come back to this.

Wellesley made his decisions quickly and orders were issued for the allied troops to advance. Burgoyne noted on 28 April 1809, that the order to advance to Pombal had been received, but that it arrived one day late. Officers were billeted in houses when on the move and Burgoyne did not appear to share many of his contemporaries' enthusiasm for female company when options for rest were limited, remarking that night, 'two pretty girls … were so obliging as to sit conversing with us until eleven at night, while we were dying for sleep and were to rise the next morning at three'.[6]

The allied forces concentrated around Coimbra in the first days of May 1809. Burgoyne was ordered make a survey of the city, assisted by three other engineer officers, Lieutenants Boothby, John Archer Williams, and Edward Fyers. He rode round the city with Fletcher on 4 May 1809. The purpose was to determine if it was possible to defend the city from a French attack. It was still possible that Soult could push south and threaten Coimbra, so understanding what defences could be put in place quickly was essential.

Burgoyne's caring attitude is again seen during the stay at Coimbra when another engineer officer, Lieutenant Rice Jones fell ill with the ague and 'Captain Burgoyne removed me into his own quarters at Coimbra and rendered me every little assistance which a sick person required'.[7]

Wellesley's plan was to advance on Oporto with his main force of about 24,000 whilst detaching Marshal William Carr Beresford with about 6,000 troops to cut off the likely line of retreat. Beresford's troops left first on 6 May 1809 and by 10 May were in position at Lamego.

Whilst Soult was completely unaware of Beresford's force, on 8 May 1809, he was given information on Wellesley's advance when the French traitor, Argenton, was arrested. Argenton had just met with Wellesley and had seen his troop movements around Coimbra which he divulged to Soult.[8] Soult, now on the defensive, alerted his advanced guard south of Oporto. He also ordered his troops to the north to retire to Amarante and ordered Loison, at all costs, to keep the road to the east through Amarante open for a retreat. Realising that it would take several days for his forces to concentrate, he was left with little choice but to stay at Oporto.

An attempt to surround the French advance around Aveiro failed on 10 May, and on 11 May, after a sharp skirmish at Grijo, the French retired across the Douro into Oporto and burnt the bridge of boats, believing this would keep them safe.

6 Wrottesley, *Burgoyne*, p.39.
7 H.V. Shore, *An Engineer Officer under Wellington in the Peninsula* (Huntingdon: Trotman, 2005), p.24.
8 For a description of the 'Argenton Conspiracy' see Oman, *Peninsular War*, Vol.II, pp.321-3.

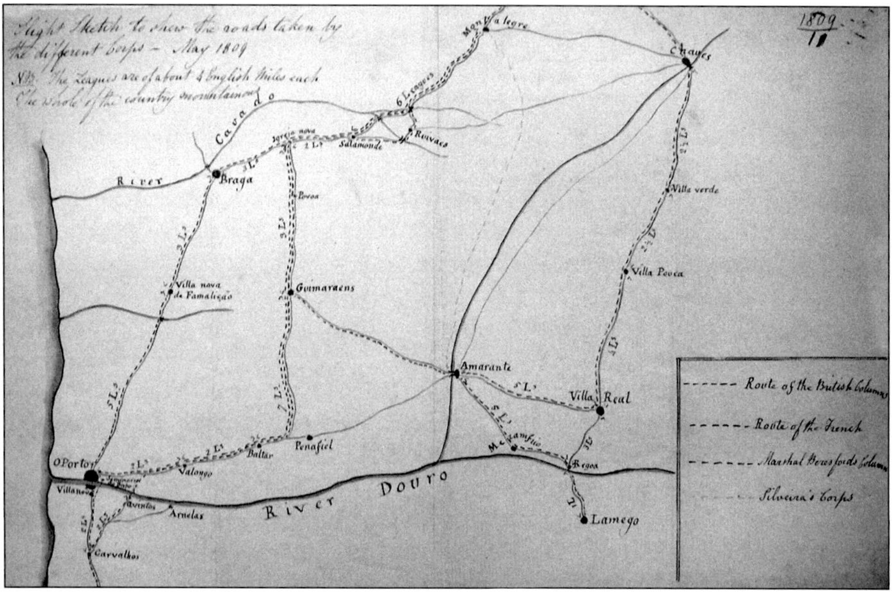

Sketch to show roads taken by different corps in Oporto campaign. (Royal Engineers Museum)

Arriving on the morning of 12 May 1809, the bulk of Wellesley's forces were out of sight around Villa Nova on the south bank of the Douro. He sent a small force under Major General John Murray four miles upstream to Avintes having heard that the main ferry boat could be repaired.[9] In the meantime, Wellesley was given further information that there were unguarded wine barges on the north bank nearer the city. Wellesley grabbed this opportunity and pushed troops, led by the 1/3rd Foot, the Buffs, across the river who then occupied the abandoned but defensible seminary on the high ground. When the French realised what was happening, they were too late to stop the crossings and were forced to retire precipitately losing much of their baggage and artillery.

Burgoyne says very little about his personal actions during the attack on Oporto. He took no part in the main action having been sent upriver, with John Murray's force, to Avintes to look for boats. Many were found due to the inattention of the French guards and John Murray pushed his troops across. Burgoyne's diary described briefly how he 'had been sent to collect boats at A Vintes [Avintes] and Arnelas, which having done, I was returning when I heard the firing, and got over the water just after General Hill's Brigade had landed'.[10]

9 Two battalions of King's German Legion, some German riflemen, two squadrons of the 14th Light Dragoons and two guns.

10 Wrottesley, *Burgoyne*, p.41.

It is likely that Burgoyne crossed at the seminary as he records that he loaned his mule to Captain George, Marquess of Tweeddale to fetch a surgeon for Lieutenant General Edward Paget who was wounded during the French attack on the seminary. Another engineer officer, Hamilton, who was also with John Murray, crossed at Avintes and was subsequently badly injured when the 14th Light Dragoons charged the retreating French.[11] A third engineer officer, Rice Jones, who was with Burgoyne, was sent back to Villa Nova to report that boats were available at Avintes. He does not mention Burgoyne returning to headquarters.

The French having been ejected, the engineers worked to restore the bridge across the Douro at Oporto which was completed on the evening of 13 May 1809.[12]

On 14 May, Burgoyne was ordered to join John Murray's brigade which had followed the retreating French. He joined them at Valongo and then continued towards Parades. It was here that Soult heard the terrible news that his subordinate, Loison, had lost Amarante and his retreat route was blocked. Soult was forced to turn north on to the poor tracks across the mountains in terrible wet weather. Burgoyne reported that 'we found several guns and howitzers, most of them mounted and spiked and a great number of ammunition wagons some blown up and others entire'.[13] The pursuit continued to Guimarães and then across the mountains again to Povoa de Lanhaso, then on to Salamonde and Montalegre. On 17 May 1809, Burgoyne assisted in repairing a bridge between Salamonde and Ruivães. Mulcaster must also have been present, as he recorded repairing the bridge. Both armies were in great need of provisions. The French were stealing anything they could find in the villages they passed through; the British had marched too fast for the commissary to keep up. Burgoyne was lucky in being invited to mess with Captain Robert Lawson's Brigade of artillery, 'otherwise in this country, I should be badly off indeed'.[14]

The pursuit was abandoned on 19 May 1809. There was no way the British could keep up with the French who had abandoned all their baggage. It was also on this date when Wellesley heard that Victor had finally stirred from Merida and had attacked the bridge over the Tagus at Alcantara,[15] a possible first move for an invasion of Portugal from the east. Fortunately, an arch on the bridge had been destroyed.

Even at this early stage in the war, there is a certain cynicism in Burgoyne's diary entries; he noted on 19 May 1809:

11 Thompson (ed.), *Mulcaster*, p.35.
12 TNA WO55/958 Fletcher to Morse, 24 May 1809.
13 Wrottesley, *Burgoyne*, p.42.
14 Wrottesley, *Burgoyne*, p.44.
15 Oman, *Peninsular War*, Vol.II, p.434.

> Had we made the same exertions in following the enemy on this occasion, which we did [in the] last campaign in Spain to retreat from them, one would suppose more might have been done; *but it is probable Sir Arthur know best.*[16]

Burgoyne wrote an account of the Oporto campaign later in the year.[17] It does not comment on his personal actions but provides his critique of the campaign, particularly focussing on the pursuit and its consequences. Only part of it was published by Wrottesley. Burgoyne made a number of criticisms of the handling of the campaign:

- The French stayed far too long at Oporto.
- The allied crossing should have been at Avintes with a demonstration opposite Oporto.
- The allied pursuit was too slow, allowing the French to retreat with little interference.
- Wellesley not giving Beresford more time to get into position to intercept the retreating French.
- The Spanish General, Pedro Caro, Marqués de la Romana was not given warning of Wellesley's intentions.
- Abandoning the pursuit when it was possible to completely destroy the forces of Soult and Ney.

Let us look at each of these points, in turn.

The French stayed far too long at Oporto.

Burgoyne was strongly critical writing 'one cannot conceive how Soult's corps could possibly escape total destruction … but from want of information or some other accountable reason, he blindly remained in Oporto until he ran the greatest risk of being entirely cut off'.[18] As we have already seen, Soult was aware of the advance of Wellesley from Coimbra. However, he was not aware of Beresford's long flank march to cut him off. Soult believed that the force under Loison, that he had despatched east, would keep the main route open for his retreat. Soult needed to wait to give his detachments to the north time to concentrate. With the 'impassable' Douro to his front and his line of retreat secure, the risk of waiting seemed low.

16 Wrottesley, *Burgoyne*, p.44: author's italics.

17 REM 4601-74, f.131, A Narrative of the Capture of Oporto in 1809 by Lieutenant General Sir Arthur Wellesley, with Remarks [Not Dated, but after Talavera]; emphasis added.

18 Wrottesley, *Burgoyne*, p.44 and REM 4601-72, f.131, Burgoyne's commentary on the Oporto Campaign.

The placing of guards on the banks of the Douro was negligent and for that, Soult can rightly be blamed. There is no way that the allied forces should have been able to cross at Villa Nova and Avintes without the French being aware and resisting the attempt. Once the allies were across, his plan for a controlled withdrawal was ruined and he was left with no option but a precipitate retreat. At this point all was not lost as he had a secure route of withdrawal, or did he? Loison's failure to keep him properly informed of the situation was similarly negligent and compounded by not telling Soult that the route was blocked until after the unplanned retreat had started. Now the situation was a complete disaster.

A second and probably less likely reason for Soult's delay was the cause of the Argenton Conspiracy. It has been claimed that Soult was trying to create his own empire in northern Portugal and the long delay was to allow the idea to progress to a point where Soult could claim the throne of this new northern Lusitanian country. Argenton's conspiracy was to encourage Soult to do this, so that the French army could revolt against his actions. There is evidence to suggest that Soult was considering such a step, but here, the only consideration is whether it caused Soult to delay too long at Oporto when he should either have advanced as ordered by Napoleon or retreated in the face of the allied army. Even if Soult had declared himself ruler of this new Kingdom, it would not have stopped Wellesley throwing him out of the city.[19]

Assuming that the reason for staying was operational rather than political, Soult did not stay too long. He needed time to allow his forces to concentrate and for his escape route to be confirmed. His failures were not guarding the Douro around Oporto and not ensuring that Loison had secured his route of retreat.

The allied crossing should have been at Avintes with a demonstration opposite Oporto.

When Wellesley approached Oporto, he would have been unsure what the French intended to do. It is possible that the French could have retired as he approached. On arriving at Villa Nova on the south bank of the Douro, he first sent troops eastward under John Murray, having been told that a crossing was possible around Avintes. It was at a later point that Wellesley was alerted to the possibility of crossing near the city. The poor watch set by the French gave the allied forces an hour to establish themselves before they were attacked. Had the French defenders been alert, the crossing was likely to have failed completely with significant losses.

There is some merit in Burgoyne's criticism. Wellesley was aware that some of the French forces had left on the morning of the 12 May. A strong crossing at Avintes would have severely disrupted the French retreat. Oman argued that had John Murray's force been larger and better handled, the French would have suffered significantly more casualties. It must be remembered that there was no

19 Oman, *Peninsular War*, Vol.II, p.274 for a description of Soult's actions.

information available to the allies on a defensible position around Avintes, so a strong French counter-attack could still have repulsed the allied crossing. A French retreat would have been difficult, but, if Soult had held his ground, then a contested river crossing could have been very dangerous. There was no danger to the French of a crossing at Oporto, if the river front had been guarded.

Had the opportunity of crossing at Villa Nova not been presented to Wellesley, then he would have made the main attempt to cross at Avintes, as Burgoyne had suggested. However, Burgoyne's comment: 'but then the *brilliant achievement* of forcing the passage of a considerable river in the presence of the enemy *would have been lost*';[20] appears grossly unfair. He appears to suggest that Wellesley's decision to cross at Villa Nova was taking an unnecessary risk for the sake of glory. The present author finds it impossible accept that accusation.

The allied pursuit was too slow, allowing the French to retreat with little interference.

By the end of 12 May 1809, Soult's disorganised army was ten miles from the city, at Baltar. Wellesley's forces were still spread across both sides of the Douro. Whilst most of the infantry were across on the 12th, the artillery, transport, and baggage were still on the south bank. Until the bridge was re-established late on 13 May, everything had to be moved across the river on barges; a slow process. The allied army had marched 80 miles in the last four days, fought two actions, and the men were in need of food. Wellesley had little choice but to delay the main advance until 14 May. He was also unaware that Beresford held the Amarante road. Meanwhile, John Murray continued to press the French with a small force.

Burgoyne's account quoted from the King of Prussia's instruction to his generals: 'It is the fault of the general-in-chief when he is short of food. When he gives a battle he has a design, and if he has a design, he must prepare all that is necessary for the execution; therefore, care should be taken to have bread or biscuit for eight, [or] ten days'. Whilst this may be true in the perfect world, the realities of logistics in the Peninsula and the inexperience of Wellesley's commissariat made it a serious challenge to keep his troops fed. On reaching Oporto, Wellesley's supply line was already extensive and his forces were moving into a wasteland where French troops had been stationed for several weeks. The route to the north of Oporto was entering a mountainous area of Portugal where supplies would be limited even at the best of times and his supply line would continue to grow. In the unpublished portion of Burgoyne's narrative, he continued the quotation from the King of Prussia: 'For the fatigues, if they were not too excessive, it will be necessary in extraordinary days to do extraordinary things'. Wellesley's troops had marched 80 miles to reach Oporto. The pursuit continued for seven more days before Wellesley recalled his troops. Had Wellesley pushed on most of his troops

20 Wrottesley, *Burgoyne*, p.45, emphasis added.

immediately, he would have done so without artillery and baggage, leaving his troops at risk if Soult had turned and faced him (unlikely, but possible). Also, the allied troops by then would have been marching hard for 10 days, covering up to 200 miles in appalling weather with supplies steadily decreasing. The 'fatigues' appear to be excessive.

When Soult realised early on 13 May that he was trapped, he made the decision to abandon most of his heavy baggage and strike across the mountains. There was no way that the allied army could keep pace with a fleeing French army, which marched faster than a British army even when fully equipped.

It is possible that John Murray could have pressed the French harder. He showed a cautious attitude when he crossed the Douro at Avintes, letting the French pass without any serious attempt to impede them. It should also be remembered that the French were familiar with these roads; the British were not. It was probably unfair to say that the pursuit was too slow.

Not giving Beresford more time to get into position to intercept the retreating French.

On this point, Burgoyne is wrong. Beresford, when he advanced, expected the Amarante road to be in the possession of Silveira's Portuguese forces. When he approached, he found that Loison had dislodged them. However, after two skirmishes on the 10 and 11 May 1809, Loison had been ejected and Beresford was in full control of the route. Soult's headlong flight through the mountains was because Beresford controlled the route east. If Beresford had set off earlier to give him more time to get into position, there would have been an increased risk that his movements would have been detected.

Romana was not given warning of Wellesley's intentions.

At the time of Soult's retreat, Romana was operating against *Maréchal* Michel Ney in northern Spain, based near Oviedo. Romana had his own problems. The French had launched an attack against him and, on 18 May 1809, had caught Romana before he could concentrate his forces.[21] Romana was forced to flee to Gijon, where he boarded a Spanish man-of-war. Wellesley had written to Romana on 9 May 1809, informing him of his intention of attacking Soult at Oporto.[22] He included details of the position of Beresford and the likely routes of retreat for Soult, informing him that Loison had taken Amarante. There does not appear to be any further communication until Wellesley was informed of Romana's reverses later in the month.

It is clear that Romana did have knowledge of Wellesley's intentions, but was in no position to support the allied operations.

21 Oman, *Peninsular War*, Vol.II, pp.378-382.

22 Gurwood (ed.), *Despatches*, Vol.III, p.224, Wellesley to Romana, Quinta de la Graciosa, 9 May 1809.

Abandoning the pursuit when it was possible to completely destroy the forces of Soult and Ney.

Burgoyne considered two arguments for not continuing the pursuit. The first, that when Soult combined with Ney, they would be too strong for Wellesley's force. The second that the advance would have left Lisbon open to Victor.

Burgoyne suggested that the combined French force would have been no more than 20,000, which is too low. Certainly, Soult's force would have been in poor condition and with little equipment, but was still about 19,000 strong. Ney had an additional 17,000 troops but many of these were tied up holding key points in the unruly provinces. Ney at this time was many miles away chasing Romana on the northern Spanish coast.

Had Wellesley continued his pursuit, he would have had around 30,000 troops including Beresford's Portuguese, before the expected deductions from a rapid and hard advance in poor conditions. Many of his soldiers were untried in battle. His force would be operating on a slender supply line over 200 miles long, through mountainous country with no secure source of supplies. It would have been a huge risk to advance that far.

Wellesley's's instructions from the British government were to clear Portugal, which might include crossing the border. Any advance into Spain required further government approval.

Burgoyne's argument that Victor was too weak to advance on Lisbon has some merit, but it was based on the premise that the 10,000 allied troops under MacKenzie, supported by the Spanish forces under Cuesta, would contain the French. It also concluded, based on captured French dispatches, that the route to Lisbon would not be able to feed the advancing French whose extensive lines of communication back to Madrid would also be a serious risk. The later argument is a surprising one as Burgoyne had discounted the risk of long British supply lines whilst advocating Wellesley chasing Soult into Galicia. The French were much more capable of living off the land as they had no concern for the local inhabitants and were happy to steal and murder to get food.

> If he [Victor] had even penetrated to Lisbon, it would have been at considerable loss and could only have been esteemed a predatory excursion from which, far from important results to the general interests of the French cause on the Peninsula could have resulted.

Burgoyne continued:

> a striking difference between the operations of the French and British since the commencement of the Spanish war has been, that the plans of the French have embraced one great object, that of the conquest of the Peninsula. Every operation has tended to that great end, nor have they allowed petty objects to turn them from their way.

Whilst Burgoyne made the point that the French should act cautiously until the result of the Austrian war was known, Napoleon had no such view. He wanted Lisbon taken and Portugal and the British destroyed. That is what Soult was attempting through his invasion from the north and Victor was supposed to support the advance by threatening Portugal. Victor had shown no great inclination to advance in the preceding weeks, but he was reported to be moving west.

As mentioned above, Wellesley's's strategic objective was to evict the French from Portugal, along with the unwritten instruction not to risk the British army. Whilst there may have been a low risk of Victor taking Lisbon, it was a risk Wellesley could not take as it was the focal point of resistance in Portugal. The loss of Lisbon would almost certainly require the evacuation of the British army, again. Burgoyne's commander, Fletcher, noted on 19 May, 'Marshal Victor has, it is said, taken Alcantara, on his way, it is supposed, towards Lisbon. We shall consequently retire as fast as possible to cut him off from the capital'.[23]

Although many of Burgoyne's criticisms can be refuted, it is important to see his thinking about the allied operations. He was not only concerned about his professional duties but had an active interest in the wider strategic and tactical operations. As an engineer officer attached to headquarters, he had better-than-average access to information and could form opinions on what was being done. His views altered throughout the war as his experience grew.

Burgoyne was back in Oporto by 23 May 1809, but he would not be allowed any rest as orders were waiting for him. The next eight weeks were spent on two extensive reconnaissances; the first to investigate the length of the Douro River and the second to survey the northern border of Portugal.

Why was Burgoyne ordered to do these surveys? Wellesley was very aware that Soult and Ney were still in northern Spain and could again threaten an invasion from the north. It made sense to carry out detailed surveys of northern Portugal, especially as Soult had retreated by unknown routes. A French advance could be made the same way, although with difficulty. Wellesley needed a much better understanding of the country. Other officers were given similar tasks including Lieutenant John Williams RE who was sent to do a reconnaissance of the river Tamega, a tributary of the Douro.[24]

Fletcher's orders to Burgoyne were quite simple, leaving him to determine the best way of achieving the objectives. These orders are documented in full below to show the depth of work that was underway to supply information to the allied armies. The orders for the first survey were:

> I have to desire that you will reconnoitre the Douro from Oporto to the River Agueda. You will naturally attend to the nature of the banks,

23 TNA WO55/958, Fletcher to Morse, 19 May 1809.

24 TNA WO55/1561/4, Report on the Tamega from Chaves to its confluence with the Douro, 10 June 1809.

> its fords, now and at other seasons of the year, and mention whenever communications lead from it to other parts of the country and endeavour to learn by enquiry or otherwise how far they are practicable for artillery; the best situations for throwing bridges across and the means at hand for constructing them will form part of your report. Having done this, you will join the Headquarters of the British army.[25]

The River Agueda marked the frontier with Spain and joins the Douro at Barca d'Alva, a name that appears frequently in letters and despatches. It became a major logistics hub for the allied army as it advanced eastward. It is still a major hub today for river cruises on the Douro.

Burgoyne started a new notebook for this survey. It contains a great deal more information than was contained in the final report, dated 4 June 1809.[26] Whilst there is some exaggeration, Burgoyne noted that:

> According to all accounts, the river [Douro] in the winter rises prodigiously, some of the common people told, in places to a height of 200 feet and it is said to run at the rate of 12 miles an hour. The navigation is then very dangerous and only to be attempted by the boatmen well accustomed to the river. A great many British soldiers lost their lives last winter in descending the river with improper boatmen.[27]

As well as the survey details on the Douro, Burgoyne included details of the commerce in the area. As an example, he reported on Covilhão:

> Covilhão [is] the principal manufacturing town in Portugal, contains 1,500 houses, 13 parishes, two convents, one large manufactory of cloth called the Fabrica Real and four private ones, one manufacturer of hats and another of oilskin. It is very old and situated on the side of the mountains of Estrella at a considerable height above the Zezere from which, it is about four miles distant; a very old and good stone bridge crosses it on the road to Fundão and Castelo Branco, from which latter city is nine leagues distant.
>
> This situation is advantageous for manufactories from the fertility of the country and the quantity of wood and water in the immediate neighbourhood. The manufactures [sic] are conveyed by mules to Abrantes and there are put into boats on the Tagus for Lisbon. Each mule conveys from

25 REM 4601-74, Fletcher to Burgoyne, Oporto, 23 May 1809.

26 REM 4601-72, f.1809/3. Also, draft copy REM 4601-74, f.66.

27 REM 4201-68, Journal, 27 May 1809.

150 to 250 pounds [68-114 kg] weight, goes to Abrantes, 22 leagues in four days and gains 18 or 20 shillings.

1 Palm [0.22m]

1 Cova = 3 Palms [0.66m]

1 Arruba = 32 [British] pounds [14.7kg]

Each piece of cloth is about 45 covas long and seven palms wide. The Kersimare [Kerseymere – fine woollen cloth] the same length and about half the width. Each piece of coarse cloth or Ferdamento weighs about four arrubas and each arruba is sold to the merchants for about 18 shillings. About 2,000 pieces of this Ferdamento is made in a year and in the last eight years, 9,000 pieces of fine cloth were made in the Fabrica Real. The Kersimere is sold to the merchants at 6s 9d each cova.

In the Fabrica Real they have 76 looms for broad cloth and 66 for narrow and when trade goes on briskly, about 500 people are employed in the building and about 400 altogether about the country. At Fundão is some manufacturers dependent upon this; five different qualities of cloth are made in the Fabrica Real which was built by the government under the Marques of Pombal and granted to a company in Lisbon who now have it. The men who work by the day gain from 1s to 1s 6d per day, others paid by the work they do, much more. Upwards of 200 looms are in the place in all.

A number of Jews are established here and have two manufacturers of cloth.

The hat manufacturer employs 20 men and makes about 24 hats a day. At present, they want materials, i.e. skins which are brought from Russia; in this work are men who gain 4s 6d per day.

The cloth manufactories do not at present do much, owing to the unsettled state of the country; in the Fabrica Real are not more than 200 men employed and them entirely in cloth ordered for the troops. The wool is given by the manufactory to the country people who spin it in the villages, all the rest of the work is done in the building.

Burgoyne arrived back at headquarters at Abrantes on 10 June 1809. Two days later, orders for a second reconnaissance arrived and these were much more explicit:

I have to request that you will proceed from hence to reconnoitre the River Minho, in doing which, you will attend to the following points.

You will examine the nature of the banks of the river, its breadth and ascertain by enquiry, the parts which are fordable during the summer months and how long they continue so and suggest the best means for their [defence?].

You will report on the state of the towns of Tuy, Valença, Monção and Melagasso [Melgaço] and propose whatever you may think necessary for their improvement. You will mention the number of troops, the number and nature of ordnance (in addition to those you may find there) and the number of rounds for each that you would recommend for their defence. You will particularly examine and report upon the pass of Melgasso [Melgaço].

From Melgasso [Melgaço] you will proceed to Chaves by Monte Alegre [Montalegre] and the frontiers of Portugal. You will describe the places and particularly examine how far it would be possible to defend the former town (Chaves) and mention the garrison you would propose for it as well as the number and nature of artillery and quantity of ammunition.

There is said to be a strong position at Monte [left blank], about two leagues in front of Chaves which you will examine and describe in your report, suggesting the means for its defence.

During your inspection you will generally observe the passes in the mountains lying on your route and report your opinion as to their importance and the number of men and the number and nature of artillery (if any) you would propose to occupy them. Having arrived on the Minho you will make separate reports on each considerable [place?] and request the several commanding officers to forward them as soon as they conveniently can to the Commandant of Oporto desiring him to send them on.

You will send two copies of each, one to be addressed to Colonel D'Urban of the Portuguese army at the Headquarters of Marshal Beresford, inclosing [sic] a report for the Marshal and another to me for the information of the Commander of the Forces.

During your tour, you will examine the pass of Ruivães. You will also inspect Vila Pouca [de Aguillar] and the passes from thence towards Vila Real.

The general object is by leaving the right on Villa Real or between that and the Douro and extending to Malgasso [Malgaço] and from thence to the [embouchures?] of the Minho, to prevent an enemy from entering within that line and also to attend to the defence of Chaves separately.

You will make sketches of the fortified places on which you will describe the ground within about 1,500 yards of them and distinguish the relative heights of the works and of the hills (if there are any) by [figured?] references. The sketches of the works only, will be on a scale of about 300 feet in an inch. General sketches four inches to a mile.

The state of the roads you may pass, whether practicable or otherwise for artillery and whether they can easily be repaired, will naturally fall within the object of your reports. You will endeavour to form an opinion on the number of houses the different towns and villages may contain as also of churches and convents in case it may become necessary to quarter troops in them.

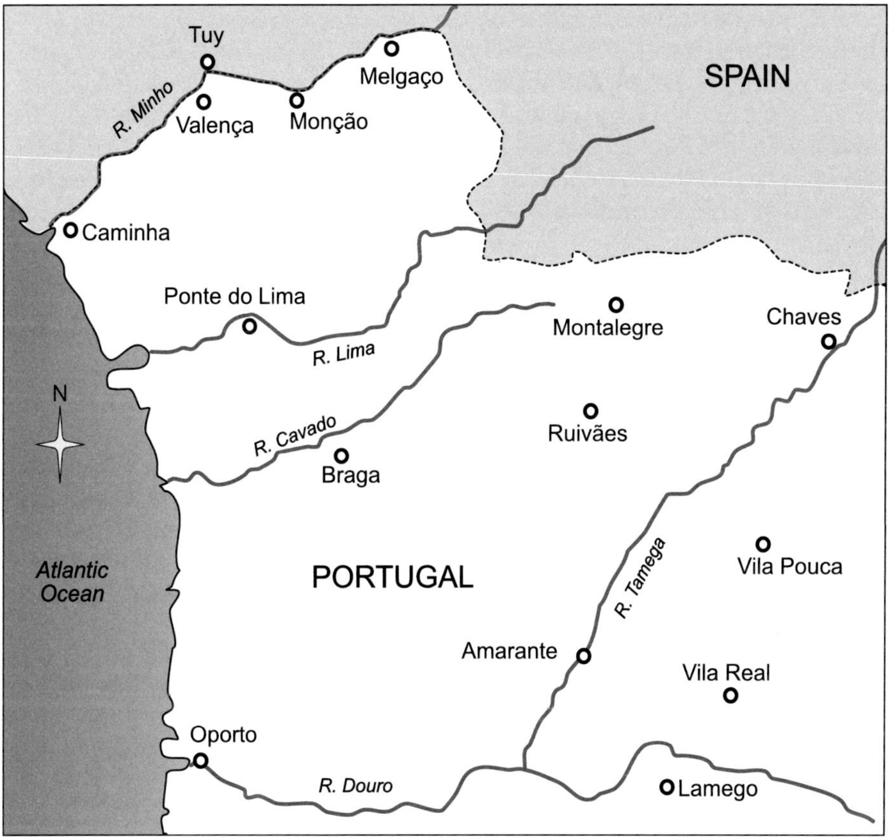

Northern Portugal.

In addition to the separate reports you have been directed to make you will also make a general memoir of your reconnaissance, sending one copy to Colonel D'Urban and another to me for the information of the Commander of the Forces above mentioned.

Having completed the objects of these instructions, you will join me at the Headquarters of the British Army.[28]

What is unusual about these orders is that an explanation is given as to the reason for the survey. Although Burgoyne could have worked out for himself why he was being sent, the explanation would have helped him in preparing his report.

28 REM 4601-72, Fletcher to Burgoyne, Abrantes, 12 June 1809.

As for the previous reconnaissance, Burgoyne's notebook is full of details of the rivers, roads and towns.[29] These surveys provided vital information for Wellesley's military operations. Soult had invaded Portugal from the north, so a good understanding of the border region would allow Wellesley to evaluate the risks of further invasions from this direction. The Douro River became an essential communication route later in the war. Burgoyne's reconnaissance not only described the river but also the commerce and resources that were available for use by the allied armies and this will have helped when setting up services to use the river for transport.

Burgoyne set off with fellow engineer Lieutenant Alexander Thomson on 14 June 1809. They moved rapidly north through Thomar, Condeixa, and Coimbra to Oporto and then travelled to the border at Caminha, a distance of about 200 miles, arriving on 26 June 1809. The next month was spent visiting all the places mentioned and generally spending two or three days at each. The officers arrived back at Almeida on 26 July 1809.

At Valença, which Burgoyne described as the 'principal town and fortress on the Minho in Portugal', he reported that all the guns had been spiked with their carriages destroyed, the main defences were in good condition but the outworks 'were in a ruinous state'.[30] Burgoyne also noted that the breach made by the French needed repairing but overall the place was defensible with little work required to make it very strong.

The defences at the Spanish town of Tuy were in a 'ruinous state'; those as Villa Nova de Cerveira 'good for nothing'; Monção 'could not make an adequate defence' Melgaço 'is enclosed by an ancient wall … round this is a line of field works … now in ruins'.[31]

Below is his description of the Ponte de Misarela, which was one of the choke points on Soult's retreat from Oporto:

> From Monte Alegre to Ruivães, five leagues. The road lies along the side of mountains which are steep and fall to the right into an extensive ravine; at three leagues, the road goes between a high, bold, rocky hill and the mountains forming a strong position for its defence; then again along the side of the mountains which are open, uncultivated and here and there, woods of chestnut.
>
> At four leagues, cross a deep, rocky ravine by the Ponte de Mizarela, a light stone bridge of one arch over the Cavado, here falling precipitately over rocks, the banks of rock and the mountains on each side steep, rocky and woody; the road to the bridge on each side exposed for some distance to the other; might be broke up with effect and at present, in parts not

29 REM 4201-68, Journal 1809. Also, his formal report: REM 4601-72, dated 4 June 1809.

30 REM 4601-74, f.67, Report of the Fortress of Valença, dated 3 July 1809.

31 REM 4201-68, Journal, 7 July 1809.

> wide enough for any but very light guns; the whole very defensible on either side and difficult to turn.[32]

The ability of British officers to ride alone through Spain and Portugal gave Wellesley a great advantage over the French, who had to send large bodies on every task to avoid being killed by the population. Reconnaissance was not an option for the French. There were still risks for British officers when travelling and accepting Portuguese hospitality. Burgoyne commented: 'The great wooden bedsteads, with ornamented board heads are very alarming, as usually producing more bedfellows than one wishes'.[33]

There were also practical difficulties in carrying out orders. Officers who worked away from the army or main locations were expected to provide for all their needs. They might get accommodation and food, but they had to be prepared that they might not. Transport was the biggest cost and difficulty. Whilst some of the cost would be provided by the government, it did not cover the full costs and it could be years before outstanding expenses were cleared. An officer had to be able to pay for his needs. During his first reconnaissance, Burgoyne stayed at Lamego for two days sharing a billet with fellow engineer Charles Boothby. In his diary, he noted his transport situation. He had three small horses 'none of them fit for my purpose'. He bought another captured horse cheaply (16 dollars) when Oporto was taken, which proved to be lame and could not be ridden for some time. He also had another 'fine' mule which cost 36 pounds, which was lost during the capture of Oporto. He sold a pony for the same as he paid for it (60 dollars). At Lamego he swapped another bad horse for a 'fine mule' for a total cost of 120 dollars.[34] The total cost to Burgoyne was in the region of £100, which was about six months' pay! In addition, an officer needed at least one servant who had to be paid and provided with transport.

By the end of July, Wellesley had detailed reports on the rivers and towns that made up northern Portugal, significantly enhancing his ability to counteract any future French advance through that region.

Burgoyne handed his reports to Marshal Beresford in the northern fortress of Almeida the same day that Wellesley fought the Battle of Talavera. He now moved south to join the allied army and encountered the rapidly-reorganised French forces under Soult that were marching to attempt to cut Wellesley's communications with Portugal. In trying to avoid the French forces by travelling through the mountains, he lost his servant, his baggage and their horses.[35]

32 REM 4201-68, Journal, 12 July 1809.
33 Wrottesley, *Burgoyne*, p.47.
34 Wrottesley, *Burgoyne*, p.48.
35 Wrottesley, *Burgoyne*, pp.49-50 fn.

On his journey south, he would have heard the news that a battle had been fought. He must have been very anxious, particularly as he was having to make his way through significant French forces as he approached Talavera. His relief of hearing about the victory would have been tempered with two pieces of bad news. The first was discovering Edward Fyers 'with a bad fever and insane'.[36] He was the son of William Fyers, one of the most senior Royal Engineers at the time. Fyers was sent home in 1809 and, sadly, he was committed to an asylum in 1819. In the meantime, he had been promoted to captain and on being committed, he was transferred to the Invalid Engineer Corps.

The second piece of bad news was discovering his friend Boothby had lost a leg at the Battle of Talavera. In the confusion of the French night attack, Boothby had found himself between the attackers and defenders and it was likely that 'friendly fire' had injured him. Boothby was left at Talavera with the wounded and taken prisoner when Wellesley was forced into a precipitate retreat on hearing of Soult's advance against his lines of communication.

When Wellesley heard that Soult was approaching from the north, he assumed he would have few troops with him as he did not believe he would have had time to reorganise his forces. Soult, with 50,000 troops, not the 15,000 Wellesley thought he had, advanced from Salamanca through the pass of Baños and was in Plascencia on 1 August, in a position to cut Wellesley's communications with Portugal. Wellesley moved off on 3 August intending to intercept Soult. When he received a captured despatch on 3 August and realised the strength of the French,[37] he was forced westwards, crossing the Tagus at Arzobispo on 4 August and then moving south-west to Trujillo, Merida, and finally to Badajoz where the exhausted army was now allowed to rest.

Burgoyne's diary shows that he did not understand the danger. On 3 August he wrote that Wellesley was moving to attack Soult who was believed to have 30,000 men with him. If Soult was that strong, there was no way that Wellesley would have attacked him with only his British troops who numbered around 15,000. Wellesley believed that Soult had 12-15,000 men available. On 4 August 1809, Burgoyne noted that it was thought necessary to cross the Tagus at Arzobispo 'in consequence of the Spaniards quitting their post'. The truth was that Wellesley and Cuesta had realised that they were outnumbered and being outmanoeuvred.

Having rapidly moved his army to the south side of the Tagus at Arzobispo and ensured that the next crossing point at Almaraz was secure, Wellesley was now able to retire unmolested, the Spanish holding Arzobispo for several more days.[38]

Burgoyne retired with the army towards the Portuguese border near Badajoz. There is evidence that he made another trip to the north of Portugal as he replied

36 Wrottesley, *Burgoyne*, p.51.

37 Oman, *Peninsular War*, Vol.II, pp.563, 573.

38 The Cardenal and Alcantara bridges over the Tagus had already been broken.

to a letter from Fletcher stating he was at 'Mondego' on 15 September 1809. The village of Mondego is in northern Portugal in the area that he had recently visited. Fletcher wrote from Badajoz on 8 September and it was a week before Burgoyne received the letter, so he was clearly some distance away from Badajoz. Fletcher's letter asked for details on the defences of Ciudad Rodrigo. This is surprising as Burgoyne had written a detailed account in December 1808 and this should have been available to Fletcher.

In October 1809, Burgoyne was ordered to Badajoz, noting that all the engineers apart from himself and Lieutenant Anthony Emmett had been ordered to Lisbon to start work on the defences that became known as the Lines of Torres Vedras. Burgoyne played no part in the construction, remaining at Badajoz until the end of December. However, he had not been completely idle during this period. Along with three other officers, he had purchased 20 Merino sheep to send home with the intention of breeding them.[39]

The army which had been cantoned around Badajoz since August, started moving towards the northern Portuguese border on 9 December 1809 with the last elements leaving on 25 December. On the same day, Burgoyne started his journey north to Campo Mayor and Arronches. Campo Mayor, he noted, was:

> [A] large town and fortified but the ground round it is favourable for its approach and attack particularly at the east end. Its figure is oblong having two long sides and two short; the short one fronting the west is very high, has an old castle on it of no consequence and the works on that side are in worse state than on the others; from this side the ground falls to the east which is the lowest part. This place contains very few guns or stores, all the places on the frontier having been dismantled to supply Elvas. In the town near the great church is a small chapel completely lined with human skulls and bones, regularly arranged in niches in the wall and some are entire figures with some flesh still on them.[40]

His journey continued through Portalegre, Gáfete, Gavião arriving at Abrantes on 29 December. He again, recorded his observations of the town:

> Abrantes occupies the summit of a high hill; the long side towards the river, the other long side opposite and the short side facing the east fall [sic] very steep with interacting ravines and very woody. The west end falls more gradually in different hills and woody. Lines are constructed all around with a good ditch and counterscarp in irregular figures the west being the most accessible side. More pains have been taken in that

39 REM 4201-68, Journal, 20 December 1809.

40 REM 4201-68, Journal, 25 December 1809.

> part and an advanced line constructed to look better down the fall of the hill. Convents and other large buildings are meant to serve as entrenchments should the lines be forced. At the east end is an old castle on the highest part of the hill. The town is large, and a garrison will be required of 6,000 men and 60 guns according to Patton's [Captain Peter Patton RE] demand. The counterscarp very substantial, of the rough stone as taken out of the ditch, which stone of a slaty [sic] quality and chips off in flat pieces and is built with a very great slope. £3,200 has been now expended and the work may be said to be half completed. The approach from Spain to Abrantes is difficult and the few roads by which an enemy may come on the right bank of the Tagus are very bad and present strong positions for defence; as Abrantes ought not to be taken unless heavy artillery is brought against it, that circumstance renders it strong and thereby, with its situation of importance in a defensive campaign.[41]

Burgoyne continued his journey north through Thomar, Leiria, and Pombal to Coimbra, arriving on 3 January 1810.

41 REM 4201-68, Journal, 30 December 1809.

6

1810 – The Third French Invasion of Portugal

1810 was an important year for Wellington.[1] His early successes in 1808 were overshadowed by the Convention of Cintra. Again, in 1809, his early success at Oporto and his debatable victory at Talavera was offset by the retreat to the Portuguese border where his army remained for the rest of the year. In 1810, Wellington knew there would be a strong French attack to destroy the British support of the Spanish and Portuguese wars of independence.

Burgoyne with the other engineer officers played a vital but generally hidden role in the delay and final destruction of the French army. At two points during the year he carried out extensive reconnaissances of the likely routes of the French advance; he repaired the defences of Fort Concepción on the Spanish border and then destroyed it at the critical moment; he investigated sites on the Mondego where the allied army could fight the French; he mined several bridges on the south side of the Mondego and finally made a last-minute reconnaissance of the Mondego to advise Wellington on the best way to delay the French advance. His fellow engineer officers built the Lines of Torres Vedras, carried out many more reconnaisances, and built field defences on the battlefield at Bussaco. Activity in 1810 was much more than sitting on the border waiting for the French army to arrive.

Following Napoleon's defeat of Austria in 1809, Wellington was certain that large French reinforcements would arrive in Spain in 1810 to attempt to destroy the Anglo-Portuguese army. The advance was likely to come by the northern route past the fortresses of Ciudad Rodrigo and Almeida. He needed to delay the French as long as possible to give time for the Lines of Torres Vedras to be completed.

Orders for the army to move north from Coimbra were given on 9 January 1810 and Burgoyne travelled to Mealhada on 10 January before travelling over the Bussaco ridge the following day. He noted:

1 Wellesley had been created Viscount Wellington on 26 August 1809; he will be referred to in the text as Wellington from now on.

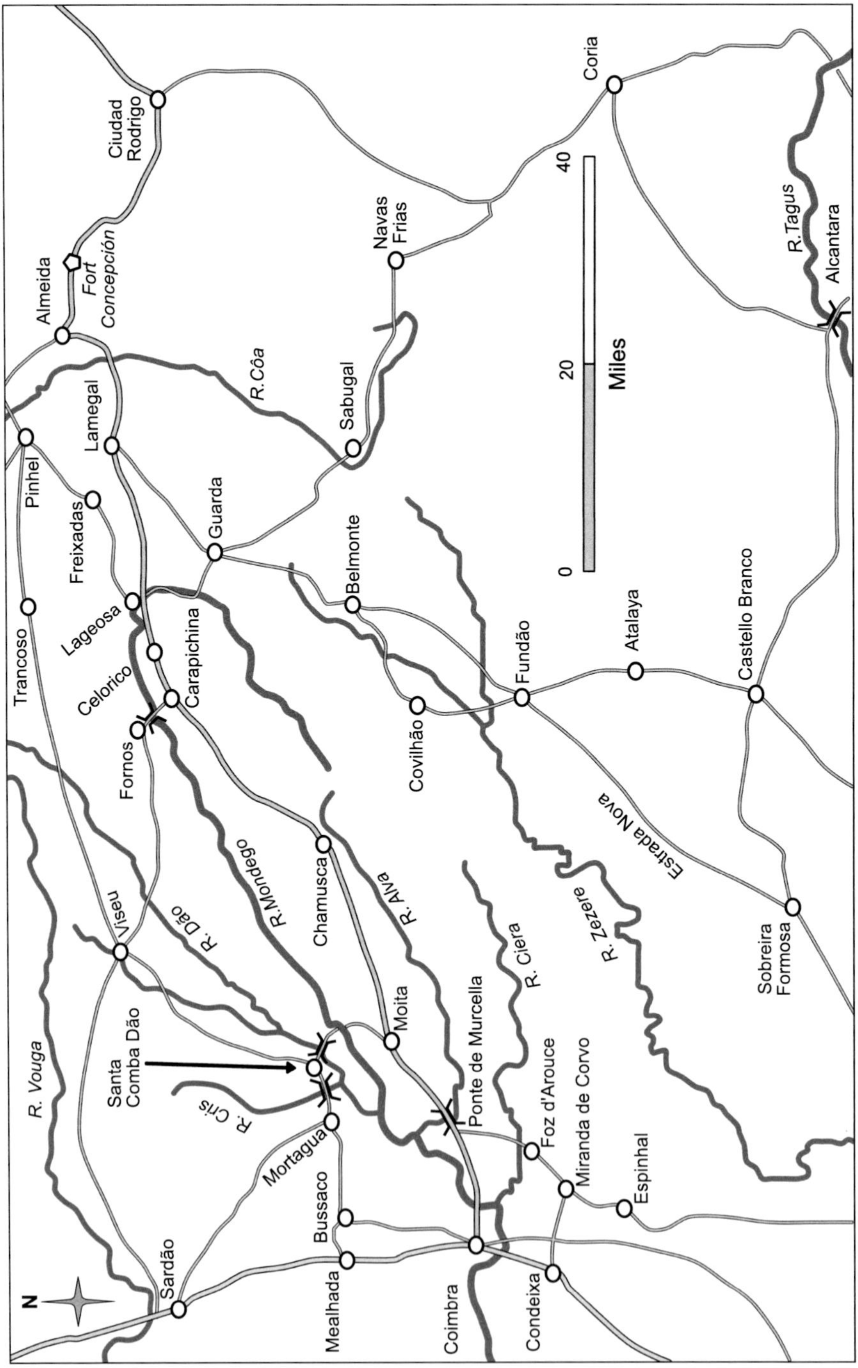

1810 campaign; area between Coimbra and Ciudad Rodrigo.

> At 3½ miles or one league, Venda Nova, of 30 huts and a church; then a very steep ascent for two miles, road in parts rocky with difficult spots for carriages to pass; country uncultivated and with much fir wood; small villages of huts to right and left of road from one to two miles distant, on the summit is a chapel and a large wood of pines, firs etc., enclosed by a good wall of a considerable extent, within this enclosure, which is called Buzaco is a convent of Carmelites, the rules of which are very severe, the monks go barefoot, cannot eat meat at any time or speak to one another except one day in a week or fortnight; it is voluntary their coming to this from other Carmelite convents in the Kingdom which are not so severe. This mountain forms part of the chain reaching from the Mondego to the Vouga.[2]

Burgoyne, with Wellington's army, would be back here in nine months. His journey continued through Santa Comba Dão, crossing the rivers Cris and Dão before arriving at Viseu, all the way he was making detailed notes of the roads and the terrain.

The Commanding Engineer, Richard Fletcher, had remained in Lisbon supervising the building of the Lines of Torres Vedras. Burgoyne was now the senior engineer with the army. On 14 January 1810, Burgoyne received orders from Colonel George Murray, the Quartermaster General. Wellington wanted a reconnaissance of the bridges and fords on the Rivers Cris and Dão in Portugal to understand what impact destroying the bridges would have on a French advance:

> I wish that an officer of the [Engineers] Department was employed as soon as possible to survey the course of the Cris and to ascertain its course, by how many bridges and fords it is crossed, where the roads crossing it head to; whether it fills in winter, and how long it remains full; and whether the destruction of the bridge between Mortagua and Sao Comabadao [Comba Dão] and the destruction of the road leading from the bridge on the right of the river would be a serious impediment to the use of the road from Vizeu to Coimbra by Mortagua and Mealhada.
>
> Let him calculate the means of destroying that bridge and road.
>
> I would wish to have the same information regarding the Dão which joins the Cris immediately below Sao Combadao.[3]

Having just travelled along the road from Coimbra to Viseu through Mortagua and Santa Comba Dão, Burgoyne concentrated on surveying the River Dão. It is

2 REM 4201-68, Journal, 11 January 1810. This entry is not included in Wrottesley's biography. The mountain chain continues south of the Mondego.

3 REM 4601-72, Memorandum from Colonel Murray, 14 January 1810.

worth looking at his notes as this was the route that Massena followed during his advance later in the year. He described his approach (from the west) to the River Cris as follows:

> Then by a bad road over gentle hills … descend a long hill and cross the Rio Cris by a fine, high bridge of stone of four arches across a rocky ravine then wind up a steep hill for 1½ miles by a bad road with sharp turnings; this hill has been thought impracticable for any guns heavier than light 6-pounders without other means than horses, from its sharp turns and bad footing for the beasts; then descend gently for one mile to Santa Combadão

He continued:

> After passing the Cris the road to Santa Combadão is to the right, but the direct road from the bridge to Tondella, the next stage towards Viseu, is to the left and winds up the hill by a similar road to the one above described and with the same difficulties.[4]

The other main bridge, at Santa Comba Dão, carried the road south to the Mondego. Similarly, to the bridge over the Cris, the road crossed:

> the Dão by a high, good stone bridge of five arches; the river now only runs through one arch; it is rapid, has many falls and winds much in this part; its bed is of sand and great rocks; the banks rocky and sides of the ravine through which it runs high and steep and much wooded.[5]

There was no bridge over the Mondego near here, which, Burgoyne noted, 'as far as can be seen above and below runs through a very steep, bare, rocky ravine with very short abrupt bends'. There were also two other rivers following the same north-east to south-west route, the Dinha and the Asnes, both flowing through ravines. This was not a good area for moving artillery or crossing rivers. On the same day that Burgoyne had received his orders to survey the rivers, Captain George Scovell, on the QMG staff, had received almost identical orders to survey the Asnes down to its junction with the Dão.[6] Wellington was clearly using all his experienced officers to collect information.

Burgoyne remained in the vicinity of Viseu for the next few weeks. Wellington, whose headquarters were at Viseu, left on 31 January 1810 for a quick visit to Lisbon

4 REM 4201-68, Journal, 11 January 1810.

5 REM 4201-68, Journal, 16 January 1810.

6 Kenton White, *The Key to Lisbon* (Warwick: Helion, 2019), p.52.

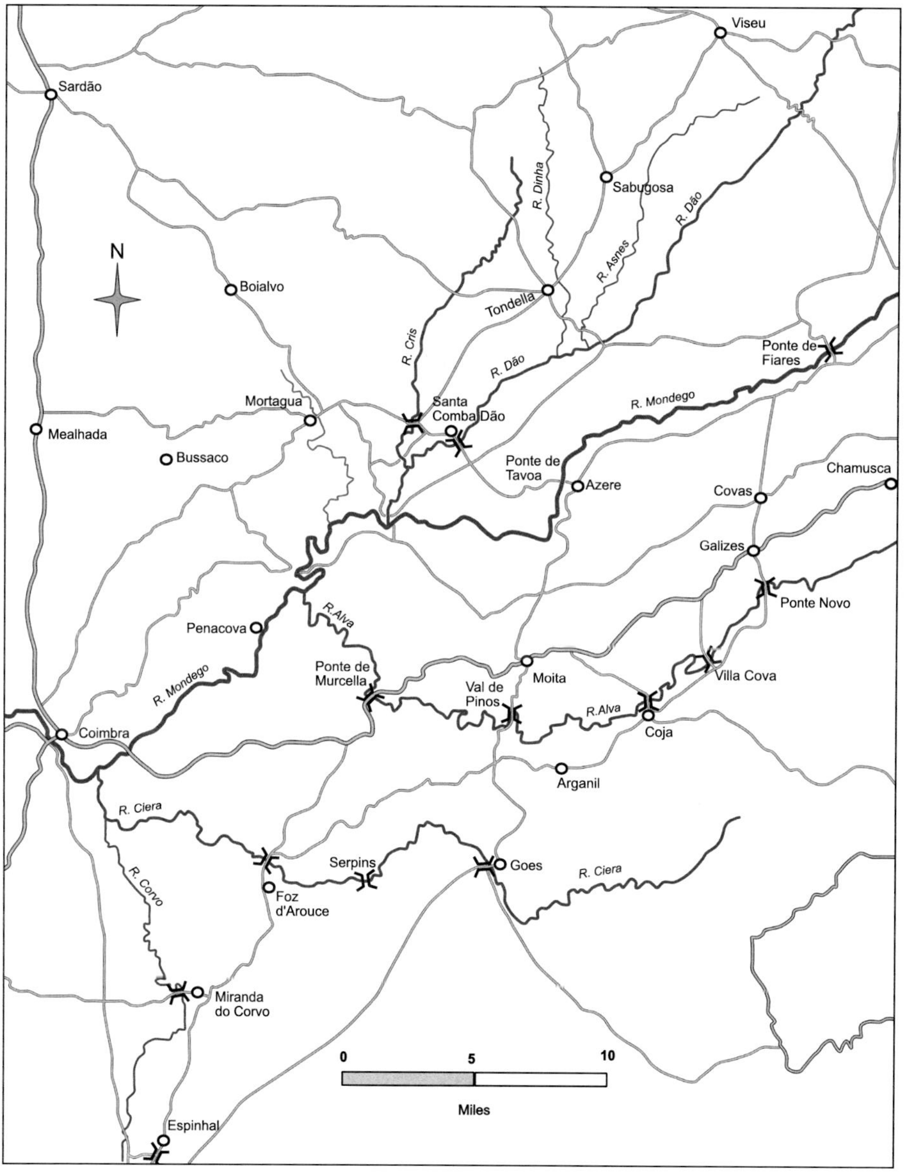

Bridges around Coimbra.

to review progress on construction of the Lines.[7] During the period he was away, the French made an advance on Ciudad Rodrigo, demanding its surrender on 13 February, but without any means of enforcing the demand. When it was refused, they withdrew. However, this advance caused a stir and Burgoyne commented:

> [A]n *aide-de-camp* of Sir John Sherbrooke was sent off in the middle of the night, a few nights ago, with a despatch to Lord Wellington; and it is now said the army will be on the move immediately. Lord Wellington left Lisbon on the 10th inst. and is expected here to-morrow'.[8]

The general feeling at headquarters, in Wellington's absence, was that there would be an advance and Burgoyne noted that the lack of cavalry would put the allies at a disadvantage.

On 17 February, Burgoyne recorded that Lord Wellington 'has expressed his perfect satisfaction at the exertions of the Engineers there'.[9] As Fletcher was still in Lisbon working on the Lines, it would suggest that Burgoyne had access to the latest information at headquarters.

Wellington repeated two orders around this time. The first was to repair the road from Ponte de Murcella to Thomar via Espinhal to allow the passage of artillery.[10] He described it thus: 'it really is a most important line of communication, without which all our combinations for defence, and any offensive measures we may adopt must be imperfect'.[11] A few days later he explained the significance of the road:

> If it is not done [repaired] I must draw in from this frontier, as soon as Soult shall cross the Tagus, if he should cross that river from Plasencia; or I may lose my communication with Hill, or even with Lisbon. If that road were made as it ought to be, I should be at a distance of only three marches from the Tagus, of which only one forced; whereas, now, I cannot reach that river by making less than nine marches.[12]

Wellington had previously ordered the road from Ponte de Murcella to Almeida, via Chamusca, to be repaired on 26 January 1810.[13] In mid-February, Wellington

7 BL ADD MS36303, f.10.
8 REM 4201-68, Journal, 15 February 1810.
9 REM 4201-68, Journal, 17 February 1810.
10 REM 4201-68, Journal, 17 February 1810.
11 Gurwood (ed.), *Despatches,* Wellington to Beresford, Viseu, 19 February 1810. Wellington had also ordered this work to be done on 26 January 1810. The second order was issued because the work had not been done.
12 Gurwood (ed.), *Despatches,* Wellington to Charles Stuart, Viseu, 19 February 1810.
13 Gurwood (ed.), *Despatches,* Wellington to Baccelar, 26 January 1810.

was faced with several French forces that were in a position to threaten Portugal. Junot and Loison were on the northern Portuguese border near Bragança; Ney was at Ciudad Rodrigo; Soult was at Plasencia and Mortier was at Badajoz. Wellington was facing the northern French forces and if events developed in the south, he would have to move quickly. This was why he was concerned about the condition of the road from Ponte de Murcella to Thomar.

Wellington's second order was to destroy the Estrada Nova which ran from Belmonte to Sobreira Formosa avoiding the difficult route from Guarda to Abrantes via Castelo Branco and Nisa.[14] Wellington did not want the French to have access to an easy route through central Portugal. Any French force approaching from the north would be forced to follow the Mondego towards Coimbra and then turn south.

Burgoyne's position with the army was viewed with some (friendly) jealousy by his fellow engineers. Mulcaster, who had been working on the Lines of Torres Vedras for three months wrote:

> I believe I told you in my last that I had no idea [hope] of joining the army till it returns [retreats to Lisbon]. You may guess my mortification at hearing that you are again in motion and according to Goldfinch to advance. I wish the redoubt, intrenchents and all their appurtenances were in hell together. I begin to think all your luck is now coming in a bunch.[15]

Mulcaster had heard rumours about the French advance on Ciudad Rodrigo in February and thought that it might lead to an action, which it did not. Burgoyne's lot was not very 'lucky', being made up of carrying out surveys, which was not really engineers' work, and, it appears, a lot of spare time. Lucky in this case meant being with the army.

Things remained quiet, although Burgoyne continued to be concerned about his transport after his losses in summer 1809. With the campaigning season rapidly approaching, good horses were essential. On 16 February he complained about the inability to get good feed, there only being rye and rye straw available, 'the worst species of forage, especially for English horses, who do not thrive even on the best forage these countries afford'.[16] On 18 February, he noted that the ration of straw had been reduced. On 2 March, he reported that his best horse had fallen and appeared lame, although the following day, after seeking advice, it was found

14 Gurwood (ed.), *Despatches*, Wellington to Wilson, Viseu, 18 February 1810. Wellington in another letter of the same date to Beresford asked for four Portuguese engineer officers to be made available for the destruction of roads.

15 REM 4601-74, Mulcaster to Burgoyne, Torres Vedras, 21 February 1810.

16 REM 4201-68, Journal, 17 February 1810.

the issue was worn shoes causing the fall, not lameness. On 23 March 1810, he reported:

> My stupid man, in exercising the horses and jackass, has let the latter stray, and lost him; which, independent of his being the best Neddy ever seen, and who served me faithfully near a year without ever giving a moment's trouble, leaves the great bulk of my baggage without conveyance; and just at the moment there are strong rumours of a move very shortly. Lord Wellington always enquired most kindly after this jackass, from having come up with him one day on a long march, and not being able to pass him with all his efforts, the little beast, as often as he attempted it, setting off in a gallop, though with a very heavy load and his Lordship had the pleasure of driving him for a considerable time, until I happened to come up, and ordered him to be stopped.

Fortunately for Burgoyne a reward of eight dollars, one month's pay for a soldier, recovered the animal.[17]

As March progressed, there was an increase in outpost activity with the French pushing patrols and foraging parties as far forward as Almeida, but still no sign of a French advance. The weather throughout the month was awful and Burgoyne commented that he was lucky to be in good accommodation.

Burgoyne wrote to Pasley on 26 March 1810. Pasley was recovering in England from wounds received during the Walcheren campaign. Burgoyne commented:

> [H]owever injudiciously and ill Lord Wellington behaves to his generals and heads of departments in general by taking away a great deal of their responsibility and consequent pride and exertion in conducting their departments well; he has universally treated Fletcher with the greatest consideration and attention as appears from the colonel's own account.[18]

The engineers were very unsure of their position in Wellington's army. Burgoyne's comments on Wellington's treatment of his generals were not unusual, few were trusted to act independently. Fletcher himself was anxious about how he would be treated when Wellington landed in April 1809 but, over the next 12 months, they built a good working relationship. Burgoyne continued:

> [T]hough still from the nature of the past service and the disorganized (as I may call it) state of the Corps, not having our duties regularly defined,

17 REM 4201-68, Journal. Last few quotes between 16 February and 23 March 1810.
18 BL ADD MS41962, ff.197-200.

> we have hitherto done little more than work indirectly for the QMG Department.

There is probably some truth in the comment about working for the QMG Department. Apart from some bridging (which was officially Royal Staff Corps work) there had been little engineering work until the Lines of Torres Vedras were started. Much of the engineers' time had been spent on surveys and reconnaissance which was the responsibility of the QMG Department. However, this work was seen as vital to the operations of the army and capable officers from every branch of the military were used to collect topographical information.

Burgoyne's letter was critical of Wellington's decision to station the troops near Badajoz in the Autumn of 1809, commenting:

> [O]ur halt at Badajoz until the sickly season was very nearly over, in which neighbourhood we lost an amazing number of men, and our own subsequent entry in Portugal, Lord Wellington's favourite country and scene of his former victories and heroism!

This criticism appears unfair. At that time of his retreat, there were two significant French forces in central Spain, those of Soult and of King Joseph. It was possible that they may have chosen to follow Wellington's forces to the Portuguese border. In fact, in August 1809 Wellington was making plans to move or destroy the bridges at Abrantes and Villa Velha if the French advanced on Portugal.[19] There were also political reasons which would have made any further retreat difficult to justify. Whilst Wellington had been very unhappy with the co-operation with the Spanish under Cuesta, another lengthy retreat like Moore's the previous year would have strained Spanish relations even more.

Burgoyne thought that Wellington could not or would not hold the Lines of Torres Vedras because he had asked for the transport tonnage required to withdraw the whole army. He suggested that Wellington was the only person who thought that it was possible to embark the army in the face of the enemy. Burgoyne's rather acidic view of Wellington's reasoning was: 'I will show them [the British nation] I can do anything Sir John Moore could do'; that is, to fight a battle before withdrawing the army by sea.[20] Again, this criticism is unfair. Wellington would have been negligent if he had not prepared for the eventuality that retreat would be necessary. He was still heavily outnumbered by the French in the Peninsula and if they could resolve their supply problems he could be faced with a superior force and left with no alternative other than destruction or withdrawal from Portugal. If Wellington had no intention of defending Portugal, which he believed was

19 Gurwood (ed.), *Despatches,* Wellington to Villiers, Beresford, 12 August 1809.

20 BL ADD MS41962, Pasley Papers, Burgoyne to Pasley, Viseu, 26 March 1810.

possible, then it is hardly credible that he would have embarked on the very expensive task of building the Lines of Torres Vedras.

Life at Viseu remained quiet, apart from some confusion when Wellington decided on 14 April 1810 to relocate his headquarters to Cea [Seia], a small village in the foothills of the Serra d'Estrella. Three days later the order was reversed and headquarters returned to Viseu. Wellington's explanation was that he wanted to have 'better communications with the advanced divisions, but I am much afraid that there is such want of stabling, that I shall be obliged to move them back again'.[21] Two days later, Wellington confirmed he was moving headquarters back to Viseu but also changed the arrangements for messages from the advance posts so that he had any correspondence the following morning. Burgoyne commented that the move was:

> [A] great inconvenience to most of the Heads of Departments in shifting their offices, clerks, papers etc. and after remaining three days and arranging the change in the different couriers, returning to Viseu, appeared very extraordinary

The more scurrilous explanation as written by Burgoyne:

> Lord Wellington, having heard of a fine house there, occupied by a nobleman's family, the lady of which was very engaging, and the daughters handsome, musical, and entertaining, determined to remove there; but finding in the house not so good accommodation as he expected, from twenty-one children who were in it; the lady, from having had no less than twenty-five children, something the worse for wear, and the young ladies very much kept up, in the true old Portuguese style—his Lordship got immediately disgusted, and returned to Viseu, *where the nuns of the convent in that town are so much more entertaining.*[22]

The words in italics were not printed in Wrottesley's biography. There is a similar account in a letter from the engineer Captain George Ross who was working on the Lines of Torres Vedras:

> We hear that a Fidalgo at Cea has pretty daughters, I mean that the Head Quarters have moved there. But that the handsome nuns at Vizeu are not so prudish as the Fidalgo's daughters.[23]

21 Gurwood (ed.), *Despatches,* Wellington to Craufurd, Cea, 15 April 1812.

22 REM 4201-68, Journal, 18 April 1810.

23 REM 4501-86, Ross to Dalrymple, Mafra, 25 April 1810. In the letter, Ross comments that he had recently received a letter from Burgoyne.

Rather than proving the truth of the tale, this is more likely to show that such stories were being swapped by the engineer officers. The move does appear unusual. As Wellington said, the accommodation was insufficient for himself and the headquarters staff who were spread over the surrounding villages. Wellington would have known all this before he decided to move to Cea and if he did not, then his QMG would. It would have made more sense to move headquarters to Celorico, as Wellington did ten days later.

The French finally advanced and started a loose blockade of the Spanish border fortress of Ciudad Rodrigo on 26 April 1810; only on the east bank of the Agueda and south of the city. It was many more weeks before the French were ready to start the siege. In the early hours of 27 April 1810, orders were given for Wellington's headquarters to move from Viseu to Celorico, probably in response to the start of the French blockade. Whilst Wellington rode on ahead, Burgoyne travelled with the army noting that the road, in many places, was not passable for artillery. Burgoyne remained with the army watching the French activities. The weather remained very wet and this slowed down the arrival of the French siege guns.

Having started the blockade on 26 April, there was little French activity until 30 May 1810 when Ney arrived. He had been forced to wait whilst he collected supplies for his forces. *Maréchal* André Masséna arrived on 1 June 1810, but only stopped long enough to approve the plan of attack before returning to Salamanca. On 5 June, the French completed the blockade by crossing to the west bank of the Agueda. Siege guns started arriving and by 25 June 1810, when the batteries opened, Ney had 50 siege guns available.

We will come back to the siege later.

Repairs at Fort Concepción

After four months of relative inactivity, the 'lucky' Burgoyne was finally given an engineering task. Towards the end of May, as the likelihood of Ciudad Rodrigo falling to the French increased, Burgoyne was ordered to the Portuguese fortress of Almeida, which faced Ciudad Rodrigo across the border.

Wellington had decided to repair Fort Concepción. This was a major stand-alone fortification which had been built by the Spanish in the 17th Century, facing the Portuguese border fortress of Almeida, four miles away. It had been occupied by the French when Spain was invaded, but when the revolts started in summer 1808 it was abandoned and partially destroyed, with the guns being moved to Almeida. Burgoyne's report on Almeida of October 1808, recorded that 20-30 guns in the fortress had come from Fort Concepción.

Wellington had written to Brigadier General William Cox, the governor of Almeida, on 27 May 1810, informing him that 18 guns were to be sent to Fort Concepción; 12 of them were Spanish and probably some of those removed by the French in 1808. Wellington continued:

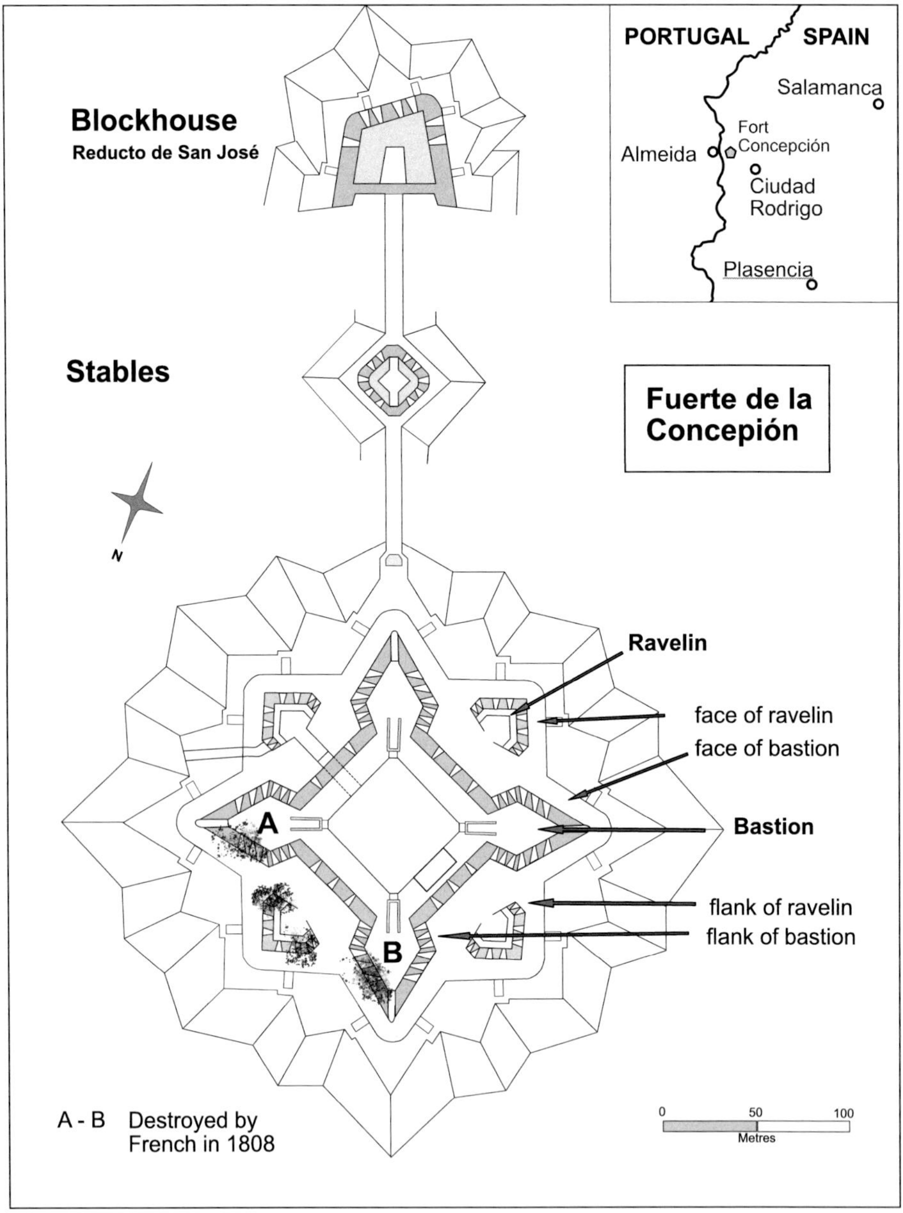

Fort Concepción showing French damage in 1808.

> The [Portuguese] engineers of Almeida to be employed as soon as possible in building up the breach; first in the body of the place; secondly, in the ravelin at Concepción. Nothing more will be required than to build up the wall in any masonry with any materials on the spot; to clear away rubbish from the ditches and to stockade the ditches in front of the parts breached and to be built up ... the AQMG from General Picton's division will be sent ... to have the casemates cleaned out, aired, etc., for the reception of the troops.[24]

The final part of the orders was probably due to there being an outbreak of fever a few weeks earlier in the fort and the nearest village, Aldea del Obispo, which were being used as a hospital by the Spanish. Burgoyne had commented in his journal that:

> 100 inhabitants died during the last two months; it is owing to a Spanish hospital which was established there and very badly regulated, the sick being quartered promiscuously with the villagers. The fort has had a jail fever since a number of French prisoners were in it last year.[25]

Wellington's orders for the officer in command at Fort Concepción were 'to defend to the last extremity and you may be certain that you will be relieved'.[26]

On 29 May, Burgoyne noted in his journal:

> Called on Lord Wellington, and requested leave to go to Almeida, when he said it was the very thing he wished, that he meant to occupy Fort Concepcion, and in consequence, had directed Brigadier General Cox, the Governor of Almeida, to set about getting the breaches made by the French in 1808 ... repaired with rough masonry, and stockaded. His Lordship therefore wished me to go and see how they were getting on, and report to him.

On 31 May 1810, Burgoyne and Cox rode to the fort and he noted that 'The breach has been built up by the Spaniards in a very rough manner, all except about half of one of the flanks, at which a few men are now employed.'[27] The same day four companies of the 1/45th Foot, the 9th Portuguese Regiment and a brigade of Portuguese artillery arrived. This artillery was only placed there until the guns arrived from Almeida.

24 Gurwood (ed.), *Despatches*, Wellington to Cox, Celorico, 27 May 1810.

25 REM 4201-68, Journal, 23 March 1810.

26 Gurwood (ed.), *Despatches*, Wellington to officer commanding, Celorico, 28 May 1810.

27 REM 4201-68, Journal, 31 May 1810.

Main entrance to Fort Concepción from the ditch. (Author's Collection)

Burgoyne with a junior Portuguese engineer officer set to work on 1 June, using 100 men, including 10 carpenters and eight masons, supplied by the Portuguese regiment. Up to that point 'only a few (16 or 18) Spanish peasants' had been working on the breach. He made a quick sketch of the fort,[28] and wrote up his observations:

> Fort Conception is situated on a hill close above the little rivulet Tourões which in this part separates Spain and Portugal, and one league or five miles from Almeida on very good road. It is a square and of masonry with ravelins, covert way and glacis. To the north are two square masonry casemated redoubts in a straight line occupying a ridge of the hill; these redoubts are not flanked and are connected by a communication having an epaulement on each side. The fort contains a great number of bomb-proof casemates and plenty of water in cisterns. The bastions are full. The breaches were made in two flanks and the ravelin of one front which is on one side of the most assailable bastion; in one flank the breach was high and has been roughly stopped up; in the other, the powder must have been

28 The plan of Fort Concepción in Jones' *Sieges*, misplaces the entrance, putting it on the southeast face of the ravelin, instead of the northeast face.

> very low and two-thirds of this flank is destroyed with a small part of the adjoining curtain. The ravelin is almost entirely in ruins.[29]

In a letter to Wellington, Burgoyne recommended that he should stay to oversee the works that were under the direct control of a Portuguese engineer from Almeida. He also warned Wellington that the ravelin was badly damaged and would take some time to rebuild.[30]

The initial work was in line with Wellington's orders which showed a concern about it being taken before the repairs could be complete. So, the first task was to build a stockade around the breaches 'with palisading taken from the covert way of the most defensible sides of the fort'.[31] Work then started on clearing the ditches and using the stones in the ditch to repair the wall.

By 2 June, the foundations of the large breach had been cleared and work started to rebuild the walls of the bastions. Work also started on repairing the gun positions in both damaged bastions. The same day came a change of plans from Wellington. His concern was building about the intentions of the French and he considered that the French might advance on Almeida before they had taken Ciudad Rodrigo: Wellington wrote to Cox and Burgoyne reported him as having said:

> [I]f the enemy intend to besiege Ciudad Rodrigo and attack us at the same time, they must be in great strength, and then it may be necessary to evacuate Concepcion; in that case it will be of consequence to Almeida to have it as completely destroyed as possible. He begs him, therefore, to consult his engineer upon this point. Accordingly, I have agreed with the governor to prepare a mine in the face of the bastion opposed to the breached flank, which will be commenced to-morrow by sinking a shaft in the rear of the banquette.[32]

Burgoyne was now concurrently making repairs to the damaged fort and also preparing mines to destroy it if that became necessary.

The temporary stockades in front of the two breaches were completed by 6 June 1810. On 7 June, the main breach was repaired to a height of 10 feet and was completed to 20 feet on 10 June 1810. Work started immediately on the minor breach, initially by pulling down the rough repair and then starting again. This was complete on 16 June 1810. Work now started on repairing the parapets on both walls.

29 REM 4201-68, Journal, 1 June 1810.

30 REM 4601-74, f.75, draft of letter from Burgoyne to Wellington, not dated.

31 REM 4601-74, f.75, Report of the Means and Options for the Demolition of Fort Conception.

32 REM 4201-68, Journal, June 1810.

Work on the mines progressed slowly. Burgoyne had written to Wellington to warn him it would take time as there were no miners present, so he was having to show the Portuguese soldiers what to do. He noted:

> A company of sappers would have very soon prepared the whole of the fort and bastions for demolition, but with the Portuguese regiment, not a man of whom had ever seen anything like such operations, the progress was slow and difficult, the soil was loose and unfavourable, but showing a little apparent tenacity when first sent out, it was only by the experience of occasionally nearly burying themselves by these galleries breaking in upon them, that the men could be induced to take the timely and proper operations with their frames. The galleries were 5ft high and 2 ½ wide and the frames two feet apart.

Work started on sinking the shaft on 3 June 1810, but the soldiers almost immediately encountered the foundations of a previous building on the site and had to move and start again. On 7 June the shaft was only five feet deep when work had to be suspended due to a lack of wood for frames and plank. These were being delivered from Almeida and they were not coming through quickly enough to keep up with the work. On 8 June the shaft was 12 feet deep and work started on the gallery to get to the back of the newly rebuilt wall. Burgoyne complained on 11 June that he could not 'go on with the mine for want of frames to line it with, which are all made in the arsenal at Almeida, where they are slow and stupid. Governor Cox is stingy, and naturally so, wishing to keep as much in his own place as possible'.[33] Even Burgoyne understood why Cox was unwilling to reduce the stores in Almeida.

By 18 June 1810, the work on the walls and the mines was nearing completion and Burgoyne wrote to Wellington to report that the fort was now safe from assault. Some years later, Burgoyne recalled that the damage caused by the French at Fort Concepción was limited:

> In destroying works, it should be borne in mind that if a breach is made in an escarp of masonry, by the usual mode of powder just sufficient to throw down the wall and part of the rampart, it may be very rapidly repaired by clearing away the rubbish and building it up again with the same square stones which will be found in the ditch nearly in sufficient quantity to carry it to its original height as we found at fort Concepción, where the breaches left by the French were built up again in a fortnight without much means or exertion.[34]

33 REM 4201-68, Journal, entries from 3-11 June 1810.

34 REM 4201-68, Memorandum, pp.30-31.

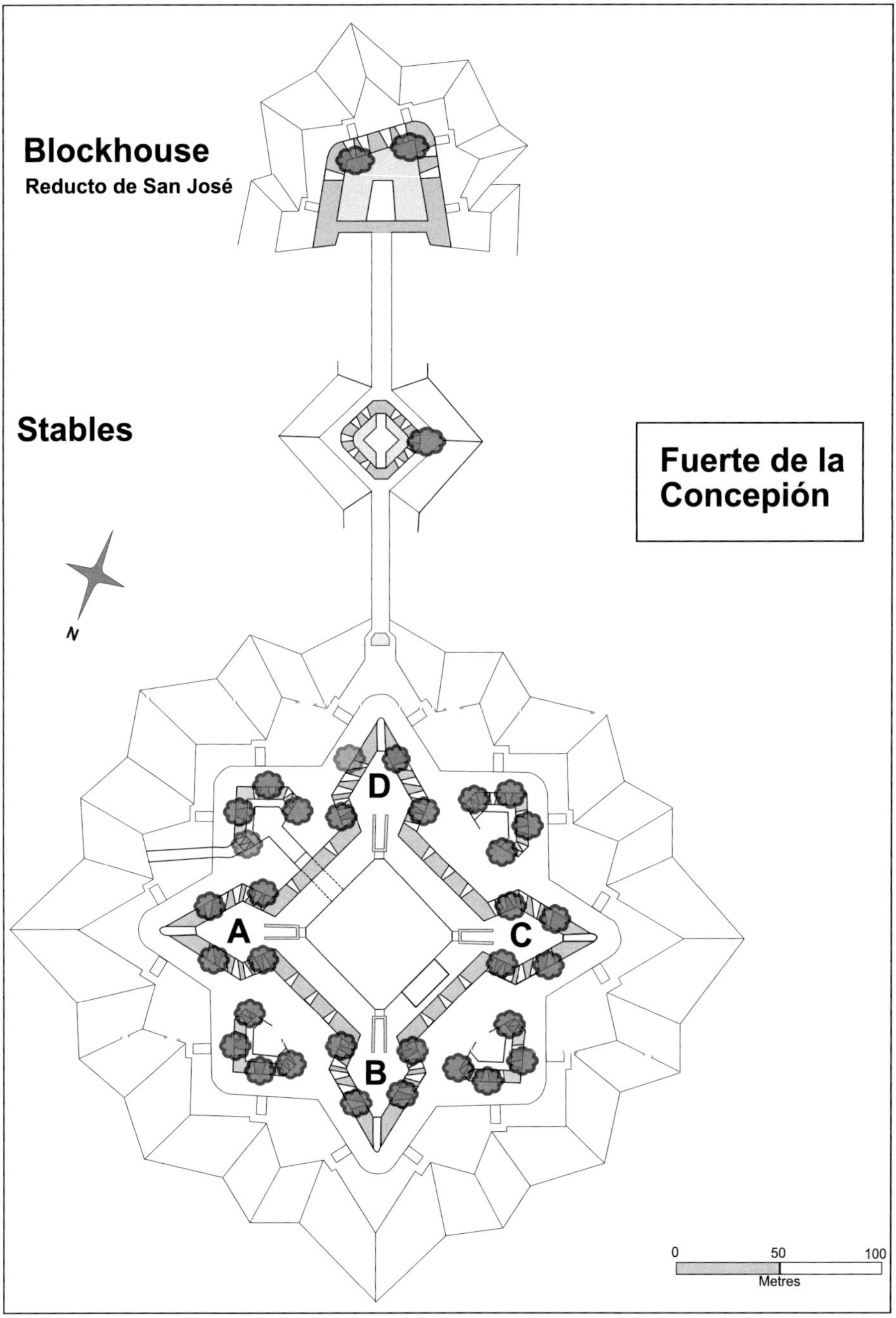

Position of mines in fort and outworks, July 1810.

Wellington's reply to Burgoyne, perhaps prompted by the speed that the repairs had been carried out, was to mine all parts of the fort for destruction:

> We see from what we have ourselves done, that the destruction of the works before destroyed is not of much consequence, and it is desirable that if there is time to make the preparations, the remainder of the works should be destroyed also.[35]

Wellington was now certain that the fort would not be occupied when the French advanced. Burgoyne immediately started work on several other mines. Realising he did not know how soon they would be required, he asked for all the necessary powder and placed it in various casemates in the walls of the fort, where it would still cause significant damage if exploded whilst they worked to complete the proper mines. Mines were started in the three other bastions with a gallery to each face; three mines were started in the stables and two mines in the blockhouse. As each mine was completed the shaft and galleries were filled with rubble to increase the effect of the explosion. The plans for the stables and blockhouse were changed when it was found that they were both built on solid rock. Later, mines were also installed in each of the four ravelins.

Burgoyne started loading the mines on 27 June 1810. In each of the four bastions, mines were placed in both faces and flanks (four mines in each bastion). He did not record how much powder was placed in each bastion. In each of the four ravelins, mines were placed in the casemates in both faces and flanks (four mines in each ravelin), 90-100 sixty-four-pound barrels of powder were used in each ravelin. In the blockhouse 100 sixty-four-pound barrels were placed in the two casemates. In the stables, 60 sixty-four-pound barrels of powder were placed in one casemate.

In estimating how much powder was used, it would seem likely that at least as much powder was used in the bastions as in the ravelins (it is probable more was used as the bastions were much more important). This would mean approximately 1,000 barrels of powder were used (64,000 pounds or 29,000 kilograms).

Lieutenant George Simmons was ordered on guard duty in early July with his company of the 95th Rifles. He wrote 'Curiosity led me to explore some places underground. I found in a corner of a large place … a cask of brandy and three casks of fine biscuit'.[36] It was not only the rank and file who were tempted when they found unguarded stores! It was also pretty foolish to wander around a place that was mined with 1,000 barrels of powder. Everything was ready by the beginning of July. The allied army now needed the French to make the next move.

35 REM 4201-68, Journal. Copy of Wellington's letter included in entry dated 19 June 1810.
36 Willoughby Verner (ed.), *A British Rifle Man* (London: Greenhill, 1996), p.73.

Present State of the War in this Country

Burgoyne started a new journal on 14 June 1810, during the time he was working at Fort Concepción. His first entry was an overview of the present state of the war in Spain and Portugal. His understanding of the numbers and location of troops is quite surprising, because of its depth and accuracy. He estimated the size of the French facing Wellington as greater than 40,000 and Wellington's forces around 30,000, although he recognised that nearly half of this number was composed of untried Portuguese troops.[37] He then wrote that:

> The river at Ciudad Rodrigo makes a bend ... and within it, some bold commanding heights overlooking the plain around. These heights the enemy are entrenching. The relief of Ciudad Rodrigo will therefore become most difficult, if not impossible ... Ciudad Rodrigo is a very poor fortress, but well supplied with artillery and ammunition. Its wall and main line may be breached from a height of not more than three hundred yards distance ... a very short time may therefore be expected to see the fall of this place, after the arrival of the French heavy ordnance.

He continued:

> Why it is thus deserted to its fate, after solemn promises being given to relieve it, appears extraordinary; it will be a great acquisition to the enemy in their future operations against this country ... If we are not able to attempt some effort in favour of this devoted place now, I fear we cannot expect much success in our operations[38]

The assertion that Wellington promised to relieve Ciudad Rodrigo is wrong. At no point did Wellington say he planned to hold the frontier or come to the aid of besieged fortresses. His whole strategy for 1810 was to draw a superior French army into Portugal to a place where they could not attack him or feed their army. If an opportunity to attack the French occurred, he would consider it. Both he and most other British officers expected the French to advance against him with superior forces. Burgoyne was not alone in criticising Wellington's inaction; British, Spanish and Portuguese were all calling for Wellington to do something. Almost the same day the Burgoyne wrote this, the Spanish Governor of Ciudad Rodrigo, Don Andrés Herrasti, was writing to Wellington, again asking for him to advance

37 See Oman, *Peninsular War*, Vol.III, p.243, for size of armies; Wellington, 32,000, Massena nearer 50,000.

38 REM 4201-68, Journal, 14 June 1810.

to relieve the fortress. Wellington's reply was that it would depend on the strength of the enemy and 'to the necessity of attending to other important objects'.[39]

The other criticism in Burgoyne's summary was:

> During the winter, a force under Junot of from 10 to 18,000 men, now joined to Ney's, was occupied in taking Astorga ... This was a fine opportunity for Lord Wellington, whose force was entire and at hand, to have pushed to Salamanca, and destroyed or taken the *depôt* forming there; and there is every reason to believe the enemy expected such an undertaking and were prepared to destroy it themselves.

Such an action would have been very risky. Even with Junot absent, there were still significant French forces around Salamanca. As well as Junot, there were other French troops who could move to support Ney. Half of Wellington's army was untried, he was short of cavalry in good cavalry country, he would have had great difficulty collecting supplies for this attack and, as Burgoyne said, they were expecting him to do it. It seems that British officers were suffering from too much inaction.

The Siege of Ciudad Rodrigo

Seven weeks after the first French troops arrived in front of Ciudad Rodrigo, the first parallel was opened on 15 June 1810 and on 19 June, the construction of the first batteries on the Grand Teson was started. The French guns opened on 25 June with effective fire being returned by the Spanish defenders who managed to inflict damage on the batteries and blow up at least one magazine. Burgoyne, 20 miles away at Fort Concepción, heard the explosion and by the following day it had been confirmed that the explosion 'was in the French lines'.[40] Clearly, communication from Ciudad Rodrigo was still good. The same day, Wellington confirmed that the fort was to be destroyed when the French advanced.

Herrasti refused a summons on 28 June and the French worked to move their siege guns forward but suffering significant casualties in the process. By 8 July there was a large breach in the north-west corner of the fortress and the counterscarp had been blown-up. Herrasti, seeing the French troops forming for an assault, surrendered on 10 July, but great credit should be given to the Spanish defence which had delayed the French for about 10 weeks.

The French now turned their attention to Almeida and started pushing patrols and foraging parties forward, with the allied advanced posts being just in front of

39 Gurwood (ed.), *Despatches,* Wellington to Herrasti, Celorico, 6 and 19 June 1810.

40 REM 4201-68, Journal, 25 June 1810.

Damage to stables and blockhouse. (Author's Collection)

Fort Concepción. On 21 July 1810, the French advanced in force to determine if the allies were intending to defend the fort and when Burgoyne blew the mines in Fort Concepción, they got their answer. A total of 35 individual mines were exploded across the bastions, ravelins and outworks. Burgoyne noted with some pleasure that the fort was almost totally destroyed:

> Good breaches were effected in the faces of the bastions and small ones in the flanks. Of the ravelins, nothing remained standing but a small part of the salient angles. The first detached work (that in the lozenge form) was as if cut in two diagonally, the half where the powder was lodged being blown down. Of the outer detached work, the whole of the front face and part of the sides were destroyed.[41]

The destruction of the fort was not without its moments. Burgoyne's fellow engineer Edmund Mulcaster had just come up to join the army. He had received permission to join the cavalry advance guard and was with the 14th Light Dragoons on 21 July when the French advance occurred. The acting commander of the regiment was Major Felton Hervey, Lieutenant Colonel Neil Talbot having been killed in a

41 REM 4601-74, f.75. The two outworks today are exactly as Burgoyne described them in 1810.

pointless skirmish, ordered by Craufurd, a few days earlier. Talbot had been buried on the glacis at Fort Concepción. As the cavalry were pushed back, Mulcaster's diary noted that he was ordered:

> [T]o tell Gos [Burgoyne] to lose no time in setting fire to the mines [at Fort Concepción]. Finding nobody there I was riding up the ramp when I heard the burning of the portfire and saw the smoke issuing from the gallery. I therefore rode with all possible speed out of the fort to the dragoons who were continuing to skirmish. The fort exploded about quarter of an hour after I left it and the mines appeared to answer fully; all the flanks, one face and the outworks being breached.[42]

Burgoyne's journal told a similar story. Captain Thomas Brotherton of the 14th Light Dragoons noted that his skirmishing troopers were so close to Fort Concepción that he 'lost several horses and men by the explosion'. He also noted with regret that he saw the body of his colonel who had been buried on the glacis a few days before 'blown into the air'.[43]

After the retreat of Masséna in 1811, Fletcher inspected the damage and John Jones recorded: 'We found that large breaches had been made in all the faces of the bastions but one, that the flank defences generally were destroyed and the two detached outworks to the south-east had been completely blown away'.[44]

Burgoyne's period as the senior engineer with the army came to an end on 15 July 1810, when Fletcher re-joined the army from Lisbon. The day after Fort Concepción was destroyed, Burgoyne was assigned to Major General Thomas Picton's 3rd Division, a position to which he was regularly assigned during the rest of the war. Burgoyne noted he was 'received most politely by General Picton and invites me to live with him' (that is, to join his staff).[45] His initial stay with the division, however, was very short.

Wellington realised that the time was approaching when would have to retire to the Lines of Torres Vedras. His planning had started many months before. Burgoyne's survey of the rivers in January 1810 was part of this planning. Wellington wanted to make sure that no alternate routes were readily available to the French. On 28 July 1810, Fletcher ordered Burgoyne to mine four bridges on possible routes of retreat.[46] These were at Ponte de Murcella (River Alva), Val de Pinos (River Alva), Foz de Arouce (River Ciera) and Espinhal (River Corvo). All these bridges were south of the Mondego. The two that Burgoyne had surveyed in

42 Thompson (ed.), *Mulcaster*, 21 July 1810.

43 Bryan Perret, *A Hawk at War* (Chippenham: Picton, 1986), p.24.

44 REM 5501-59-1, Jones Manuscript Journal, 13 April 1811. There were three engineers called Jones. John Jones will be referred to as 'Jones'; The other two as Rice Jones and Harry Jones.

45 REM 4201-68, Journal, 23 July 1810.

46 REM 4601-74, Fletcher to Burgoyne, Alverca, 27 July 1810; see also Wrottesley, *Burgoyne*, p.97.

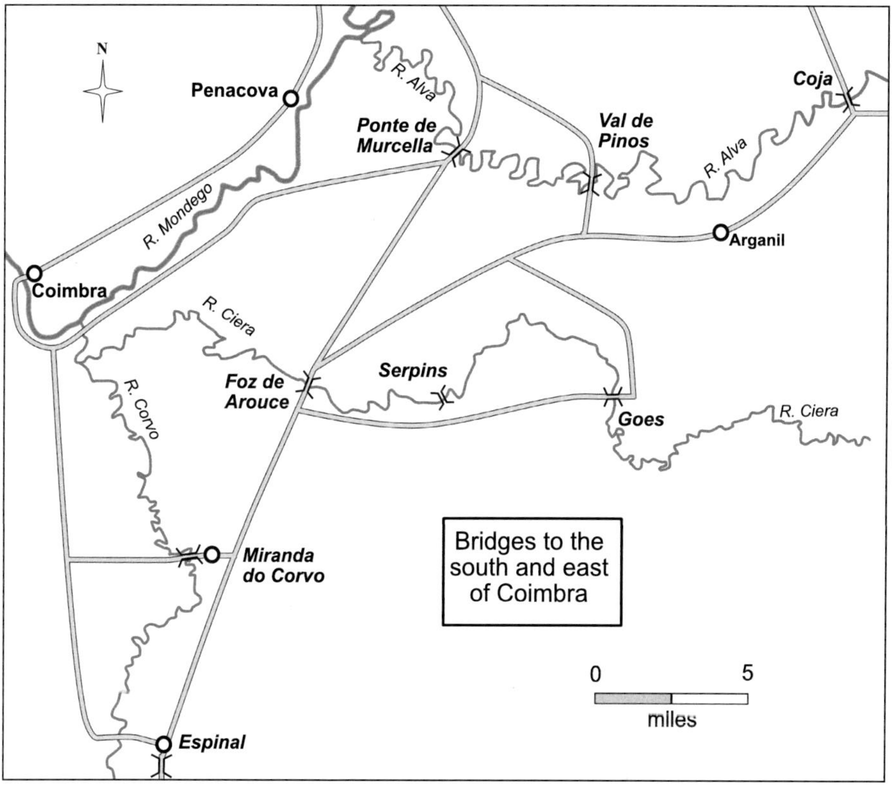

Bridges to south of Coimbra.

January 1810 were both north of the Mondego on the most likely route that the French would take. At this time, Wellington did not know whether the French would advance to the north or south of this river. He needed to be prepared for either possibility.

Burgoyne travelled to Ponte de Murcella with fellow Royal Engineer officer and regular companion, Alexander Thomson, arriving on 30 July. His first impression was that destroying the bridge there would achieve little as the river was easily fordable. However, 'took measures to undertake it, to be on the safe side'. The lack of sappers meant that Burgoyne had to employ local peasants to carry out the work.[47] Burgoyne had to pay the workmen out of his own pocket with Fletcher stating that if the money was not reimbursed, he would pay Burgoyne himself![48] The work at Ponte de Murcella was very slow due to the masonry being extremely hard. This

47 REM 4601-74, Burgoyne to Fletcher, 1 August 1810; Fletcher to Burgoyne, Celorico, 4 & 5 August 1810.
48 Wrottesley, *Burgoyne*, p.100.

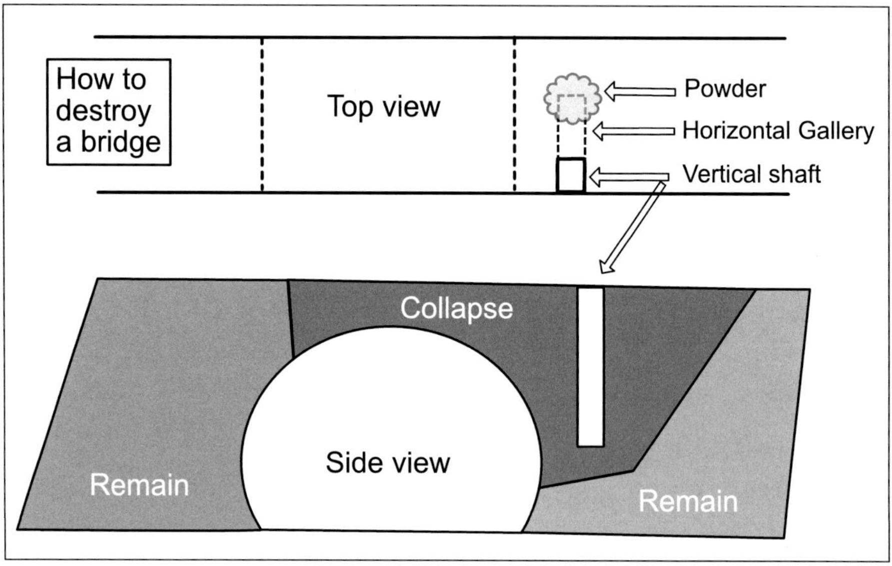

How to destroy a bridge.

was something that the engineers found all through the Iberian Peninsula, when concrete was used rather than loose stones. Burgoyne commented that 'It took a week to make a hole seven feet deep to the arch of the bridge through old composition of stones and hard mortar'.[49] Thomson, who went to Val de Pinos, had better success, quickly driving a horizontal shaft in the side of the arch.[50]

The diagram shows the ideal position for a mine.[51] Placing a mine at the top of the arch, whilst simpler, just destroys the top of the arch and makes repairs much easier because the gap is smaller. By placing a mine at the base of the arch, the whole side of the arch and part of the supporting pillar will collapse.

The mine was loaded at Val de Pinos on 1 August 1810, and the next day Burgoyne rode to Foz de Arouce where he inspected the bridge there and also another, four miles upstream at Serpins. He reported back to Fletcher that the river was fordable in both places at this time of year. Wellington asked for the bridges to be mined anyway. Finally, on 9 August 1810, the bridge at Ponte de Murcella was ready to receive the mine. Over the next few days, Burgoyne loaded the mines in the other bridges and arranged for guards to be posted to stop anyone interfering with them

49 REM 4201-68, Notebook, p.54.

50 REM 4201-68, Journal, 31 July 1810.

51 Diagram based on sketch in article, William Reid, 'Destruction of Stone Bridges', *Royal Engineer Professional Papers*, Vol.1, p.148.

(primarily the locals looking for powder). Two barrels (180 pounds or about 80 kilograms) were placed at each bridge.

In the meantime he had received further instructions to mine the bridge over the River Ciera at Goes, it also having been decided at headquarters that there was no need to mine the bridge over the Alva at Coja.[52] Burgoyne described the bridge at Goes as 'lofty with three stone semi-circular arches … running through a bold ravine, but now very fordable'.[53] He completed the mine on 17 August before riding back to Picton's Headquarters at Povoa de Concelho (10 miles north-east of Celorico), arriving on 22 August 1810. On his way back to Picton, he passed through Coja. He noted that the road to Coja 'would only be passed by artillery with difficulty'. Burgoyne had also sent his subordinate, Thomson, to report on the bridge, who reported that it was 'fordable in almost every part around the bridge'.[54] There was no point in mining this bridge as the road was very difficult for artillery and the river was fordable.

Burgoyne had now spent nearly a month visiting many of the major roads and rivers in the area to the south and east of Coimbra. This gave Wellington an unparalleled understanding of the terrain and how troops could be moved through the region. Masséna had to rely almost entirely on the poor Lopez maps of the country.[55] Wellington could not afford to be outmanoeuvred by the French and every possible route was being checked to ensure he did not receive any surprises.

After the French pushed the allied forces from in front of Fort Concepción, communication had been maintained with Almeida right up to 24 July. On 23 July 1810, Simmons of the 95th was 'having a jovial evening' with fellow officers in Almeida when, about 8:00 p.m., everyone who was not staying to defend the place was ordered to leave.[56] On the morning of 24 July 1810, the French attacked the positions of the Light Division on the River Côa, just west of Almeida. Ney brought his whole corps of 24,000 into action against Craufurd's 4,000. Craufurd has unwisely left most of his division on the French side of the Côa, against the wishes of Wellington. When attacked by superior numbers he was forced to make a fighting withdrawal across the single small stone bridge, suffering over 300 casualties.

There had been some discussion and planning on how to keep communication between Almeida and the bridge over the Côa. On 30 June 1810, Burgoyne noted:

52 REM 4601-74, Fletcher to Burgoyne, 6 & 7 August 1810.

53 REM 4201-68, Journal, 17 August 1810.

54 REM 4601-74, f.72, Thomson to Fletcher, 18 August 1810

55 See Dick Tennant, 'Maps in the Peninsular War', <https://www.napoleon-series.org/military/organization/Maps/PeninsularWar/c_MapsPeninsularWar.html> viewed 17 May 2019, and Tomas Lopez, *Geographic Atlas of Spain in the Peninsular War*, at <http://oa.upm.es/14061/2/INVE_MEM_2011_120868.pdf>, viewed 21 June 2019.

56 Verner (ed.), *British Rifleman*, p.76.

> General Cox sends for me to Almeida, to consult with him on a project of Lord Wellington's, for maintaining a part of the garrison in a position outside the place, for the purpose of preserving a communication with the bridge of the Côa; the left of this position to be on a windmill about 900 yards in front of the place, which is built extremely strong, and is to be made a tower, with a gun mounted on it. The right descends towards the Côa, and is to be on a convent, also to be entrenched and have two guns; this convent is also about 900 yards from the place, and about 1,500 from the mill. A small hill in front of the convent commanding the bridge is to be made into a post, and one or two guns [to be placed] there. The ground is broken, steep, and rocky, and the plan appears to me, to be dangerous and impracticable, particularly considering the nature of the garrison, consisting of one Portuguese regiment of the line (the 24th) and three miserable militia regiments, without discipline or subordination.[57]

Clearly some of this work was carried out as Mulcaster noted on 21 July 1810 that they 'are mounting a gun on a windmill about 900 yards from the covered way and entrenching it'. Three days later, he noted that 'Firing [was] observed today from the windmill near Almeida'.[58] Burgoyne, did have a point about the quality and size of the garrison. Stationing a significant number of troops outside the walls in the presence of a much stronger enemy risked the loss of valuable defenders. When Ney attacked, there were soldiers from the 1/52nd Light Infantry, not the Almeida garrison, in the windmill. There is no evidence that the convent was used as a strongpoint.

The Siege of Almeida

The French were now in a position to besiege Almeida, but, lacked the vital equipment of a siege train. The move from Ciudad Rodrigo was very slow due to the shortage of draught animals, the guns not arriving until about the middle of August. Another three weeks was lost. If Almeida could hold out as long as Ciudad Rodrigo, then the French might not be able to start their advance until October and that would make their move into Portugal more difficult due to the deteriorating weather.

57 REM 4201-68, Journal, 30 June 1810. Fortescue shows the convent on the road to the bridge. Oman shows the road to the bridge being further to the east and not passing the convent.

58 Thompson (ed.), *Mulcaster*, pp.116-7. In W.S. Moorsom (ed.), *Historical Record of the Fifty-Second (Oxfordshire Light Infantry) from the Year 1755 to the Year 1858* (London: Richard Bentley, 1860), p.120, it is stated that the gun in the windmill only fired once and then fell through the floor: no source is given.

Remains of castle at Almeida. (Author's collection)

Ney broke ground on 15 August 1810, and over the next 10 days, 11 batteries were constructed holding around 50 siege guns. They opened fire on the fortress on the morning of 26 August 1810 and later that day, disaster struck when the main powder magazine exploded, killing hundreds of soldiers and civilians and destroying the castle, most of the powder supply and many houses. Two days later, Almeida surrendered, the place being indefensible.

Oman described Almeida as a stronger fortress than Ciudad Rodrigo, with only two major defects; the glacis was too low to protect the walls and the castle which contained the main magazine was 'flimsy'.[59] Burgoyne, in his survey in October 1808 also noted these weaknesses but reported that the glacis was only too low around two of the six bastions. The castle he described as 'incapable of defence', meaning it could not withstand battering with modern weapons for long. However, as a powder store is was probably as strong as any magazine albeit a bit more visible and exposed. Burgoyne's recommendation to build other powder stores appeared, in hindsight, to be good advice. The explosion of the magazine was an accident caused by bad luck and bad practice in handling powder, not a major fault in the defences.

59 Oman, *Peninsular War*, Vol.III, p.268.

Writing on 28 August 1810, Burgoyne, who was now back with the 3rd Division, was completely ignorant about the cause of the surrender and could not understand how it had happened so quickly. Later that day he heard the news of the explosion of the magazine, commenting 'this accident probably accelerating its fall'.[60] Wellington's hope that the French would be delayed until October had just been dashed.

Supply issues again caused delays and the French did not advance until 15 September 1810. Wellington expected the French to march to the south of the Mondego on the best road. That was why Burgoyne had spent the last few weeks looking at and mining all the river crossings to the south of the river. Wellington had a defensive position selected at Ponte de Murcella and did not want the French army taking any route south of the Mondego other than by Ponte de Murcella.

Looking at Masséna's Lopez maps, the route to Coimbra on the south side of the Mondego did not look any more attractive than the routes to Viseu. The Lopez map shows the three routes being considered; Pinhel, Trancoso, Viseu (north of Mondego); Celorico, Fornos, Viseu (north) and Celorico, Chamusca, Ponte de Murcella (south). Masséna had marked in red pencil some roads not shown on the Lopez map. Each of these routes suggested the same standard of road. Criticism of Masséna's routing decisions and his Lopez map are quite common. Masséna was aware of the limitations of his topographical information. His aide de camp, Jean Jacques Pelet, remarked that all the information and 'strategists' they had access to 'could not answer the only thing we asked them. Can a carriage go on this road? Is this river deep? Is this range of mountains impracticable?'[61]

If one looks at two other well-known, contemporary maps, one gets exactly the same impression of the quality of the routes. The Carta Militar, which was only issued by the Portuguese in 1808,[62] and the Peninsula map in Wyld's Atlas, which was surveyed during and immediately after the war, both show all three routes as being 'better' quality roads. The advantage Wellington had was that he had trained military observers riding the roads and producing reports based on their direct observations, exactly as Pelet wished above.

The French should have known the northern route was not good. Junot's chief engineer in 1808, *Colonel* Humbert Vincent, had sent one of his officers to survey the routes and he reported:

> An inhabitant of Ponte de Murcella that was supposed to be educated, having assured us that the path by Viseu … was very good and passable

60 REM 4201-68, Journal, 28 August 1810.

61 Donald Horward (ed.), *The French Campaign in Portugal. An Account by Jean Jaques Pelet* (Minnesota: University of Minnesota, 1973), p.136.

62 Pelet noted that they had access to 'a poor little map by a Portuguese Major'. Perhaps they had a copy of the Carta Militar. It was Junot who had expedited its production. Horward (ed.), *Pelet*, p.135.

> at all times for cars, we hastened to recommend it and we went through Sta Comba Dão, Tondela, Viseu, Chans and Fornos. Greater difficulties were found than on the left bank [of the Mondego], the country more broken and consequently, the slopes are steeper and more numerous, and the rock is almost everywhere bare. The only reason that could make this road, though a little longer than the first, is that the country is more productive and more populated. It should be noted, however, that it does not offer any resources for the cavalry.
>
> We see from these details that it is absolutely necessary to give up passing the artillery and the carts by the paths which we followed, and if one believes the reports of the inhabitants, there are no better ones in this province. If we wanted to have the baggage transported by the country cars, there would still be difficulties almost insurmountable. These cars carry very little and go only two or three leagues a day. It would be more difficult to gather the number of carts that one would need to transport everything than exists to Ciudad Rodrigo.[63]

Oman is critical of Masséna for not scouting ahead, although he noted the difficulties French reconnaissance parties had to face. There is some justification in this view. However, the distances involved were not great and a strong cavalry reconnaissance would have quickly shown that the two northern routes were very poor. Oman noted that Masséna had been warned that Wellington had fortified the southern route.[64] Oman also criticised Masséna for taking the northern route as it was two additional marches for the troops, before noting the possibility that Masséna thought that provisions could be found at Viseu. Pelet stated that Masséna chose the northern routes to avoid Wellington's defensive position on the Alva around Ponte de Murcella and Vincent's report confirms the view of the existence of supplies. The decision to go through Viseu to collect provisions is understandable. However, no evidence has been located that defences were built at Ponte de Murcella, although, as an extension of the Bussaco ridge, the Serra de Murcella was every bit as formidable as Bussaco.

There were no substantial towns on the route to the south of the Mondego, and Wellington's forces had been occupying this area for much of the summer, so the French would have expected that there would be little chance of picking up additional supplies.

63 A Vincente, *Le Génie Français Au Portugal Sous L'Empire*, (Lisbonne: Estado-Maior do Exercito, 1984), pp.219-220, author's translation.

64 Oman, *Peninsular War*, Vol.III, p.348. Horward (ed.), *Pelet*, p.138 also notes this. The present author has not found any details of such defences being prepared and concludes that Oman used Masséna/Pelet as his source. The ridge to the west of Ponte de Murcella is a continuation of the Bussaco ridge and equally formidable even without field works.

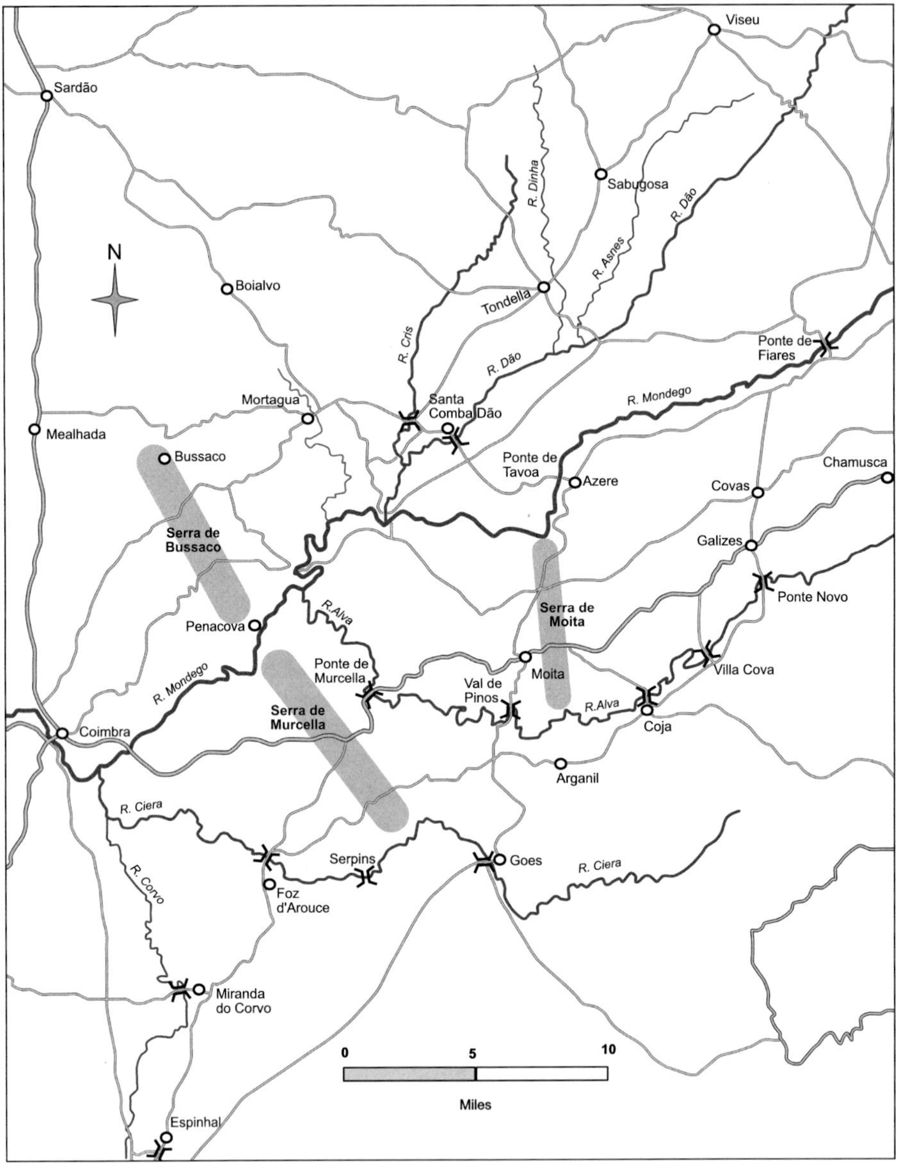

Country around Coimbra.

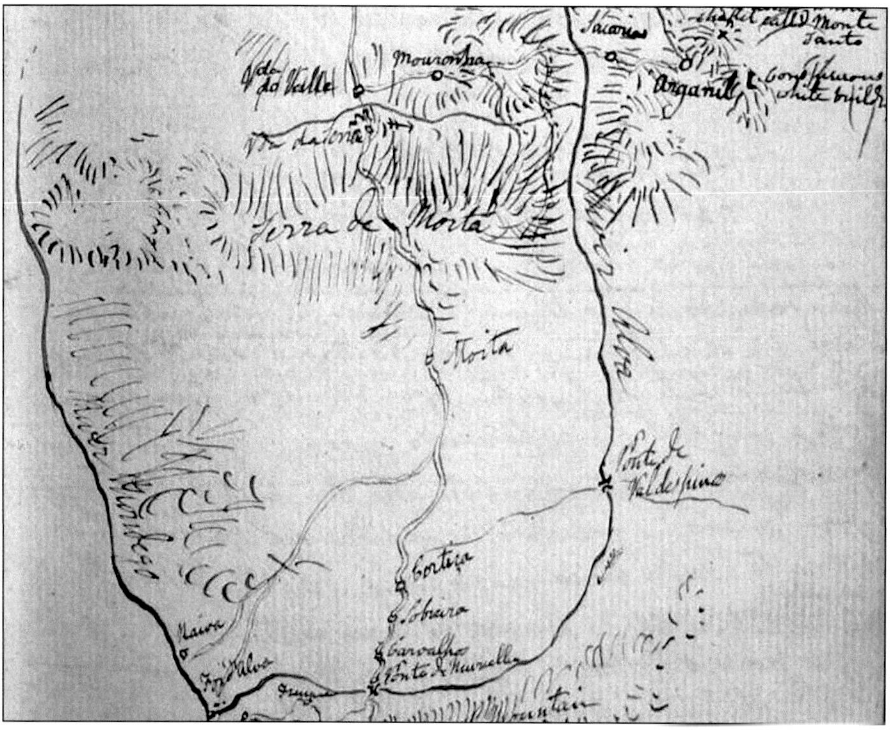

Burgoyne's sketch of area between Serra de Moita and Ponte de Murcella. (Royal Engineers Museum)

Following the surrender of Almeida, orders to retreat were issued the next day although the allied advance guard remained in place for many days. Burgoyne withdrew with the 3rd Division along the main road to Ponte de Murcella. This was done at a leisurely pace over several days; the French showing no immediate plans to advance. At this point Wellington knew the French advance had started but was still not sure whether Masséna would advance to the north or the south of the Mondego.

Wellington was seriously considering making a stand against the French and had selected likely sites on the south bank. On 17 September, Burgoyne:

> Received an order in the evening from Colonel Fletcher, dated Lourosa, 17th September, to examine the Serra de Moita as a position fronting either way, with its communication with Arganil, and also the ridge extending from above Ponte Murcella to the Mondego, and meet him to-morrow evening at Ponte de Murcella.[65]

65 Wrottesley, *Burgoyne*, p.107.

The Serra de Moita was a high ridge across the main road, several miles in front of Ponte de Murcella. It formed a very strong position from which to stop a French advance to the south of the Mondego. The ridge between Ponte de Murcella and the Mondego was a continuation of the Bussaco ridge on the south side of the Mondego and was similarly strong for defence. Burgoyne rode over both these heights on the 18 September and when he met Fletcher, the only comment recorded was that the position on the Serra de Moita was of no use because of the present movements. Fletcher must have been told that Masséna had turned north, although his logic was faulty as it was still possible (but very unlikely) that Masséna could have moved south from Viseu and re-cross the Mondego at Taboa.[66] As mentioned above, some writers have recorded that defensive positions had been prepared at Ponte de Murcella but there are no records of construction of defences at this place. Conversely, defences were built on the Bussaco ridge which also do not get mentioned in most accounts.[67]

On 19 September 1810, Burgoyne received orders to 'proceed immediately to Coimbra and report whether destroying the bridge there would cause much impediment to the enemy's artillery'.[68] On the same day, Mulcaster was ordered to destroy the two bridges at Santa Comba Dão that Burgoyne had surveyed in January 1810. These were on the direct route from Viseu to Coimbra, which was one of two possible routes that the French could take. There was still a possibility that Masséna could have moved north of the Bussaco ridge and joined the main Coimbra–Oporto road at Mealhada, then turning south. If this had happened, then Wellington needed to know if the Mondego around Coimbra was defensible and this was the reason for Burgoyne's orders. The order to proceed immediately showed how important this information was to Wellington.

The following day, Burgoyne reported back that he had seen bullock carts crossing the river above and below the bridge and destroying the bridge would serve no purpose. With mounting frustration, Burgoyne wrote five times before he received a response on 23 September 1810. He knew battle was imminent and did not want to miss it. Disappointingly, a second order now arrived to examine the River Mondego from Coimbra to the sea, again focussing on crossing points:

> Lord Wellington wishes you to reconnoitre the River Mondego below Coimbra; by going down it in a boat to ascertain how far and in what places it is fordable and that you will also particularly examine the left bank, and then the right bank and that you will report upon the whole as soon as possible. His Lordship seems very anxious for your report how far

66 The crossing point at Ponte de Tavoa (Taboa) would have been a ferry, not a bridge.

67 See Thompson (ed.), *Mulcaster*, p.130, Shore (ed.), *Engineer Officer*, p.72 and REM 4201-68, Journal, 23 September 1810.

68 Wrottesley, *Burgoyne*, p.108.

Burgoyne's sketch of battle of Bussaco. (Royal Engineers Museum)

> the destruction of the bridge at Coimbra would prove an impediment to an enemy, that he may decide whether to order it or not.[69]

It is surprising that although Burgoyne had sent five copies of his report on the bridge, using different routes, they did not appear to have been received at headquarters. Burgoyne's journal contains sketches of this river journey and on 25 September a consolidated map was sent to Wellington showing 17 places where artillery could cross.[70] The Mondego at Coimbra was not going to be good for defence; fortunately this was not required.

By 20 September 1810, it was clear that Masséna was advancing on the Santa Comba Dão road that leads to Bussaco, and Wellington was now able to concentrate his forces on the heights. Burgoyne, having finished his reports, rushed back to Bussaco arriving on 26 September and re-joined Picton's division.

This division was placed in the centre of the allied position covering one of the two roads which crossed the Bussaco ridge. On the 27 September 1810, the French made separate attacks up the two steep roads but were driven back. The first attack was against Picton's division around 6:00 a.m. and the later attack further north against the convent.

69 REM 4601-72, Fletcher to Burgoyne, Bussaco, 23 September 1810.
70 TNA WO55/1561/4, 25 September 1810.

To the surprise of many, the Portuguese troops behaved well and made a major contribution to the victory. Burgoyne commented:

> In the course of this day the 1st Portuguese Regiment of the line distinguished itself by advancing down the hill in line and driving a strong body of the enemy from the road, and the 4th Regiment of *Caçadores* also behaved extremely spiritedly and with great skill. In short, in all parts where they had an opportunity, the Portuguese regiments of the line and artillery behaved very well.[71]

The following day the allied army waited to see if the French would renew the attack, but Masséna, quite rightly, was not willing to make another frontal attack. Sending out scouting parties, he identified a minor road from Mortagua to Sardão which would allow the French to turn Wellington's position. Whilst Wellington was convinced that the French would continue their advance, the movements were not immediately understood, although the French could be seen moving from the foot of the Bussaco heights. Wellington ordered some of his divisions to withdraw but some were left in place. Burgoyne recorded:

> [I]n the course of this day, [a] great part of the French cavalry, which were in the rear, and a division of infantry, were observed from our commanding ground to be moving round our left. Lord Wellington had previously [looked?] how the left might be turned and found that it could not be so, but by a route of six leagues of bad road.[72]

Evidence of Wellington's intention to retreat can be seen in the meticulous orders that were issued by Murray, the army's QMG, including coloured maps for the route of each part of the army.[73] Burgoyne's commanding officer, Fletcher, was one of a number of officers who were sent out to find and track the French movements after the battle.[74] Confirmation of their marching via the Mortagua–Sardão road came on 29 September and the general withdrawal commenced.

Burgoyne remained with the 3rd Division, which retreated to Coimbra on 29 September crossing the Mondego the next day and marching to Condeixa on the main road to Lisbon. The retreat continued ahead of the French who remained in Coimbra to thoroughly sack it. There were still significant supplies in Coimbra due to the civilians ignoring the orders or waiting too long before leaving.

71 REM 4201-68, Journal, 27 September 1810.

72 REM 4201-68, Journal, 28 September 1810.

73 John Harding-Edgar, *Next to Wellington: General Sir George Murray* (Warwick: Helion, 2018), pp.185-188 and plate iv.

74 TNA WO55/958, Fletcher to Morse, 30 September 1810.

Unfortunately for Masséna, the first corps to enter the city were out of control and much food and drink was wasted before order was restored. His plan to obtain significant additional supplies was lost.

Burgoyne noted on 2 October that 'The people of the country are quitting their houses by order of the government, and are on the roads in all directions, most of them without means of subsistence; they say the penalty of not obeying this order is death'. Part of Wellington's plan was to leave no resources available to the advancing French army. This meant that the population were forced to leave their homes and move towards Lisbon. This caused great hardship to the population but probably better than the brutality suffered at the hands of the French by the civilians who chose to stay. Burgoyne's Journal continued the following day: 'This order appears to be most ill-judged; the people will flock to Lisbon, and there, will be in the greatest distress, besides the ill effects it will have on our reputation'.[75]

Burgoyne was right on both counts but there was little alternative. The other consequence of the civilians leaving their properties, was looting by the retreating British troops. Burgoyne noted that Picton made great efforts to stop it, including refusing to let his troops be quartered in the towns and making them sleep in the open.[76]

The 3rd Division passed through Roliça, the site of the first battle of the war, on 6 October 1810, and the following day the division arrived at the town of Torres Vedras and the start of the defensive lines. The French arrived a few days later and were shocked at the scale of the defences. Apart from a couple of probing attacks in mid-October they made no attempt to breach the Lines until troop losses and starvation forced them to retreat six months later in March 1811.

Before leaving 1810, there is one other activity to mention in which Burgoyne was heavily involved. A number of officers with recent operational experience felt that the training given to engineer officers and the structure of the corps were not fit for purpose and were vocal in their criticism of the situation and the lack of interest in changing it. The engineer officers, primarily based in the Peninsula, discussed the formation of the Society for the Procurement of Useful Military Information, whose aim was to share knowledge to improve the professionalism of the Corps.[77] The main complaints were about the lack of preparation of officers for field-based activities and the lack of sappers. The instigator of the formation of the Society was Charles Lefebure and other engineer officers involved included John Jones, John Squire, and Edmund Mulcaster, all officers who played a leading role in the Peninsula.[78] Discussions first started in early 1810 with the intention

75 REM 4201-68, Journal, 3 October 1810.

76 REM 4201-68, Journal, 5 October 1810.

77 REM 4601-74, Mulcaster to Burgoyne, Ponte do Rol, 18 January 1810.

78 The original six were: Squire, Burgoyne, Jones, Ross, Dickinson and Mulcaster. The group grew from six to 18 in January 1811 when Birch, Nicholas, Goldfinch, Fanshawe, Pasley, Boothby, Thackeray, Parker, Lewis, Marlow, Douglas and Arnold were admitted.

of sharing practical experience and creating a library of relevant works. It is surprising that none of the senior corps officers were involved. When Lefebure was killed in April 1810, Burgoyne took a leading role in the development. Discussions continued through into 1811 but then there was no more correspondence on the subject. By this time, Pasley had joined the group and his experiments at home led to the formation of the School of Military Engineering in April 1812 an event that satisfied much of the concern of the officers. The need for proper training and recording of experience is best demonstrated by the fact that of the six original members, four died during the Peninsular War, losing all their valuable experience apart from what was shared amongst the group.

7

The Lines of Torres Vedras

Construction of the Lines of Torres Vedras began in October 1809 after Wellington's visit to the area. His memorandum of 20 October 1809 outlined the work required, which, apart from the building of many forts, included scarping hillsides, damming rivers and the building or destruction of roads. The original plan was for a single line of defences; what is now called the second line. In front of this line were three strongpoints designed to slow down the French advance before they approached the main defensive line. These three strong points were at Torres Vedras, Sobral, and Arruda. Due to the delays in Masséna's advance, there was more time than expected to build additional forts and the forward strong points were extended and eventually became the first line. As well as these two lines of defence, a third line was constructed at St Julião de Barra, west of Lisbon on the Tagus estuary. This was to cover the embarkation of the allied army, if that became necessary.

Many of these new forts were built after the French arrived. There were over 150 forts built, of which 128 had been completed when the allied army arrived at the beginning of October 1810. Wellington's plan was to use militia and *ordenança* (Portuguese levies) in the forts and keep his army concentrated behind the Lines to respond to any French attack; a plan that seemed to be lost on many of his officers.

The Lines of Torres Vedras were initially divided into six districts, each with a general officer in charge, a regulating (engineer) officer and a commissary officer. The six districts were:

1. From Torres Vedras to the sea
2. From Sobral de Monte Agraço to the valley of Calahandriz
3. From Alhandra to the valley of Calahandriz
4. From the banks of the Tagus near Alverca to the pass of Bucellas
5. From the pass of Freixal to the right of the pass of Mafra
6. From the pass of Mafra to the sea.[1]

1 Gurwood (ed.), *Despatches,* Memorandum to Colonel Fletcher, Rio Mayor, 6 October 1810.

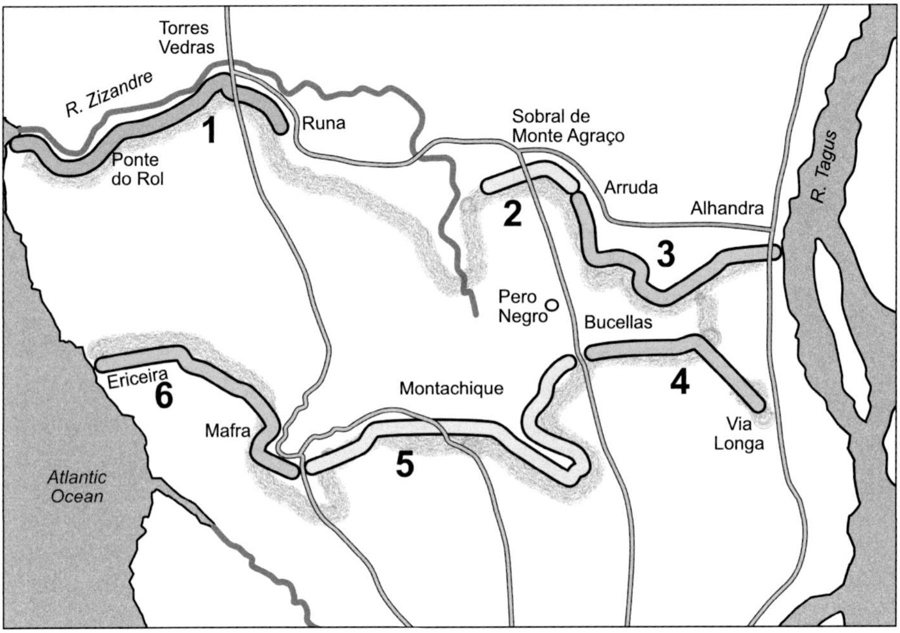

Lines of Torres Vedras with six districts, 1810.

The area between Sobral and Runa was initially judged to be secure enough without forts, but once the decision was made to hold the French at the front line, this gap was filled and in 1811 a seventh district was created (and confusingly, all the districts were then renumbered).

On 8 October 1810, his first day on the Lines at Torres Vedras, Burgoyne was told that Major General John Sontag would command the district (District One) and recently promoted Captain Mulcaster had been appointed Regulating Officer. In the absence of both these officers, Burgoyne worked with Major General Picton to arrange the deployment of the Portuguese soldiers and militia into the forts around Torres Vedras.

Later in the day, Burgoyne received an order appointing him Regulating Officer to District Four (which was changed to number five when they were renumbered). Assigned to work with him was Lieutenant Frank Stanway RE. Burgoyne's orders from Wellington stated:

> The business of your situation ... is to manage the troops ... when they will be sent into the district to occupy the redoubts; to take charge of the mines with which to blow up the roads and bridges and to carry [out] my orders in the district.[2]

2 REM 5501-108-8, Wellington to Burgoyne, Rio Maior, 6 Oct 1810.

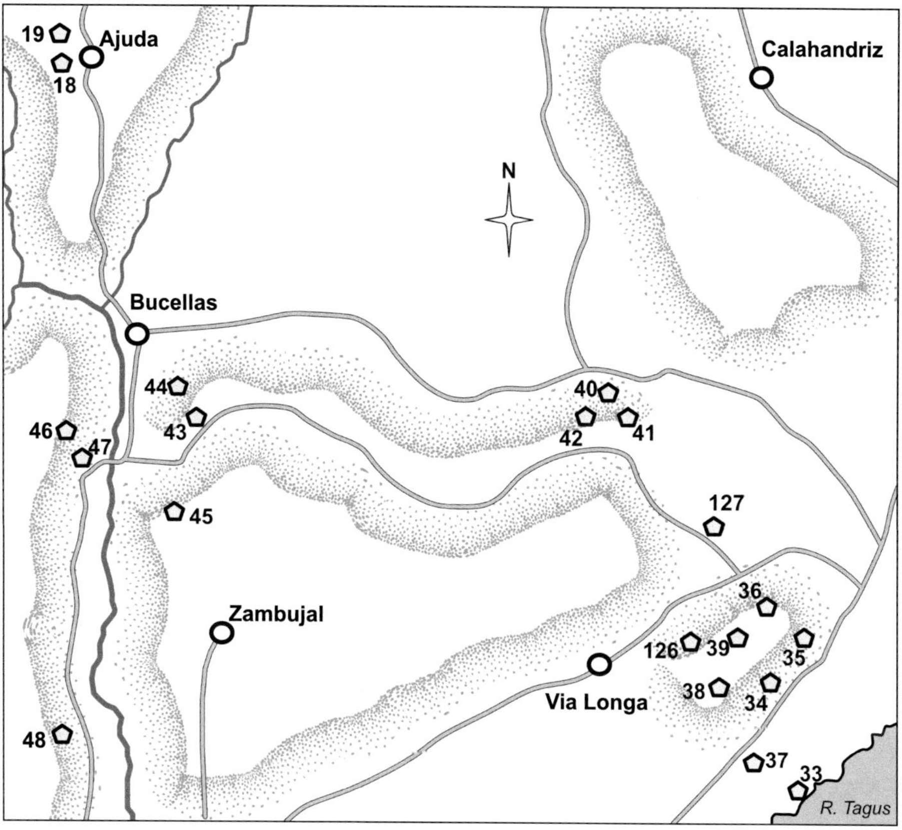

District 4 of the Lines of Torres Vedras, 1810.

At the time of his appointment, he noted the district:

> [C]ontains sixteen redoubts and batteries, on which are mounted thirty-seven 12-pounders and twenty-two, 9-pounders, and the works are calculated to require 2,660 infantry. At present, 1,100 militia infantry, 500 ordenança artillery, and eight Portuguese artillery of the linc are allotted to it.[3]

The district eventually contained 20 forts with 72 cannon, requiring 3,500 militia to man them.

Burgoyne would have been busy for several weeks completing the provisioning of the forts and organising the troops, but he makes no mention of the work he

3 REM 4201-68, Journal, 8 October 1810.

was doing on the Lines at any point in the next six months. This is quite surprising and probably reflects his unhappiness at working on such tasks. Like his fellow engineer officers, he wanted to be on active operations with the army, not stuck doing 'boring' engineering work, even though that was their role. Confirmation of his view is clarified in a letter written to Lord Derby in May 1811, which starts, 'For the last three or four months, I have been most disagreeably situated in this neighbourhood [the Lines], while the army has been working hard on the frontier'.[4] The last 'three or four months' meaning since Masséna retired. He probably felt the same about the previous five months. As before, in other periods when there were no active operations, the diary entries slow down: it is likely that little was being done. Burgoyne's journal over this period instead followed the activities of other forces on active operations.

As already mentioned, Wellington had also ordered the area in front of the Lines to be cleared, with the population ordered to Lisbon and anything useful to the French to be destroyed. This caused great hardship and many thousands of civilians died of starvation through the winter. The success of this 'scorched earth' policy was not complete, with a number of comments that the French were able to find supplies. The fact they could remain stationary in front of the Lines for five months confirms some success in finding supplies. Burgoyne commented, on 1 November 1810:

> It is evident that though the enemy might suffer on their first arrival in this part of the country for want of provisions, that they must now be very well off, the country they are now occupying is a very fertile one and the harvest was got in entirely when they arrived. No measures were taken for driving the country... on the contrary the wretched inhabitants had barely time to get off themselves and I myself was witness to messages coming to a General of a Division informing him of quantities of corn etc. which they were forced to leave ... so far from being in want, they must be living luxuriously ... Therefore, all things considered the idea of starving the enemy out of their ground is out of the question.[5]

There were several other officers who made similar comments about provisions being left during the retreat. Whilst the Portuguese government had agreed to the strategy of clearing the country, it was understandable that people would be reluctant to implement it and especially to implement it early. The problem for the French forces was not if there were supplies available as they advanced, it was how to replenish them when they were used up. The disorder at Coimbra showed that Masséna would have great difficulty, and there was little co-ordination between

4 Wrottesley, *Burgoyne*, p.132.
5 REM 4201-68, Journal, 1 November 1810.

the roving French bands that scoured they Portuguese countryside for the next few months.

Even a few weeks inactivity did not seem to sit well with British officers and there was confusion and frustration as to why Wellington with his 'larger' forces did not attack the French in front of them. Burgoyne, having detailed the relative sizes of the armies, commented 'It is said our troops are to be cantoned, and made as comfortable as can be for the winter!!!'.[6]

In mid-November the French retired from immediately in front of the Lines and the allied army moved into more comfortable quarters, also allowing some of the militia to be sent back to Lisbon. Burgoyne's journal has few entries between December and March and does not pick up again until the Masséna's retreat started in March 1811.

6 REM 4201-68, Journal, 1 November 1810.

8

1811 – Stalemate

The year started quietly, with the allies watching the French and waiting to see if any attempt would be made to attack the Lines of Torres Vedras or launch a separate attack as demanded by Napoleon. Due to this concern that the French would cross the Tagus and move into the Alentejo region where there would be greater access to supplies, an allied force under Lieutenant General Rowland Hill was despatched. In December 1810, Hill fell ill and was temporarily replaced by Major General Stewart before Beresford was appointed. Burgoyne commented 'Marshal Beresford ... now commands the division formerly under General Hill. General Stewart ... having during his short [period in] command ventured to give opinions to Lord Wellington'.[1] As Burgoyne was not attached to headquarters this was probably a view being passed round the army. This was not the first time that Burgoyne had commented on Wellington's unwillingness to accept 'advice', which would have been of concern to engineer officers whose role was to give Wellington just such advice.

March 1811 saw the French finally accepting that they had to retreat from in front of the Lines. Wellington quickly followed and kept the demoralised French moving north.

On 20 March 1811, Burgoyne was given overall command of the Second Line, with Lieutenants Richard Boteler, John Pringle, and Anthony Marshall reporting to him. Similarly, Captain William Holloway was in charge of the Third Line and Captain John Williams the First Line.[2] Burgoyne's journal traces the military operations but continues to make no mention of what he was engaged in. He was certainly unhappy to have been left behind, when the army followed Masséna. The decision to leave him on the Lines may have been because he was with the army the whole of the preceding year when most other engineer officers were 'stuck' working on the Lines.

1 REM 4201-68, Journal, 29 January 1811.
2 REM 5501-59-1, Jones MS Journal, 20 March 1811.

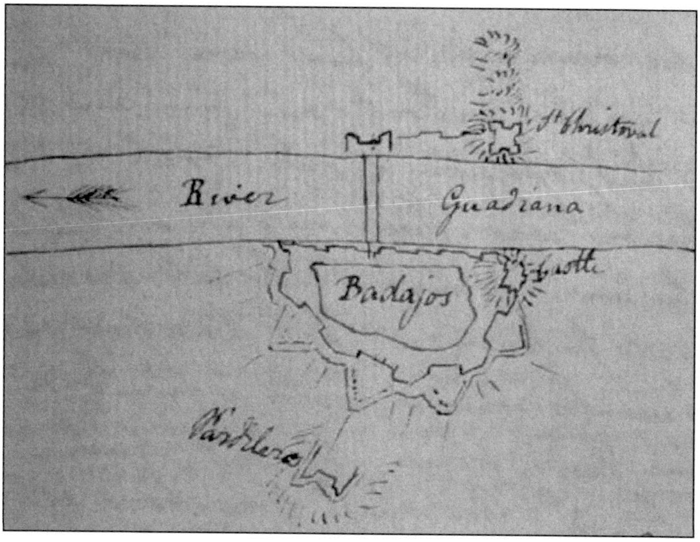

Sketch of Badajoz from Burgoyne's Journal. (Royal Engineers Museum)

The attention of the engineer officers moved south even as Wellington moved north. The Spanish fortress of Badajoz had unexpectedly surrendered to the French on 10 March 1811. A French attack on Lisbon from this direction now became more likely. This could not have come at a worse time for Wellington who had just started his move north in pursuit of Masséna's retreating army.

An allied force under Marshal Beresford was sent to retake the fortresses of Campo Mayor, Olivenza, and Badajoz. The first two were quickly taken and the senior engineer present, Captain John Squire, then asked for more engineers to tackle the much harder task of re-taking Badajoz. Burgoyne was one of the officers specifically asked for, although he was not called up to the siege.[3] Burgoyne noted on 23 April, that three engineer captains recently arrived from England and three other captains at Lisbon had been ordered up to Elvas, 'it is expected that Badajoz will be besieged'.[4] A few days later, he noted that twenty officers of engineers will be employed at the siege of Badajoz. His frustration at not being one of them must have been mounting.

Badajoz was fully invested on 8 May 1811, with Burgoyne still working on the Lines. The siege had barely started when it had to be raised due to the approach of a French army under Soult and the bloody Battle of Albuera was fought on 16 May 1811. There was much frustration amongst the engineers present, who felt that the allied commander, Beresford, had not listened to their recommendations.

3 REM 4601-71, Squire to unknown, Arroches, 23 March 1811.
4 REM 4201-68, Journal, 23 April 1811.

Burgoyne was clearly getting regular updates on what was happening and commented:

> Had the plan originally proposed been allowed to be carried into execution, it is the opinion of many of the Engineers there that the place would have been taken in six or seven days, that is, before it was necessary to raise the siege.[5]

However, the biggest delay in starting the siege was more political than operational. With the death of the Marqués de la Romana in January 1811, it was necessary to agree a plan of operations with the Spanish forces which were operating in the same area as Beresford. Wellington had written to the three Spanish commanders, Francisco Javier Castaños, Joaquín Blake, and Francisco Ballesteros, outlining his proposals for the operation to retake Badajoz and had given Beresford strict instructions that the siege was not to be started until all three Spanish generals had agreed to Wellington's proposals. This agreement from the Spanish generals was not received until 8 May 1811, the date the trenches were started. It is likely that many officers were not aware that Beresford was waiting for agreement from the Spanish commanders, but Fletcher as Chief Engineer must have known. He wrote an update on the siege for his superiors on 15 May, the day before the Battle of Albuera, saying:

> I am sorry to acquaint you that the siege of Badajoz has been raised. We broke ground before the advanced works on the 8th instant, on the 9th, I earnestly entreated Sir Wm Beresford to allow me to commence operations against the body of the place, from feeling that it might be done with a reasonable degree of safety, and a wish to lessen the probability of being disturbed by Marshal Soult, before the place should surrender. The Marshal would not however finally consent until the evening of the 12th when we opened a parallel within about six hundred yards of the place and were going on with every prospect of speedy success, when at one o'clock in the morning of the 13th, I received an order to discontinue the work and to withdraw the parties. This arose from some reports of the advance of the enemy. Four of five days at the utmost must have given us a practicable breach had we commenced as proposed and urged, as far as could be done with propriety, we must have been in possession of the place at this moment.[6]

5 Wrottesley, *Burgoyne*, p.131.
6 TNA WO55/958, Fletcher to Morse, Badajoz, 15 May 1811.

The unhappiness expressed by the engineers about the actual siege was about the delay in starting work against the castle between the 9 and 12 May. Beresford was already hearing rumours about a French attempt to relieve the fortress and this appears to have led him to delay the work for the attack on the castle. Since the other attacks were carried on, it is hard to see a reason for delaying what was intended to be the main attack. Even without this delay, there were few guns available for the siege and many were in poor condition; there were few engineer officers and no sappers. It is highly unlikely that the siege could have been completed before the French arrived, especially in the light of what happened when the castle wall was attacked during the second siege. Fletcher's comment about 'some reports of an advance' is also misleading. It was not 'some reports', it was actual confirmation that the French were advancing rapidly on Badajoz.

The Second Siege of Badajoz

Finally, on 27 May, Burgoyne received his summons to join the siege of Badajoz, arriving there on 2 June 1811. Burgoyne's diary describes the siege but makes no mention of what role he had. Jones recorded he was director of the attack on the castle at Badajoz.[7] Also surprisingly, there was no analysis after the siege was raised, Burgoyne would certainly have had opinions on its organisation.

The plan for the second siege was broadly the same as that used in the first siege; to take Fort San Cristóbal on the northern bank of the Guadiana, then breach and assault the eastern wall of the castle.[8]

The south side of the fortress was re-invested on 19 May and the northern side on 25 May 1811. Major Alexander Dickson RA, who was responsible for collecting the siege train, estimated that it would not be ready until around 30 May, by which time there were already rumours that the French were moving to relieve the fortress.

On the night of 29 May, the first trenches were started, for the false attack on the Pardaleras fort. This was the site of the French attack earlier in the year. Despite being the preferred direction of attack by everyone, it had been rejected, as it was judged there was not sufficient time to first take the Pardaleras fort and then take the fortress itself before the French relief arrived. Despite much criticism of this decision and blame attached to the engineers, this decision was accepted by Wellington and Beresford in May and confirmed by Wellington in June. The attack against San Cristóbal and the castle was riskier but judged to be quicker.

7 Jones, *Sieges*, Vol.I, p.31.

8 See the present author's extensive analysis of the confusion around the plan originally ordered and the plan actually followed in Thompson, *Wellington's Engineers*, pp.90-105.

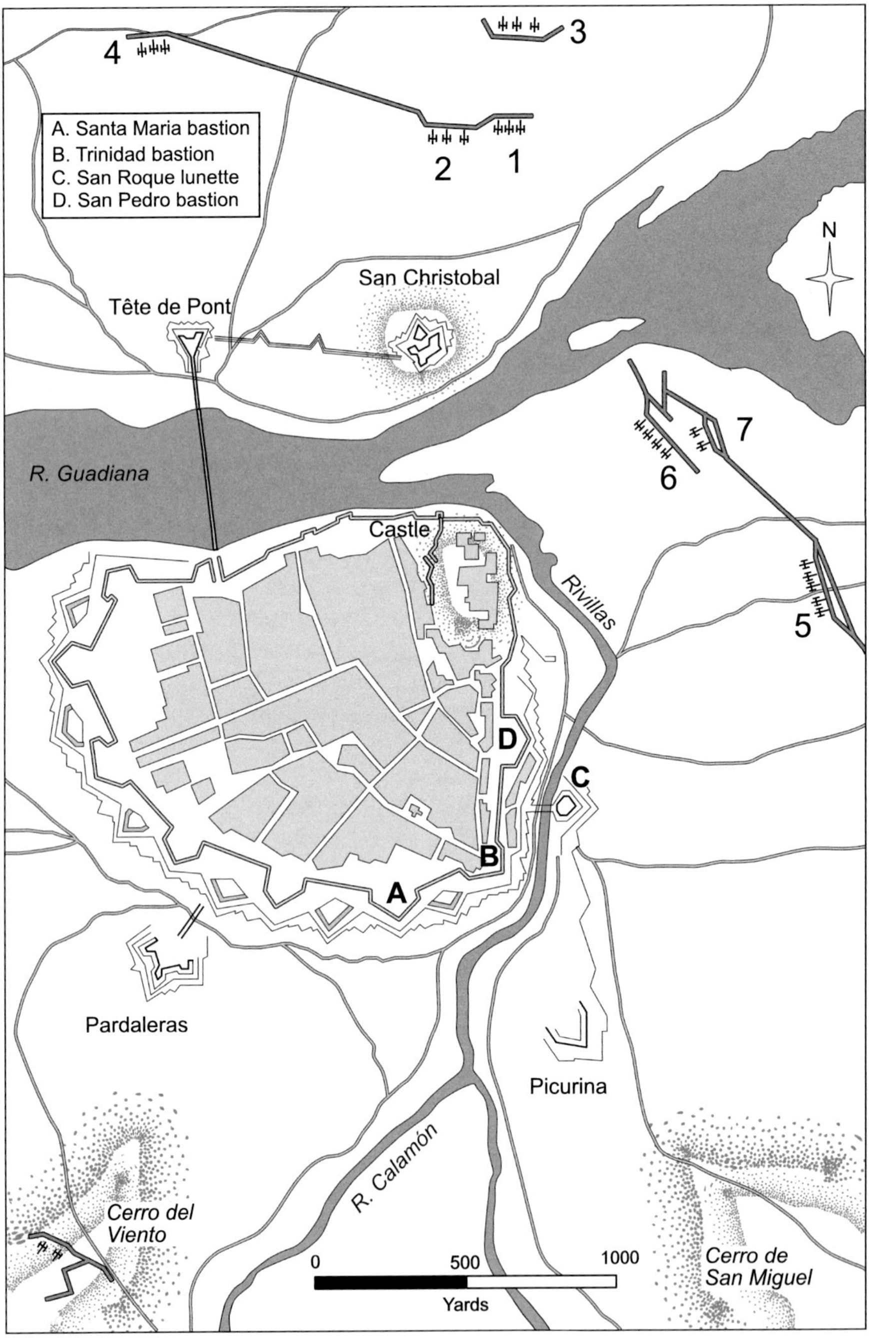

Second siege of Badajoz, 19 May – 10 June 1811.

Work continued throughout the day on the false attack and the following night the trenches were also opened for the main attacks against the castle and Fort San Cristóbal. No battery appears to have been erected against the Picurina fort as was done during the first siege. By the time Burgoyne arrived on 2 June and took up his post as siege director for the castle attack, the batteries had been completed although not in their planned position. To save time, a decision had been made to erect the batteries in the first parallel rather than wait for the construction of the second parallel, which would have put them closer. The guns were installed overnight and were ready by 8:00 a.m., there now being a slight delay whilst the batteries for the attack against fort San Cristóbal were completed. Burgoyne noted:

> At 10 or 11am, the batteries opened, those on this side to endeavour to breach the old castle wall and keep up a vigorous cannonade which was but slightly returned by the enemy who do not seem to expected the attack on this side having directed great efforts to the side of Pardilleros [Pardaleras], that which they had previously chosen themselves for attack and where we conducted the false attack.[9]

Although no work had been done on the false attack on the Pardaleras since 31 May,[10] the French had clearly spent some time preparing for an attack from this direction. Both Burgoyne and Dickson noted that more French guns were brought round during 3 June to fire on the castle attack. Burgoyne, like Dickson and Jones, noted that the accuracy of the allied guns was poor, although it improved during the day as the gunners got used to their individual guns' quirks. In Jones' manuscript journal, he wrote that 'not one shot in six struck the castle wall'.[11] Squire, who was the engineer in charge of the attack on San Cristóbal, noted that 'the artillery, guns, shot and powder are most wretched'. He continued:

> About 10:30 [on 3 June 1811], My Lord arrives. Accompany him to the low ground to observe the breaching battery on the left of the river [against the castle]. He seemed in high spirits … I remarked that I thought the battery on the other side was at too great a distance to make much impression on the wall. "Oh", replied, My Lord, "only 600 yards and that is near enough to make a breach when you can see the foot of the wall." … In fact, he seemed quite satisfied with the prospect and said he saw the wall tumbling down in large pieces. I confess, I observed only a very slight imperfection made by our fire.[12]

9 REM 4201-68, Journal, 3 & 4 June 1811.
10 REM 5501-59-1, Jones MS journal, 31 May 1811.
11 REM 5501-59-1, Jones MS journal, 3 June 1811.
12 NAM 2016-07-24, Squire Journal, 3 June 1811.

Despite Squire's pessimism, the old castle wall crumbled as expected. What was not expected was that behind the wall was a solid bank of earth that was resistant to the cannon fire. When it did break, it tended to do it in vertical slabs, leaving another vertical wall of earth behind.[13] The engineers' confidence that they could have quickly taken the fortress during the first siege, if they were given more time, had been proven wrong.

After a visit by Wellington, it was decided to build the second battery (No.6.) to the right of the original one and about 150 yards closer. This was Burgoyne's first task. Seven guns were moved into it and it opened fire on 5 June 1811. Still the earth behind the castle wall resisted. A slope was being created, but very slowly. A third battery [No.7] was now started 'about 50 yards in advance and something to the right of Number 2 [No.5 on Jones' plan and map], a zig-zag approach is carried up to it of about 300 yards to avoid the enfilades of Picarina [Picurina] and San Christobal'.[14] In an understatement, Jones recorded 'the heavy grape which the garrison showered down from the castle annoyed the workmen extremely and caused many casualties'.[15]

Engineer officers repeatedly risked their lives to monitor the progress of the battering. Mulcaster crossed the Rivillas stream on the night of 5 June to confirm that there were fords that the troops could use for an assault. Three days later, Patton made another reconnaissance and was badly wounded, dying on 17 July 1811. Burgoyne himself made a reconnaissance of the castle breach on 9 June.[16] On the other side of the Guadiana, Forster explored the breach in fort San Cristóbal on the night of 4/5 June.[17] He died in the failed assault on the night of 6/7 June. Rice Jones made a further exploration of the breach before the assault on the night of 9 June 1811.

The breach in San Cristóbal was declared practicable on 6 June and an assault was ordered for that night. The attacking force was only 180 men and by the time they approached, at midnight, the defenders had cleared the foot of the breach and had blocked up the breach. The ladders they carried for mounting the breach were too short to mount the walls. After an hour trying to find another way in, the survivors retired.

13 Jones, *Sieges*, Vol.III, plate II, shows the gradual build-up of a slope over several days of fire.

14 REM 4201-68, Journal, 5 June 1811. Burgoyne used a different numbering system for the batteries. I have stayed with Jones' as the most common.

15 Jones, *Sieges*, Vol.I, p.49.

16 REM 4201-68, Journal, 10 June 1811. Burgoyne gets slightly confused about dates. It suggests these journal entries were written later.

17 NAM 2016-07-24, Squire Journal entry, night of 4 & 5 June 1811. Squire's words are that 'Forster reconnoitres the ditch, which he reports to be no obstacle'. Was he investigating access to the ditch rather than access to the breach? As there was two days between his reconnaissance and the assault this seems possible. If he was checking the breach, that should have been done just before the assault.

Squire's journal records that on the morning of 7 June, Wellington had ordered another assault on San Cristóbal as soon as the breach was declared practicable. The next day, 8 June, Wellington ordered an assault that night. The initial urgency was because the French had placed field pieces in the back of the fort that were firing across the river and causing casualties on the castle attack. Fletcher told Squire that he had altered the approach that was enfiladed by the field pieces and there was no longer any urgency. Squire asked for a 24-hour delay before the next assault, to give more time to improve the breach: this must have been agreed by Wellington. On 9 June, Squire argued that the assault on San Cristóbal was only needed just before the main assault on the castle and was told that Wellington wanted possession of San Cristóbal as soon as possible as there was a French force approaching and he wanted to summon the fortress 'with some hope of its surrender'.[18] The second assault was launched around 9:00 p.m.: although the attacking force was larger, it again failed.

After two failed attempts to take fort San Cristóbal, the siege was again abandoned on 10 June, due to the approach of French forces and the need to stop drawing upon stores from Elvas which could itself now soon be under siege.

There is plenty of criticism of the planning and execution of these two sieges. However, the key reason they failed was a lack of time. Steps have to be followed in sieges; there are rarely short cuts. Wellington's requirements were to conduct the siege in 16 days, or less. The strategy adopted was the only one that the engineers could see would meet this time requirement. Attacking the south side was a better option but it could not be done in the time available.

There is one element that could have made a difference and Oman did recognise it. Both attacks against San Cristóbal were made with very small forces; 200 for the first and 400 for the second. The defenders were approximately 200 during the first assault and 400 during the second. Each face of the fort is roughly 100 metres long. The small number of defenders must have followed the attackers round the walls during the assault. Neither assault planned a secondary attack, the 'hope' being that assaulting the breach would work. If a more substantial assault force had been planned; with multiple points of attack; with ladders able to reach the tops of the wall, there were not enough defenders to resist. San Cristóbal could have been taken on 5 June. Capture would have allowed the allied artillery fire to plunge into the castle, making it defenceless, and so improve the chances of a successful assault. Badajoz could have been taken by 10 June.

What is very surprising is Burgoyne's complete silence on this siege after his involvement. His journal records information from the first siege that he must have received from officers who were present. There are no journal entries commenting on the plan or execution of the second siege. The present author has not found any letters on the subject, to, or from him. The silence is almost as if he was trying to

18 NAM 2016-07-24, Squire Journal, 6-9 June 1811.

disassociate himself from the whole operation or, possibly, he felt he arrived too late to make any significant contribution. However, this was the first siege he had been involved in since Malta in 1800 and, being on a larger scale, it would have increased his knowledge and understanding of the practical processes involved in such operations. This experience would be valuable over the next two years.

Having failed to retake Badajoz, the safety of Elvas became paramount. Fletcher the commanding engineer moved to Elvas to evaluate the state of the defences. The engineer officers were dispersed, some going to Abrantes and several back to work on the Lines. Burgoyne would have been greatly relieved to see that Captain John By RE was ordered to take command of the second of the Lines of Torres Vedras. Burgoyne and Ross stayed with the main army and Squire returned to Lieutenant General Hill's corps.

Wellington had moved most of his forces south leaving Picton's 3rd Division blockading the fortress. On 15 June, he was on the battlefield of Albuera, waiting for the expected French advance. On 17 June 1811, he withdrew to a defensive line from Ouguela to Puente de Caya via Campo Mayor, having confirmed that Soult and *Maréchal* Auguste-Frédéric Marmont had met at Merida. The French relieving forces entering Badajoz on 20 June. The combined French armies numbered around 60,000 and were much stronger than Wellington's forces. An attack on his army or on Elvas was very likely.

On 21 June, Burgoyne joined the 3rd Division at Campo Mayor and described the defensive position taken up by the allied army:

> Campo Mayor is about 1,000 yards in front of the right of the centre of the position and in front of the right is a round, bold, commanding hill, with olive woods on it, which would be occupied and disputed. Towards the left, near the Atalaya [Tower] de Ouguela, the ground is more broken and has olive wood and vineyards on it which extend a considerable distance in front. Farther on the left, about 2 ½ miles is Ouguela, an old fort, now made a post, being well enclosed with walls and situated on a small height; close under it runs the River Gebora, dividing Spain and Portugal.

Burgoyne also noted that he had been ordered to construct an abbatis around the Atalaya, to construct three batteries and make repairs to the outwork, Fort San Pedro at Campo Mayor.[19] The use of Royal Engineers to make field works is interesting. Officially, such work was the responsibility of the Royal Staff Corps, but Wellington used whoever was available. There were certainly elements of the Staff Corps present as Lieutenant John Westmacott was wounded in the failed assault on San Cristóbal on the night of 6/7 June.[20] The Royal Engineer brigade major,

19 REM 4201-68, Journal, 21 June 1811. Not printed in Wrottesley.

20 NAM 2016-07-24, Squire Journal, night of 6&7 June 1811.

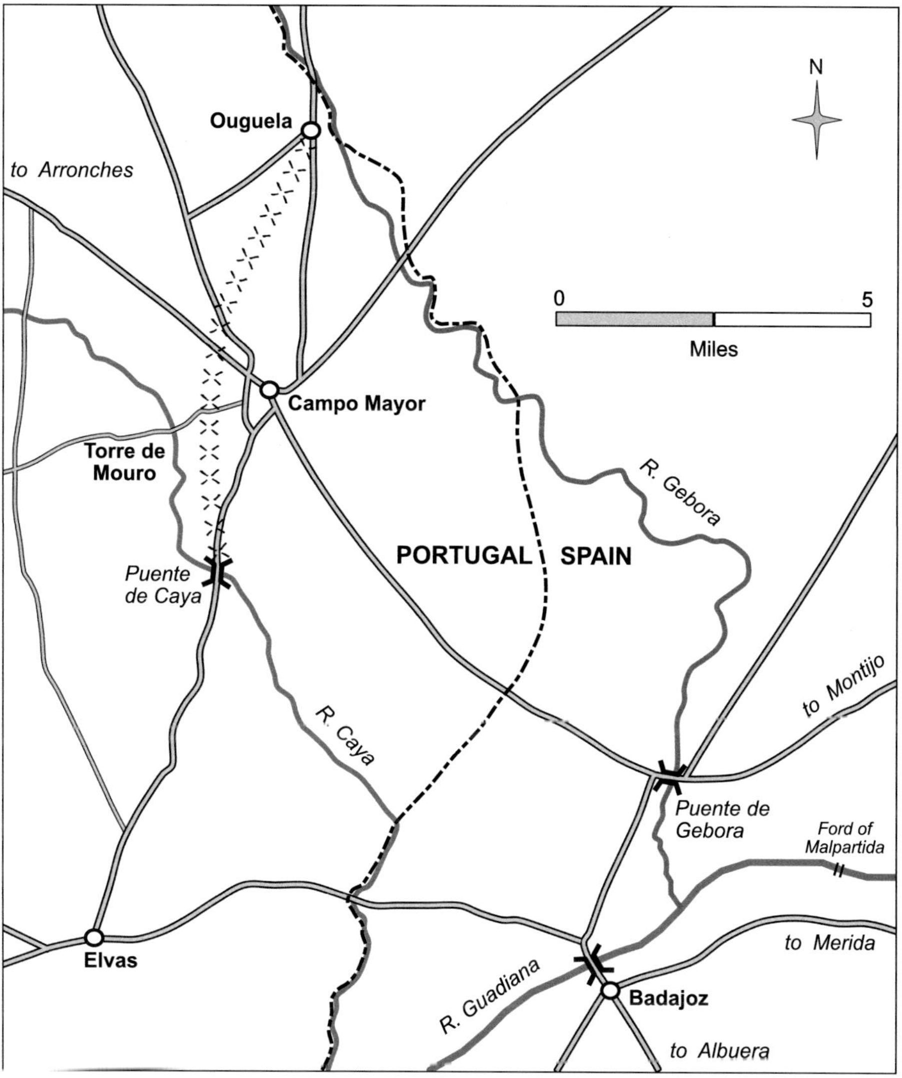

Allied positions on the Caya, June 1811.

Jones, commented that there was a delay in starting the batteries as the Conductor of Stores with responsibility for the entrenching tools could not be found. Then he took a long time to arrive and when he arrived with the tools it was found that somebody had decided to dismiss the working party.

Whilst Burgoyne was working on these defences, Fletcher was working with the Portuguese engineers, making proposals to strengthen Elvas. It was still possible that the French would attack the final border fortress in allied hands and the

Fort of Ouguela. (Author's collection)

threat had encouraged the Governor to make some improvements.[21] Wellington had complained to Beresford about the condition of the fortress and was also working hard to restock supplies in the fortress, which should have been done by the Portuguese government.[22]

Having relieved Badajoz, the French now pushed forward to find the location of Wellington's forces. On 22 June a large French reconnaissance was launched which approached Juromenha, Elvas, and Campo Mayor. During this reconnaissance, Dickson, who was at Campo Mayor, recorded that:

> A large body of cavalry advanced close ... I was there at the time on duty and finding a favourable opportunity, opened two or three guns of the place upon them, which obliged them to take a more respectable distance.[23]

Jones also commented that the feeling was that the 'Reconnaissance seeming to be the prelude to a general action, working parties were employed all night to strengthen the position by means of emplacement for guns, etc.'[24]

These working parties continued day and night for the next five nights. This might explain why Burgoyne's journal entries stopped for the next two weeks. Wellington would have been extremely concerned about the possibility that the more numerous French could attack him, and the improvements to the defences at Ouguela and Campo Mayor as well as the field works would have become a priority. His inferiority in cavalry and artillery would have also increased the urgency.

On 26 June, two more batteries were ordered to be constructed and also repairs to the outwork of San Jean. On 27 June 1811, two further engineers, Lieutenants Rice Jones and Stanway, were sent to help Burgoyne.[25] Dickson commented on the progress of the repairs to the defences at Campo Mayor: 'The breach is now in a state of security and they are scarping down the rampart of the old outwork ... and when completed will be a tenable post and keep the enemy at a greater distance'.[26]

The defensive work carried out on the Caya River is another good example of the mostly hidden work carried out by engineers (probably including the Royal Staff Corps) which contributed to Wellington's success. Many books do not even mention the building of these defences. However, the question is, did these defences discourage the French from attacking? One could argue that they were

21 Leslie (ed.), *Dickson Manuscripts*, Vol.III, p.408.

22 Gurwood (ed.), *Despatches*, Wellington to Beresford, Quinta de Sao João, 18 June 1811. The redoubt mentioned near fort Santa Lucia was built and can still be seen.

23 Leslie (ed.), *Dickson Manuscripts*, Vol.III, p.406.

24 Jones, *Sieges*, Vol.I, p.75.

25 REM 5501-59-2, Jones MS Diary, 22 June 1811.

26 Leslie (ed.), *Dickson Manuscripts*, Vol.III, p.408. A similar comment is made in NAM 2016-07-24, Squire Journal, 29 June 1811.

never tested so they were unnecessary, but one would hardly say that about the Lines of Torres Vedras, about which the same claim could be made. Similarly, the claim that defences were built around Ponte de Murcella in summer 1810 was given by the French as one of the reasons they took the difficult northern route to Coimbra, thereby delaying their advance – even though they were never built, the threat was enough to make the French change their plans.

By the end of June, Wellington had confirmation that Soult with some of his troops were moving south, back towards Seville. He no longer expected an attack by the French, either on his army, or on Elvas. A significant French force remained around Badajoz until mid-July to complete the filling of its stores, then Marmont retired north. Wellington also quickly moved his army away, the Caya valley being known as unhealthy.

Burgoyne re-joined Picton's division, which left Campo Mayor on 17 July 1811 and moved north with the rest of the army to cantonments near the Spanish border about 20 miles southwest of Ciudad Rodrigo. Burgoyne recorded that the move was because Wellington hoped to take Ciudad Rodrigo with a brief blockade having heard it was short of food. Two weeks later, he added, 'We are too late however, a convoy having [just] entered the place'.[27]

During the march, Burgoyne was detached on 27 July to investigate the roads to the ferry crossing on the River Tagus at Barca de Montalvão, east of Villa Velha. The order came from headquarters and again Burgoyne appeared to be the engineer of choice to carry out important survey missions.

In a sign that the lack of sappers was recognised as a major problem in the army, Burgoyne was ordered on 28 July 1811, to instruct 200 men of the division 'in the art of carrying out the sap etc'.[28] Wellington needed to take control of the Portuguese border again. Having failed twice to re-take Badajoz, he turned his attention to the northern fortress of Ciudad Rodrigo. Few were in any doubt that this was the next target. As early as May 1811, Burgoyne had noted the shipping of the new British siege train from Lisbon to Oporto and although the public message was that they were for the defence of Oporto he correctly deduced (or had been told) that they were for the coming siege of Ciudad Rodrigo.[29] Once the siege train had arrived at Oporto, Wellington met with the artillery and engineer commanders on 19 July, whilst still on the Caya, and gave orders for the move of the siege train and ammunition from Oporto to Almeida. This was a massive logistical exercise involving hundreds of boats and thousands of mules and carts over a period of five months.[30]

27 REM 4201-68, Journal, 8 August 1811.

28 REM 4201-68, Journal, 28 July 1811.

29 Wrottesley, *Burgoyne*, pp.130, 133. Wellington's order to General Howarth to move the guns was given on 14 May 1810; Gurwood (ed.), *Despatches*. 1st Edition only.

30 Leslie (ed.), *Dickson Manuscripts*, Vol.III, pp.417; Thompson, *Wellington's Engineers*, pp.120-1; Gurwood, *Despatches*, Wellington to Framingham, Fletcher and Kennedy, 19 July 1811 which ordered Dickson to

The experiences of the two sieges of Badajoz had made the issue of the lack of trained sappers very public. It was admitted that the preferred point of attack could not be attempted, partially due to the lack of sappers, and the subsequent failure made this lack of expertise the focus of criticism. The lack of trained sappers was well-known and understood amongst the engineer officers. At different times, proposals had been put forward by John Jones, Charles Lefebure, Richard Fletcher, Robert Morse, and Charles Pasley. The major difficulty was that the Royal Military Artificers (RMA) were originally formed to provide garrison-based artificers; there was no provision for field-based soldiers. Their primary role was maintaining the great fortresses in Britain and across the empire. This was why there was great reluctance by the Board of Ordnance to providing artificers to serve with the army.

However, campaigns in the early 19th Century, particularly Wellington in the Peninsula, were highlighting the deficiency. Whilst it would be another year before the solution would be in place, there was recognition and attempts were being made to mitigate the problem. Since 1806, the size of the RMA had been 12 companies with an establishment of 1,500. Seven were based in the United Kingdom (including one in Ireland), one in the Channel Islands, two in Gibraltar, one in the West Indies, and one in Canada. On 28 May 1811, the warrant was signed for an expansion of the RMA, which was nearly doubled to 2,900, with 32 companies in four battalions.[31] More important than just the numbers, was the decision that four companies were assigned to serve with the army in Portugal. For the first time, these companies would be deployed in full rather than the previous practice of sending out small detachments from different companies.

Burgoyne was appointed on 12 August 1811 as the first officer to command an RMA company attached to an army in the field. The other three companies were initially assigned to continue work on the Lines of Torres Vedras.[32] It would be some considerable time before the soldiers making up the various companies were brought together, although Burgoyne noted that Mulcaster 'is ordered to march my company of Royal Military Artificers up to the army'.[33] This was most likely a small number of men who had been assigned to the company rather than the full company. The structure was now in place; what remained was to train the artificers to carry out the duties of sappers in the field.

Wellington could not wait for sappers to start arriving from England and his order to Burgoyne to start training soldiers into this role was to ensure some

move the artillery; REM 5501-59-2, 19 July, where Lieutenant Marshal RE, was ordered to Oporto to move engineer stores.

31 Mark S Thompson, 'The Rise of the Scientific Soldier' (PhD Thesis, University of Sunderland, 2009), pp.51-56.

32 REM 5501-59-2, Jones Diary, 12 August 1811. Apart from Burgoyne's company, two were assigned to the Lines north of the Tagus and the final company to work on the defences to the south of the Tagus.

33 REM 4201-68, Journal, 30 August 1811.

understanding was available when Ciudad Rodrigo was attacked. Burgoyne commented:

> My principal business now is training 200 men of different regiments to the duties required in a siege, which, to our disgrace and misfortune, we have no regular establishment equal to, notwithstanding the repeated experience of the absolute necessity of such a corps to act under the Engineers in a campaign. For want of such an establishment we are frequently led to the loss of valuable officers, and very undeserved discredit. The undertaking I am set about will only be temporary and will supply very imperfectly this deficiency.[34]

The failures at Badajoz were causing some friction. Burgoyne writing privately to fellow engineer, John Squire, said:

> There is an account current that his Lordship says, "if he undertakes another siege, he will be his own engineer." Whatever faults were committed at Badajoz, I suspect he was not aware of them, and I think it is very doubtful whether he knows them now. *This is a [consequence?] of his system of insinuating blame where he [cares not?], whether deserved or not.* It appears to me probable that he did say so.[35]

The sentence in italics criticising Wellington was omitted from Wrottesley's biography. This was not the first or the last time that Burgoyne expressed sharp words about Wellington. The engineer officers were very sensitive about being blamed when they felt they had been given insufficient time and resources, and their recommendations had not been followed. This would happen again.

Whilst Burgoyne says little about his training of the troops, clearly there was significant activity going on. Jones' diary noted that Lieutenant Peter Wright RE had been ordered up from Abrantes on 29 July 'to assist in training the men to sap'. Wright had also been attached to Burgoyne's company of artificers.[36] Jones noted on 16 August, that 'Captain Burgoyne was completed with all the requisites to enable him to teach his party to sap and they are now regularly instructed'. It is not clear what Jones means by 'regularly' instructed. The 3rd Division had been on the move since 17 July and did not reach its cantonments until 14 August. Burgoyne did not report starting the training 'in fascine

34 Wrottesley, *Burgoyne*, p.136, Burgoyne to his sister, Albergaria, 14 Sep 1811. Captain Ross RE had been given similar orders for the 1st Division; see REM 4501-86, Ross to Dalrymple, Nave de Aver, 24 September 1811.

35 REM 4601-72, Burgoyne to Squire, 1 September 1811 and Wrottesley, *Burgoyne*, p.135.

36 Wrottesley, *Burgoyne*, p.135; REM 5501-59-2, 29 July 1811. Wright arrived on 19 August.

and gabion making and sapping etc' until 15 August 1811. In early September, Burgoyne 'proposed to Headquarters, to pay at six pence apiece for ballast baskets, to contain a cubic foot of earth, to such of my people as choose to make them ... Ten pounds would be well spent ... in the event of a siege'.[37] This idea was approved and 400 were made. He complained a month later that the French advance to resupply Ciudad Rodrigo had taken 'the trouble to burn every stick of my fascines and gabions'.[38]

On 24 August 1811, Fletcher and Jones visited Burgoyne at Albergaria to 'inspect the progress of the party learning to sap'.[39] The next day, Lieutenants Anthony Emmett and William Reid were ordered from Almeida to assist in the training work. They had originally been ordered up to assist in the repairs of Almeida. If three more scarce engineer officers were sent to assist Burgoyne, then this work was judged to be vital by headquarters.

Fletcher visited again on 10 September 1811 and the next day ordered Ross, who was attached to the 1st Division, to start a similar training process with another 200 soldiers. A small number of RMA artificers were sent to assist.[40] Jones' manuscript diary also suggests that this training was also ordered in the 4th Division, but no further details are known.

Burgoyne spent much of the next few weeks speculating on the opportunity of besieging Ciudad Rodrigo. In the letter to his sister, dated 4 September 1811, he thought that the siege was unlikely as Wellington was not strong enough to conduct a siege and fight off Marmont at the same time. He then went on to say:

> I hope with all my heart that we may undertake this said siege of Ciudad Rodrigo. If we do, I think there is little doubt but we shall take it, for I perceive in the army such a want of spirit about the operation [i.e. sieges] since our bad success in our last, which was also our first, that there appears to be little prospect of it being commenced, without the chances being well calculated beforehand.[41]

Burgoyne's comment about 'want of spirit' in the army when undertaking sieges would be repeated more than once in the following year.

Wellington, knowing that the French would soon advance on Ciudad Rodrigo to attempt to resupply it, had asked Fletcher, on 5 September 1811, to look at fortifying positions around Fuenteguinaldo and work started on the 8 September. Burgoyne, who was not involved noted: 'By attacking us in these positions, the enemy would

37 Wrottesley, *Burgoyne*, p.136 and REM 4601-72, Burgoyne to Squire, Albergaria, 1 September 1811.
38 Wrottesley, *Burgoyne*, p.145 and REM 4601-72, Burgoyne to Squire, Albergaria, 4 October 1811.
39 REM 5501-59-2, 24-25 August 1811.
40 REM 5501-59-2, 10-11 September 1811.
41 Wrottesley, *Burgoyne*, pp.136-7.

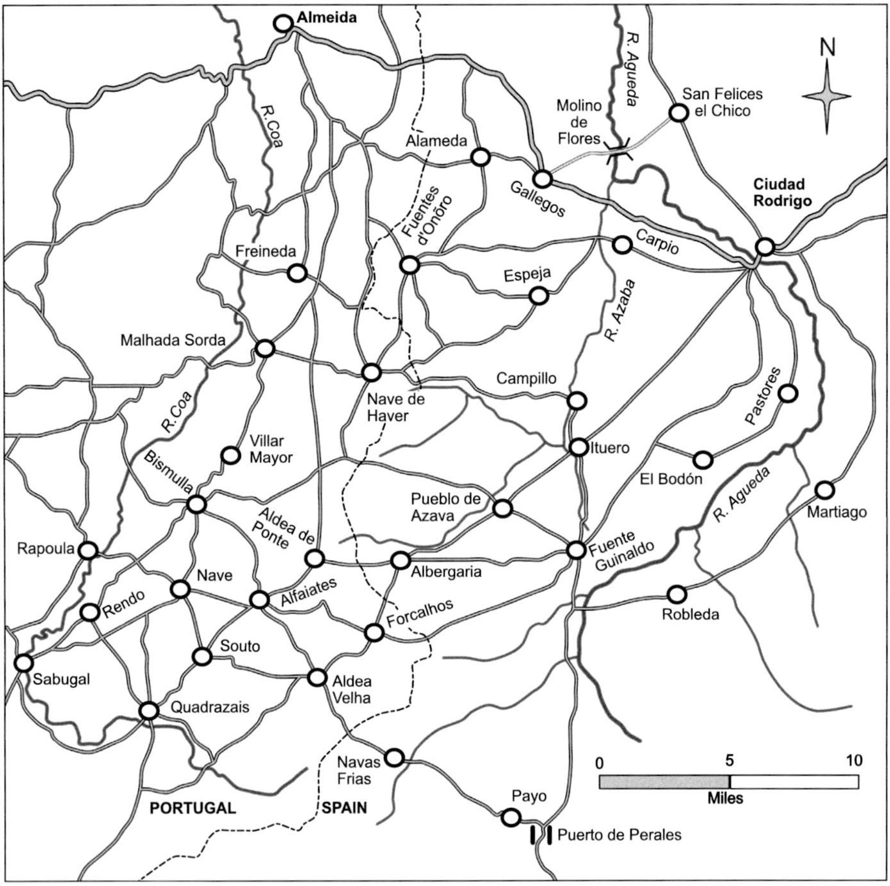

Operations around Ciudad Rodrigo 1811.

have much to lose by defeat, and little to gain by success'.[42] Wellington was aware that the French forces assembling were stronger than his and the erection of field defences was a sensible precaution even though he believed that any French advance would only be for the purpose of resupplying Ciudad Rodrigo. The initial construction work was hampered by poor soil and there appears to have been a delay until 23 September after which soldiers from the 4th Division worked almost non-stop to complete them. In addition, on 14 September, Fletcher and Wellington looked at constructing defences further forward at El Bodón.

On 18 September 1811, the 3rd Division moved forward to El Bodón within about 10 miles of Ciudad Rodrigo. Burgoyne was close enough to observe the

42 REM 4201-68, Journal, 18 September 1811.

fortress by telescope, reporting on its condition and the work underway by the French.[43] Wellington had concentrated most of his army, hearing that the French would soon make another advance to resupply the fortress. On 24 September 1811, Marmont forced a convoy through using his whole army plus some reinforcements from other French forces. The French, instead of just supplying the fortress, then surprised Wellington by making an advance on his positions.

On the continued advance of the French on 25 September, Wellington showed an unusual reluctance to concentrate his forces which were spread out over twenty miles between the Agueda and Azaba rivers. He had selected two defensive positions, one around Fuenteguinaldo and another further back on the Côa River near Sabugal. However, he chose to leave some of his troops further forward; the 3rd Division around El Bodón and the Light Division around Martiago. The remaining divisions were left dispersed. On the morning of the 25 September, Marmont surprised Wellington by launching two reconnaissances in strength. The reconnaissance sent towards Fuenteguinaldo found the 3rd Division spread out over six miles.[44]

For the rest of the day, the hard-pressed battalions retreated, with the small allied cavalry making repeated charges to delay the French force, finally arriving at the entrenched positions at Fuenteguinaldo and the support of the 4th Division and the British heavy dragoons. Burgoyne's comment of 8 September maybe came back to him 'By attacking us in these positions, the enemy would have much to lose by defeat, and little to gain by success'. The French obviously felt the same and withdrew. Would they have withdrawn if the field defences were not there? One would think not.

Oman described Wellington's actions on this day as rash and said he was lucky not to suffer serious casualties. The French, not realising how exposed the allied forces were, did not bring up any infantry until later in the day. Had they done so earlier, the consequences would have been serious. The allies were still not safe. Wellington now had about 15,000 troops with him, but he could be faced with much of the French force of 60,000 on the following morning. However, the Wellington 'myth' was working already. The French watched the allied force all day, believing that Wellington had more troops hidden and were unwilling to attack him. Overnight, Wellington withdrew to a position near Alfaiates and by the morning, the bulk of his divisions were present. Fortunately, again for Wellington, the French had also started withdrawing and it was late in the night when Marmont was told that Wellington had withdrawn. The French withdrawal was halted and the leading elements found Wellington in his preferred position in front of Sabugal. However, he now had all his forces with him in a 'Bussaco' style position. Marmont – quite rightly, this time – chose not to attack and the French

43 REM 4601-72, Burgoyne to Squire, El Bodón, 20 September 1811.

44 See Oman, *Peninsular War*, Vol.IV, pp.563-571.

forces started their withdrawal having achieved their objective of resupplying Ciudad Rodrigo. However, he missed a great opportunity to attack the allied forces with a significant advantage.

Burgoyne wrote extensive entries in his journal describing the terrain and the events. On the night of 24 September, he stated 'the situation in which we remained during the night appeared extraordinary *and critical*' (the words in italics were not printed in Wrottesley's biography). He had watched '25,000 French, including 5 or 6,000 cavalry' form in front of them, 'the 3rd Division unsupported except by General Victor Alten's Brigade of cavalry (the 1st Hussars and 11th Light Dragoons) in front and dispersed in its small scale as the whole army was on a large one'. Burgoyne was rightly critical of Wellington's dispositions on the day, commenting:

> [C]onceive a Bonaparte in our front, within fifteen miles of any part of our extended line, most of it of open country, with his rapid night marches. I confess I thought there was more than one way of striking a good coup. Fortunately, however, [for us] I think they proceeded in the old steady style.[45]

Burgoyne complained that; 'our force was evidently threatened, yet Lord Wellington would not allow the division to be collected [initially]'. He continued to describe the retreat to El Bodón and then on to Fuenteguinaldo and the location of the redoubts, for which by now the army was surely very grateful. When safe in front of Sabugal, having withdrawn again from Fuenteguinaldo, Burgoyne noted 'that this is one of Lord Wellington's positions for meeting the enemy'.[46] The position in front of Sabugal had Rendo on the left, Alfaiates in the centre and Aldea Velha on the right, with a loop of the River Côa covering both flanks. Burgoyne's analysis and recording of these events was quite accurate and highlighted the risks that Wellington took. His understanding of the situation shows a maturing military mind that Wellington would grow to trust over the next few years.

There is one other aspect of this skirmish that needs to be looked at. During the early, anxious part of the day, the 2/5th and 77th Regiments and the 21st Portuguese Line were forced to withdraw in the face of 2,500 French cavalry, marching and forming square several times. In typical Burgoyne style, he downplayed his role, not mentioning it in his journal, but it was noticed by others. Wellington himself commented:

45 Wrottesley, *Burgoyne*, p.140.

46 See Wrottesley, *Burgoyne*, pp.139-145, although I have used Burgoyne's original journal, not the printed version.

> After the business at El Bodon, Marmont told my *Aide-de-Camp* who went in with a flag of truce, that he observed we were forced to attach a British officer to encourage the Portuguese regiment on that day and keep it to its duty, and that was Burgoyne.[47]

Another engineer officer who was present, Emmett, commented:

> Lord Wellington passed by the regiment and posted himself on the right to see what passed: telling Burgoyne in passing to keep by the regiment and see if he could keep it together.

Burgoyne later described it like this:

> This business of El Bodon was on the 25th of September 1811, and Lord Wellington himself was present; our small force retired for six miles across a plain, in presence of a much superior body of the enemy, particularly cavalry. There being some difficulty in moving the 21st Portuguese Regiment, I volunteered to interpret to them all orders, and regulate their movements, and ultimately, the Portuguese colonel being an inactive old fool, I took complete command of the regiment through the day. They were frequently threatened but never absolutely charged, though it would appear by Marmont's observation, that he particularly watched for an opportunity upon them, as the part on which he was most likely to make an impression. Lord Wellington appeared very well pleased at the time, but I imagined it was all forgotten. This remark of Marmont's, however, appears to have fixed it in his memory as a point in my favour.[48]

Wellington's use of Burgoyne is interesting. Burgoyne was not on his staff and one would have thought that Wellington would have been more inclined to use one them, or more likely a member of Picton's staff. Did this mean that Burgoyne possessed some skills that other staff did not? Could this have been Burgoyne's Portuguese language skills or had Wellington seen something else? Or finally, could Burgoyne have made the whole tale up? The latter is unlikely, no other incident having been found where Burgoyne appears to have invented his involvement. However, Burgoyne would have been wearing his blue engineer uniform not a distinctive red British uniform that would have stood out amongst the blue coated

47 Wrottesley, *Burgoyne*, p.253. This story was told two years later, and Burgoyne believed it swayed Wellington to let him join the army for the 1813 campaign, rather than being left to repair Ciudad Rodrigo. At this time Fletcher had gone home for the winter and although Henry Goldfinch was the senior engineer, Wellington probably still spoke to Burgoyne as an officer he had come to trust.

48 Wrottesley, *Burgoyne*, p.253.

Portuguese. Picton was further to the rear at this time and the Portuguese brigade commander may not have been present, his two regiments being in different locations. So, it is possible that Burgoyne was in this advanced position near the 21st Regiment when Wellington recognised him and ordered him to assist.

The commander of the 21st Portuguese Line at this time was José Maria de Araújo Bacellar. He was 54 years old and had been with the regiment for many years, certainly before Junot's invasion. Picton had complained about the state of discipline in the regiment in 1810,[49] although there was no complaint about their performance at Bussaco. In April 1812, the 21st were part of Colonel Manly Power's Portuguese Brigade which was sent to restore order in Badajoz after the assault. The brigade ignored orders and dispersed to join the plundering. Power was publicly reprimanded for the behaviour of his troops. Within days, Baccelar had resigned and been appointed governor of a minor fort in northern Portugal.[50] Perhaps Burgoyne was right.

This was the first example of Wellington using Burgoyne in an important role outside of engineering. It certainly shows that Wellington had already developed a trust in Burgoyne's capabilities. Burgoyne's position as senior engineer with the army in the first half of 1810, followed by his regular presence at headquarters, will have brought him to Wellington's attention. He appeared to get more than his fair share of tasks where Wellington needed good information and confidence that a job would be done properly. Wellington was not used to having officers around him of whom he was confident that they would do what he required, but Burgoyne was one officer who appeared to fill this role.

One result of the unexpected push by Marmont was that repairs to Almeida were given a new importance and Fletcher made several trips in the coming weeks to ensure that work was progressing as fast as possible. Apart from the possibility of Almeida being taken by a *coup-de-main* there was also concern about moving the siege train forward to Almeida if its security could not be guaranteed. To speed up the repairs, Wellington agreed to allocate 800 soldiers from the Transcoso Militia to work on the fortifications, a tenfold increase in the work force. Two days later, 400 soldiers from the 6th Division were added.[51] Captain William MacCulloch RE, who was at Almeida, organised the new working parties.

At the beginning of October the 3rd Division, with Burgoyne, returned to Albergaria, about 20 miles southwest of Ciudad Rodrigo, and remained there quietly for the rest of the month. It does not appear the sapper training had

49 Beresford, *Beresford*, p.111.

50 My thanks to Moisés Gaudêncio, Bob Burnham and Marcus de la Poer Beresford for details on the 21st Portuguese Regiment and its commander. Baccelar was appointed Governor of Esposende in 26 April 1812, immediately after the siege of Badajoz and retired as colonel in September 1812. It is thought that the second-in-command was Major Thomas Staunton St Clair but it is not clear whether he was present at El Bodón.

51 REM 5501-59-2, Jones Diary, 5 & 7 October 1811.

restarted after Marmont's advance. Whilst there is no evidence that Burgoyne was involved in any other task, there is a cryptic note in Jones' journal on 26 October 1811, saying 'Burgoyne returned to his division'.[52]

In November, Burgoyne was ordered to resume training soldiers from the 3rd Division as sappers.[53] As before, there is no further mention of this training work after receiving the order nor of his command of a sapper company.

Clearly Burgoyne was not finding his work too onerous; on 13 December 1811, he joined a party under Major General Charles Colville, which had been ordered to try and capture some large herds of cattle which were being grazed on the Spanish side of the Sierra de Gata. 'I took the opportunity of getting a look at the country. The weather was delightful, and it was a very pleasant excursion to me'.[54] The raid was a complete failure, but Burgoyne had an opportunity to ride through the passes of Perales and Gata and see the pass of Acebo, gaining current information on the state of them. The route from Payo to the pass of Perales, he described as a gradual ascent of about four miles on a good road with a steeper descent on a 'tolerable good road' to Villasbuenas da Gata. He did note that there was one place where water had excavated a channel across the road. Colville and Burgoyne then spent the night at Gata before ascending that pass and returning to the allied lines. The ascent from Gata he described as three miles, the road in bad condition but practicable for artillery. His final comment was that because of the number of smaller roads and tracks it would be impossible to find the correct route without a guide.[55]

52 REM 5501-59-2, Jones Diary, 26 October 1911.

53 Wrottesley, *Burgoyne*, p.149 and REM 4201-68, Journal, p.168, 11 Nov 1811.

54 Wrottesley, *Burgoyne*, p.150. The raid is also covered in John Colville, *Portrait of a General* (Salisbury: Spellmount, 1980), pp.75-6. Colville commanded a brigade in the 3rd Division.

55 REM 4201-68, Journal, 12 -14 December 1811. Colville, *Portrait of a General,* p.76, is more negative about the Gata pass, saying it was easier to ascend than descend and most of it was done on foot.

9

1812 – The Siege of Ciudad Rodrigo

1812 was the fifth year that Burgoyne had been in the Peninsula. Since his first arrival in August 1808 he had spent 37 of the 40 months in the Peninsula, the only gap was the brief return to England after Moore's campaign. 1812 was also a significant year for Burgoyne personally. For six months of the year, he was again the senior engineer with Wellington's army in which capacity he undertook two siege operations and supported a difficult retreat. Personally and professionally, it was a very challenging year and would have required all his engineering and diplomatic skills to navigate the challenges he faced. The John Burgoyne in December 1812 would have been a much wiser person than the officer who started the year.

The first task and the one that everyone knew was coming (but not when) was the siege of Ciudad Rodrigo. Wellington was waiting for the right opportunity. The siege of Ciudad Rodrigo was probably the only British siege during the Peninsular War that was successfully planned and executed. Unlike the two earlier sieges of Badajoz, Wellington knew this siege was inevitable and could plan it as part of his overall strategy.

Siege of Ciudad Rodrigo – The Preparation

Preparation for the siege of Ciudad Rodrigo started in May 1811, when Wellington gave orders for the movement of the new English battering train from Lisbon to Oporto by sea.[1] The guns had recently arrived from England and were still on board the transports. The critics who say that Wellington should have moved a siege train to Badajoz in May 1811 should look at the scale of the operations to complete such a task.

The siege train was made up of thirty-four 24-pounder and four 18-pounder cannon, eight 10-inch iron mortars, two 8-inch brass howitzers and twenty 24-pounder iron howitzers, totalling 68 pieces of ordnance. Wellington's

1 Gurwood (ed.), *Despatches*, Wellington to Howarth, Villar Formoso, 14 May 1811. NB 1st Edition only.

Move of siege train to Almeida.

memorandum of 19 July 1811 detailed the move of the guns up the Douro to Peso da Régua, near Lamego. Then nearly 900 carts with an additional 800 bullocks were needed to move the train and supplies from the Douro to Vila de Ponte.[2] Even with this large number of carts, two journeys were required. In addition, 200 carts were needed for the engineer stores and then more for 1,600 barrels of powder.[3]

Collecting this amount of transport together was a major task and keeping the carts and bullocks together for an extended period leading up to the siege was even more difficult. The scale of this operation was even larger than the numbers above suggest. John May's report of 28 August 1811 identified 4,170 journeys by oxen pairs to move the siege and engineering trains forward.[4] There were 1,910 ox carts and 4,920 oxen physically present with the siege train at Vila de Ponte at the end of September 1811![5]

Moving the guns forward was under control of Dickson, and Marshall managed the movement of the engineering stores. Once shipped to Oporto, Dickson arranged for nearly 200 boats to take the equipment up the Douro to Peso da

2 Jones, *Sieges*, Vol.I, p.358, details the siege guns selected by Wellington to be moved to Oporto. The transport requirement listed in the memo of 19 July, was for 48 guns only and did not include the twenty 24-pounder howitzers, which were added later.

3 Leslie (ed.), *Dickson Manuscripts*, Vol.III, pp.417-8. About 270 carts would have been needed for the powder.

4 Jones, *Sieges*, Vol.III, table facing p.363. The report is mentioned in Leslie (ed.), *Dickson Manuscripts*, Vol. III, p.456 but not included. May reported on the number of oxen journeys required to move the siege train forward, not the number of oxen present. In summary, 2,071 oxen pairs for the first trip; 1,367 for the second trip and 732 to increase the ammunition up to 800 rounds for cannon and 400 for howitzer (although it is unclear whether this happened); making 4,170 oxen pair, journeys in total.

5 Jones, *Sieges*, Vol.III, p.364.

Régua. Before he could do that, he had to convert all the limbers to be pulled by oxen and make boxes to carry the shot and shells.

The siege train was then unloaded and transported by road to Lamego. From there the original plan was to move the train to Transcoso but later the decision was changed to store them at Vila de Ponte. Dickson had travelled up the road from Transcoso to Lamego and reported that the road between Moimenta da Beira and Transcoso was not suitable for heavy artillery.[6] The siege train was at Vila de Ponte by mid-September but did not move forward for two months. During this period, work was done to repair the gun carriages and improve the roads in the area. Finally, on 14 November, the order was given to move the siege train forward to Almeida, Wellington now being confident that it was safe there. Dickson struggled, unsuccessfully, to bring all the siege stores forward. He was forced to prioritise the movement of the equipment in the order: (1) guns, (2) powder and ammunition for the cannon, (3) ammunition for the howitzers and mortars.[7] Most of the final item were not delivered to the siege due to lack of transport and the awful road conditions. Wellington carried out the siege without howitzers and mortars and there were consequences.

On 18 December 1811, Wellington confirmed his intention to besiege Ciudad Rodrigo by ordering the construction of fascines, gabions and pickets by the troops from the 1st, 3rd, 4th and Light Divisions as well as Pack's Portuguese Brigade. The troops who made these items were volunteers and were paid for the work.[8] Engineer officers were sent to each of the units to oversee the work. Burgoyne managed the cutting of planks for the gun platforms near his base at Albergaria.[9]

Burgoyne criticised the planning, noting that the troops who were tasked to prepare fascines and gabions were up to 25 miles away, whilst there was good supply of material within 10 miles of the fortress. The winter weather and the lack of transport would make moving the materials difficult. He did seem to have a point as the 1st Division was many miles away, between Guarda and Penamacor, although the other divisions were closer.

Wellington continued to collect information on the state of Ciudad Rodrigo. On 27 December 1811, Fletcher met with Don Carlos D'España who recommended the south side as being the easiest to approach, although he did also comment that the walls were strongest at this point, that there were some fortified buildings, and that the suburbs on this side of the town were entrenched. Two days later Fletcher was given a return of the artillery in the town which had been stolen from the French artillery commander.[10]

6 Leslie (ed.), *Dickson Manuscripts*, Vol.III, pp.432-3, 435.

7 Leslie (ed.), *Dickson Manuscripts*, Vol.III, pp.501-530.

8 Jones, *Sieges*, Vol.III, p.90 and REM 5501-59-2, 17 December 1811.

9 Burgoyne was cutting the planks at Puebla de Azaba; the siege stores were being collected at Gallegos, San Felices el Chico and Las Agallas (about two miles east of Martiago).

10 REM 5501-59-2, 27 & 29 December 1811.

Oman wrote, that on 29 December 1811, Wellington had received information which confirmed that Napoleon was redeploying his forces in Spain with the intention of supporting *Maréchal* Louis Gabriel Suchet's operations in Valencia; French forces around Ciudad Rodrigo were being reduced.[11] This was the opportunity Wellington had been waiting for. Jones had also written on 28 December 1811, that Wellington 'had determined to commence the siege instantly [sic] he could get up the smallest proportion of stores and ammunition'.[12]

One of the difficulties Wellington faced was how to get the siege train across the Agueda River. The existing bridges were either under French control or were inaccessible to heavy artillery. The river was steep and rocky in many places and in winter would be fast flowing with substantial changes in water level depending on the amount of rain. The challenge was given to Major Henry Sturgeon of the Royal Staff Corps. Nearly 150 soldier-tradesmen from four divisions were ordered to Almeida to construct the bridge on 18 November 1811.[13] Emmett remarked in his diary on 28 November 1811, that Sturgeon was preparing a bridge of trestles for the passage of the Agueda.[14] The point selected for the bridge was called the ford of Marialva [Marialba], near Gallegos de Argañán. At this point, the river was around 400 feet wide. The bridge was to be built of 22 trestles, each trestle weighed down with stones and secured to a pile by heavy chain. Each trestle was streamlined to help resist the force of the water. The road level on the bridge was twelve feet above the normal water level. It would appear that the order to lay the bridge was given on 1 January 1812, the same day that the army was ordered to move forward for the siege.[15] Colville, writing on 1 January 1812, reported that the bridge would be ready in about a week.[16] There are different descriptions of exactly where the bridge was placed. Jones and Oman said it was at Marialva. Colville correctly said it was at Molino de Flores which is about one mile north of Marialva.[17] Even today there are tracks approaching both sides of the river at this point.

Wellington laid out detailed plans for the concentration of troops and guns, starting on 1 January, with the intention of investing the town on 6 January. Unfortunately, heavy snow delayed the investment to 8 January 1812. Although the troops were in place, it had proved impossible to move the siege train and

11 Oman, *Peninsular War*, Vol.V, p.162.

12 REM 5501-59-2, 28 December 1811.

13 General Order, 18 November 1811, as quoted in Jones, *Sieges*, Vol.III, p.365.

14 REM 4601-57-1, Emmett's Diary, 29 November 1811.

15 Jones, *Sieges*, Vol.III, p.93.

16 Colville, *Portrait of a General*, p.77. He called the ford Molino de Flores.

17 The ford's position is marked incorrectly on the map in Oman, *Peninsular War*, Vol.IV, p.200. The actual position is near Cuéllar almost on the direct line between Gallegos and Saelices (San Felices) el Chico. Thanks to Bob Burnham for clarifying its position.

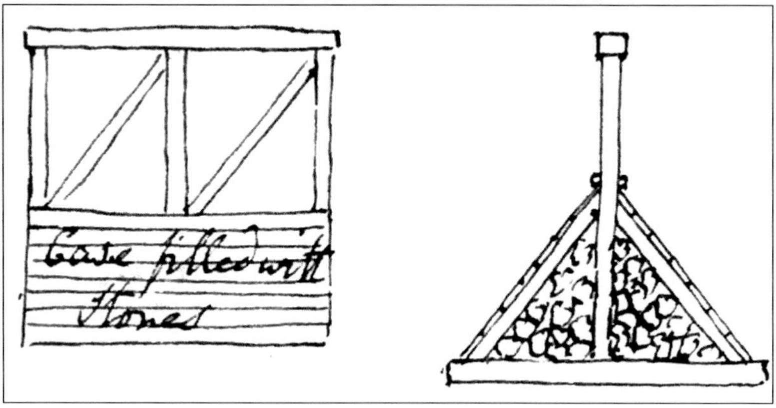

Burgoyne's sketch of trestles used in bridge. (Royal Engineers Museum)

supplies forward. Burgoyne described the weather on 4 January 1812 as 'terrible, snow on the ground and rain and sleet falling with a high wind'.[18]

Engineer resources for the attack comprised of Fletcher in overall command with 18 other officers and 18 men from the Royal Military Artificers.[19] A company of Royal Military Artificers under the command of Lieutenant Edward de Salaberry had been ordered up from Lisbon on 20 December 1811, but they had not yet arrived.[20] Burgoyne and Ross were assigned as siege directors, each taking 24-hour shifts to manage the work. Additional support was made up of 12 assistant engineers and 180 soldiers, all from the 3rd Division.[21] These were the men who had been given basic training under Burgoyne in the preceding months. On 1 January 1812, Burgoyne was ordered to organise the soldiers into three divisions of 64; each division being broken down onto eight brigades of eight soldiers, giving twenty-four work units. Their officers and NCOs were split amongst the units.[22] The engineers and assistant engineers were formed into seven brigades who worked in shifts during the siege. The four infantry divisions involved in the siege also took 24-hour shifts in the trenches.

18 Wrottesley, *Burgoyne*, p.153.

19 Although at least two arrived late. Captain Williams and Lieutenant De Salaberry did not arrive until 15 January 1812. Jones, *Sieges*, Vol.I, p.118.

20 REM 5501-59-2, 20 December 1811. The original order was for Lieutenant Piper to bring the company up, but on 25 December he was assigned to the pontoon train and Lieutenant de Salaberry was substituted. Jones, *Sieges,* Vol.I, p.118, They arrived on 15 January 1812.

21 In other sieges, Wellington had allowed a number of infantry officers to volunteer to act as Assistant Engineers in the sieges. I believe the Assistant Engineers at Ciudad Rodrigo were officers from the 3rd Division who were attached to the 200 trained soldiers. Jones MS Journal, REM 5501-59-2, recorded that on 3 January 1812, 'Lord Wellington positively refused to attach a single officer of the Line to us for the siege'.

22 REM 5501-59-2, 1 January 1812.

Siege of Ciudad Rodrigo

The fortress was finally invested on 8 January 1812 by the Light Division. Fletcher reconnoitred and reported to Wellington that the trenches could not be started until the Renaud Redoubt had been taken. He recommended it to be stormed that night. This was achieved with great efficiency by troops under the command of Colonel John Colborne. Jones commented that the assault was made easier because the French had placed the palisades (wooden stakes) in the ditch near to the counterscarp (outside wall of ditch) and the attackers were able to use fascines to make a bridge straight over the top.[23]

Burgoyne, who was on duty that night, had also made a close reconnaissance of the town and drew a sketch in his notebook of the place where the wall was to be breached, noting it appeared to be a 'good stone wall'.

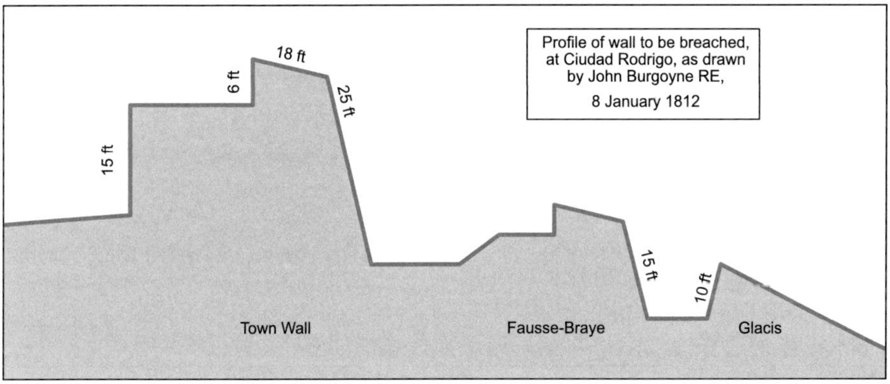

Wall profile at Ciudad Rodrigo, January 1812.

Work started on the trenches immediately and the following night the breaching batteries were started. Three batteries for eleven guns each, were begun to create the main breach. The original plan was to place the first breaching batteries on the Great Teson hill and then move nearer digging a second parallel on the Little Teson from which other batteries would be constructed.[24] Ross, the other siege director, was killed early on the night of 9 January and was initially replaced by the Brigade Major, John Jones for the next night with responsibility then passing to Captain Charles Ellicombe RE, an officer with less experience.

On 10 January, the position of battery No.1 was found to be partially masked by the Reynaud redoubt and five of the guns had to be moved to battery No.3. Jones

24 Jones, *Sieges*, Vol.I, p.99.

Ciudad Rodrigo defences. (Author's Collection)

remarked, with some irony, 'that it was thought less labour to remove five of the guns [to another battery] ... than to cut away the redoubt'.[25]

The siege guns left Almeida on 10 January, crossed the new trestle bridge and were at Ciudad Rodrigo by 11 January 1812. Work continued through the 11 and 12 January 1812 to complete the trenches and batteries, in the face of continuous cannon and shell fire from the defenders. The lack of howitzers and mortars meant that there was no counter-battery fire. Overall progress was good, but the troops were suffering due to the freezing weather and because they had to march from their camps that in some cases were 10-12 miles away. *En route* some had to ford the River Agueda, so they spent most of their 24-hour shift, cold and wet.

There was a change of plan on 13 January, when Wellington asked Fletcher if the second, closer, set of breaching batteries could be dispensed with, as he had received news that Marmont might be moving to relieve the fortress. This was agreed, although work continued on the second parallel to keep Wellington's options open if Marmont did not advance.[26]

That night the convent of Santa Cruz was stormed as it directly threatened the second parallel. On the morning of the 14th, the French made a sortie from the fortress and briefly took control of the trenches. They had noticed that there was

25 Jones, *Sieges*, Vol.I, p.103.

26 Jones, *Sieges*, Vol.I, pp.110-111; Oman, *Peninsular War*, Vol.V, p.171.

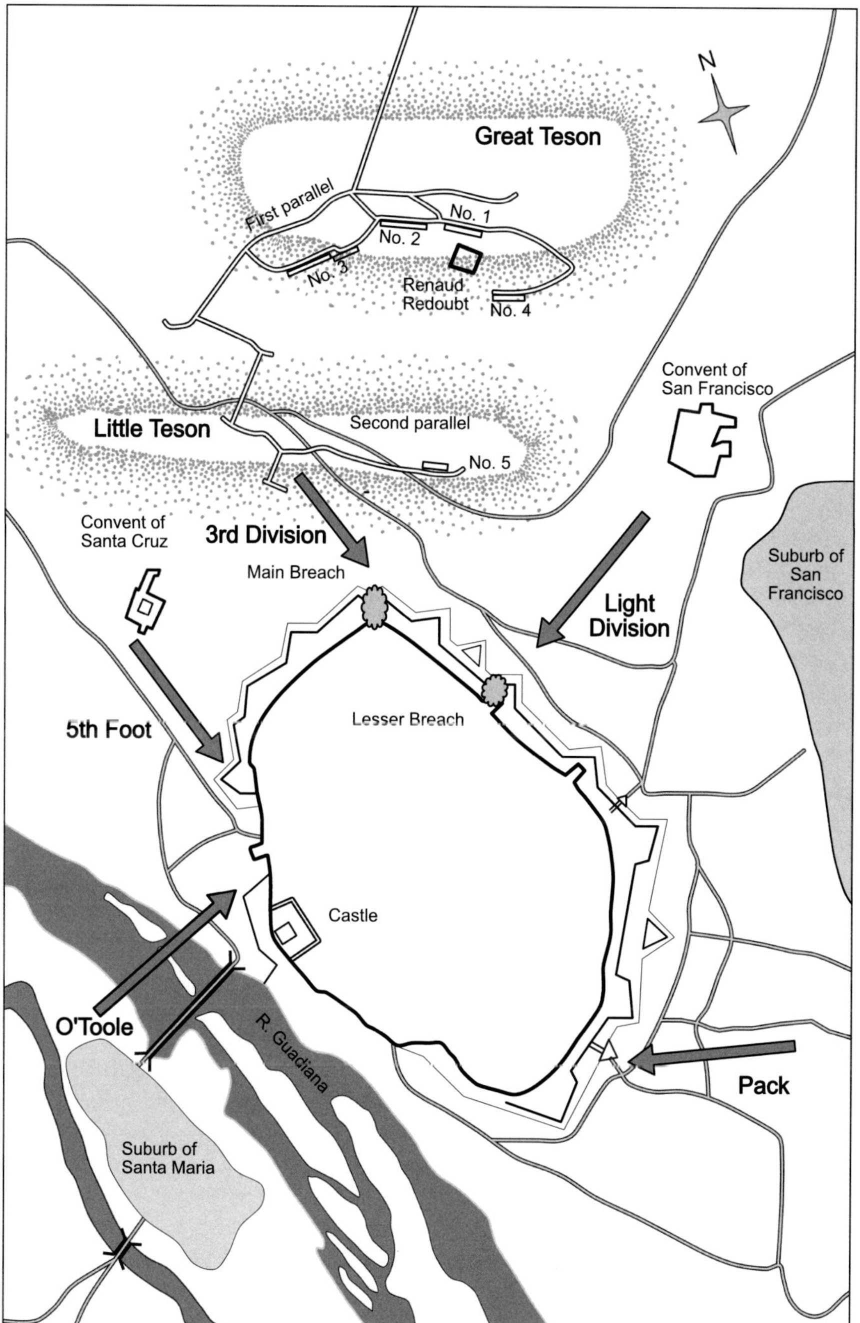

Assault of Ciudad Rodrigo, 19 January 1812.

a period when the troops were relieved that the trenches were nearly empty, the troops coming off shift being understandably keen to get away and into some warmth. Damage was done to the second parallel, but the prompt action by a small number of troops led by Lieutenant General Graham restored the situation.[27] The breaching batteries opened later that day. Burgoyne described it as follows:

> On the evening of the 14th, our batteries opened and made an hour's very bad practice, partly however from opening the embrasures in a hurry. In this operation, while standing on the parapet, poor Skelton [Lieutenant Thomas Skelton RE] received a mortal wound, a round shot taking his hip and the hand he had upon it ... On the same night Mulcaster received a musket ball through the fleshy part of his thigh (of little consequence but disables him for the present) while superintending the zig zags on the right, on which they keep up a constant fire of musketry and occasionally grape.[28]

There was another error in the siting of guns, as it was now found that two 18-pounders could not see the foot of the wall of the convent of San Francisco which they were supposed to attack. A new battery, No.4, was started to create a second breach in the wall and this opened fire on 18 January. The new guns had an immediate impact and the next day the tower and wall collapsed, creating the second practicable breach. Wellington inspected the breaches and wrote orders for an assault that night.

The 3rd Division was to storm the main breach and the Light Division the lesser breach. There were also two other attacks planned to distract and spread the defenders. The main storming parties were led to the breaches by Sturgeon, Ellicombe, and Wright.[29] The assault was planned for 7:00 p.m., that evening and both attacks succeeded, the troops then dissolved into a disorderly mob to ransack the town. Order was restored by the morning and work commenced at once to restore the fortress to a defensible state.

Observations on the Siege of Ciudad Rodrigo

The siege of Ciudad Rodrigo is seen as the most successful of the Peninsular War sieges with pre-planning ensuring a new siege train was available; a lightning advance followed by an effective siege, leading to the fortress being taken in

27 Thomas Graham had joined the army from Cadiz and now commanded the 1st Division.

28 REM 4601-72, Burgoyne to Squire, 16 January 1812.

29 Wellington (ed.), *Supplementary Despatches*, Arrangements for the Assault of Ciudad Rodrigo, 19th January 1812, Vol.7, p.253.

only 11 days. It succeeded almost before the French knew it had started. However, there are events that need further evaluation. Wellington's decision to attack on 1 January 1812, was a consequence of intercepting orders from Napoleon reorganising the French command structure and simultaneously detaching troops to the east coast of Spain.[30] The consequence was that the French forces covering Ciudad Rodrigo were reduced and moved further away, thereby increasing their response time to any actions by Wellington. Although Wellington had been making preparations for the siege, this was clearly a snap decision, as on 30 December 1811, Dickson wrote 'Wellington thinks in about a fortnight we shall have sufficient [ammunition] here to commence operations'.[31] Two days later, he wrote that the 'operation will be undertaken immediately … and … the trenches will be open in six or seven days'.[32] Dickson, who was many miles away, was slightly behind with the decision-making. John Jones noted in his journal on 28 December 1811 that 'Wellington determined to start the siege instantly he could get up the smallest possible proportion of stores and ammunition'.[33] The engineers were also caught unprepared and several officers were ordered to immediately join the army for the siege.[34]

Once again Wellington was starting a siege with a very small window of opportunity, which meant that the normal rules of sieges had to be ignored. The weather was atrocious, and the stores were not ready. One engineer remarked: 'Lord W is anxious to break ground tomorrow night, for which he has not afforded the means'.[35]

This quick decision meant that there was no transport to deliver the mortar and howitzer ammunition and Wellington took the risk of starting the siege with a limited ability to carry out counter-battery fire. This would explain why there was no attempt to silence the French guns until the day of the assault. After the siege, Wellington appeared to justify this decision as a new tactic: 'We proceeded at Ciudad Rodrigo on quite a new principle of sieges. The whole object of our fire was to lay open the walls'.[36] The disadvantage of this principle was that many more allied troops were injured through the consistently effective fire from the numerous French guns. The French were certainly surprised by the lack of

30 Leslie (ed.), *Dickson Manuscripts*, Vol.IV, p.562, Dickson to MacLeod. The reasons and consequences of the French moves are discussed at length in Oman, *Peninsular War,* Vol.V, pp.187-195.

31 Leslie (ed.), *Dickson Manuscripts*, Vol.III, p.534.

32 Leslie (ed.), *Dickson Manuscripts*, Vol.IV, p.562.

33 REM 5501-59-2, Jones MS Diary, 28 December 1811.

34 REM 5501-59-2, 31 December 1811. Captains Ross, Macleod and Williams and Lieutenants Emmett, Thomson and Reid. There was also Lieutenant de Salaberry who was marching up with the company of Royal Military Artificers. Williams and de Salaberry (at least) did not arrive until late in the siege.

35 REM 4501-86-4, Ross Letters, 7 January 1812.

36 Gurwood (ed.), *Despatches,* Wellington to Richmond, 29 January 1812.

counter-battery fire.[37] Colville, commanding the 4th Division, commented that Fletcher had requested counter-battery fire on 18 January and that when the guns were directed at the French batteries just prior to the assault they had an immediate effect. Colville also noted that whereas he thought counter-battery fire was necessary, Wellington did not.[38] Was this what Wellington meant, when he said he would be his own engineer? The fact was, there was no new principle for sieges: it was a lack of transport that caused Wellington to carry out the siege without counter battery fire.

Burgoyne commented, that in the diary of a French engineer officer obtained after the siege, it was reported that:

> the Governor ordered splinter proof timbers to be laid … against the houses of the three squares nearest the attack … This was for the shelter of the garrison. He did not know therefore, that we had no mortars or shells owing to the want of conveyance to bring up so many stores.[39]

The date of this is interesting as it suggests Burgoyne wrote up his journal at a later date and not as it happened. He could not have been in possession of this diary until after the siege was completed. This is another of the omissions from Wrottesley's biography.

Throughout Jones' account of the construction of the trenches and batteries he makes reference to the damage and casualties caused by French howitzer and mortar fire. Significant casualties were caused by Wellington's decision not to bring forward similar guns for counter battery fire. There are also a number of comments by engineers about the scale of the batteries which had to be built extra thick to withstand the battering by the defenders. Had there been any mortars and howitzers in Wellington's siege train then perhaps the additional work would have been unnecessary, and progress would have been quicker.

One of the main reasons why Ciudad Rodrigo was taken so quickly was because it was a second-rate fortress with nothing like the strength of Badajoz. Burgoyne, after a visit to the fortress in 1808, described it as 'incapable of defence … its works … possessing nearly every fault a fortification can have'.[40] In 1810, Squire described Ciudad Rodrigo as 'merely a walled town',[41] and after it was taken, he wrote to Pasley: 'We succeeded in taking the place more from its own weakness, than from any means we possessed'.[42] Wellington took full advantage of this weakness and was able to breach the walls from the position of the first batteries.

37 Fortescue, *British Army,* Vol.VIII, p.356.
38 Colville (ed.), *Portrait of a General*, pp.83-84.
39 REM 4201-68, Journal, 9 January 1812.
40 BL ADD57544, f.184, Burgoyne to Moore, 10 December 1808.
41 BL ADD63106, Squire Letters, ff. 3-4, Squire to Bunbury, 27 May 1810.
42 BL ADD41963, ff.13-16, Squire to CW Pasley, Portalegre, 3 March 1812.

The governor and the garrison were similarly weak. Barrié, the governor, was 'the only general of brigade available at Salamanca when his predecessor, Renaud was taken'.[43] Renaud described Barrié as a 'miserable fellow, perfectly unfit for the job'.[44] His performance matched the expectations set: 'all British accounts agree in condemning Barrié for his lack of energy'.[45] There was no serious resistance to the taking of the redoubt, the convents or the fortress. Barrié has to take responsibility for this.

The greatest success of the siege and the single event that made the siege so quick was Colborne taking the Renaud Redoubt on the first night. Typically, four to five days would have been needed to prepare to attack and take such an outwork. It is worthy of note that to take this small redoubt Colborne used more troops than Wellington did during the two failed attempts on the much stronger Fort San Cristóbal at Badajoz. The outcome at Badajoz may have been different had a similar strategy been used.

The size and quality of the guns used during the siege also had a significant effect on the outcome. Wellington had none of the problems with inaccuracy and overheating that had plagued the old brass guns at Badajoz. Had he been able to bring up the howitzer ammunition, there would probably have been substantially fewer casualties both before and during the assault.

The performance of the engineers tells a different story from the previous two sieges. At Badajoz, the engineers had neither time nor resources to complete their task. At Ciudad Rodrigo they had better guns and more time, although time was still a constraint. Whilst the result was positive, there were some worrying mistakes. Three significant errors were recorded: a battery being placed behind the Renaud Redoubt; the guns to attack the convent of San Francisco being too low to see the base of the wall; and the embrasures for the main batteries being misaligned when originally opened. The first error, the misplacing of the battery, was made on the night of 9/10 January, when Ross who was siege director for the night was killed.

Burgoyne's journal contains further criticisms of battery No.1, which are here repeated in full so that they can be evaluated:

> In the night the parallel is prolonged to the right, the right battery is prolonged for five more guns to the left and by a little echelon to the front of as much as the thickness of a parapet and communications are made from one battery to another. This additional battery on the right is because the left battery being placed behind the redoubt and retired

43 Oman, *Peninsular War*, Vol.V, p.165. Fortescue also comments that Dorsenne had no confidence in Barrié. Fortescue, *British Army*, Vol.VIII, p.355.

44 REM 5501-139-1, f.4, Burgoyne to Pasley, 12 February 1812.

45 Fortescue, *British Army*, Vol.VIII, p.367.

> on the hill; it is thought some of the guns will not be able to fire over all the batteries, being so much sunk in the inside. After working two nights hard, it is thought to be impossible to remove sufficient of the parapet, rampart etc. of the redoubt to make this battery serviceable. Indeed in the end after nearly completing this battery, laying some of the platforms and even taking them up and raising them, none of the guns could be brought to bear from it, and it was abandoned. Even the two guns against the convent after firing some rounds found they could not see the foot of the wall of it, for the hill, and were of no service whatever.[46]

We have already seen that Burgoyne could be very abrasive in his comments and criticisms and at first glance this looks another example. The initial comment that five guns had to be moved to battery No.3 because they were behind the Renaud Redoubt is acknowledged by many sources. There also appears to be confirmation that his criticism of the siting of the two guns to fire on the convent of San Francisco was correct. Although couched in vague language, Jones admits that:

> The object of the latter [the two 18-pounders to fire on the convent] was to lay open the garden and other walls, which had been converted into exterior defences; but the swell of the ground between the battery and the object [the convent walls] prevented the guns striking sufficiently low [continued in footnote] This is an error very likely to occur in placing artillery in batteries on heights, as frequently a person standing upright will see an object over a swell of ground, which a gun placed on the front of a platform will not; this requires particular attention in field-works where garrison carriages are used.

Both engineer and artillery officers must have been fully aware of the situation described and the failure to place the guns correctly was an error. What about the final part of Burgoyne's criticism? He wrote that the battery was abandoned. It was originally traced for 11 guns: five were moved to battery No.3; the two guns facing the convent were not placed correctly. That leaves four more 24-pounders to make up the 11. When the guns were placed in the batteries on the night of 13/14 January, 16 cannon were placed in battery No.3 and nine cannon in battery No.2. The only guns in battery No.1 were the two cannon to fire on the convent which, as we have already seen, were placed wrongly. Burgoyne seems to have a point and other accounts appear to overlook the scale of the errors.

46 REM 4201-68 Journal, 10 January 1812. This is another entry that refers to events in the future, strongly suggesting that the journal was written up later. It is possible that, like Dickson, Burgoyne made notes and then wrote up in full when he had the opportunity.

Burgoyne and his comrades do not specifically identify who they thought was at fault. Fletcher certainly marked out the batteries previously at Badajoz and it is difficult to believe that he was not present when this, the most vital stage, was being carried out, even if Ross actually did the work.

Similarly, the failure to open the embrasures properly occurred after the engineer in command, Lieutenant Skelton, was killed whilst standing on the top of the parapet encouraging the troops to perform the task. His death was unlikely to have helped with the troops willingness to expose themselves to French fire. Burgoyne noted that when the batteries originally opened on 14 January, many of the shots were passing over the top of the town. Jones' published *Journal of the Sieges* noted Skelton's death but not the problem with the embrasures. however, his unpublished diary noted 'the want of [a] qualified … Engineer … to superintend the opening of the embrasures … caused such a delay that the day was lost'.[47] This problem was corrected that night and the guns were firing effectively from the following morning.[48] The loss of Ross so early in the siege probably had a continuing effect. Ellicombe, who replaced him, was a senior officer but had no operational experience. After some years in Ceylon he had been in Britain for the three years prior to his coming out to the Peninsula.

All three errors were avoidable and should have been identified earlier.

In a letter to Squire after the siege, Burgoyne added: 'Our headquarters party have sent home a journal of the siege, in which I presume this battery does not make its appearance – it makes a very ugly one in my journal. Williams tells me that he saw the [official] Journal of the siege and that he gave great offence to Jones by pointing out some inaccuracies, as that it was put down there that the seven-gun battery on the left opened on the 17th, instead of the 18th.[49] Burgoyne was correct: the official report sent home, which was clearly written from Jones' manuscript journal, probably by Jones himself, did not mention the problems with battery No.1. It reported that the plan was to have only six guns in battery No.1 and 16 in battery No.3, avoiding the issue of explaining why five guns were moved to battery No.3. Neither is there any mention of the problems with the guns that were placed in No.1. Williams was also correct, the official journal did report battery No.4 opening on the 17 January, when it actually opened on 18 January.[50] Jones' critical comment in his journal on 14 January: 'the same want of Sappers and Miners caused so much delay in the placing of gabions', was rewritten to: 'much time was consumed in instructing the men in how to place gabions'. The reports sent home were being sanitised.

47 REM 5501-59-2, Jones MS Diary, 14 January 1812.

48 Wrottesley, *Burgoyne*, p.164, and REM 5501-139-1, Burgoyne to Pasley, 12 February 1812.

49 Wrottesley, *Burgoyne*, p.161-3, Burgoyne to Squire, Albergaria, 7 February 1812. The official journal of the siege is in TNA MPH 1/243.

50 Interestingly, Jones had corrected all these errors in the 1st Edition of the *Sieges*, published in 1814.

Whilst Burgoyne was highly critical of the errors, he took no personal responsibility for them, which as one of the siege directors he should have. Ultimately Fletcher must take responsibility as the commanding engineer. None of these errors had a material effect on the timescale or the outcome of the siege, but they must have had some effect on the reputation and confidence of the engineers.

Burgoyne was critical of most elements of the siege of Ciudad Rodrigo, even though this was seen as the most successful allied siege of the war. The Commanding Royal Engineer at the siege, Fletcher, gave high praise to Burgoyne who 'gave me every assistance, and executed the works under his charge with great zeal and ability'.[51] Burgoyne's initial comments in his diary were quite mild: 'Our works were certainly not carried on with great expedition'.[52] In private letters he was much more critical. He wrote lengthy letters to Squire and Pasley criticising most aspects of the siege, including the preparation (the gabions and fascines were made without proper supervision and too far away, leading to poor quality and delivery problems) and the daily operations (the siting of the batteries and guns, the want of arrangement in bringing up stores and the organisation of the working parties). In a letter to Squire, Burgoyne complained: 'We go on most miserably, no superintendents, no arrangements, it is said that Wellington objects to give any assistance the Colonel proposes, but I can't think this would be the case to a man of firmness'.[53] In a later letter he wrote:

> his Lordship can have but little confidence in Colonel Fletcher, as it appears from what we hear that he objects to nearly every proposal made by him … for some reason or other Colonel Fletcher had not influence enough to get the smallest assistance from the army.'[54]

This appears to be the first suggestion that there was a lack of confidence in Fletcher's command both amongst his subordinates and from Wellington. This is a marked change from what Burgoyne said two years earlier about the relationship between Wellington and Fletcher: 'he [Wellington] has universally treated Fletcher with the greatest consideration and attention'.[55]

Burgoyne's criticism was not restricted to his engineering superiors. The lack of trained soldiers from the Royal Sappers and Miners was again evident. Burgoyne commented, 'One company of artificers of about 30 men were up who knew nothing and were made no use of except 3 or 4 individuals'.[56] The sappers present were part of Burgoyne's company of RMA. Perhaps he should have taken more

51 Wrottesley, *Burgoyne*, p.164.
52 Wrottesley, *Burgoyne*, p.160, 19 January 1812.
53 REM 4601-72, f. 1813/1. Burgoyne to Squire, 16 January 1812.
54 BL ADD MS41962, f.197, Burgoyne to Pasley, 26 March 1810.
55 BL ADD MS41962, f.197, Burgoyne to Pasley, 26 March 1810.
56 REM 5501-139-1, Burgoyne to Pasley, Albergaria, 20 Feb 1812.

responsibility for their effectiveness as they had been with him since before the siege started.

Burgoyne also believed that Wellington summoned the French governor too early and that the French would have been much more likely to ask for terms had they had been summoned on 19 January 1812, just before the assault, when there were two significant breaches.[57] Napoleon had given his military Governors strict instructions not to surrender, although it was clear by this point that the fortress could not be saved. This is probably a valid criticism as many lives might have been saved if Wellington summoned the fortress on the 19 January and the French surrendered. It was worth a try.

The commitment (or lack of it) from the soldiers that became very evident at Burgos was also an object of criticism. Burgoyne noted:

> The principal reasons [for the delays] is the wretched, spiritless, grumbling way in which the British soldiers work, which instead of being checked is frequently rather encouraged by the manner of the officers, who do not seem to think it a point of duty or honour to interest themselves in the exertions of a working party.[58]

He suggested that having a general officer with the troops in the trenches would help to maintain discipline and progress. This was actually done in some future sieges; perhaps Burgoyne had an opportunity to suggest it to Wellington.

In terms of resources for the siege, all the senior engineers, Burgoyne, Jones and Ross, commented on Wellington refusing to provide line officers to assist.[59] This should, in fairness to him, be offset against the fact that the engineers had been allocated around 200 soldiers and officers from the 3rd Division who had been given some rudimentary training in the previous few months. In addition to this, the division on duty each day had to furnish a group of carpenters and miners.

In summary, the siege of Ciudad Rodrigo was a great operational success that materially strengthened Wellington's position and put the French firmly on the defensive. The success was due to three main factors: the weakness of the fortress, the strength of the allied battering train and the lack of energy of the French governor. Overall, the engineers had performed their duties well, but, as Fortescue wrote, 'the engineers themselves … were by no means faultless in their plans'.[60] As mentioned above, the first signs of criticism within the engineers were also appearing.

57 Wrottesley, *Burgoyne*, p.163. Burgoyne to Squire, 7 February 1812.

58 REM 5501-139-1, Burgoyne to Pasley, 16 Feb 1812.

59 E.g. REM 5501-139-1, Burgoyne to Squire, 12 February 1812; REM 5501-59-2, Jones' Diary, 3 January 1812.

60 Fortescue, *British Army*, Vol.VIII, p.365.

Burgoyne's temper was not helped, when, due to an oversight, his name was omitted from Wellington's dispatch and only engineer Captains John Jones and George MacLeod were mentioned. Both received brevet promotions and only after the omission was spotted was the same promotion given to Burgoyne.[61] The promotion of Macleod in particular would have caused annoyance as he was mentioned in connection with the troops from the 3rd Division who had been trained as sappers. Wellington's despatch said:

> It is but justice to the 3rd Division to report that the men who performed the sap belonged to the 45th, 74th and 88th Regiments, under the command of Captain Macleod of the Royal Engineers and Captain Thompson of the 74th, Lieutenant Beresford [a cousin of Marshal Beresford] of the 88th and Lieutenant Metcalfe of the 45th and they distinguished themselves not less in the storm of the place than they had in the performance of their laborious duties during the siege.[62]

This is not correct, and it is understandable that Burgoyne was upset. Burgoyne was responsible for the training of the sappers in the 3rd Division and was also one of the siege directors. Wellington's despatch clearly suggests that MacLeod was responsible. MacLeod did lead the sappers during the assault on the 19th. The other siege Director, Charles Ellicombe, guided Vandeleur's Brigade of the Light Division to the breaches during the assault but was not mentioned in Wellington's despatch. It is difficult to see why MacLeod was singled out. Pasley commented:

> You have been unlucky in having two junior officers promoted over you who were employed on the same service. MacLeod's case in particular is a great shame. His father took advantage of the very mention of his name and settled the matter in a moment.[63]

MacLeod's father was Major General John Macleod RA. Burgoyne summed up his feelings saying:

> With respect to myself, you may conceive I am not a little hurt at the omission of my name in favour of Jones, and whether it arises from accident, favour, or that I over rate my own abilities and exertions, conceiving I do not deserve so marked a slight, it has certainly not added to my peace of mind.[64]

61 Burgoyne's brevet promotion to major was backdated to 8 February 1812.

62 Gurwood (ed.), *Despatches*, Wellington to Liverpool, Gallegos, 20 January 1812.

63 REM 4601-74, Pasley to Burgoyne, 2 March 1812.

64 REM 5501-139-1, Burgoyne to Pasley, Albergaria, 20 Feb 1812.

This omission mattered, as the two engineer captains mentioned in Wellington's despatch obtained brevet promotion. Probably, of more importance to Burgoyne, was that not being mentioned, when he should have been, would be interpreted by many as a deliberate act signifying that Wellington was dissatisfied with his performance. Wellington and Fletcher should have been aware of this. The mistake was an oversight and was quickly remedied by Wellington, but, as Burgoyne said, it did nothing for his peace of mind.[65] It was noted that Wellington's despatch mentioned nine artillery officers but only three engineer officers. The engineer officers wondered if Fletcher was promoting his corps as well as other commanders were promoting their own.

Burgoyne wrote a long, confidential letter home to Pasley giving an update on operations and expressing freely his opinions on the performance of the engineers, their leaders and the army. In the letter he said:

> [Y]ou will probably ask why I did not state them at the time, but the fact is that I am kept as much in the dark on future arrangements and at as great a distance as the youngest subaltern and disagreeing so entirely on the systems pursued, you will conceive how arrogant it would have appeared, and how little likely to be attended with effect had I affected to propose a whole plan of proceedings. What little I could do in the course of my regular duty, I of course did.[66]

Perhaps his frustration came from feeling he was not informed or involved on the conduct of the siege. The letter finishes with the statement: 'I am all anxiety for your second volume'. The second volume being Pasley's critique of the Board of Ordnance and the leadership of the Royal Engineers. The publication of Part 2 did not happen, but 1812 would see the formation of the School of Military Engineering which addressed the issue of training for sappers.

Pasley's reply, sent in March 1812, opens with congratulating Burgoyne on being the first officer to train sappers that have acted against an enemy.[67] He went on to describe progress in the establishment of the School of Military Engineering saying there was a stalemate as the Board of Ordnance would not approve his promotion and he would not accept the role without the promotion!

If Burgoyne's letter to Pasley, which was essentially a copy of what he recorded in his diary, is looked at in another light, that is, not as a complaint but a reflection on the siege, then several learning points can be seen. Burgoyne, whilst being

65 TNA WO3/601 Torrens to Wellington, 21 February 1812, confirming Burgoyne would get his brevet promotion. Torrens letter refers to Wellington's of 22 January 1812, so it would appear that the omission was almost immediately identified, and Wellington wrote to have it corrected. Thanks to Dr Rory Muir for pointing out this correspondence.

66 REM 5501-139-1, Burgoyne to Pasley, Albergaria, 12 February 1812.

67 Wrottesley, *Burgoyne*, p.165 and REM 4601-74, Pasley to Burgoyne, 2 March 1812.

critical, is also evaluating the processes and considering alternatives. The siege of Ciudad Rodrigo was a major siege and there was much to be learnt. The list below shows elements of the siege that Burgoyne picked out as needing refinement.

Siege materials, equipment and transport:

> Making fascines & gabions at remote and dispersed sites. The quality could not be checked and transporting them placed further pressures on the limited transport available. Burgoyne suggested that many of the items made were abandoned. Production was based on the location of divisions, not the location of materials, which were not always compatible.
>
> Lack of transport. This was a problem throughout the whole war. There was insufficient transport to bring up the siege equipment and materials. On several occasions, divisional transport was borrowed to ease temporary problems.
>
> Not using mortars and howitzers. The extensive armoury in Ciudad Rodrigo was allowed to fire on the besiegers for almost the whole siege without response. Unnecessary casualties will have been caused.
>
> Not using counter battery fire. As above. There was an immediate effect when it was started on 18 January. John Jones noted in his *Autobiography* 'the fire of the garrison, unopposed by counter-batteries, was unceasing, well-directed and concentrated on the point of operations'.[68]
>
> Problems with scaling ladders and the best design. Most used were made on the spot and were liable to break when scaling the highest of the walls. In Burgoyne's letter to Pasley he suggested a design and asked Pasley (who was in England) if he could investigate options.

Management of siege:

> Making summons too early. The summons was usually made just before the assault when the breaches were ready. Wellington did it earlier. It is likely the French would have refused anyway, but it should still have been tried.
>
> Consequences of excavating the interior of batteries. If batteries are placed so that the interior has to be excavated, there is a massive increase in the amount of material to be moved and the time taken. It should be avoided wherever possible.
>
> Best way of making, reinforcing and opening embrasures. When this is done in a hurried fashion as at Ciudad Rodrigo there is a need for constant repairs.

68 Jones, *Autobiography*, p.50.

Not enough care in the siting of batteries. This should be well understood by engineer and artillery officers. The fact it was overlooked at battery No. 1 should have concerned all present and should be remembered at future sieges.

Using sappers to lead assaults and improve access to breaches. This was seen as a great success. Hence the constant complaint about the lack of trained sappers and miners.

Limited use of muskets to keep down fire of defenders. Again, like counter battery fire, it would have reduced allied casualties and the amount of repair needed for the trenches.

Organisation:

Poor organisation in siege park and moving of materials. Material was moved in a haphazard way. Groups of soldiers carrying material for the same destination should have been collected and led to the place saving much time and confusion.

Organising working parties by military unit and not by the number of troops required. There was at least one occasion when the division on duty could not provide the working parties. This was much easier for the army commanders, but there could have been more effective ways that reduced the hardship for the soldiers.

Troops cantonment too far away from siege. A great deal of time was wasted marching; fording a freezing river cannot have helped health or morale; the troops spent more time in the open in poor weather.

Command and People:

Lack of trained sappers and miners. This was seen as an issue at Badajoz in 1811. It was also seen as an issue at Ciudad Rodrigo. Apart from being true, it gave everyone a convenient excuse when things went wrong.

24-hour shifts for artillery were too long. This was hard work and the shifts should have been 8 or 12 hours.

Poor command of troops in the trenches; changeover and sortie. Shift changeover was identified as an issue in terms of work rate and in terms of risk of attack. The French noticed the situation very quickly. No-one on the allied side appears to have taken responsibility for managing the troops during the changeover. The poor weather would have been a contributing factor, but the periods when the trenches were unoccupied should have been stopped.

Attitude of the soldiers and in many cases, their officers. Siege work was seen as not honourable work for the soldier. As William Grattan put it, the engineers might like siege work, but: 'Not so the infantry soldier, who is

> obliged to stand to be shot at, with a pick axe or shovel in his hand instead of his firelock and bayonet'.[69]
>
> No general officer in the trenches. There was no army officer in overall command. This was reflected in the poor discipline in the trenches.
>
> Not enough engineers/assistant engineers (overseeing troops). This would always remain a problem. Whilst Wellington had assigned 200 officers and men from the 3rd Division, this was still not enough. It would not have impacted on the divisions at all, to have a few officers assigned as assistant engineers when they were in the trenches. It would have given the officers some 'ownership' of the siege and its progress.

Most of these issues would occur again and, having experienced them, Burgoyne was probably in a better place to counteract them, especially when he was the commanding engineer as would happen later in the year.

The frustration around the lack of trained sappers and miners was coming to a head. Writing home to Lord Liverpool after the siege, Wellington said:

> I would beg to suggest to your Lordship the expediency of adding to the Engineer establishment a corps of Sappers and Miners. It is inconceivable with what disadvantage we undertake anything like a siege for want of assistance of this description … we are obliged to depend … upon the regiments of the line; and although the men are brave and willing, they want the knowledge and training which are necessary.[70]

Fletcher had written a similar letter to the Board of Ordnance about two weeks earlier.[71] In the Peninsula, Wellington could only complain to Fletcher. This cannot have helped their relationship. Jones said he also wrote to the Board of Ordnance and was suitably chastised for the suggesting the inactivity of the Board of Ordnance was the equivalent of Nero fiddling whilst Rome burned.[72] The lack of sappers and miners would be addressed soon, but not soon enough.

Casualties among the 19 engineer officers were two killed and five wounded. Two of the wounded sailed to England and did not return to the Peninsula.[73]

Although Burgoyne was not directly involved, work to fill the trenches and start repairs began the morning after the assault. As the north side was clearly the weakest point, additional work was carried out there. At the main breach, a new wall was built

69 Grattan, *Connaught Rangers*, p.108.

70 Gurwood (ed.), *Despatches*, Wellington to Liverpool, 11 February 1812.

71 TNA WO55/959, Fletcher to Morse, Ciudad Rodrigo, 29 January 1812.

72 Jones, *Autobiography*, p.51; TNA WO55/981, Jones to unknown (headed, Dear Sir), Ciudad Rodrigo, 28 January 1812.

73 Ross and Skelton killed. Mulcaster, Marshall, Macculloch, Thomson and Reid wounded. Thomson and Macculloch returned to England.

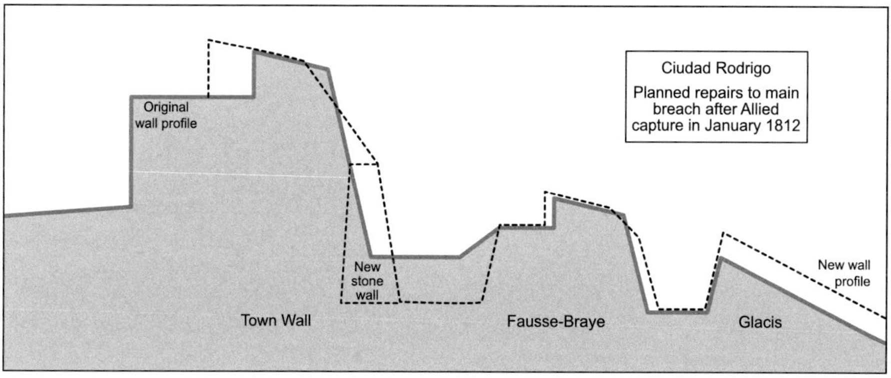

Ciudad Rodrigo, new wall profile.

in front of the old one and reprofiled, the ditch between the main wall and *fausse-braye* was deepened and the glacis raised. At the lesser breach, the square tower was replaced and the *fausse-braye* altered in the same way as at the main breach.

Burgoyne described the work as follows:

> The profile of the great breach as it is proposed to repair it will be thus:
>
> A ditch is to be excavated in the fausse-bray [sic] in front of the escarp of eight feet deep from the bottom of which will commence the new escarp which will be carried up in all sixteen feet and six feet in front of the old escarp; from the summit of the parapet to the top of the escarp the earth will fall at its proper slope. The fausse-bray will secure this new escarp from breaching and by raising the counterscarp a few feet, the fausse-bray will be equally secured; but after all other parts of the same line will remain exposed.
>
> In the little breach, the fausse-bray is to be repaired as before, but the breach in the tower of Amajuelas of the upper wall will be repaired similar to the other breach in profile and its plan altered to enlarge it … It will contain three guns to face the Teson.[74]

In front of the fortress, work started on 23 January to enlarge the Renaud Redoubt, and three other defensive works were built on the Little and Great Tesons.[75] The first, on the Little Teson was started on 25 January 1812. After an examination

74 REM 4201-68, Journal, 18 February 1812. These profiles are what you will see today.

75 The redoubt on the little Teson is now built over; the two outer works are still visible on the ground. The Renaud Redoubt is still visible, in outline, on aerial images. REM 5501-59-3 shows a sketch of the Renaud Redoubt with dimensions.

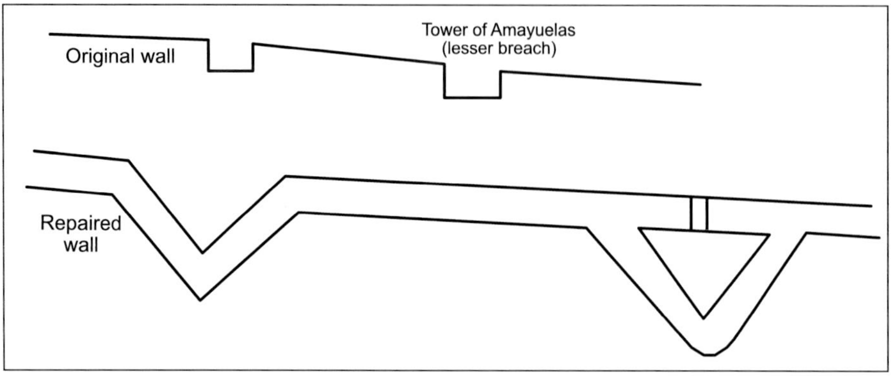

Ciudad Rodrigo, repair to lesser breach.

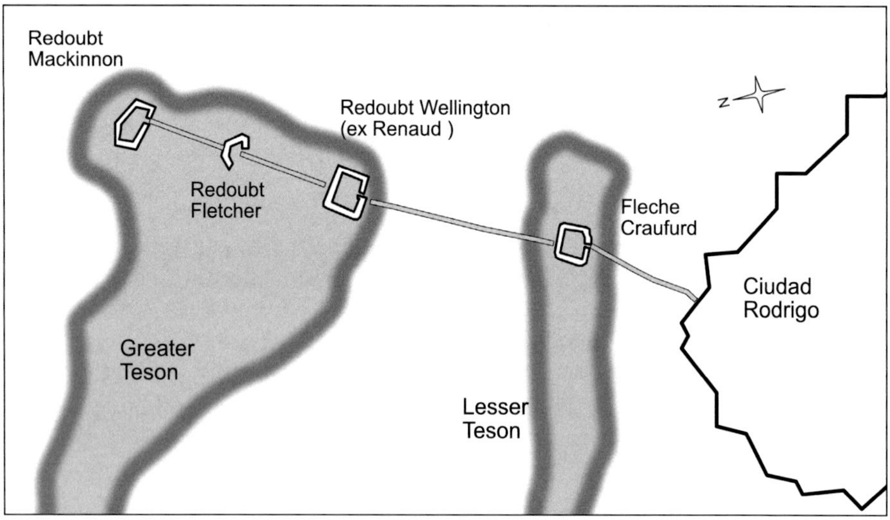

Redoubts built by British after siege of Ciudad Rodrigo, 1812.

of the fortress with *Capitán General* Castaños on 31 January 1812, Wellington ordered a redoubt for 220 men to be built on the rear edge of the Great Teson. This redoubt was 510 yards from the Renaud Redoubt and was placed to cover the ground behind the Great Teson which was hidden from the town. On 7 February 1812, the fourth work, a small fleche, was marked out between the Renaud Redoubt and the new outwork.[76] A covered communication was built between the three outworks on the Great Teson.

76 All these details come from Jones MS Journal, REM 5501-59-3. Jones' published Journal says the fleche was ordered on the 1 February not 7 February.

Wellington ordered the convents of San Francisco, Santa Clara, and San Domingo to be strengthened as fortified places. The convent of Santa Cruz was to be demolished. On 19 February, Jones marked out a new redoubt in front of the convent of San Domingo. A new ditch and scarping was started on the south and south-west of the town.[77] Wellington did not want to lose it again. These works were progressed and by the beginning of March, much of the work had been completed.

Whilst the building work continued and after a few weeks of quiet, orders arrived towards the end of February for the army to start a slow march south towards Badajoz. Three of the four fortresses covering the main routes into Portugal were now in allied hands. It was not difficult to guess what was coming next.

77 REM 5501-59-3, 19 February 1812.

10

1812 – The Siege of Badajoz

Wellington held two planning meetings with the heads of the Quartermaster General, Artillery and Engineering departments on 28 January and 15 February 1812. The first meeting on 28 January was to discuss the movement of a siege train to Badajoz. The main task discussed at the meeting was how to move the new British siege guns south from Ciudad Rodrigo to Elvas. There was no good road for a journey directly south and it was accepted that the heavy 24-pounder cannon could not make this march due to the state of the roads and the difficulty in feeding the large number of oxen that would be required. The lighter 24-pounder howitzers and 29 travelling carriages for siege guns were sent by road,[1] but the heavy cannon had to go back to the Douro for shipping to Setúbal, south of Lisbon, and onwards to Elvas.[2] The siege stores held at Lisbon were also ordered to Elvas by the same route.

To put together the siege guns for Badajoz, Wellington was once again forced to make compromises. There were 16 new, British, iron 24-pounder cannon at Lisbon. Wellington wrote to Admiral Sir George Berkeley, asking if the navy could supply another twenty 24-pounder cannon.[3] Berkeley could not do this and offered twenty 18-pounders instead, a significantly inferior weapon. Even worse, it turned out that the guns offered were worn Russian 18-pounders with a different bore from English cannon, which would further reduce their power and accuracy.[4] Dickson, on behalf of Wellington, argued very forcefully with the navy that the

1 Jones, *Sieges*, Vol.I, p.147.

2 Wellington's order to move the 24-pounder cannon from Almeida to Elvas was dated 26 January 1812. Dickson suggests that they were never moved from Almeida, Leslie (ed.), *Dickson Manuscripts*, Vol.IV, p.580, Dickson to MacLeod, 29 January 1812.

3 Berkeley was the commander of the Portuguese station, based at Lisbon, and Wellington's primary contact with the Royal Navy.

4 The 24-pounder cannon sent by sea from Ciudad Rodrigo were not used at the siege of Badajoz. Oman is wrong to say that the 24-pounders from Oporto arrived on 7 February: that was impossible, being only 11 days after the order was given to move them from Almeida. Dickson reported the arrival of the sixteen 24-pounders from Lisbon, not the guns from Oporto. Oman, *Peninsular War*, Vol.V, p.224.

Russian guns 'are not in conformity to the spirit of Lord W's wish' and that guns 'as are employed on British Men of War' should be sent without delay.[5] However, no alternative to the Russian guns was offered until too late. In addition, Wellington was again planning to undertake a siege with limited counter-battery capability. There were sixteen 24-pounder iron howitzers (the equivalent of a 5.5-inch field howitzer; these were not siege guns), and no mortars. This deficiency would again cause unnecessary casualties amongst his troops.

There appears to have been less planning for the siege of Badajoz than there was for the siege of Ciudad Rodrigo. Wellington must have known this was a likely next step for his army. Even if it was only an option, it should have been planned for. The difficulties of moving heavy siege guns from Almeida to Elvas will have been well understood. The reason that the guns went by sea and river to Almeida for the siege of Ciudad Rodrigo was because transport by road was very slow, even when possible. Wellington, from his experiences in 1811, knew that Elvas could not provide the necessary weapons. Blaming the navy for not being able to provide weapons that Wellington had not sourced is unfair. Wellington had started collecting and moving the pontoon train in December 1811 for a siege at Badajoz but did not appear to have made similar planning for sufficient siege guns.

This is not the Wellington we normally see, who planned everything in great detail. Perhaps, events occurred much faster than he envisaged. When he saw the opportunity to attack Ciudad Rodrigo in early January, he quickly took it. He now saw the opportunity for carrying out a quick strike on Badajoz before the weather improved. Whilst he was not explicit about this, he argued that the flooded rivers and the spring growth of grass would both act in his favour and at the same time slow the French. The strike had to be quick and that did not leave time for the full siege train to be moved south. This meant compromises, again.

The second planning meeting held on 15 February 1812, was to agree the plan for the siege. John Jones who was present at the meeting recorded:

> The Spaniard [Castaños] and his Lordship were for making the same attack as the French. Fletcher proposed attacking the bastion of Santa Trinidad from the ground in front of the Picurina redoubt, but not being able to state his reasons, viz., the British engineers not having establishments of either sappers or miners and being therefore unequal to the task of contending with the mines on those fronts [which had been placed by the French defenders], no-one of the council would accede to his opinions, but Wellington being reminded of our deficiencies agreed to the project saying "he regretted extremely our deficiencies and it obliged him to undertake an attack he did not approve [of], but that knowing our means, he believed it to be the only attack in our power to get through".

5 Leslie (ed.), *Dickson Manuscripts*, Vol.IV, pp.587-90.

> What a reflection on those who have governed the engineer service for the last 19 years of war.[6]

After the meeting on 15 February, MacLeod was ordered to Elvas to immediately start preparing fascines and gabions.

Burgoyne was not involved in these planning decisions and moved south with the 3rd Division, arriving near Elvas on 15 March 1812.

The fortress was invested on 16 March 1812 with Burgoyne and Squire being the two siege directors. These were the officers who were siege directors at the previous siege of Badajoz. Wellington, learning from the last siege and answering one of Burgoyne's complaints, appointed three general officers to take duty in the trenches.[7] There was some delay on the morning of the investment as Graham's covering force of three divisions crossed the pontoon bridge to the south bank of the Guadiana before the investing force was able to do so.

The siege of Badajoz is covered in detail in several books, so what is presented here is a summary, followed by discussion of the differences to the standard accounts as taken from the manuscript rather than the printed journals of the officers involved.[8]

The first parallel was opened on 17 March 1812 in front of the Picurina fort. The weather was very wet and windy. The poor weather continued for a week and made work in the trenches nearly impossible. There was probably more effort expended trying to empty water out the trenches than there was extending them. The pontoon bridge that was used to bring in supplies was swept away on the 22 March and was not re-established for three days, Burgoyne commenting that the Guadiana had risen 15 feet.[9]

The first two batteries, Nos 1 and 2, to attack the Picurina fort, were started on the night of 18/19 March. At noon the following day, the French launched a sortie and managed to briefly take control of the trenches. No significant damage was done but over 500 tools were lost as the French soldiers had been offered a reward for every tool they brought back.[10] During the sortie, the commanding engineer, Richard Fletcher, was wounded and controlled most of the rest of the siege from his bed. This cannot have helped the planning and execution.

6 REM 5501-59-3, 15 February 1812.

7 Colville, Bowes and Kempt. REM 4201-68, Siege of Badajoz, 16 March 1812.

8 For descriptions of the siege, see Oman, *Peninsular War*, Vol.III, pp.217-264; Frederick Myatt, *British Sieges of the Peninsular War* (Tunbridge Wells: Spellmount, 1987), pp.92-117; Ian Fletcher, *In Hell Before Daylight. The Siege and Storming of the Fortress of Badajoz, 16 March to 6 April 1812* (London: Baton Press, 1984).

9 REM 4201-68, Siege of Badajoz, dated 23 March 1812.

10 Lamarre, *Relation des Sieges et Defences d'Olivenza, de Badajoz et de Campo Mayor en 1811 et 1812* (Paris: Anselin et Pochard, 1825), p.226.

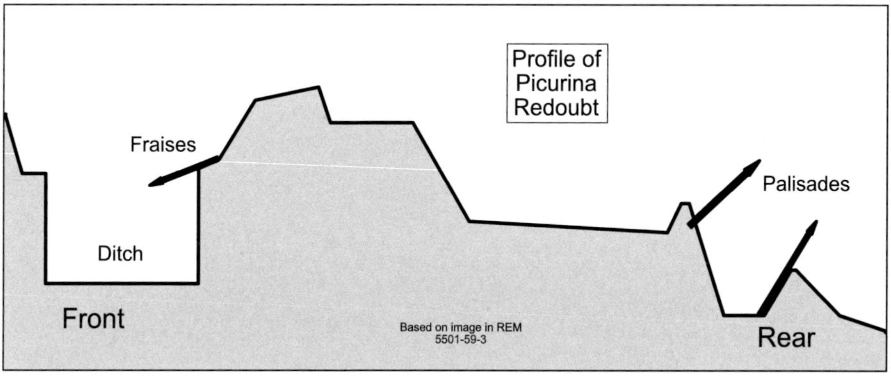

Badajoz, Picurina fort profile as drawn by Burgoyne.

On the night of 20/21 March 1812, three more batteries were commenced, Numbers 4, 5 and 6. The following night, battery No.3 was started. These batteries were intended to suppress the defensive fire that could bear on the Picurina fort from the bastions of Trinidad and San Pedro and the San Roque lunette.

It was not until 24 March that the right bank of the Guadiana (the San Cristóbal side) was invested. The French had been placing field guns to enfilade the trenches from that side of the river and had caused many casualties necessitating changes to the trench layout.

Batteries 1-6 were armed on the night of 24/25 March and opened the following morning. Fortunately for Wellington, the weather improved and eased the difficulties faced by the attackers, although, on 27 March 1812, Jones commented that the bright moonlight was hampering work, as the French could see what was being done. Without any real signs of damage to the fort or its supporting guns, the Picurina fort was stormed that night and after a stiff resistance was taken.

This now allowed the opening of the second parallel and the construction of the main breaching batteries. On the night of 26/27 March, batteries number 7, 9 and 10 were started to contain twenty cannon and three howitzers. A further breaching battery, No.8, was started on 28/29 March. Battery No.9 opened against the Santa Maria bastion on 30 March 1812, and batteries 7, 8 and 10 opened the following morning.

The walls of the bastions proved very hard, but progress was made over the next few days. One of Wellington's great concerns was the flooding of the area in front of the intended breaches. The French had dammed the Rivillas stream behind the San Roque lunette and the water backed up for several hundred yards past the south-eastern corner of the fortress. The French had also diverted the stream into the ditch near the Trinidad and Santa Maria bastions.

It was seen as vital that the dam was breached, and a trench was pushed down towards the lunette. Casualties in the trenches were high and Jones complained that 'The want of proper instructed workmen [i.e. trained sappers] to push on

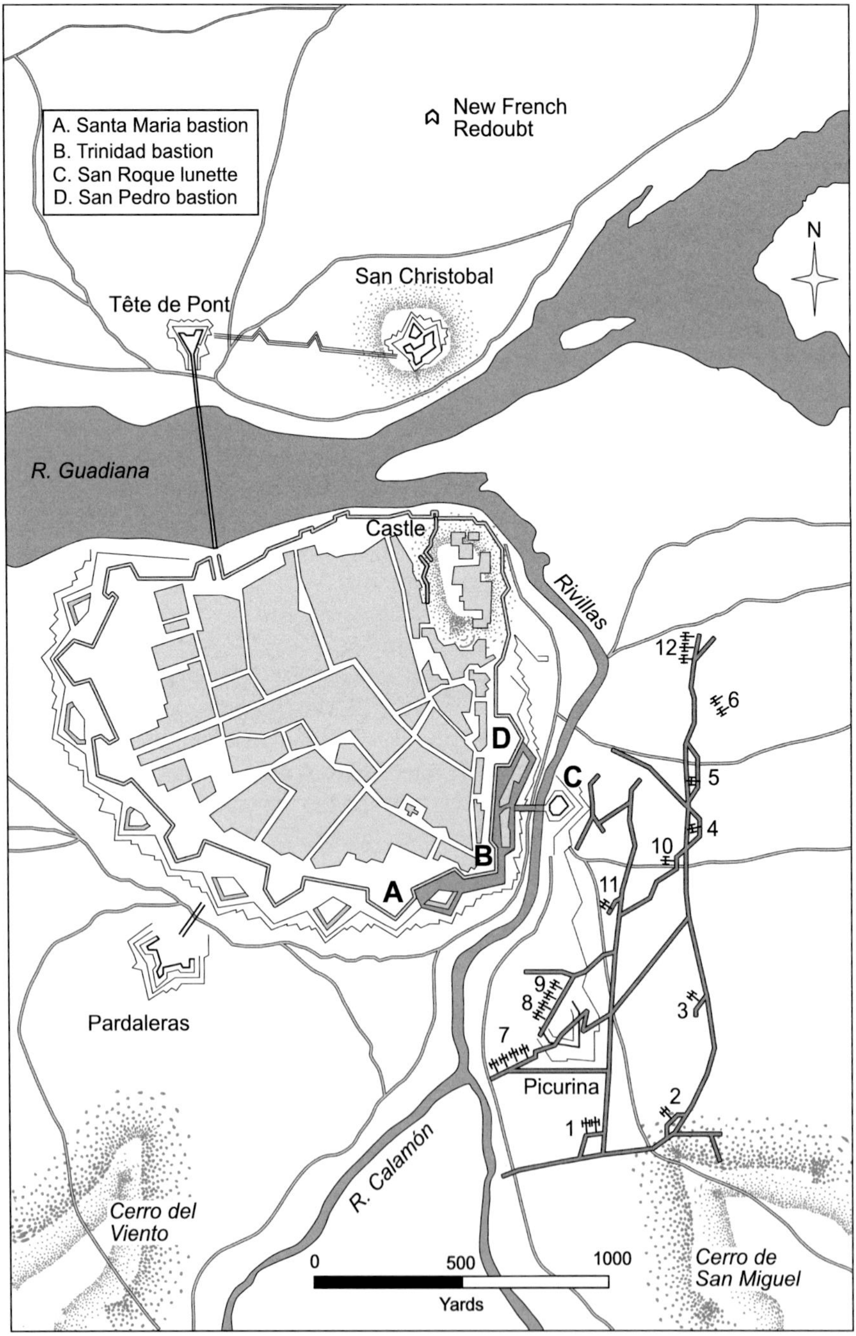

Batteries at third siege of Badajoz, 1812.

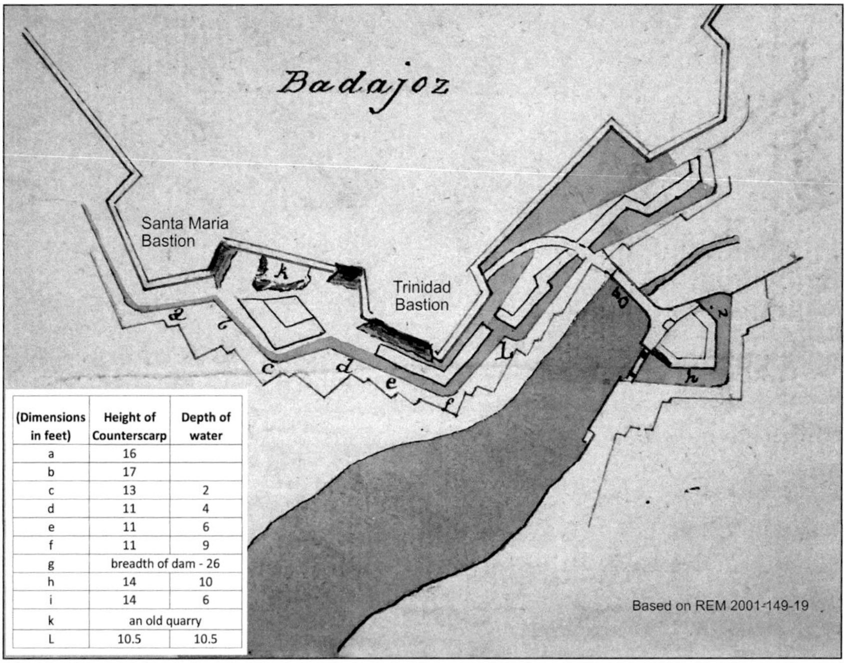

(Dimensions in feet)	Height of Counterscarp	Depth of water
a	16	
b	17	
c	13	2
d	11	4
e	11	6
f	11	9
g	breadth of dam - 26	
h	14	10
i	14	6
k	an old quarry	
L	10.5	10.5

San Roque Lunette, Badajoz, 1812.

the sap to the ravelin of St Roque rendering the completion of that attack nearly hopeless'.[11]

On the night of 2 /3 April 1812, a party of 28 men led by the engineer Lieutenant Frank Stanway crept forward and laid 450 pounds of powder against the dam, but the explosion did not destroy it.

Jones described the operation:

> [I]t becoming daily a greater object to draw off the water from the inundation, Wellington ordered a strict reconnaissance … his Lordship determined to try a bold enterprise and to attach a *pétard* to the masonry and blow it in. With that intent, five barrels of powder were emptied into two cases and twenty sandbags filled with earth to place on top of them

Stanway, having been challenged three times on his approach:

> deposited the boxes of powder, but did not think it of any consequence to put the sandbags over them … the explosion not taking place, as he

11 REM 5501-59-3, 2 April 1812.

> expected, he returned … and found the water had extinguished the slow match … [he lit it again] and in due time the powder exploded.[12]

The attempt is described differently in Jones' published version: 'the powder could not be placed precisely at the foot of the … wall and in consequence failed to blow it down'.[13] The attempt to sap down to the dam was given up at this point and Wellington accepted the very restricted access his troops would have to the breaches.[14]

On 4 April 1812, Burgoyne examined the fords across the Rivillas, under the castle walls, and confirmed that troops could cross. He recommended that an attempt should be made against the castle, but it was judged too risky.[15] Two days later, Burgoyne would lead the 3rd Division along this route.

On 5 April, the two breaches were declared practicable and the assault was ordered for that evening, only to be cancelled at the last minute when the decision was made to open a third breach. Burgoyne's diary said all were astonished and disappointed with the decision. There are some alternate views on who made the decision to postpone the attack. Jones' account in the *Sieges*, says that Wellington reviewed the breaches around noon and made the decision to assault that night, the 5/6 April. He then asked the commanding engineer, Fletcher to look at the defences the French had constructed behind the breaches. Fletcher, just out of his sickbed, reported that the new defences were significant and 'it was determined to carry the original plan into effect and turn all the guns of the batteries on the old wall … between the two breaches, so as in one days firing to obtain an opening into the place which should turn the retrenchment'. Jones did not specifically say that Fletcher made the recommendation to delay the assault for 24 hours.[16] In Jones' unpublished journal, he wrote that Wellington and Beresford made a reconnaissance at 4:00 p.m., saw that the retrenchments were formidable, and decided to delay the assault and open a third breach. Fletcher was not mentioned.[17] In Dickson's unpublished account of the siege, he recorded that Wellington 'declared the breaches perfectly practicable, [and] at the same time determined to defer the assault another day, to afford time to open a third breach in the curtain'.[18]

12 REM 5501-59-3, 2 April 1812.

13 Jones, *Sieges*, Vol.I, p.189.

14 Burgoyne suggested that there was a plan to storm the St Roque lunette on the night of 3 / 4 April but that it was given up. REM 4201-68, Siege of Badajoz, 3 April 1812.

15 Wrottesley, *Burgoyne*, p.174.

16 Jones, *Sieges*, Vol.I, p193. The original plan was to make a third breach at the last moment to circumvent and interior defences. Jones, after Fletcher's death at San Sebastián, wrote that he believed that Wellington blamed Fletcher for the high casualties at the siege of Badajoz because he recommended the delay. I find it difficult to believe that Wellington would have delayed 24 hours, if he thought the breaches were practicable, especially when he knew that French forces were approaching to relieve the fortress.

17 REM 5501-59-3, 5 April 1812.

18 REM 5501-59-25, 5 April 1812.

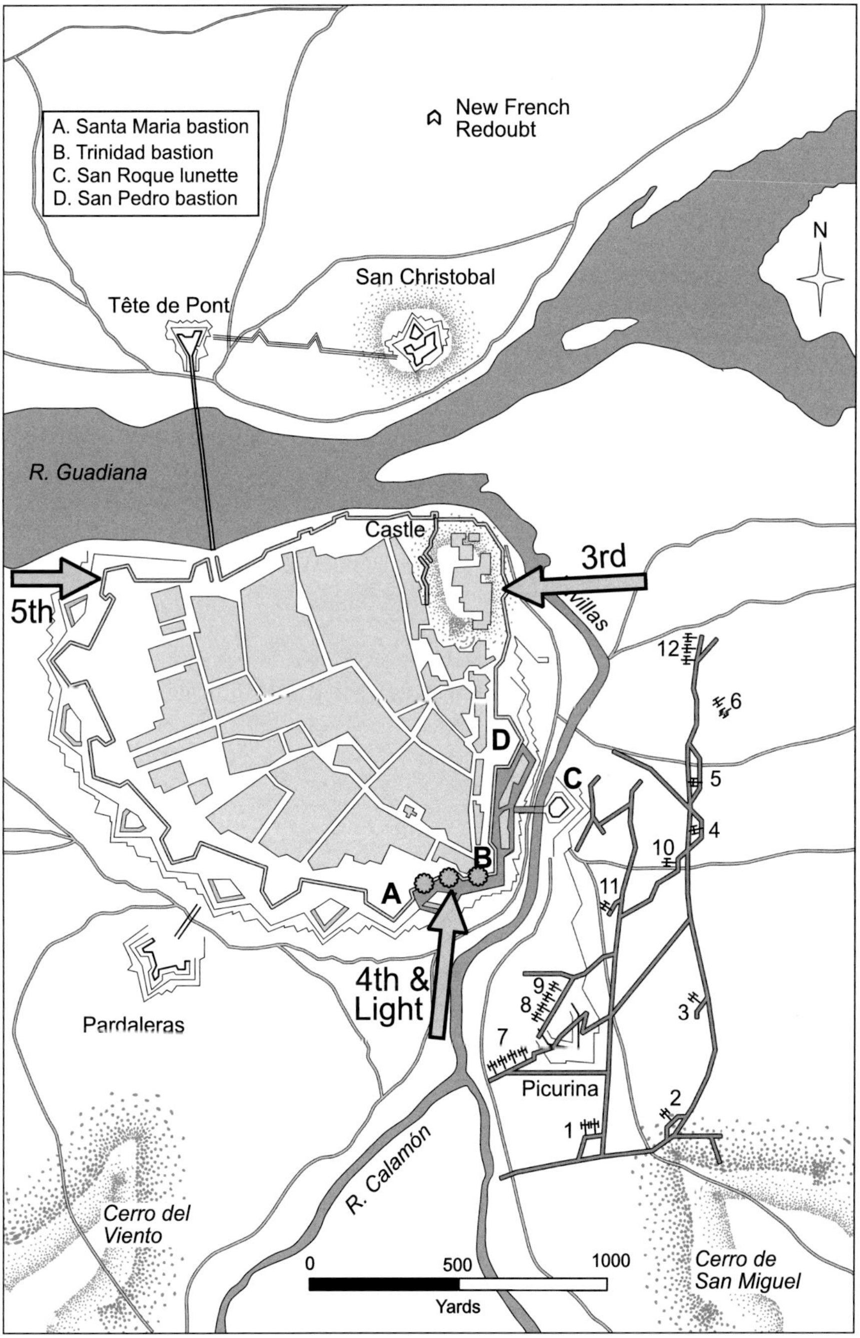

Assault at third siege of Badajoz.

The assault was made on the night of 6 April 1812, Burgoyne guiding the 3rd Division to their assigned point of attack. Like at Ciudad Rodrigo, Burgoyne was completely silent on his role although he does appear in other officers' accounts of the night.[19] He certainly appeared to have great luck in avoiding injury. Of the 24 engineer officers present (of whom four arrived at the close of the siege), four were killed and eight were wounded. Of these, three officers were killed and two wounded during the assault. Burgoyne was clearly in the thick of the fighting as he was with Picton, the commander of the 3rd Division. Picton and his two brigade commanders were wounded; 53 other officers in the division were killed and wounded (about 1/3 of the total).

Captain McCarthy, who was acting as an Assistant Engineer, described the scene when organising the erection of the ladders against the castle wall:

> During which I was visited by General Kempt and Major Burgoyne although this place and the whole face of the wall, being opposed by the guns of the citadel, were so swept by their discharges of round shot, broken shells, bundles of cartridges and other missiles and also from the top of the wall, ignited shells etc., that it was almost impossible to twinkle the eye on any man, before he was knocked down.[20]

The assault was successful but with terrible casualties. The primary attacks by the 4th and Light Divisions on the main breaches failed, but the secondary attacks by the 3rd and 5th Divisions manged to enter the town and tip the balance in favour of the attackers. Fortunately, Burgoyne came through again without injury, and, being mentioned in Wellington's despatch, received his second brevet promotion in three months, rising from captain to lieutenant colonel (in the Army only, not in the Corps). John Jones also received two promotions for the same events and these two officers were looked at with some jealousy by other less fortunate engineer officers.[21] Colonel Henry Torrens, Military Secretary to the Duke of York, writing to Wellington commented:

> You will perceive that the officers of Artillery and Engineers who were promoted at Ciudad Rodrigo, have been advanced upon the present occasion to the rank of Lt Colonel! When this becomes public, I anticipate a great sensation and clamour at the Ordnance.[22]

19 See MacCarthy, *Recollections of the Storming of the Castle of Badajoz*, as quoted in Wrottesley, *Burgoyne*, pp.178-181.

20 As quoted in Wrottesley, *Burgoyne*, p.180.

21 The officers would not have found out about their promotion for some months. The brevet promotions were not officially confirmed until 4 May 1812 and it would have been several weeks more before they were informed. TNA WO55/981, Crewe to Mann, 4 May 1812.

22 TNA WO3/602, ff.60-63, Torrens to Wellington, 28 April 1812.

Torrens was writing on behalf of a friend and engineer officer, Captain Stephen Chapman, who was also known to Wellington from his earlier services in the Peninsula. Torrens was asking if Wellington could do anything to accelerate Chapman's promotion. Another engineer officer, Pasley, who would soon be appointed to command the new School of Military Engineering, was also writing to everyone he knew to secure a brevet promotion before the siege of Badajoz finished, as it was expected that the engineer officers involved would get promoted. Whilst the brevet ranks did not count towards seniority within the Royal Engineers, the rank did within the army and society. These things mattered a great deal in the early 19th Century.

Observation on the Siege of Badajoz

There were a number of questionable decisions and mistakes made during the siege by the engineers, artillery and the army. The weather was a significant hindrance through the first week of the siege. Wellington accepted that risk: it was one of the reasons he gave for attacking at that time of year as it would impede the French response. The sieges in 1811 against Badajoz also had weather problems and the pontoon bridge was also lost. The issues of crossing the Guadiana should not have come as a surprise to anyone and there should have been spare pontoons ready for any likely problems.

The French sortie on 19 March did not appear to be handled well. The covering party whose role was to be ready to respond to a sortie, was not ready and fell into confusion, before weight of numbers finally pushed the French back into the town. The fact that a lookout was set up and a cavalry unit was added to the covering party, after the sortie suggests that the initial arrangements were not comprehensive. It was only a matter of weeks since the allied besiegers at Ciudad Rodrigo had been surprised by a sortie. It should not have happened again so soon, especially when everyone knew that the French Governor, Philippon, had proved himself very active in 1811.

Was it an error not to invest the north bank straight away? It allowed the French to position guns to enfilade the trenches and caused many casualties. This omission required additional work to alter the direction of the trench before the decision was made to invest the northern bank.

Both Burgoyne and Jones commented on problems with the working parties. Filing in and out of the narrow trenches was very time consuming and delayed the working parties. Much of this movement would have been done in the dark which will have further added to the delays. Burgoyne, as he did at Ciudad Rodrigo, commented on the delays caused by working parties, who were moving stores, not being collected and moved together to their task. This meant that soldiers arrived in disorganised small groups rather than as a body.

The destruction of the dam at the San Roque lunette was seen as vital. It could be argued that more effort should have been made to take and destroy San Roque.

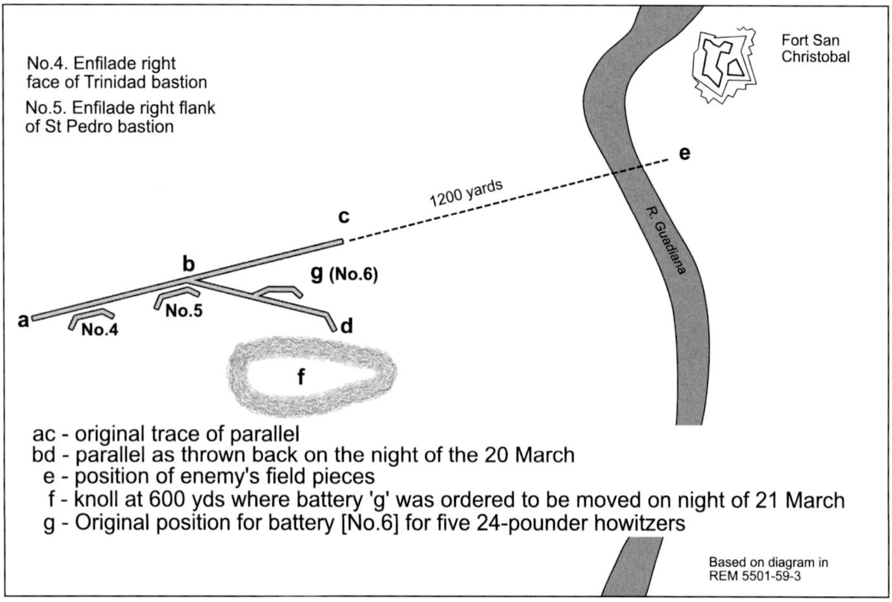

Right of trenches at third siege of Badajoz as drawn by Jones.

The flooding was of great benefit to the defenders as the approach to the breaches was now longer and very constricted. Whilst the situation was not identical, San Roque was taken quickly on the night of the main assault.

There is criticism of the decision to delay the assault on 5 April. The retrenchments behind the two main breaches were formidable. Would another 24 hours under intense fire have allowed further strengthening of the retrenchments? The point of the third breach was that there was no time to retrench the extra breach and it would have spread the defenders thinner. The other question is, would Wellington have deferred to Fletcher if he did not agree with the recommendation? Jones wrote that Wellington asked Fletcher to examine the retrenchments. Fletcher reported they were significant, which will have been the same conclusion that Wellington came to when he examined the breaches on 5 April.

As at Ciudad Rodrigo, Wellington had no mortars in his siege train and did not use all the howitzers until the last day. The consequences were the same; the defenders had to worry less about counter-battery and anti-personnel fire. Throughout the siege the attackers commented on the strength of the defensive fire, the casualties caused and the delays to work caused by shells landing amongst the trenches and batteries. The attack on Picurina and the main assault could have been less costly with effective mortar fire during the siege. Having mortars would have helped to damage the defensive positions in the breaches before the assault. This would appear to be a continuation of Wellington's 'new tactic', first used at Ciudad Rodrigo.

The artillery came in for criticism. On the evening after the breaching batteries opened, orders were given for them to fire grape shot and spherical case through the night to stop the enemy making repairs which they did not do. On the morning of 1 April 1812, it was seen that the French had raised additional defences in front of the face of the Trinidad Bastion (a counterguard) stopping the direct fire of the breaching batteries. A strongly worded order was issued by Lieutenant Colonel Framingham, the Commander of the artillery, threatening to report any officer who did not follow orders to Lord Wellington.[23]

Most descriptions of the construction of the batteries for the siege are based on Jones' *Journal of the Sieges*. There is a different and less flattering picture if the events are taken from the original manuscript journals rather than the published versions.[24]

On 18/19 March 1812, the first two batteries were started. No.1 was to enfilade the communications from the town to the Picurina fort. No.2 was to fire directly at the front of the fort. The following morning, both Jones and Burgoyne note that battery No.1 was abandoned, although they give different reasons. Jones wrote that it: 'was found to be so far retired down the slope of the hill that it could not see the object and was therefore abandoned'. Burgoyne recorded that it was 'discontinued, the soil being rock'. No other complaint was made about the ground being 'rock' in the construction of any other battery. Burgoyne was on duty on the night of 18/19 March and his diary also noted that there were no tracing fascines available, which were used to mark out the planned work.

Both Jones and Burgoyne record that battery No.1 was restarted on the night of 20/21 March, 'close to the left of the former one and 60 yards in front of the parallel'. This mistake and correction do not appear in the published versions.

Also, on the night of 20/21 March, three new batteries were started, Numbers 4, 5 and 6, to attempt to reduce the defending fire that could bear on the Picurina from the Trinidad bastion, the San Pedro bastion and the San Roque lunette.

Again, the following morning, Jones and Burgoyne record that there were mistakes in siting these new batteries. Burgoyne wrote 'the three batteries on the right are ill placed … by alteration, however, two of them will do. Jones' explanation was more comprehensive:

23 Jones, *Sieges*, Vol.I, p.186. These words were provided to Jones by Alexander Dickson, commanding the artillery during the siege, so this was not an inter-service complaint.

24 Most of this interpretation of the work to construct the batteries comes from Jones' and Burgoyne's manuscript journals. REM 5501-59-3 and REM 4201-68, note books on the siege of Badajoz. To try and reduce confusion, the account given here does not employ the battery numbering used by Jones and copied by most other authors. At the time the batteries were not numbered and that is why some appear to be built out of sequence. Specific comments are not referenced; they can be found against the appropriate date in the MS journals.

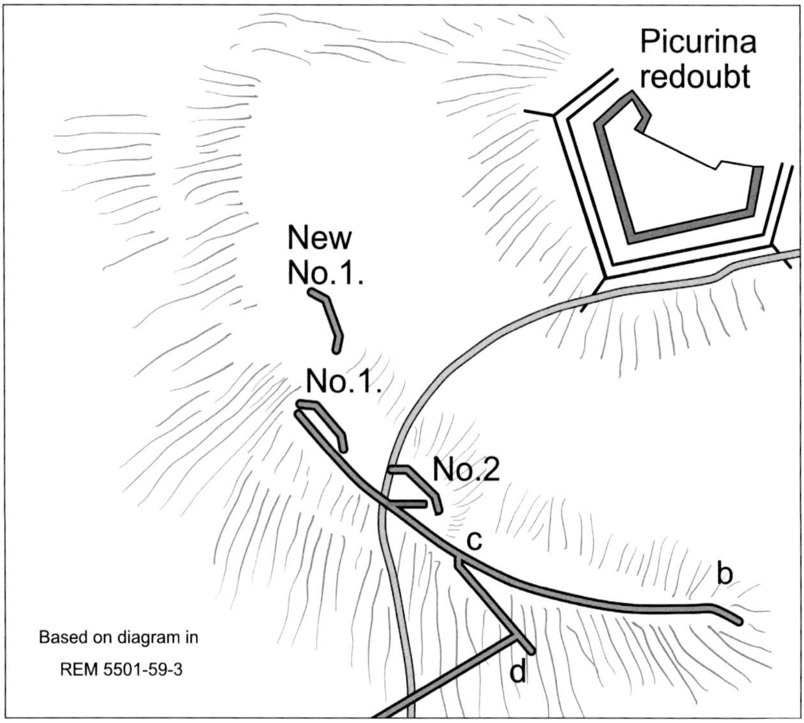

Fault in siting battery No.1 as drawn by Jones.

> [T]he enfilading batteries on the flat had not been correctly marked out. That intended for the prolongation of the flank [of San Pedro, No.5] being placed about 250 yards too much to the right, and that intended for the prolongation of the right face of the bastion Trinidad, [No.4], about 20 yards too much to the right and that for the right face of the ravelin of St Roque, [No.6], being altogether in a hollow and good for nothing. On looking over the batteries, it was found that the battery marked out for the face answers very well for the flank, so it was agreed by the Directing Officer that the party should continue to work on it this day and enlarge it for two guns more, and that the other battery should be commenced at night for the face of the bastion and ravelin, [and] the latter [No.6, to be moved] on [to] the knoll.

A diagram in Jones' manuscript Journal confirms that battery No.6 was intended to be moved to a height well behind the trenches.[25]

25 See previous diagram, 'Right of the trenches at third siege of Badajoz', where the knoll is marked.

The next night, Jones complained that the working party was 350 short of the requirement and:

> [N]o steps whatever had been taken to mark the proper directions for the new enfilading batteries. The battery for the right flank of the bastion of St Pedro [No.5] was therefore picketed out when it was too dark to be certain of the direction and the battery (g) [No.6] on the right, being in exactly the same state as in the morning without any works having been taken on the rise (f), it was decided to go on with it, in its original situation, it being too dark to mark out afresh, although there is little probability of it answering any good purpose, but to make certain of keeping down the fire of the ravelin a [new] direct battery [No.3] was picketed out for four 18-pounders.

Jones appears to be complaining that the last three (eight hour) reliefs of engineers had not progressed anything. There had been constant heavy rain for days now and it is understandable that progress was limited in constructing the batteries due to the state of the soil, but it does not explain why more was not done by the engineer officers to mark out the work required for the following evening. Several mistakes had been made in setting out the batteries, the same mistakes as were made at Ciudad Rodrigo. It is easy 200 years later to criticise these mistakes, but tracing out batteries at night, in terrible weather, cannot be easy. Neither was keeping soldiers working in these appalling conditions. Nevertheless, it is hard to see how some of the errors were not picked up. The surprising thing about all these mistakes is that none of the engineer officers appeared to accept responsibility or apportion blame. With Fletcher being wounded, these batteries were marked out by Jones, Burgoyne, or Squire and yet there is no explanation as to why these errors happened. There is no doubt that the bad weather was a significant contributory factor, but one would expect that scientific soldiers would have been able to cope with that. Was the pressure to make quick progress justifying guesswork when accuracy was needed?

The official report of the siege sent by the Commanding Engineer, Fletcher, dated 18 April 1812, does not mention any of the errors that occurred during the siege. As with the report after the siege of Ciudad Rodrigo, it was sanitised.[26]

During the attempt to breach the dam at San Roque, the *pétard* (explosive) was not placed properly. It was well understood that placing weights over explosives increased the effect. Jones' account suggested that Lieutenant Stanway advanced with 20 soldiers carrying sandbags to place over the explosives and then did not use them, which seems odd. A more likely explanation is that, after being challenged three times, Stanway made the decision to continue with a smaller party,

26 TNA WO55/959, Fletcher to Mann, 18 April 1812.

just carrying the explosives, leaving the largest part of the group carrying the sandbags behind. This would have increased his chances of reaching the dam but would have reduced the impact of the explosion. There is no way of knowing, today, if placing the sandbags would have made a difference. Certainly, Burgoyne was of the opinion that the masonry of the dam would have been too strong, if it was able to hold back the large inundation.[27]

Burgoyne made a number of observations about the execution of the siege, during the operation and also later when he recorded some 'remarks'.[28] He thought that the French sapper sergeant who had deserted and previously provided valuable information on the mining of the south-west face should have been brought up to provide additional information.

He suggested that there were limited supplies of spherical case ammunition. He may have had a point, as the total usage during the siege was 1,300 against 32,000 round shot. Limited grape and shell will have further reduced the counter battery and anti-personnel capabilities of the allied artillery. For the sake of speed, Wellington was accepting greater casualties amongst his troops.

Burgoyne's observation that the pontoon train was too small for a siege of this scale was also valid. Wellington knew the weather could be bad at that time of year. The army lost the pontoon bridge at the siege the previous year, which caused significant delays. The British pontoon was very unreliable, so having spares would have been a sensible precaution. There were other pontoons available which could have been brought up. For the key bridges across the Tagus there was an engineer stationed permanently with them who could react quickly to any change in circumstances. The engineer who brought up the pontoon train, Lieutenant Robert Piper RE, was assigned to one of the brigades working on the siege and had to be sent back, after the pontoon bridge had sunk. It would have been better to leave an engineer with the bridge who could have made the decision to withdraw it before it sank.[29] Wellington's communications with the northern bank were severely degraded after the pontoon bridge sank, with there not being enough pontoons to re-establish the bridge and the compromise was flying bridges using the remaining pontoons.

Allowing Graham's force to cross the Guadiana on the same day as the investing force, caused delays and the original intention of starting the trenches on the night of 16/17 March had to be delayed until the following night. There was really no reason why Graham's force could not have followed the investing force as Wellington was sure of the positions of the various French forces and a delay of one day for Graham would have made no difference.

27 REM 4201-68, Siege of Badajoz, 2 April 1812.

28 REM 4601-74, f.78-79.

29 As an example, the pontoon bridge at Villa Velha had 12 boats on 12 April 1812, but, after heavy rain, needed 17 on 17 April. Wrottesley, *Burgoyne*, pp.182-3.

Burgoyne's biggest complaint was the lack of tracing fascines in the first few days which made marking out the trenches and batteries more difficult and inaccurate.

Having now seen the construction of batteries at three sieges, Burgoyne was forming views on the accepted construction methods. He had noticed significant damage was caused to the embrasures in the batteries from the firing of the siege guns. Small gabions and sand bags could not withstand the blast of the large siege guns, and, within a few rounds, the sides of the embrasures were disintegrating exposing the gunners to the defenders' fire. He suggested that the use of long fascines that lined the whole length of the embrasure were the solution.

At Ciudad Rodrigo and again at Badajoz in 1812, he noted issues when sinking the interior of the batteries. Firstly, it was a huge amount of effort to excavate three feet of earth and secondly, in low-lying ground, in wet weather, the batteries tended to fill with water. He suggested that only sinking the interiors by one foot would help with both issues. He recorded similar thoughts on the construction of escarps and the magazines.[30]

Burgoyne had noted at Ciudad Rodrigo that the organisation of working parties was inefficient. The working parties were not homogenous groups that could immediately act together, but soldiers from several different regiments with their own officers. The work required arrangement into task specific groups which could not fit easily with the normal command structure. So, soldiers would often be separated from their own officers, which caused confusion and the opportunities to avoid work. Burgoyne commented on workers 'shirking', especially at night and in bad weather.

Throughout, Burgoyne was of the opinion that the castle should have been attacked again. Whilst the wall was high, it could be seen to its foot and he believed there were points where it could be breached successfully. After his reconnaissance of the Rivillas stream on 4 April, he recommended an attack by this route, but his recommendation was rejected.

Aftermath of the Siege

From an engineering perspective, the main outcome of the siege was a strongly worded letter home from Wellington to Lord Liverpool complaining about the lack of sappers and miners. Its arrival coincided, to the day, with the signing of the warrant for the establishment of the School of Military Engineering. Lord Liverpool wrote back, telling Wellington he would have trained sappers in a matter of weeks: he did not. The first increase in Royal Military Artificer numbers was in November 1812, when 135 sappers were embarked for the Peninsula.[31] Lord

30 REM 4201-68, Siege of Badajoz, 24 March 1812.

31 TNA WO54/727, RMA Embarkation Returns.

Liverpool had probably been told by the Board of Ordnance in April 1812 that the School of Military Engineering had been established at Chatham and that trained sappers would quickly follow. It was unrealistic to suggest that trained sappers would be quickly available. The first group of trained sappers from the School of Military Engineering did not embark until August 1813.[32]

Wellington's letter dated 7 April 1812, when the horror of the assault and the casualties were fresh in his mind, launched into an unwarranted attack on the competence of the engineer officers, appearing to blame them for the high casualties. Whilst the base complaint was true, that the lack of trained sappers and miners impacted on siege operations, the inference that this was the cause of the high casualties is very debatable. It could be argued that the primary causes of the high casualties was through Wellington embarking on sieges with limited time to complete them and carrying them out with poor or insufficient guns, howitzers, and mortars. The later attacks on the Salamanca forts and on Burgos are two further examples of this lack of preparation and resources, with predictable results. There were other generals in Wellington's army who did not agree with his approach.

The French and British sieges in 1810, 1811 and 1812 were very different in their nature. The French took their time, being confident they would not be interrupted and generally took the places without the need for an assault. The British raced against time knowing that relief for the garrison was on the way. The cost difference between the two methods was measured in blood.

Whilst Burgoyne's long letter to Pasley after the siege of Ciudad Rodrigo, is at first glance, a letter full of complaints, when it is read again along with his comments about the conduct of the siege of Badajoz one can see that he was evaluating the operations and identifying areas that could be improved. Burgoyne had now taken part in three sieges in the last 12 months and had seen different resources and strategies applied. Although two of the sieges had been successful, there had been significant loss of life. Anything that could reduce the casualties or speed up the process would be beneficial. There would be two more sieges in 1812 and Burgoyne would command at both. Could he apply any of these lessons to future operations?

One of the other outcomes of the siege was the reduction in the number of senior (i.e. experienced) engineer officers available. The Brigade-Major, John Jones, and the two siege Directors, Squire and Burgoyne had come through untouched. Of the seven other senior engineers present with the rank of major or captain, two were killed (Mulcaster and Nicholas) and three wounded. A month later, there was one less as Squire had died of exhaustion. With the loss of Ross at Ciudad Rodrigo, the Royal Engineers had lost four experienced officers in four months.

32 This was the second company of the second battalion, 94 strong including their officers. TNA WO54/727, returns, August 1812.

This left very few experienced engineer officers, although Burgoyne appeared to be the officer of choice for important tasks.

On the orders of Napoleon, Marmont had initially been forbidden to come to the aid of Badajoz. His orders were to strike at Ciudad Rodrigo and the allied communications with Portugal. He had advanced against Ciudad Rodrigo and Almeida but had realised that both were too strong to allow a *coup-de-main*. A force was also sent against Castelo Branco and this raised concerns that the critical allied pontoon bridge across the Tagus at Villa Velha might be captured or destroyed. Wellington was intending to move his army in that direction but needed an immediate response to the threat on the bridge

On 10 April 1812, Burgoyne was ordered to ride immediately to the pontoon bridge at Villa Velha. His orders were to remove the bridge if the French approached. Setting off at midnight, Burgoyne raced the 80 miles in 33 hours, arriving on the morning of 12 April. Burgoyne found no senior officer willing to make the decision to remove the bridge, as they had no instructions from Wellington. Burgoyne commented:

> [I] found the Portuguese captain of engineers, in charge of the bridge, in great distress, having received an order from Marshal Beresford to remove the bridge when the enemy should arrive, that is, in his immediate presence. Knowing how impossible this would be, from the nature of the business, and the few proper people he had, he determined on preparing to burn it, as the only recourse, in the immediate presence of the enemy, for the French had entered Castelo Branco yesterday [20 miles away], about 7,000 strong at 4pm and were expected down at Villa Velha hourly.
>
> Neither General Carlos Lecor, who commanded in the province, and had two or three regiments of militia, nor General Baron Alten with the 1st Hussars, also near Castelo Branco, would take upon themselves to give an order for removing the bridge, not knowing the situation of our troops.[33]

Burgoyne, as instructed by Wellington, immediately ordered the removal of the bridge to a safe place, which was completed in a couple of hours. Two days later the threat was over, the French having retired, probably having heard that Badajoz had surrendered. The leading elements of the allied army were also approaching Villa Velha. The bridge was back in place by the 15 April 1812 and Burgoyne was back at headquarters, noting briefly that he was now, again, the senior engineer with Wellington's army.

Fletcher had been wounded on 19 March 1812 and commanded the engineers from his bed through the remainder of the siege of Badajoz. Wellington ordered

33 Wrottesley, *Burgoyne*, p.182.

Fletcher to remain at Badajoz to carry out the repairs. There were some suggestions that Fletcher was left there as a sign of Wellington's displeasure over the handling of the siege, but it is more likely that he was left there to recover from his injuries and also to make sure the critical fortress was repaired as quickly and effectively as possible. From the correspondence, it was clear that Fletcher was still in charge, as Wellington continued to write to him on engineering matters. It would make no sense for Wellington to leave Fletcher at Badajoz as a punishment and then have to suffer the inconvenience of having to write to him every time a decision was required. The northern fortress of Ciudad Rodrigo had been handed over to the Spanish to repair and Wellington was already getting negative reports on the progress. Rather than have more of the same, Wellington needed someone he could trust at Badajoz: his future strategy depended on him retaining possession of these border fortresses, they could not be risked again.

Having been close to Wellington on numerous occasions over the last two years, Burgoyne was clearly forming an opinion of how Wellington operated. Whilst his comments tend to be critical, his understanding of how Wellington worked probably helped him develop a good working relationship with him. Writing to Squire, he noted that Lecor, the commandant at Villa Velha, had been chastised by Wellington for taking the initiative to move the sick and wounded from Castelo Branco as the French advanced, without orders to do so.[34] Burgoyne agreed that Lecor had made the right decision, as the allied sick would have been captured on 11 April when the French entered Castelo Branco. This was the sort of behaviour by Wellington which meant that none of his subordinates would make an independent decision.

This is possibly why Wellington respected Burgoyne, and also Alexander Dickson. They were willing to make decisions when other senior officers were not. There was always the risk of incurring Wellington's wrath if they got it wrong, but it did not stop them doing what they believed was right. The willingness of these two officers to think independently may be the nature of Ordnance officers who were trained to rely on their own judgement, because, often, there would be no-one else there to take responsibility for decisions. The next six months would see Burgoyne's decision-making capabilities tested to the full.

34 REM 4601-72, Burgoyne to Squire, Niza, 18 April 1812.

11

1812 – Peninsular Command, Salamanca

Wellington's army continued a slow march north from Villa Velha to the country around Ciudad Rodrigo and Almeida. This was to ensure that the French made no further attempts on the fortresses until both places were fully supplied and capable of a lengthy resistance.

There now followed a period of quiet for the army of several weeks, whilst Wellington planed his advance into Spain. However, Burgoyne had no free time. The issue of supplies for the army and for the northern fortresses became important again and Burgoyne was sent to examine the work done by his fellow engineers to improve the navigability of the River Douro up to the border.[1] Although the Douro had been pronounced navigable up to Barca d'Alva in late 1811, Wellington had received complaints that this was not true. As he intended to victual both the fortresses and his army using the Douro, the navigability of the river became critical to his strategy. On 23 May 1812, Wellington ordered Burgoyne to investigate the different views.[2]

Burgoyne wrote back within two days, with an initial report based on speaking to locals and confirmed the river was navigable between São João da Pesqueira and the border at Barca d'Alva, except when there had been heavy rains.[3] To confirm this opinion, he then travelled the length of the Douro from Peso da Régua to Barca d'Alva by boat, a journey that took 12 days, recording full details of the journey.[4]

This survey took three weeks, with Burgoyne arriving back at headquarters on 15 June 1812, just as the army approached Salamanca. With hindsight, one wonders whether Wellington had other motives for asking for another detailed survey of the Douro up to the border. We will come back to this question.

1 Burgoyne's report, REM 4601-74, 13 June 1812.

2 Wrottesley, *Burgoyne*, p.190.

3 REM 4201-68, Journal, Torre de Moncorvo, 25 May 1812. Typical journey time 5-10 days upriver; one day back. Oxen and sails were required to move boats upriver. The work previously done by the engineers was to clear obstructions in the river and repair tow paths.

4 REM 4201-68, Journal, 30 May-12 June 1812.

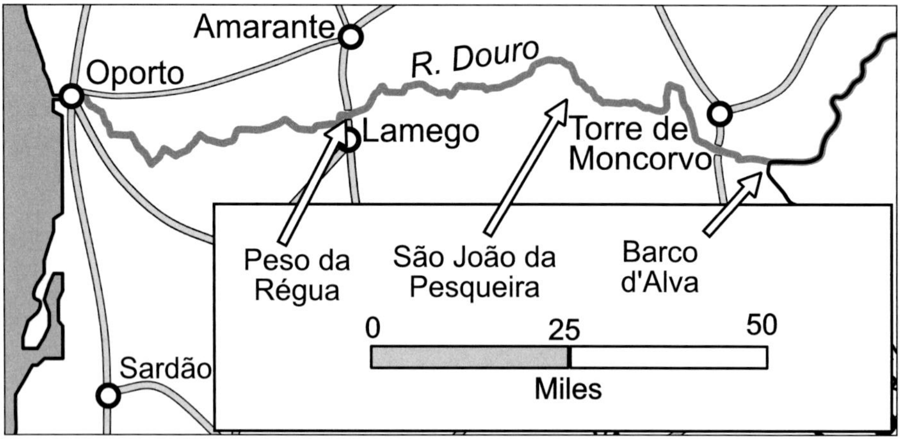

Navigation of river Douro.

Although Salamanca was not a walled city that could be properly defended, the French had prepared a number of strong buildings to resist any attack. Wellington was aware this work was underway, but, like Masséna with the Lines of Torres Vedras in 1810, he underestimated the challenge he would face. This would be Burgoyne's first command under Wellington's critical eye and the resources were very limited. The battering train was made up of only four 18-pounder cannon and six 24-pounder iron howitzers.

Dickson had previously proposed to Wellington that a field brigade should be formed of six 24-pounder iron howitzers, which he described as 'a formidable battery in the field'.[5] Under normal use they could fire all the ammunition used by a 5.5-inch howitzer but could also fire 24-pounder roundshot. Although having neither the power or accuracy of a true 24-pounder cannon, they would, as Dickson said, be formidable in the field against troops or minor fortifications. A 24-pounder howitzer was about the same weight as a 9-pounder cannon and would make a powerful reserve artillery brigade. Dickson took this brigade on Hill's attack on the French held bridge at Almaraz on 19 May 1812. Dickson then returned to Merida and on 28 May was ordered to immediately move the howitzer brigade to the Tagus at Alcantara, where the Royal Staff Corps under Sturgeon were repairing the fallen arch in the Roman bridge.[6] It is not clear whether Wellington's order for the brigade to advance was for it to join the field army or be part of a small battering train. Wellington used it for both in the coming weeks.

The other part of the battering train was four 18-pounder cannon. These were collected by Lieutenant Colonel John May RA from Almeida and were most likely

5 Leslie (ed.), *Dickson Manuscripts*, Vol.IV, p.635.
6 Leslie (ed.), *Dickson Manuscripts*, Vol.IV, p.653.

the four new cannon that had been brought up for the siege of Ciudad Rodrigo earlier in 1812.

Wellington did not appreciate the scale of the defences until he saw them. Even had he known, the equipment selected was all that could be easily moved with the army. Larger guns were available, but a heavy siege train could not possibly keep up with an advancing (or retreating) army and would have been at serious risk of being lost. When Wellington sent for more ammunition from Almeida, he could have ordered up more guns; he did not.

The suggestion by Burgoyne and others that poor information was why they took little siege artillery is wrong. Burgoyne commented: 'Our information, on commencing the march, having been only to the extent that some convents had been fortified ... and the means conducted with the army were very trifling'.[7] May also commented in a similar manner:

> From all the reports received they were said to be by no means strong and ill calculated to stand an assault. The reports however, turned out to be completely false and their strength far exceeded the means in ordnance and ammunition we had brought forward with us for their reduction.[8]

The likelihood was that Wellington reasonably assumed that the French would not leave significant troops in Salamanca when they withdrew. They could not possibly hold out long; were very unlikely to be relieved and would not impact at all on Wellington's movements. So, the French were just throwing troops away.

Oman was clear that the decision to bring forward such a small battering train was a mistake, commenting, 'whether Wellington himself or his artillery and engineer advisors were primarily responsible was not clear'.[9] He then adds in a footnote that Dickson was not there, so he could not be responsible. Neither were the senior engineers Fletcher or Burgoyne. Lipscombe suggests that the artillery commander, Colonel Framingham, was to blame,[10] but it would seem that the decision to take a small siege train was made by Wellington, who later acknowledged his error, writing 'I was mistaken in my estimate of the extent of the means which would be necessary to subdue these forts; and I was obliged to send to the rear for a fresh supply of ammunition. This necessity occasioned a delay of six days'.[11]

Whilst it is at least understandable that Wellington did not expect to need a siege train at Salamanca, it is less understandable that he then took a smaller siege train to Burgos, with disastrous results.

7 Wrottesley, *Burgoyne*, pp.191-2.
8 Leslie (ed.), *Dickson Manuscripts*, Vol.IV, p.669, quoting May.
9 Oman, *History*, Vol.V, p.362.
10 Nick Lipscombe, *Wellington's Guns* (Oxford: Osprey, 2013), p.231.
11 Gurwood (ed.), *Despatches*, Wellington to Liverpool, Fuente la Peña, 30 June 1812.

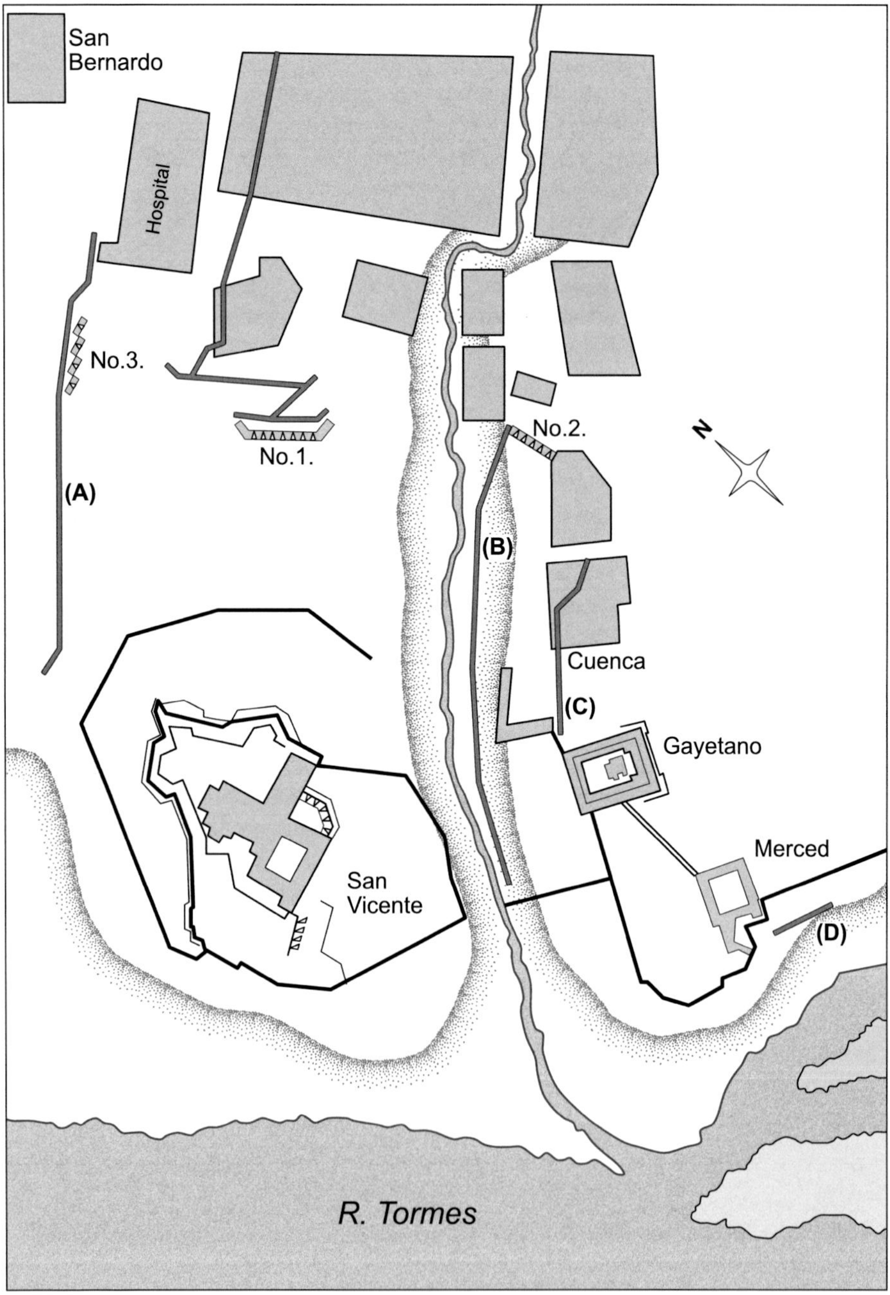

Plan of Salamanca forts.

Wellington did not appear to have a clear plan of operation for the rest of 1812. Much depended on the movements of the French and what opportunities were presented. Taking a large siege train into central Spain would have been a great risk if the French concentrated against him and its loss would be quite possible. Having said that, what Wellington did was the worst option: he took too little to be effective and too much to be moved easily.

At Salamanca, Burgoyne found three strong forts, which had been converted from convents. The ground in front of them had been cleared of all buildings to give the defenders a clear field of fire. The French had effectively flattened the university district of Salamanca to create these three strongpoints. Wellington reported that 13 of 25 convents and 22 of 25 colleges had been levelled.[12] Much of the wood and stone had been re-used to strengthen the walls, roofs and loop-hole the windows but the whole area was a wasteland of ruined buildings, some of which were burning when the allied army arrived.

The strongest of the forts, San Vicente, had been cleverly created from the convent and included all the features of a fort. It had loopholed walls, a ditch with scarp and counterscarp, and an exterior glacis. At points, batteries had been formed with embrasures to protect the defending guns and gunners. Between San Vicente and the other smaller forts, Gayetano and Merced, there was a steep sided gully through which the Rio Tanner ran. The forts were close enough together to provide supporting fire. These forts had been placed there to provide secure areas for stores and to protect the main bridge and fords near the city.

The forts were far too strong to be escaladed and required siege guns to destroy the walls. Unfortunately, as mentioned above, the heavy siege guns used at Ciudad Rodrigo and Badajoz were not available and the total resources were four 18-pounder cannon and (eventually) six 24-pounder iron howitzers with limited amounts of ammunition for both. The 24-pounder howitzer was not a siege weapon: it was a poor choice, except when there was no alternative.

As Dickson did not arrive with his brigade of six 24-pounder howitzers until 20 June, iron howitzers were borrowed from the field brigades.[13] There is some confusion about the number of howitzers that were borrowed. Jones, said that three howitzers were borrowed, but his text on the following pages mentions four.[14] His wording appears to suggest that they came from a single field brigade, but there was no such artillery brigade present. Oman also stated that three howitzers were borrowed but does not state his source. Burgoyne and Dickson said four iron

12 Gurwood (ed.), *Despatches*, Wellington to Liverpool, Salamanca, 18 June 1812.

13 There were six iron and two brass howitzers in the eight artillery brigades with the army. It is possible that Wellington would have removed the howitzers from all units other than those attached to the Light Division and the cavalry. This would equal four iron and two brass howitzers. See Lipscombe, *Wellington's Guns*, p.230.

14 Jones, *Sieges*, Vol.I, p.250, 252 and 254.

howitzers were borrowed.[15] Later two field pieces and two brass howitzers were also used to annoy the defenders.

There were 36 French guns in the forts at Salamanca against at most, 14 allied guns. For the third siege in a row, Wellington's attacking force was seriously out-gunned and his counter-battery capability was limited. His troops would have been aware of the lack of guns at these sieges. Engineer resources were also insufficient with only three officers: Burgoyne and Lieutenants Reid and Pitts. There were five assistant engineers to help, but only two had previous experience at sieges.[16] Clearly there was very limited expertise available. Assuming that the engineers worked in three eight-hour shifts, there was never more than three on duty.

To compound Burgoyne's problems, the troops left to carry out the siege work, the 6th Division, had no experience and this led to problems.

Wellington and Burgoyne examined the French defences from a number of high points around the city, including the cathedral. The decision was made to focus on the main fort, the convent of San Vicente, and battery No.1 was started on the night of 17 June 1812 by a working party of 400 men. The batteries were to be constructed using the rubble of the buildings that had been destroyed as digging out batteries in the normal manner was impossible. Lieutenant Thomas Pitts RE complained about the difficulties they faced: flour sacks were used in the absence of sand bags, 'scarce moveable', and beds from the hospital were used for the bottom of the parapets. Burgoyne was also given a working party to make fascines.[17] The engineers and assistant engineers would spend much of the next ten days trying to keep these makeshift batteries in place.

Burgoyne complained that it was with great difficulty that the inexperienced soldiers could be kept working under fire 'the Portuguese in particular, absolutely went on their hands and knees and dragged their baskets along the ground'.[18] The unintended consequence of this behaviour was that the engineer officers became more exposed to the enemy fire through leading by example and standing up when many around them would not. The short, moonlit nights did not help either.

15 See Oman, *History*, p.362; REM 4601-72, Burgoyne's Journal of siege, 17 June; REM 4201-68, Journal, 17 June 1812; Leslie (ed.), *Dickson Manuscripts*, Vol.IV, p.668. Also, Gurwood (ed.), *Despatches*, Wellington to Liverpool, 18 June 1812, clearly states that eight pieces of cannon were used i.e. four 18-pounders and four 24-pounder howitzers.

16 Jones, *Sieges*, Vol.I, 249, ignores the contribution of the Assistant Engineers which is unfair, particularly to Major Alexander Thompson, 74th Foot. and Lieutenant William Barney, Chasseurs Britanniques, who both served in this role at the sieges of Ciudad Rodrigo, Badajoz, and Burgos.

17 Whitworth Porter, *History of the Corps of Royal Engineers* (Chatham: Institution of Royal Engineers, 1977), Vol.I, p.314.

18 Wrottesley, *Burgoyne*, p.193.

An attempt was also made, on the night of 17 June, to blow in the counterscarp opposite the convent of San Vicente, but the alert guard and their dog frustrated the attempt.[19]

By the end of the first night's work, the battery was 'not quite to the height of a *genouillere* [kneepad]'.[20] Because there was insufficient cover, no work could be done to improve the battery during daylight hours on the 18 June. Instead, two 6-pounder cannon were lifted on to the roof of the hospital of San Bernardo and two brass howitzers, also from the field artillery brigades, were placed on a hill to the right of San Bernardo. The intention of both was to try and suppress the fire from the French held convents, not to attack the defences.

Battery No.1, was completed on the night of 18/19 June and four 18-pounder cannon and three 24-pounder iron howitzers were installed. Although Burgoyne stated that there were two 24-pounder iron howitzers in battery No.1, and two in battery No.2,[21] other sources state that there were originally three howitzers in battery No.1 and that one was moved to Battery No.2 on the afternoon of 19 June.[22] Two further works were started, near the convents of Cuenca, battery No.2 for two guns and, on a hill near San Bernardo for two brass howitzers.

The guns opened fire around 6:00 a.m. on the morning of 19 June 1812. By 10:00 a.m., the wall of the convent of San Vicente had collapsed. However, the base of the wall could not be seen from battery No.1 and fire continued from two 24-pounder howitzers in battery No.2. During the day, one of the howitzers was damaged and there were significant casualties amongst the gunners in battery No.2, as No.1 had stopped firing and the defenders could concentrate their fire on No.2.

One of the issues with using these howitzers in batteries, was that the openings for the guns had to be much wider due to the shortness of the barrel. The barrel was meant to protrude past the embrasure so that the blast did not damage the embrasure. This could not be achieved with a howitzer, so the opening had to be much wider. The consequence was that the artillerymen operating the guns were more exposed to enemy fire.

Overnight, battery No.2, was extended to take three more guns[23] and two 18-pounder cannon were moved from battery No.1. The howitzers alone in battery

19 This party was led by Lieutenant William Reid RE who after a long career in the engineers and colonial government became the Chairman of the Executive Committee of the Great Exhibition committee in 1851.

20 Wrottesley, *Burgoyne*, p.192.

21 REM 4601-72, Burgoyne, Journal of siege, 18 June 1812; REM 4201-68, Journal, 19 June 1812.

22 Jones, *Sieges*, Vol.I, p.252, Leslie (ed.), *Dickson Manuscripts*, Vol.IV, p.668.

23 Jones, *Sieges*, Vol.I, pp.253-4 says it was extended for three additional guns and was fitted with two 18-pounder and three 24-pounders. Leslie (ed.), *Dickson Manuscripts*, Vol.IV, p.668, says two 24-pounders were used. Burgoyne, Journal of Siege, 20 June, infers that there was only one 24-pounder. That is unlikely as they had five available (one had been damaged) and there was more 24-pounder roundshot available than there was 18-pounder. The account given here therefore follows Jones.

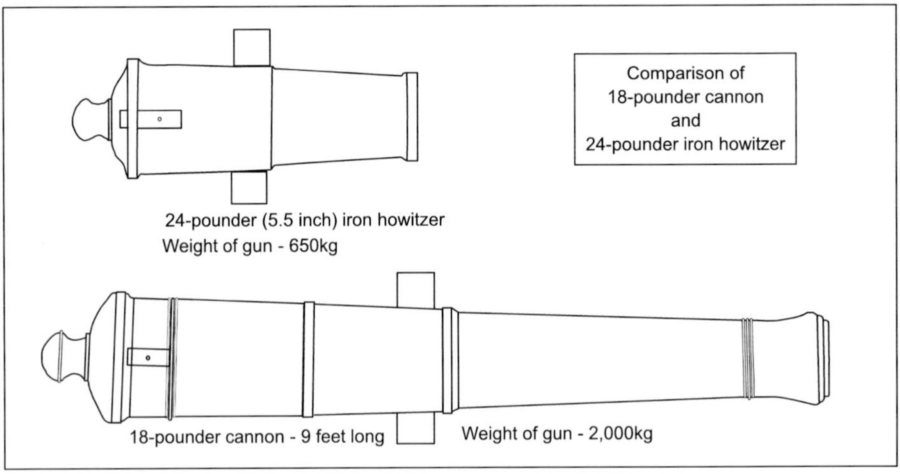

Comparison of 24-pounder howitzer and 18-pounder cannon.

No.2 had proved ineffective in damaging the wall the previous day. Dickson arrived on 20 June 1812 with his brigade of 24-pounder iron howitzers and the four borrowed from the field brigades were immediately replaced.[24] The other two howitzers were placed in battery No.2, making three in total (the damaged howitzer having been removed).

Battery No.2. opened around noon and quickly had an impact on the lower part of the wall. Later in the afternoon a substantial part collapsed, burying several of the defenders. About 140 each of the 18 and 24-pounder roundshot were fired during the day leaving only sixty 18-pounder and one-hundred-and-sixty 24-pounder roundshot.[25] A review of the breached defences concluded that an assault was not possible.[26]

Marmont chose this day to advance on the allied positions in front of Salamanca. Wellington had drawn up his troops on the heights of San Cristóbal and waited for a French attack. Many British officers could not understand why Wellington did not attack as he had a superiority in infantry and in cavalry. Burgoyne commented:

> The enemy's force was inferior to ours both in infantry and cavalry and the reason we did not attack them was supposed to be because we were not masters of the bridge of Salamanca, which the enemy's forts commanded; the country also, although it appears quite open, has in many parts, deep

24 Jones, *Sieges*, Vol.I, p.254.
25 Jones, *Sieges*, Vol.I, p.255.
26 REM 4201-68, Journal, 20 June 1812.

> water [ruts?] in different directions that would cause serious obstacles to an attacking body.[27]

On 21 June, for their safety, the 18-pounders were removed and sent to the rear and one brigade of the 6th Division and Dickson's six iron howitzers were moved up to join the main field army.[28] There was some skirmishing between the armies on 21 June, but the following day Marmont retired, having decided not to risk an attack on Wellington in a place of his choosing. The infantry brigade of the 6th Division which had been called up from the city and Dickson's Brigade both returned to Salamanca on the morning of 23 June.

Having concluded that there was not enough artillery to destroy San Vicente, an attempt was now made to breach the gorge (rear) of Fort Gayetano, since 'getting possession of that redoubt we might be enabled to make a lodgement in the breaches of San Vicente from which we might mine or set the convent on fire'.[29] Battery No.3 was started for this purpose near the convent of San Bernardo on the night of 22 June.

Due to the severe shortage of ammunition, only one 18-pounder and three 24-pounder howitzers were run into the battery on the morning of 23 June and opened fire at 11:00 a.m. The distance was 450 yards and the shot would be striking the defences at an oblique angle. As Jones described, the 24-pounder howitzers 'were defective in both force and precision' the roundshot glancing off the walls. A 24-pounder howitzer firing roundshot had the equivalent striking power of a 9-pounder cannon and as Jones commented later was little more than a waste of ammunition.[30] By 2:00 p.m., all the ammunition had been used without any significant damage to the fort. The decision was still made to assault the Gayetano and Merced forts that night.

All these actions smack of desperation to get the siege finished and the assault on the night of 23 June was throwing men at the problem of having insufficient artillery to break down the walls. Marmont had just withdrawn from the immediate vicinity of Salamanca but Wellington knew he would be back, possibly with a larger force. One officer present commented that as Wellington wanted access to the bridge, 'we are to have the forts at any cost, tonight'.[31]

Most accounts tell of the troops under Major General Barnard Bowes moving forward under overwhelming fire from the defenders and being unable to place more than two of the twenty ladders provided. Oman wrote:

27 REM 4601-72, Burgoyne Journal of Siege, 21 June 1812, written in the draft version only and subsequently crossed out.

28 Oman, *History*, Vol.V, p.368, and Jones, *Sieges*, Vol.I, p.256.

29 REM 4201-68, Journal, 22 June 1812.

30 Jones, *Sieges*, Vol.I, p.473.

31 Gareth Glover (ed.), *Wellington's Lieutenant, Napoleon's Gaoler* (Barnsley: Pen & Sword, 2005), p.130.

> [T]he casualties from the first moment were very heavy, many men never got near their objective and only two ladders out of twenty were planted against the fort. No-one tried to ascend them, the project obviously being useless.[32]

The engineers tell a different story. Burgoyne, who would have been responsible for the plan of the assault, described the attack:

> Lieutenant Reid, Royal Engineers, conducted the party to the Gayetano redoubt and got two ladders placed against the gorge, but there not being above 20 or 30 men there and the other ladders left on the way, nothing could be done. The party for storming the redoubt of Merced returned with an account that their ladders broke, but as the escarp, counterscarp and gorge of the place were not more than 15 and 18 feet high, they must have lost their way and gone elsewhere, though it was full moon and they did not start above 150 yards from the works. In fact, the men did not go about the business with any confidence, and probably from this division having been little employed, saw too much of the difficulties.[33]

The soldiers felt that they were being asked to carry out an impossible task and their relative inexperience in sieges would not have helped their confidence. One officer involved commented 'the result was precisely such as most of the officers anticipated, a failure attended with severe loss of life'.[34] One wonders whether this was a comment about the competence of the divisional commander or the lack of resources.[35]

The storming party was led forward by Reid. His account of the assault was not published until 1837.[36] He reported that he spent two days prior to the assault working out the best route to approach the gorge of the Gayetano fort. His proposal was to approach down the valley between the forts. Most of the way the troops would have cover from the ruined houses and would have been sheltered from the fire of the forts. He prepared the 20 ladders, 'which would have covered the whole extent of the rear wall to be attacked; and as … these ladders should be planted, under the protection of a firing party in the surrounding houses'. He continued, had the assault been executed as planned 'there is no doubt it would have been successful'.[37]

32 Oman, *History*, Vol.V, p.371.
33 REM 4201-68, Journal, 23 June 1812.
34 See Oman, *History*, Vol.V, p.371.
35 See Glover, *Wellington's Lieutenant*, where Bingham makes many criticisms of his commander.
36 Papers on Subjects Connected with the Duties of the Corps of Royal Engineers, Vol.I (London, Royal Engineers, 1837), pp.6-8.
37 RE Papers, 1837, Vol.I, p.6.

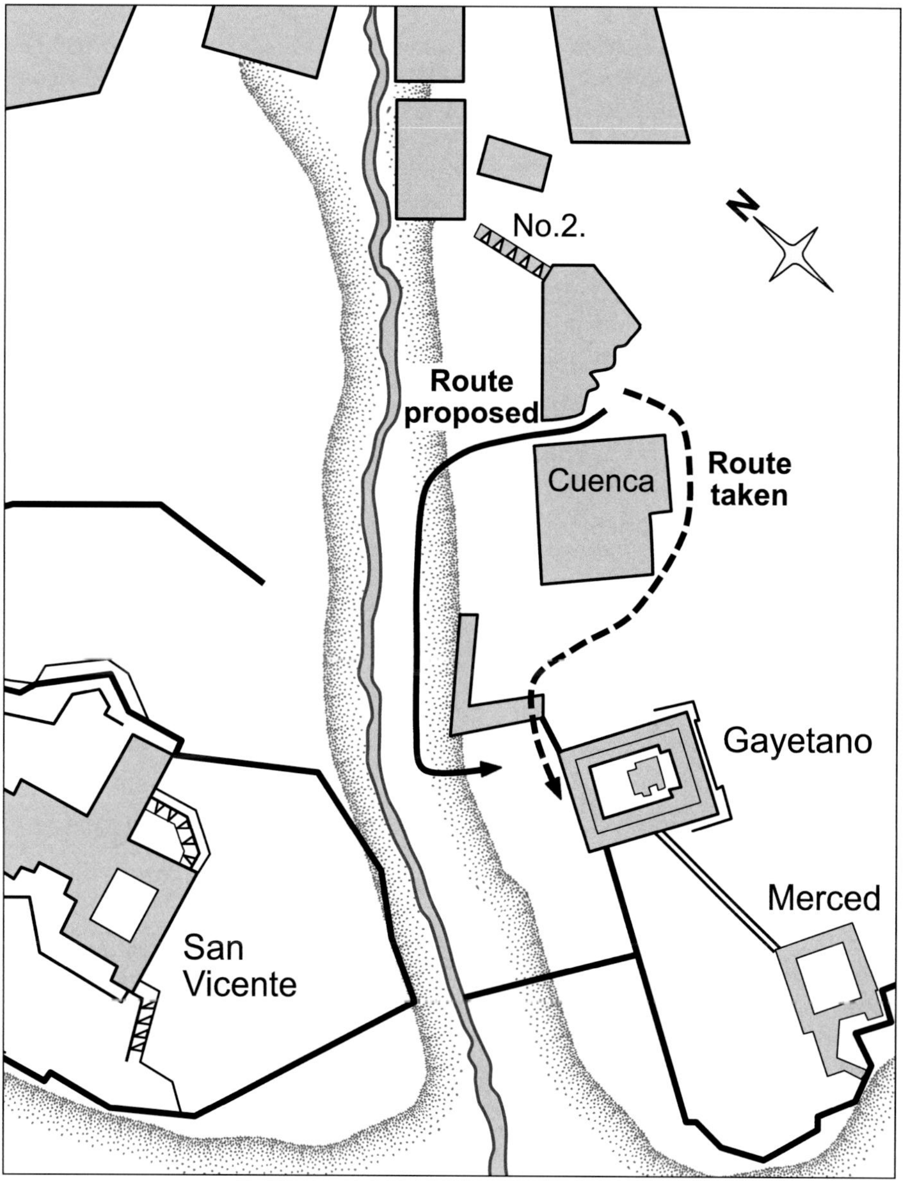

Plan of assault of Salamanca forts.

Reid described his proposals being overruled by Major General Bowes who ordered only four of the 20 ladders to be used. Bowes then changed the direction of attack so that the troops advanced across the glacis and then approached the gorge through narrow entrances in the ruined buildings, during which time they were exposed to fire from the defenders. The moonlight night also made for good visibility. Only two ladders were brought forward, the troops carrying the other ladders being wounded.

> Not ten men of the storming party followed. One of the door-ways through which they had to file, man by man was within twenty yards of the direct fire of the enemy's parapet … the officers throughout had made the most gallant exertions to bring their men forward … it was agreed to re-form their men; and after placing an officer on each side of the door-way, to force the men through it. The whole were accordingly forced through; but instead of keeping to their left and going up to the wall and the two ladders raised against it, they turned to the right and fled by the streets in the valley.[38]

Reid's view was supported by Lieutenant Colonel George Bingham who was present at the siege:

> Our storm … failed; partly from mismanagement and partly I think from not employing a sufficient number of people … the false attack of the large work (San Vicente) did not take place till the other attacks had failed. The ladders … came to pieces in the men's hands as they were carrying them. General Bowes … chose to neglect the advice of the engineer and would take the troops straight across the glacis, when by a detour he might have got within fifty yards of the place, or less, under cover.[39]

Ignoring the advice of the engineers, not using enough troops in the assault and the lack of enthusiasm of the soldiers for siege work would become recurring themes for Burgoyne. Major General Bowes, six officers, and 120 soldiers were killed or wounded in this failed attempt.

The siege stuttered to a halt and it was three days before more ammunition arrived. In the meantime, Burgoyne was ordered to dig a communication trench (A) from battery No.3 towards San Vicente to allow the attackers to fire muskets at the French artillery in the fort.[40] Early on the morning of 25 June, Wellington asked Burgoyne, Dickson, and May to report to him as he 'was anxious to have

38 RE Papers, 1837, Vol.I, p.8.

39 Glover, *Wellington's Lieutenant*, p.131.

40 See plan of Salamanca forts.

a little conversation'. He knew the extra ammunition would arrive the next day and would want to agree the course of action with the senior ordnance officers.[41] Wellington still wanted the forts taken quickly. On the night of the 25/26 June, Burgoyne started a new trench in the valley between San Vicente and the other two forts (B). The intention was to place some troops armed with muskets near the gorge of Gayetano. The French concentrated fire on these exposed troops and there were many casualties. The following night, the trench was extended, effectively cutting off San Vicente from the forts on the other side of the ravine. The same night, (26/27 June), Burgoyne commenced two other trenches. The first was from the college of Cuenca towards the scarp of Gayetano with the aim of being able to mine and blow in the scarp (C). The second was along the steep slope near the river towards the Merced fort with the intention of mining under the walls (D). The miners would have been volunteers from the Line regiments. Burgoyne described the work as follows:

> In the course of the night, likewise we opened a passage through a house on the side of the river within 20 yards of the cliff on which the redoubt Merced was situated; a hollow just under the work and large enough to hold two or three men was favourable for commencing a mine and the cliff was of a sandy stone, very easy to work in.[42]

The miners started work on the morning of 27 June 1812 and were given orders:

> [T]o gain 24 feet horizontal distance and 12 in height which according to our observations, we calculated would leave a line of least resistance above and in the redoubt of about 12 feet; Our very near fire of musketry from the houses on this side prevented the enemy looking over the works and the miners were able to communicate to and from the opening without cover ... In a few hours they had worked six feet in.[43]

All this work on trenches to approach the defences appear to suggest that there was little confidence in the ability of the artillery to destroy the walls. If the walls could not be breached with the next delivery of ammunition, the troops would have to carry them the hard way.

It was probable that at the meeting between Wellington and the ordnance officers on 25 June, it was decided to try setting the forts on fire with red-hot shot.

41 Gurwood (ed.), *Despatches*, Wellington to Clinton, Heights behind Aldea Lengua, 6:00 a.m., 25 June 1812 and Wellington to Liverpool, Salamanca, 25 June 1812.

42 REM 4601-72, Burgoyne Journal of siege, 26 June 1812.

43 REM 4601-72, Burgoyne Journal of siege, 27 June 1812.

It also appears that it was decided to assault the forts on 27 June even though the ammunition had not arrived, and any consequent damage was unknown.

In a letter written in the early afternoon of 26 June 1812 to Major General Clinton, Wellington laid out his plans for the following day.[44] The letter started, confusingly, 'I conclude you have stopped the firing for this day'. This was written at the time when the guns were being run back in to the batteries, having received the new ammunition in the morning. The batteries had re-opened fire around 3:00 p.m.; four 18-pounders in battery No.3 to breach the gorge of the Gayetano and four 24-pounder howitzers in battery No.2 to fire red-hot shot at San Vicente. They continued without break until the surrender the following day.[45] Wellington's letter continued, ordering the repair of the batteries, the continuation of the approach trenches, including the one that would allow Gayetano to be mined, to attack San Vicente with red-hot shot and the placing of further guns and muskets to supress the defenders fire during the assault.

By the morning of the 27 June 1812, both San Vicente and Gayetano were on fire and both offered to surrender after a delay to consult with their superiors. Wellington was ready to storm the forts and rejected these offers, demanding immediate surrender: when this did not happen the siege guns reopened. The French quickly surrendered when the assaults were started. Reid noted that the second assault on Gayetano was done according to his previous recommendation and worked well.[46] It had taken 10 days to take three insignificant forts with a total loss of 300 killed and wounded.

Whilst this attack was insignificant compared with the major sieges, it still had many of the same issues; a lack of resources, few trained engineers or sappers, too few guns and working against time. The manoeuvring around Salamanca and the possibility that Wellington could be forced back, made it necessary to take the forts quickly and this led to additional loss of lives. If there was no immediate threat, they could have been forced to surrender through a close blockade with fewer casualties. It is not clear why Wellington was cutting corners to take Salamanca. If he believed he needed to take it quickly before the French could concentrate, then it was every bit as likely that he could not have held it if they did concentrate. A more likely possibility is that Wellington was unwilling to risk a battle in front of Salamanca whilst the French still held the city's bridge. In the event of a defeat, his retreat would have been much more difficult and the loss of troops and equipment higher.

44 Gurwood (ed.), *Despatches*, Wellington to Clinton, Cabrerizos, 2:00 p.m., 26 June 1812.

45 There is some confusion again about the number of howitzers used in battery No.2 to fire red-hot shot. Burgoyne and Wellington say two, Dickson says three, Jones and Bingham say four. There were four embrasures in battery No.2 and Wellington wanted the convent of San Vicente on fire when it was assaulted the next day. There seems to be no good reason why four howitzers would not be used.

46 RE Papers, 1837, Vol.I, p.8.

During the planning and conduct of the siege, Wellington appeared to keep control of the detail with artillery and engineer officers responding to his directions. Neither Burgoyne nor Dickson give any indication that they had much input into the decision making. Burgoyne's journal is written like he was an observer of the events rather than someone directly involved. Being ordered to other tasks in the weeks leading up to the siege meant he was not involved in the preparations. There does not appear to be any critique of the siege, nor any letters on the subject between engineer officers. This is unusual.[47]

A few weeks later Burgoyne wrote to Pasley, who was now responsible for training sappers and junior engineer officers at the recently formed School of Military Engineering at Chatham:

> I am extremely anxious to know what you are doing and on what footing your new establishment is, for it's you we now all look up [to] for the reform [of the engineers] and new modelling we long called out for.
>
> There is a story current in this army that Lord Wellington wrote to Sir Thomas Graham on the fall of Badajoz, that he hoped to God, such another siege would never be required, that the loss was horrible, not being general as in an action in the field, but necessarily of the best people in the army and that he could attribute it to nothing but the mistaken policy of having so inefficient an Engineer establishment. Whether he said it or not, it is [a] very good cause [to put] your establishment on a proper scale; and have the means of trying experiments in the different branches of field engineering

Burgoyne was one of a number of officers who were regularly writing to Pasley, offering information and suggestions on how to set-up the new training environment. He continued:

> The way in which it strikes me... would be to subdivide the subjects as much as possible and then make each a separate treatise and to be published as soon as completed. From those which treated the subjects most fully, memoranda or general deductions might be taken and printed on one octavo sheet ... which being collected as they came out, might be made up into the memorandum book of the officer. A great assistance would be gained by this mode, that many who would not read a great book, would be very glad to read and even study a periodical work.

He then reflected on his recent experiences:

47 REM 4601-72 contains Burgoyne's report, marked private. Also, TNA WO55/959 includes a copy of Burgoyne's report dated 27 June 1812.

> I have lately had occasion to reflect on [engineering stores], by being senior officer for some months during which has occurred a little siege and suffering from our miserable depot. It consists for this army of 50,000 men (General Hill with his 20,000 men out of the question, and indeed they have nothing, not a single pick axe or shovel) ; the Engineer Depot for this grand army, I say, consists of the tools on 35 mules; that 400 entrenching tools and a few carpenters tools consisting of one hand saw and other articles in proportion … There is only a single subaltern of engineers (another who is attached to Don Carlos was present and we got hold of him by accident) and nine Royal Military Artificers, most of them of a bad class and none who have ever seen anything that could be of service and these are the means we have for besieging excellent forts and may perhaps be called upon to entrench the army.[48]

What was happening at this time, for the first time, was a direct communication from officers in the field sharing their practical experiences with someone who had the opportunity of altering training and materials quickly enough to have an impact on the current conflict. Burgoyne made a further request to Pasley:

> Another point worth your attention if you have time, is the construction of scaling ladders. Those of the [common?] joint you have already improved, but it is not generally known and has never yet been adopted, but what is much wanted, is, the best wood and what dimensions for common ladders of different lengths to be as strong and light as possible. Whether in ladders above 20 feet the great weight can be remedied and strength gained by a support in the centre.[49]

This request sound like a direct response to the issues with scaling ladders at Badajoz and the Salamanca forts. Some of Burgoyne's suggestions were a bit more radical. He noted that a number of French sappers had deserted and wondered if they could be used to share their knowledge at the school.

The attack on the forts at Salamanca was Burgoyne's first independent command in the Peninsula. The operation presented several challenges to Burgoyne. The defences were stronger than expected; there was too little artillery and too few engineer resources; the besieging troops were inexperienced, and time was limited due to the threats from the French forces.

Having taken the forts, the next task was to complete the destruction of them. Burgoyne noted on 29 June 1812 that he had been ordered to destroy the French defences in the city and he was occupied on this task for the next few days. This

48 REM 4601-74, f.46, not dated.

49 REM 4601-74, f.46, not dated.

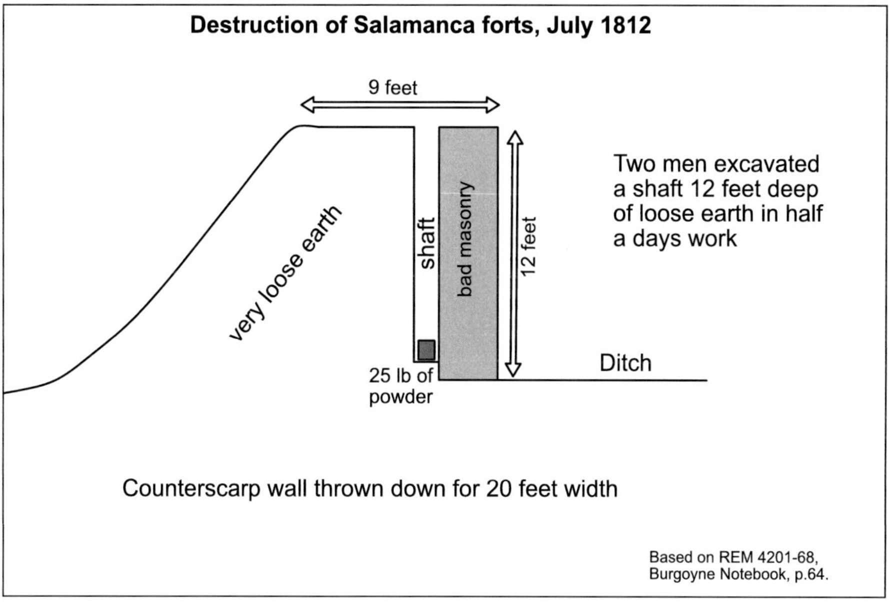

Sketch of destruction of counterscarp of San Vicente.

again questions why Wellington rushed to take the forts. Access to the main bridges across the Tormes would be convenient but it did not appear to be a major issue at this time of the year. Destroying the defences meant he had no intention of trying to hold the city if the French concentrated against him. It did of course mean that if Salamanca was lost, the French would not have ready-made defences and the cost of rebuilding the defences would probably be prohibitive.

On 30 June 1812, Burgoyne:

> Commenced mining part of the counterscarp of San Vicente; wall twelve feet high and three feet thick of bad masonry backed with loose earth. Sunk shafts close to the back of the wall to the level of the bottom of the ditch and loaded them with 20 pounds of powder, which destroyed the walls for about 15 feet [in length]. The miners can sink one of these shafts of twelve feet deep in six hours.[50]

On 3 July 1812, Burgoyne also commented on the work to destroy the old city wall and on 5 July 1812, he summarised the destruction of the forts as follows:

50 REM 4201-68, Journal, 30 June 1812.

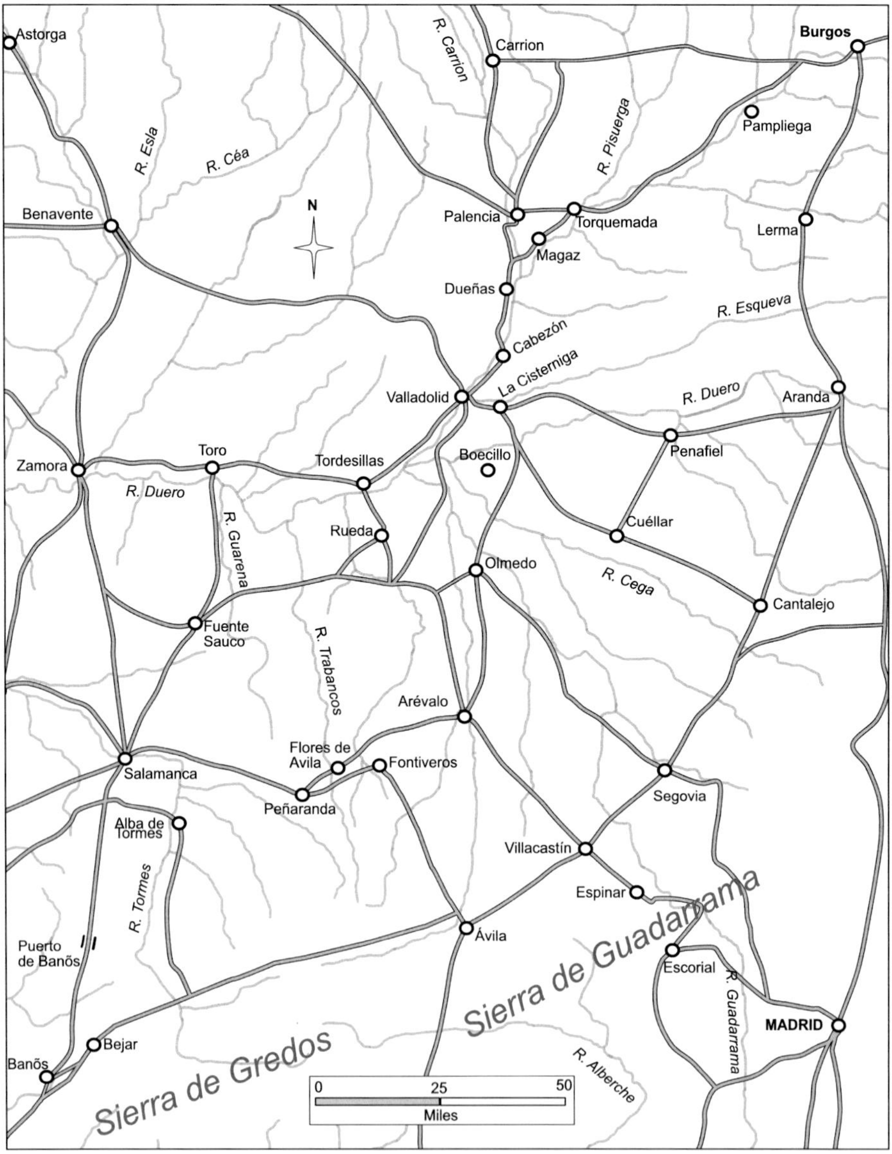

Map of Salamanca to Burgos.

> [I]n San Vicente, the whole front opposite the hospital blown down, escarp and counterscarp as well as the bastion covering the gate on the left, and large breaches in other parts of the fort; the counterscarp, all along from the above mentioned bastion towards the river destroyed. The guns and stores all removed and most of the timber.
>
> The convent of San Vicente burnt down and only the shell of the walls remaining. Large breaches are made in Gayetano and Merced redoubts and the destruction of the whole might be easily now completed by the Spaniards.[51]

Burgoyne now travelled north and joined headquarters at Rueda on 7 July 1812. Having reported to Wellington, he was then ordered to destroy more of the defences at Salamanca and Reid was sent back to complete this work. Even this early in the campaign there were comments being made about Wellington's cautious approach. Burgoyne noted, 'There have been several opportunities of attacking the enemy with superior force, but from their not being taken, Lord Wellington appears to conceive a probability of encompassing his ends without fighting'.[52]

The next two weeks were taken up with both armies manoeuvring to seek an advantage. Burgoyne remained with headquarters during this period. The movements eventually led to the battle of Salamanca on 22 July 1812 when Wellington crushed the French army under Marmont. Had this victory not occurred, it is possible that Wellington could have been forced to retire from Salamanca as his forces could not march as quickly as the French and were always vulnerable to being outflanked and cut off from their supply line.

The Battle of Salamanca

Although Burgoyne does not specifically say, it seems likely that as the senior engineer he was with Wellington during the battle. He quickly wrote two letters describing the victory. Writing to his sister a few days after the battle, he said:

> The events of the war here, and our constant state of movement and activity, have thrown me into the greatest confusion of business, public and private, but at the same time, I never was so happy or in better health.

He wrote with pride about the 3rd Division:

51 REM 4201-68, Journal, 5 July 1812.

52 REM 4201-68, Journal, 8 July 1812; Wrottesley, *Burgoyne*, p.195.

> The conduct of my old friends the 3rd Division was most conspicuous. Supported by a body of our cavalry, they made a tremendous rush, and overwhelmed everything before them. The Frenchmen threw down their arms and delivered themselves up prisoners by hundreds.[53]

Burgoyne also wrote to Pasley. Along with details of the battle, he commented on the, 'discipline of the troops and the command the officers had over them in checking their impetuosity and putting them in order after each succeeding attack, which has, we have been told, always caused Lord Wellington dread of [ordering] an attack'.[54]

The defeated French were pursued initially eastward then north beyond Valladolid, the advance guard of the allies entering the city on 30 July 1812. Wellington having briefly entered the city then turned back towards Madrid, leaving a screening force under Major General Henry Clinton near Cuéllar and the Spanish force of *Mariscal de Campo* José María Santocildes in Tordesillas. The army arrived at Madrid on 12 August 1812. Wellington again showed confidence in Burgoyne's abilities, sending him to summon the Retiro fort, a task that should have been performed by one of his staff:

> Lord Wellington sent me on with six dragoons, to summon them. They fired repeatedly at me when I attempted to go in on the side of the town ... but on the country side they let me in.
>
> The governor was hurt at a verbal message being sent him, and answered, "Les Francais ne se rendent pas si facilement". [The French do not surrender so easily.]

One possibility was that Burgoyne was sent so that he could reconnoitre the fort at the same time. The following morning Burgoyne and Wellington examined the defences and preparations were made to besiege the place. The outer walls were taken on the night of the 13 August and the French recognising that the place was indefensible, surrendered on 14 August 1812. Burgoyne noted that '180 brass guns, chiefly field pieces' were captured in the Retiro.[55] Similarly, Wellington reported that there were '189 pieces of brass ordnance in excellent condition'.[56] Neither of these comments suggests there were many modern iron siege guns present.

Wellington now had to decide his next step. He still believed his priority should be the relief of Cadiz which would have major political benefits for both the Spanish and the British and be a major loss of face for Napoleon. However, moving south

53 Wrottesley, *Burgoyne*, p.205.

54 REM 4601-74, Letter 46, Burgoyne to Pasley, not dated but around 1 August 1812.

55 Wrottesley, *Burgoyne*, p.209.

56 Gurwood (ed.), *Despatches*, Wellington to Bathurst, Madrid, 15 August 1812.

against Soult had significant risks. There were still large French forces in the north and east of Spain and his supply line could be threatened by either of these forces if he went south. This was also the hottest part of the year and the fatiguing marches south were likely to increase the sickness of his army. Attacking the Armée de Portugal again was a safer option as it was unlikely to have fully recovered from the defeat at Salamanca and there was less chance that other French forces would quickly come to its aid. The new French commander, *Général de Division* Bertrand Clausel, who had replaced the wounded Marmont, was working to recover discipline and reorganise his forces. In some ways, the decision was made for him by Clausel.

In pushing the French back to Valladolid after the Battle of Salamanca, three French garrisons were left behind the allied lines at Astorga, Zamora, and Toro. Wellington, in his instructions to Clinton and Santocildes, anticipated a French advance to relieve the garrisons and instructed both to retire if it happened.[57] Although Wellington thought it was unlikely, the French army did advance on 13 August and managed to free two of the garrisons; Astorga had surrendered before the French advanced. During this operation, Clausel remained with a small force in a very exposed position around Valladolid whilst the bulk of his troops under *Général de Division* Maximilien Foy advanced to recover the garrisons. The two French forces did not re-join until 28 August 1812. Wellington made no attempt to attack Clausel during this dangerous two-week period, remaining in Madrid. There is no reason to believe that Wellington did not know of Clausel's position and strength. A successful attack on Clausel would have been another major setback for the French and could have destroyed one of the three French forces that faced him. On the other hand, ignoring Clausel and the possibility that he could be reinforced from *Général de Division* Louis Caffarelli's French Armée du Nord, meant that Wellington's supply line through Salamanca could be threatened. Wellington decided to move north to neutralise the threat in the north with a view to being back in Madrid in time to deal with any threat from the combined armies of Joseph, *Maréchal* Louis-Gabriel Suchet, and Soult.

Wellington's actions over this period were very cautious and his intentions were not clear. Wellington did not leave Madrid until 1 September 1812. By then the French army was concentrated around Valladolid. The force Wellington took north from Madrid to confront Clausel was quite small consisting of the 1st, 5th, 6th, and 7th Divisions with the two Portuguese infantry brigades of Brigadier General Denis Pack and Colonel Thomas Bradford. In addition, there were the three cavalry brigades of Major General George Anson, Major General George Bock and Colonel William Ponsonby. To make up for the size of his force he asked the Spanish forces under *Capitán General* Francisco Castaños to join him

57 Gurwood (ed.), *Despatches*, Memorandum to be communicated to General Santocildes, Cuéllar, 5 August 1812.

immediately. The size, quality, and movements of the Spanish army were blamed for Wellington's slow pursuit of the French. It is difficult to see why any of these factors should have come as a surprise to Wellington, but the Spanish armies were always a good target for blame.

The bulk of the allied army was left around Madrid; there was always the possibility that Suchet (from the east coast) or Soult would advance on the capital or try to cut the allied lines of communication. The French forces in Spain still significantly outnumbered the allied forces.

Having pushed Clausel back from Valladolid, Wellington now made the decision to advance on Burgos. For reasons that are not explained, he now decided to undertake a siege that he was not equipped for. Burgos was not a strong fortress and would have quickly been destroyed by an effective siege train, but Wellington did not have one. Possible reasons for Wellington attacking Burgos may have been to provide a secure base for his flank and rear, if he decided to move south against Soult, or maybe to provide a secure base that would allow him to hold on to the Spanish territory he had freed from the French during 1812. Continuing to hold Madrid would have been a very visible sign to the whole of Europe of the French difficulties in Spain.

Burgoyne's journal goes very quiet in the second half of August there only being one entry between the 14th and the 31st. Both were from Madrid, so it can be assumed that he remained in the city and must have had no urgent duties to perform. He had been there briefly in 1808 but did not have time to enjoy the sights; maybe this time, he was able to do so.

Burgoyne left Madrid on 1 September 1812, with the army, travelling first to the Escurial then Villa Castin, Arévalo, and Olmedo. The allied forces crossed the River Duero on 6 September and there was a leisurely pursuit of Clausel back towards Burgos, which was not reached until 17 September 1812. The siege train, which had remained north of Madrid, moved with the army.

Zamora and Toro

Whilst travelling towards Rueda on 6 September, Burgoyne wrote: 'I was ordered by Lord Wellington to proceed immediately to report to him on the state of the French forts of Zamora and Toro and return as quickly as possible'.[58] Over the next six days, Burgoyne rode about 140 miles, not only reporting on the forts but also, as usual, on the roads he travelled on.[59]

The fort at Toro, the Alcázar de Toro, is pretty much the same today as it was when Burgoyne looked at it. Having been originally built in the 10th Century

58 REM 4201-68, Journal, 6 September 1812.

59 Burgoyne's report including sketches is in REM 4601-72, f1812-15, 11 September 1812.

and upgraded in the 15th Century, it had no modern defensive features and was described as 'an old castle of little importance'.[60] However the walls and towers were intact and it contained a well, barracks, and magazine:

> The defences made by the French consist of a loop holed wall, two feet thick round the summit and a wooden scaffolding within to stand and fire from. Round the towers, the new parapet wall has embrasures for guns … the fort is on a commanding part of the town and has almost an enfilading fire on the bridge … about 500 yards distance … it may be well battered from the Convent del Carmen at a distance of less than 300 yards. It can be of no service to us and the Spaniards have commenced dismantling it also by orders of General Castaños … Two arches of the bridge were destroyed … about July 15th last … the Spaniards have repaired these arches with timber, but as they have supported their work by uprights on the ruins of the arches, it is very probable that some winter rising of the waters may carry it away.[61]

The fortifications at Zamora were described as:

> [A] small enclosure round the castle, [with?] loop holed walls connecting the cathedral with the old town wall … the whole exposed to the height of Espiritu [sic] Santo … the Spaniards are destroying the fort by order of General Castaños and have been very active and nearly the whole of the new French works are down already. The bridge remains entire.[62]

Burgoyne re-joined headquarters at Dueñas on 11 September and continued with the army on the slow advance towards Burgos. On 13 September, he commented 'The reason of our very slow movements is supposed to be our waiting to be joined by Santocildes' army, which might have been up yesterday, but made some bungling in their movements. The whole army march on the same high Burgos road'.[63]

60 REM 4201-68, Journal, 7 September 1812.
61 REM 4601-72, f1812/15.
62 REM 4601-72, f1812/15.
63 REM 4201-68, Journal, 13 September 1812.

12

1812 – Peninsular Command, the Siege of Burgos[1]

It is not clear when Wellington decided to besiege Burgos. It appears to have been a snap decision. As late as 3 September 1812, Wellington was still writing that any decision to attack the city would depend on circumstances.[2] His staff appeared to be clearer, with Lieutenant Colonel Alexander Gordon writing on 3 October, 'the possession of Burgos is of great importance', and, two days later, 'the taking of this castle is an object of the greatest possible importance to us'.[3]

The place was invested on 19 September and Burgoyne now found himself facing a greater challenge that the Salamanca forts. To attack the fortress, he had a smaller battering train, there being only three 18-pounders and five 24-pounder iron howitzers available. Similarly, there were only five engineer officers and an insignificantly small number of Royal Military Artificers (eight). Ten officers of the line volunteered to act as assistant engineers and there were about 80 tradesmen volunteers from the line regiments.

Burgoyne noted that engineer stores were very limited with only: '600 pick axes and shovels, 100 felling axes and 200 bill hooks, with no carpenters, masons nor miners' tools, nor any other description of stores.' He also noted that if they had not found engineering stores that the French had left in the town, the besieging force would have run out before the siege ended.[4]

1 The account of the siege of Burgos in Jones' *Sieges* is based on Burgoyne's Journal of the siege, REM 4601-72, f.1812/6.

2 See Charles Esdaile & Philip Freeman, *Burgos in the Peninsular War, 1808-14. Occupation, Siege, Aftermath* (Basingstoke: Palgrave, 2015), pp.68-9. Esdaile mentions that according to John Jones RE, Wellington told Jones on 30 August that he would besiege Burgos and that Jones would command. The second point is wrong, as Jones was not the senior engineer present, and it is probable that the first point is also wrong. Jones' *Autobiography* was very self-promoting.

3 Rory Muir, *At Wellington's Right Hand* (Stroud: Sutton Publishing, 2003), pp.325-7.

4 REM 4601-72, f.1812/16.

The main duties of the siege were assigned to the 1st and 6th Divisions and the two Portuguese brigades of Pack and Bradford. The 5th and 7th Divisions were in advance of Burgos providing a covering force. As at Salamanca, the besieging divisions were new to siege work – the 6th Division's experiences at the Salamanca forts were hardly representative of normal siege warfare – and this would have an impact during the coming weeks.

Burgos was not strong, but its artillery, like at the previous sieges in 1812, were far superior to that which the allied army brought. On his arrival, Burgoyne recorded that the defenders had nine 18-pounders, and eleven light guns, with five or six mortars or howitzers.[5] Seven of the lighter guns were in the San Miguel hornwork and seven of the heavy guns mounted on top of the castle facing the hornwork on San Miguel (Napoleon battery).

From an engineer's perspective, Burgos was a very weak fortress. It had been extensively strengthened by the French after they took possession in 1808. The castle at the centre of the fortress was medieval in origin and its design predated the advent of cannon. High walls and towers were not an effective defence against an iron cannonball, although they might impress a soldier uneducated in siege warfare. Captain James Stanhope's view that it was 'infinitely stronger than Badajoz' could not have been further from the truth.[6] The castle stood on a conical hill that towered over the city of Burgos. Around the castle were three walls with ditches and palisades to provide additional strength. However, most of the walls were exposed and therefore vulnerable to cannon fire. Also, there was very little cover within the defences and most of the French troops were camped out within the fortress. Had the allied army had any mortars with them, the place would have been a death-trap for the defenders. The walls, however, were not the main strength of the defences, which came from a motivated garrison of around 2,000 soldiers and a determined Governor, *Général de Brigade* Jean Dubreton, who Wellington later described as 'a very clever fellow'.[7]

To the north of the castle of Burgos was another hill of roughly the same height, the Cerro de San Miguel. This hill had been fortified with a large redoubt capable of holding 500 soldiers. Fortunately for Wellington, it was unfinished, the greatest weakness being at the rear where only a strong line of palisades was in place to keep out attackers. There was a substantial earth wall at the front, but no palisades had been fitted. Between the Cerro de San Miguel and the town was a narrow, steep valley.

5 Wrottesley, *Burgoyne*, p.212 says two howitzers. Burgoyne's Journal of the siege, REM 4601-72, f.1812/16 says that the French had five or six mortars or howitzers.

6 Glover (ed.), *Eyewitness to the Peninsular war and the Battle of Waterloo. The Letters and Journals of Lieutenant Colonel The Honourable John Stanhope 1803 to 1815* (Barnsley: Pen & Sword, 2010), p.101. The average soldier might be impressed by the high walls, but an engineer or artiller man would know that they were an easy target for modern cannon.

7 Francis Ellesmere, *Personal Reminiscences of the Duke of Wellington* (London: John Murray, 1904), p.146.

Burgoyne rode round the fortress on the 18 September after the French had been pushed beyond it.[8] He does not say who was with him, but he must have been with Wellington. The obvious decision was that possession of the hill of San Miguel was essential to any attempt to take the town. The French also knew this, which was why they had built the substantial redoubt on it. Burgoyne's unpublished journal recorded his opinion that 'None of the lines, nor the hornwork were esteemed capable of resisting a *coup-de-main*', although this was altered in Jones' *Sieges* to 'the lines ... were not esteemed capable of resisting an assault, after they should have been cannonaded for a short time'.[9]

According to Jones, the plan agreed for the siege was:

1. Take the San Miguel hornwork.
2. Build a battery by the hornwork to breach the walls below the church of La Blanca (to the north-west).
3. Dig a communication from the suburb of San Pedro to approach the outer wall below the church of La Blanca where a mine would be exploded.
4. Assault the outer wall when the mine was exploded and make a lodgement. The battery to fire on the second line, above, whilst the assault was made.
5. Assault the second and third lines with supporting fire from the battery on the Cerro de San Miguel.
6. Turn all artillery on castle if the French had not surrendered after third line breached.[10]

For reasons that will be set out below, it does not appear that this is correct. Burgoyne's explanation of this plan of attack was as follows:

> The side selected for attack was that under the end of the church of La Blanca, because it presented the smallest front, the side of the hill there was so steep that the guns could not be depressed to see down it and each of the different lines on that side were very faulty and weak; the first being an old, unflanked wall with an earth parapet, which could be attacked in front and flank; the second, an unflanked line of earth works, the ditch and escarp of which were much exposed to the hornwork, the getting possession of which was a necessary preliminary to the attack on any side;

8 Wrottesley, *Burgoyne*, p.212. In his journal of the siege (REM 4601-72, f.1812/6), he recorded that a reconnaissance was carried out on the morning of 19 September. It seems probable that both of these were done. John Daniel, *Journal of an Officer in the Commissariat Department* (Cambridge: Trotman, 1997), p.166, says Wellington rode round Burgos with a large staff on that day (which would have included Burgoyne).

9 REM 4601-72, f.1812/16, 19 September; Jones, *Sieges*, Vol.I, p.276.

10 Jones, *Sieges*, Vol.I, pp.276-7.

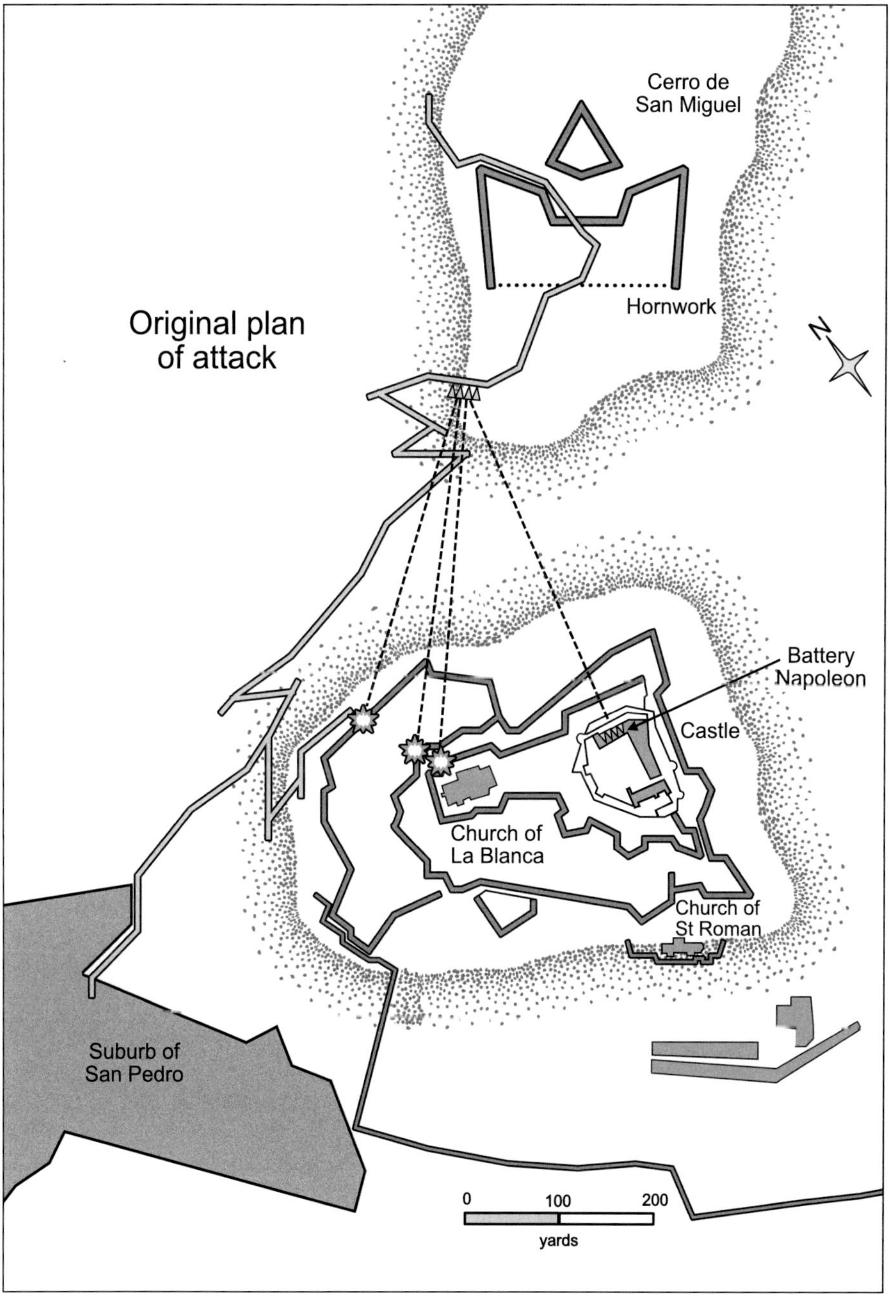

Siege of Burgos, original plan of attack.

> and the third had scarce any space, being encumbered with the church, a bad building which presented no defences.[11]

Interestingly, Burgoyne's explanation differs from that above, as described in Jones' *Sieges*, which stated the original plan was to mine the outer wall.[12] Burgoyne was clear:

> None of the lines, nor the hornwork were esteemed capable of resisting a *coup-de-main* and not having artillery or stores equal to attacking it regularly, it was in consequence proposed to attempt each line successively by assault, after the one taken precedingly [sic] was well secured to us by a good lodgement and communications; drawing all the little aid we could from our small force of artillery.[13]

Burgoyne's explanation that assault was the plan is a convincing one, as this would fit in with Wellington's views about being able to take the place without a siege. Whatever the original plan was, it was not long before it was changed.

When the fortress was invested on the morning of 19 September, the French outlying posts around the hornwork on San Miguel were quickly attacked and the French retired into the main defence on the hill. The decision was made to assault the hornwork the same night with no attempt to weaken the defences with artillery. Wellington was clearly ready to accept casualties to make quick progress with the siege.

The assault was in four parts. Two parties of 100 men from Pack's Portuguese Brigade were to assault each inner face of the hornwork's bastions. Each of these parties would be led by a ladder party from the 42nd Foot. A third party of 300 soldiers from the 42nd was to approach the main face of the hornwork and fire on the defenders to keep them down. A fourth party made up of the flank companies of Colonel James Stirling's Brigade was tasked to attack the gorge of the hornwork.

The main attack failed; the firing party was discovered early and suffered heavy casualties. The two main assaults approached the walls and placed the ladders, Pitts leading the left party. However, the main assault parties did not climb the walls and the mainly Portuguese troops withdrew. Whilst these attacks were going in at the front of the hornwork, Major Charles Cocks with the brigade light companies had made his way round to the rear of the hornwork. Some writers have suggested that this was planned as a false attack and that Cocks took the initiative to turn it into a full attack. However, Wellington's orders for the assault are quite clear,

11 REM 4601-72, f.1812/17, Note 4.

12 Jones, *Sieges*, Vol.I, p.276.

13 REM 4601-72, f.1812/16, introduction.

stating 'they should penetrate there [at the gorge] if possible'.[14] This is what Cocks did, and, having entered the rear of the hornwork, he left a small guard to stop any French leaving and attacked with the rest of his troops. It was this attack which upset the balance and the much larger French force then pushed their way past the small guard and retreated to the castle. The attack had succeeded, but at a cost of over 400 killed and wounded.

There were a number of criticisms of the planning and execution of the attack. Some reports by soldiers involved in the assault, said the ladders were too short.[15] Jones makes no mention of this, recording that the troops in the forlorn hope climbed the ladders after they had placed them, but the Portuguese troops, 'notwithstanding this stimulating example, could not be prevailed upon to enter the ditch'.[16] Burgoyne was scathing about this claim: 'As in all bungling matters of this sort, there was the old story raised of the ladders being too short, but being left standing, on the morning [after the assault] a convincing proof was afforded of their being of sufficient length'.[17]

Burgos was not the only siege where claims were made about ladders being too short. The two senior engineers present at the siege were clearly of the opinion that this was not true. There is an account by a soldier in the 42nd, who took part in the assault who claimed the ladders were 'about two feet short'.[18] The most puzzling account, from another authoritative source, is by William Reid who was present as a Lieutenant in the Royal Engineers. Reid wrote that Jones and other writers were wrong and the actual height of the wall (scarp) was 45 feet![19] This is a massive difference and if the wall of the hornwork was truly 45 feet high (vertical), it was probably the highest wall in the Peninsula, which is very unlikely.

So, how can these different accounts be explained? A cynical view would be that the senior engineers were covering their mistake in underestimating the height of the wall and thereby the length of the ladders required. Yet what about the disagreement by the engineers who were present? A careful reading of the accounts shows a different cause. When Reid stated the height of the scarp as 45 feet, he followed with the words 'measured upon the slope'. It must be remembered that the hornwork was an earthwork, not a stone fortification with vertical walls. The main wall, which is called a scarp in Jones' description, was 'hard and slippery, 25

14 Wellington (ed.), *Supplementary Despatches*, Vol.XIV, p.120.

15 See Esdaile, *Burgos*, p.87; Oman, *Peninsular War*, Vol.VI, p27.

16 Jones, *Sieges*, Vol.I, pp.278-9.

17 REM 4601-72, Journal on Siege of Burgos, Note 5.

18 Anon, *Personal Narrative of a Private Soldier who Served in the Forty-Second Highlanders for Twelve Years During the Late War* (Cambridge: Trotman, 1996), pp.141-2. This account is used by Esdaile, *Burgos*, p.87 but discarded by Fortescue without explanation, as 'worthless', *History of British Army* (London: Macmillan, 1917), Vol.VIII, p.575 footnote.

19 William Reid, 'On Assaults', *Papers on Subjects Connected with the Duties of the Corps of Royal Engineers* (London: Royal Engineers, 1837), Vol.I, p.11. Jones was still alive when this was published.

feet in height, stood at an angle of 60 degrees.[20] Reid was describing the length of the slope of the scarped wall, not the vertical height. A 25 feet high earth wall with a 45-degree slope would have a slope of 35 feet. If the slope was slightly less steep, as was likely to keep the earth in place, then we can see where Reid got 45 feet from. Reid also described the slope as being of 'rammed earth very neatly scarped with a spade'. His description of the assault on the left bastion makes it clear that the highlanders were able to connect ladders together, up the slope, using bayonets as spikes. They were not doing this on a vertical wall.

Reid finished with 'had a British regiment been ready … such a column, most likely, would have effected an entrance at that point'.[21] Reid's inference was not that the assault failed because of the ladders were too short, but, that ladders were in place on the scarp and there were no troops willing to climb the ladders (i.e. the Portuguese troops). We will come back to the behaviour of the Portuguese soldiers during the siege.

Burgoyne, in his private notes on the attack said:

> [I]t was attended with some difficulty and considerable loss … this was in my mind to be attributed both to the plans and the execution … the two storming parties advanced and did nothing; General Pack who commanded, produced another firing party and rallied the storming parties; in the meantime, the party at the gorge had entered and the enemy ran away by the opening there.

Burgoyne had recommended that the weakest points, the two flanks and the gorge of the hornwork should be attacked, but he was overruled, and the main attacks went in on the stronger front, although to be fair, this face was sheltered from the heavy fire from the fortress.[22]

Jones was similarly critical, writing: 'Luckily, the assaulting columns carried the work, and success glossed over this most unmilitary and inefficient mode [of attack]'.[23] Even Wellington's ADC, Gordon, commented that 'the business was not well managed'.[24]

The first part of the plan, the capture of the hornwork, had been completed on the first day. The engineers also suffered their first casualty, with Pitts falling off his horse and breaking his arm. Burgoyne had only three engineers available to him.

20 60 degrees is highly unlikely as an earth wall would not stand with that slope.
21 Reid, 'On Assaults', pp.10-12; Jones, *Sieges*, Vol.I, p.275.
22 REM 4601-72, f.1812/17, Note 5.
23 Porter, *Royal Engineers*, Vol.I, p.320.
24 Muir, *At Wellington's Right Hand*, p.320.

During the night, under heavy fire from the castle, the allies created a communication trench through the front of the hornwork to a parallel near the gorge (rear). A separate zig-zag was dug on the left (north-west) side of the hornwork to the location of the first battery.[25] The site of this battery had been carefully chosen, so that it was not visible from the Napoleon battery, but could see the fortifications below the back of the church of La Blanca. On the night of the 20 September, battery No.1, for five guns was started and it was armed on the night of 22/23 September. The same night battery No.2 was started to fire on the castle, although there was no immediate plan to start such an attack as it would bring an overwhelming response from the guns in the fortress. Burgoyne commented:

> For my part, I was always afraid to look the castle in the face and recommended not attempting to breach it [the castle], except as a *dernier resort*; there was no harm, however, in making the batteries and the opening one of them was only [done] very late in the business, when any sort of fantastic [sic] plan was adopted as "worth trying," instead of adhering firmly to one project, and expending the whole of our means, trifling as they were, on one point.[26]

The French, not being short of guns or ammunition kept up a heavy fire day and night making work difficult and dangerous for the allied troops. In fact, Burgoyne came within in an inch of losing his life on 20 September, when he was hit on the head by a musket shot, fortunately only bruising him.

Unfortunately, the weather broke and cold and wet weather started. This continued through the rest of the siege and made life in both bivouac and trenches unpleasant. On the night of 22/23 September 1812, Wellington ordered an attack to be made on the outer wall on the northern side on the church of La Blanca. Battery No.1 was now ready to provide supporting fire to the attack, but no account mentions the guns firing. The plan was to make two separate attacks on the outer wall at the back of the church of La Blanca; one on the northern face and one on the southern face. The northern attack would be by 400 soldiers from the 1st Division; 200 from the Guards and 200 from the King's German Legion. Their task was to escalade the outer wall. The southern attack was to be made by 130 Portuguese soldiers from the 6th Division.[27] Their task was to break through the palisading in the ditch and then make contact with the other attacking force

25 Care needs to be taken when comparing Jones' *Sieges* and Burgoyne's manuscript Journal, REM 4601-72, f.1812/16 as they use different numbering for the batteries. Burgoyne uses batteries no.1 and 2 to equate to what Jones calls No.1. Burgoyne uses batteries no.3 and 4 to equate to what Jones calls No.2. This account uses Jones numbering as this is what is generally used.

26 REM 4601-72, f.1812/17, note 6; Wrottesley, *Burgoyne*, p.234.

27 Gurwood (ed.), *Despatches*, Plan for the attack of the exterior line of the castle of Burgos, 22 September 1812, says 130; Burgoyne's Journal, 22 September, says 150.

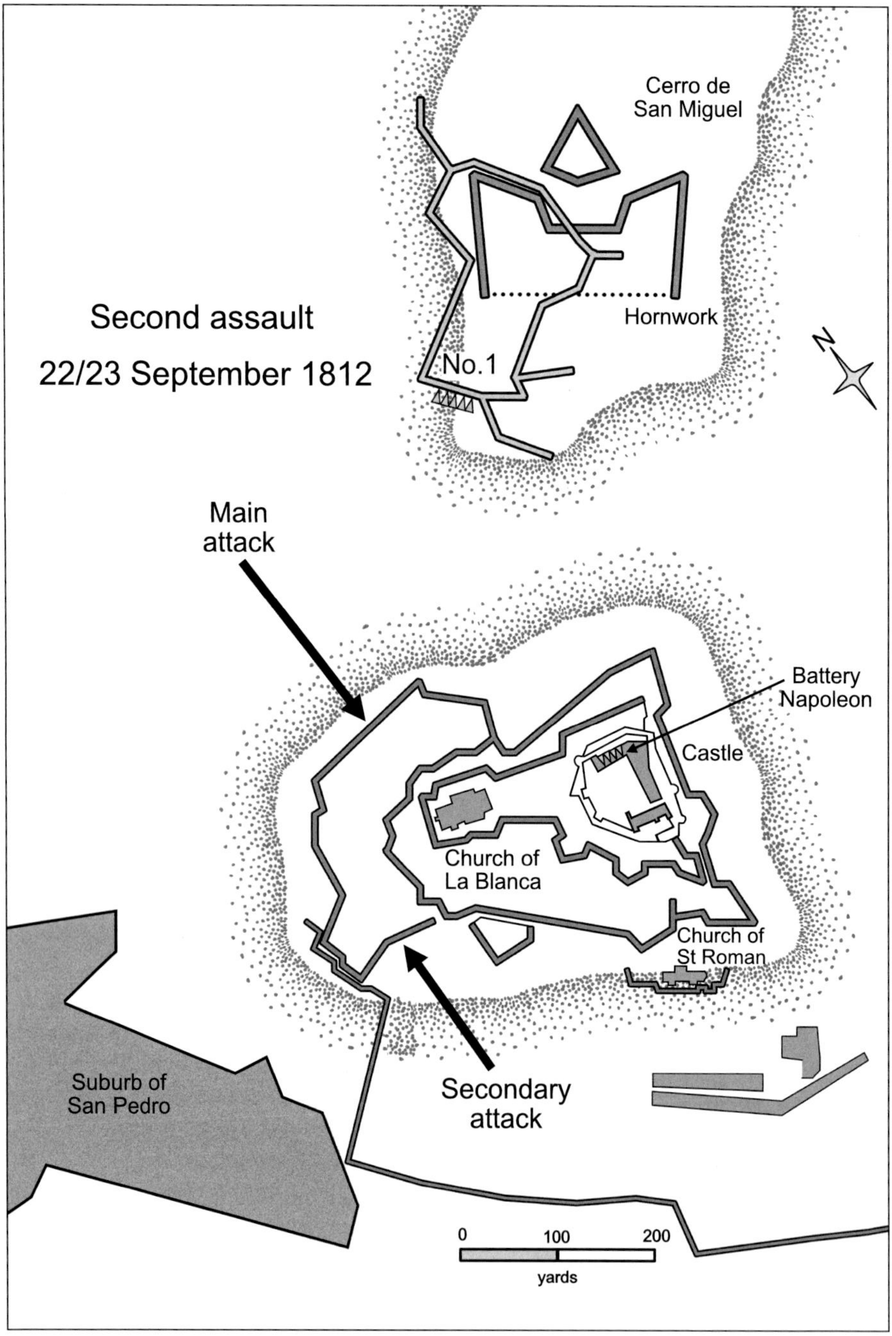

Burgos: Second Assault 22/23 September 1812.

round the outside of the outer wall to protect the right flank of the main attack and watch for any French support arriving from the upper levels of the fortress.[28] Both these attacking forces were very small.

The main assaulting force was ordered to be split into two groups with 200 to form the assaulting force and 200 to form a firing party further back to keep down the defenders on the wall. Once the assault started, the whole force became confused and when the commanding officer, Major Andrew Lawrie of the 79th, was killed the whole body retired with 129 killed and wounded. The secondary attack by the Portuguese also failed and there was much criticism that they made little effort. More than one officer went as far as to suggest that the main attack failed because of the lack of support from the secondary attack.[29]

Wellington was furious, blaming Lawrie for the failure, saying 'the troops ought to have carried the exterior line by escalade … and if they had, we had means sufficient to take the place.'[30] Was this failure the watershed point that negated Wellington's hopes of quickly taking the city? Lawrie had been given clear instructions on how to conduct the assault and appears to have not followed them as they were going to be very difficult to implement at night over unfamiliar terrain that he had no opportunity to reconnoitre. Rather than separate the firing and assaulting parties and then feed in portions of the assaulting party, Lawrie had chosen to form the whole body into a compact column to allow him to quickly move up the steep hill. The result was that when the defenders opened fire, the rear of the column ran for cover and the troops that reached the wall had no firing party to protect them. The failure of the secondary Portuguese attack would also have allowed more defenders to the main point of attack.[31]

Burgoyne described the attack, writing:

> [N]o order was kept, all was confusion; part of the men went up to the wall; and the remainder to the rear; none remained in the hollow way, nor acted as a firing party; during the latter part of the business, therefore, the Frenchmen stood on the top of the parapet, and fired down on our people crowded in the ditch, who from thence returned the fire, and thus stood some time to be killed, as Bonaparte describes the Russians, "afraid to advance, unwilling to retire, and having given up all hope of success".

28 It is not clearly stated in any one place what the purpose of the Portuguese attack was. This interpretation is taken from reading of the various accounts by Jones, Burgoyne (his journal of the siege and his journal), Wellington's Despatches amongst others.

29 Gareth Glover (ed.), *Wellington's Voice: The Candid Letters of John Freemantle* (London: Frontline, 2012), pp.126-7. See also Burgoyne's comment below.

30 Gurwood (ed.), *Despatches*, Wellington to Liverpool, 23 November 1812.

31 See Esdaile's comprehensive account of the attack, in, Esdaile, *Burgos*, pp.92-97; Also, Oman, *Peninsular War*, Vol.VI, pp.29-30. Carole Divall, *Wellington's Worst Scrape: The Burgos Campaign 1812* (Barnsley: Pen & Sword, 2012), pp.39-78.

He added:

> This project would undoubtedly have succeeded, had the Portuguese detachment done their duty, but they never reached even the first line of palisading and without that support, it was impossible the wall of twenty-four feet high could be carried by the five ladders.[32]

Any hope of a quick success was looking less likely. At 1:00 p.m., the following day, a truce was arranged to allow the wounded and dead to be removed. The question on everyone's mind now was, what next?

Burgoyne, in line with his understanding that each wall would be assaulted, reported that having failed 'it was [now] necessary to work up to the wall and attempt to mine it'.[33] Jones, having recorded that the original plan was to mine the outer wall, explained the assault by saying 'with a view to abridge the attack [i.e. the siege] and save the troops from unnecessary fatigue, Lord Wellington determined to make an effort to carry the exterior defences of the castle by escalade'. After the assault failed, Jones recorded 'it became necessary to revert to the original project of forming a breach in the outer or first line … [by] forming a mine under it'.[34] The present author is still inclined to accept Burgoyne's view. Wellington appeared to believe he could take this fortress as he had previously captured Indian hill-forts. His first assault on the hornwork had been successful and he justified the high casualties by suggesting, unfairly, that they were caused by the inexperience of the highlanders carrying out the assault. He appeared to ignore the poor performance of the Portuguese troops. Although four days had been spent getting the first batteries ready, they were still inadequate to take-on the defenders' artillery and another escalade would have looked attractive to Wellington. It would seem that the poor organisation of the British attack and the failure of the Portuguese troops was the problem. Did Wellington have the right troops with him to escalade the fort?

The deciding factor on whether the original intention was to mine the outer wall or escalade it, is the fact that the approaches from the suburb of San Pedro towards the outer wall, to dig the mine, were not started until the night after the assault had failed (23/24 September). These approaches could have been started five days earlier and there seems no obvious reason to have delayed this work if mining was the preferred choice. It would have just been five days wasted, when Wellington was supposedly in a hurry. It is suggested, therefore, that Jones' version of the plan represents editing of the facts after the event. We have seen this before in reporting on sieges.

32 Wrottesley, *Burgoyne*, p.215; REM 4601-72, f.1812/17, Note 7.
33 REM 4601-72, f.1812/16, 23 September 1812.
34 Jones, *Sieges*, Vol.I, pp.283, 286.

On the night of 23/24 September, the trenches were started from the suburb of San Pedro to connect to a parallel that was dug on the line of the 'hollow' road in the valley between the Cerro de San Miguel and the city. The first allied guns opened on 25 September, but not as part of a general attack. Two were used to try and destroy a strong palisade that was allowing French marksmen to pick off the allied workmen. The attempt was given up after firing 141 rounds without success due to the inaccuracy of the weapons. The historian Nick Lipscombe expresses surprise that Dickson appeared more interested in duty rosters than the performance of his guns at this critical time.[35]

The following night, a flying sap was pushed to within 20 yards of the wall. Burgoyne's meagre engineer resources were reduced when Williams was killed, bringing the number of engineer officers down to four, one of whom had a broken arm.

The mine was started on the night of 25/26 September from the end of the flying sap. The troops carrying out the mining operations were from the line regiments with little training. The distance of the gallery was about 60 feet. Work was also started to connect the works on the Cerro de San Miguel with the new trenches in front of San Pedro. Zig-zags were dug down the hillside and a parallel was also started for a firing party. On this date, Burgoyne's journal of the siege makes his first specific complaint about the quality of the working parties:

> On this and every other night when we broke ground, much more work was proposed and tools and men collected in sufficient number; the reason why it was not executed, was from the want of superintendents and the misconduct of the working parties, which latter reason was duly reported to the Commander of the Forces and taken notice of by him.[36]

This complaint would become frequent and led to a furious argument between Burgoyne and some officers in the regiments. We will come back to this.

By the end of 26 September, the gallery was 18 feet long. The French, realising what was being done, started work to reinforce their second line. A new trench was also started to the right of the mine with the intention of placing a second mine. The following day the mine was 28 feet long and the second mine was started. Burgoyne was frustrated by the slow work but accepted that with untrained troops and poor tools not much could be expected.

On the 28 September, the communication between the hornwork and San Pedro was completed. Burgoyne complained that it should have been completed the preceding night, but 'some of the working party had neglected their duty'.[37]

35 Jones, *Sieges*, Vol.I, p.289; Lispcombe, *Wellington's Guns*, p.250.

36 REM 4601-72, f.1812/16, 25 September 1812.

37 REM 4201-68, Journal, 27 September 1812.

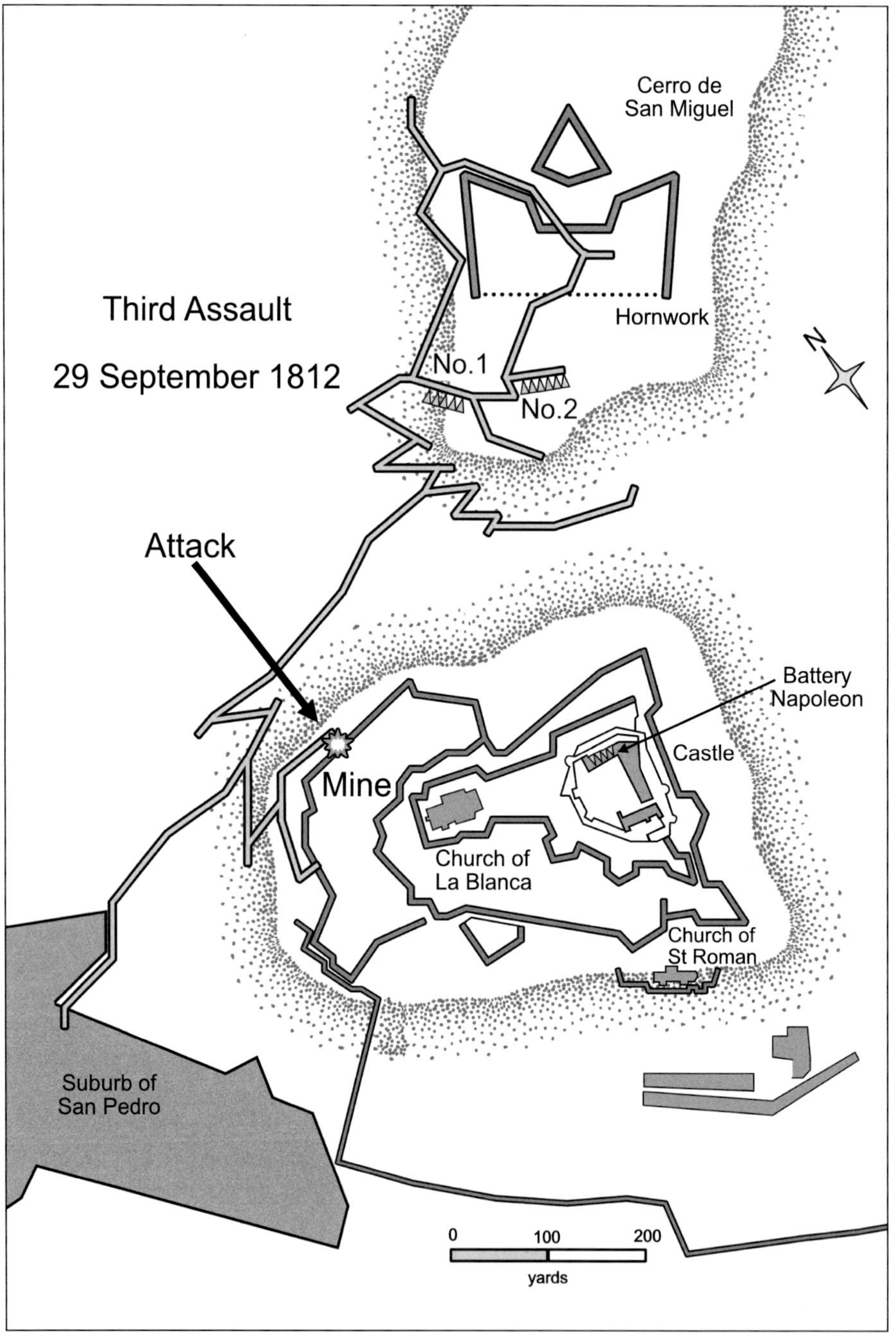

Burgos: Third Assault.

The first mine was 42 feet long and the second, making faster progress, was 32 feet long.

On 29 September 1812, the first mine hit the foundations of the wall; it was supposed to go under the foundations. Rather than dig down and under the foundations, Wellington ordered a chamber to be excavated under the foundations at this point and it was loaded with 1,080 pounds (500kg) of powder. An assault was ordered for that night, made up of 300 troops from the covering party. Exploding the mine at midnight, the walls collapsed leaving a solid earth wall behind. The advance party of 20 men reached the wall, but soon returned, reporting that there was no breach. No further attempt to escalade was made. Burgoyne recorded:

> The storming party of 300 men were to have assailed it, led by one officer and twenty men; of these a sergeant and four men gained the top of the breach, and describe [sic] the enemy as quite taken by surprise. They do not appear to have been supported, for the officer returned, and even said the wall was not injured. Two of the men who ascended were wounded in the hand with bayonets, a certain sign they were up.[38]

After the event, it was concluded that the officer leading the party turned too far to the right and missed the breach and the leading five soldiers who were at the top of it. The attack raises all the same questions as the previous ones on 19 and 22 September. The storming party again was very small and likely to be outnumbered by the defenders. At Ciudad Rodrigo and Badajoz, thousands of troops were used for the assaults; at Burgos the numbers were measured in the low hundreds. There were never enough troops assigned to the attacks to make success probable. The poor performance of the Portuguese troops made the situation even worse. This assault was also conducted without an engineer officer to lead the advance party forward. With only four available, there was no-one on hand to lead them.[39]

Wellington persevered with the plan to mine the outer wall and work on the second mine continued. Battery No.3 was ordered to be established where it could batter the wall at the point of the expected breach from blowing the mine. This was completed and the three 18-pounders were run in before daylight on 1 October 1812. A decision had been made to make the parapet of the battery very light as it was believed none of the French artillery could fire on it. Unfortunately, the French had other ideas and the battery was pounded non-stop throughout the day; the parapet ruined and two of the three 18-pounders badly damaged. None of the 18-pounders had yet fired a shot during the siege!

The behaviour of the troops in the working parties had now reached such a level that a General Order was issued on 1 October 1812:

38 REM 4201-68, Journal, 29 September 1812; Wrottesley, *Burgoyne*, p.216.
39 Jones, *Sieges*, Vol.I, p.297.

> The Commander of the Forces is concerned to state that the working parties in the trenches do not perform their duty … He desires that Lieutenant Colonel Burgoyne will report to him every morning who commanded the working parties … and whether each of the parties performed the work allotted to it.[40]

Burgoyne said it was his suggestion to make the daily reports. Work on the mine continued and by evening on 1 October it was 65 feet long. Overnight, the three 18-pounders were removed from battery No.3 to a safe place until a new battery, No.4, slightly to the left of No.3 was completed. The parapet of this new battery was to be capable of resisting artillery fire.

Again, the French out-thought the allies. Battery No.4 was battered all day on 2 October 1812 and abandoned as too dangerous even before the guns had been placed in it. Two of the 18-pounders were ordered to be moved back up to battery No.1 on the Cerro de San Miguel. The third of the 18-pounders had one of its trunnions knocked off and was considered unusable. It took two days to move the guns this short distance 'owing to the desertion of their working party, a common complaint with us; we seldom can keep above half our working party through the night'.[41] Wellington followed his earlier General Order with another on 3 October 1812:

> The Commander of the Forces … is again concerned to have again to notice that he has received complaints on the working parties ordered for last night … the working party … for the Commanding Officer of the artillery did not perform their duty. All the officers and the whole of the Portuguese detachments absented themselves … he is happy to make an exception in favour of the Guards … who have invariably performed … in the most exemplary manner.[42]

On 2 October, the second mine was now 72 feet long but was still a few feet short of the wall. Progress in the mine was terribly slow, partly from the poor behaviour of the miners and partly from a lack of oxygen at the end of the tunnel. Burgoyne noted:

> [B]oth at this and the first galleries, from their being small, very considerable difficulty was experienced after about 45 feet to keep the candles burning; at times we were forced to make the people leave the gallery for

40 Wellington (ed.), *Supplementary Despatches*, General Order, Villa Toro, 1 October 1812.

41 REM 4201-68, Journal, 3 October 1812; Wrottesley, *Burgoyne*, p.217.

42 Wellington (ed.), *Supplementary Despatches*, General Order, Villa Toro, 3 October 1812.

> half an hour to let air in; but we were fearful of losing time by adopting even the most simple machine to ventilate them.[43]

On 4 October 1812, battery No.1 opened on the breach made by the first mine. There were two 18-pounder cannon and three 24-pounder iron howitzers. Burgoyne noted with satisfaction that by the evening the breach was practicable and wide enough for 20 men.[44] At the start of the day, the second mine was now 88 feet long and it was loaded with 1,080 pounds of powder.

Wellington was now in a position to try another assault. The first breach was ready, and a second breach should be created by exploding the mine which was blown at 5:00 p.m. The two breaches were stormed successfully by the 2/24th Foot, and, 15 days after the start of the siege, Wellington had taken the first line of defences, something he felt should have happened 12 days previously. It is worth noting that this successful assault was made by a larger number of troops from one regiment under their own officers, rather than the mix of units used in the two previous failed assaults.

Work started immediately to secure the breaches and form a lodgement. During the attack, Burgoyne's only other senior engineer officer, Jones, was severely injured and took no further part in the siege.[45]

The Governor, *Général de Brigade* Jean-Louis Dubreton, continued to show the initiative that he had shown throughout the siege. At 5:00 p.m., on 5 October, he launched a sortie and caused substantial damage to the lodgement around the first breach. However, work continued overnight, and a start was made to dig a parallel on the glacis of the second French line. Whilst the French could not bring any of the artillery to bear on the allied working parties, they kept up a constant fire of musketry. Burgoyne continued to despair at the inexperience and the work rate of the soldiers:

> We could not get a dozen gabions filled in one day. Our musketry fire, kept up by the covering parties, of whoever they might happen to be composed, was noisy, wasteful, and ineffective; while the French kept a small number of steady men who fired well, and never but at a fair object; not a gabion we placed at the full sap but had ten or twenty shots through it, and an extraordinary number of our foolish firing parties were shot in the head by one unobserved Frenchman, while their attention was purposely engaged by another.[46]

43 REM 4601-72, f.1812/16, 3 October 1812.

44 REM 4601-72, f.1812/16, 4 October 1812.

45 This is the John Jones, who wrote the *Journal of the Sieges.*

46 REM 4601-72, f.1812/17, Note 14.

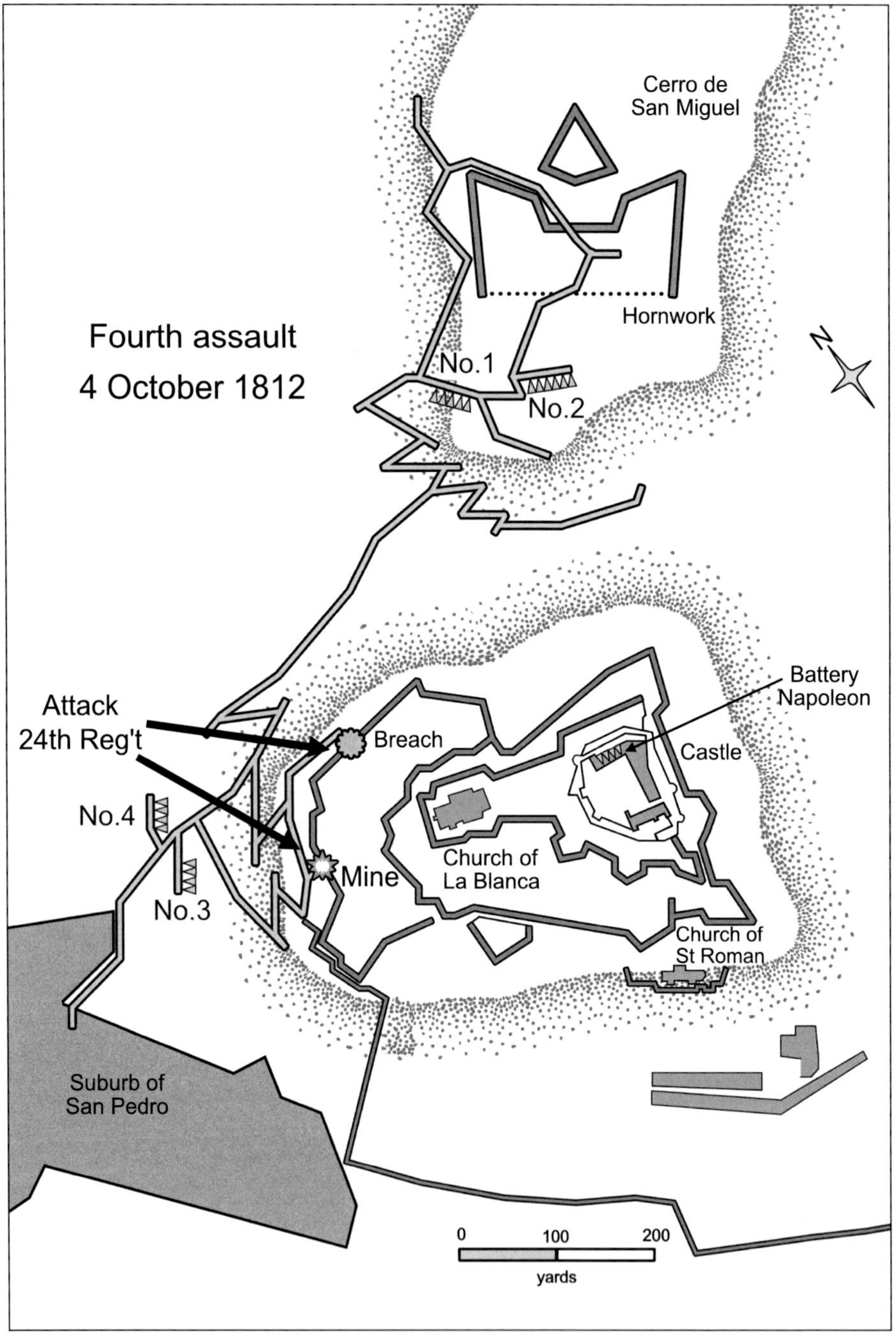

Burgos: Fourth Assault.

This frustration about taking risks clearly did not apply to himself. In later life, he recalled how he took risks in moving between trenches in the open to save time. Wearing a distinctive greatcoat, the French allowed him to do this where anyone else would have been shot at. It only needed one Frenchman to take a different view and the only senior engineer at the siege could have been killed.[47]

At mid-day on 6 October, the batteries on the Cerro de San Miguel opened to make a new breach in the second line directly opposite the hill.[48] The wall was visible to its foot at this point. Although he does not explicitly say it in his journal of the siege, Burgoyne implied that this attack was not by his recommendation:

> The attempt to effect a third breach, was, by the express order of Lord Wellington, who did not choose to trust the assault of the second line to the single attack in front; this breach being completed, contrary to the expectation of many officers considering our small quantity of artillery and ammunition. It was evidently our interest to storm the work immediately as any delay must be in favour of the enemy; but a delay of many days did occur, first, to wait for a supply from St Andero of musket ammunition … and secondly, doubts of our ultimate success had been gaining ground for some time and various little projects were suggested to accelerate the fall of the place, as worth trying and some of them put in practice, instead of preserving on one determined plan, and expending our whole means, trifling as they were on one front.[49]

There are a number of points that need to be made about this entry. Wellington's confidence in his troops appeared to be low. He was not willing to risk a single assault from the breaches by San Pedro as per the original plan and wanted a second threat to the garrison. The new breach being made opposite the Cerro de San Miguel would provide this alternative. Wellington had clearly over-ruled Burgoyne in 'expressly' ordering the breach to be made. The timing of the decision by Wellington is surprising. Wellington knew that he was short of musket ammunition. He had ordered up new supplies some days before and had remarked on 5 October that he was having to delay any assault until new supplies arrived.[50] As Burgoyne remarked above, making a breach and then delaying any assault gave time for the defenders to reinforce the breach. It would have been better to delay making the breach until the musket ammunition arrived. Time pressures appeared to be affecting decision making. With a good siege train and knowing the weak state of the wall, a breach could have been made in one day. With the

47 Wrottesley, *Burgoyne*, p.239.

48 There is a sketch in Leslie (ed.), *Dickson Manuscripts*, Vol.IV, p.754.

49 REM 4601-72, f.1812/16, 8 October 1812.

50 Wellington (ed.), *Supplementary Despatches*, Wellington to Bathurst, Villa Toro, 5 October 1812.

guns Wellington had available, it took longer and gave the defenders plenty of time to make retrenchments.

The most concerning comment was the last sentence. 'doubts of our ultimate success'; 'various little projects were suggested'; 'worth trying' and 'instead of preserving on one determined plan'. All these words suggest that a lack of confidence was building in Wellington's mind. Burgoyne must also have felt threatened. Other officers were now suggesting how the siege could be better organised and there were certainly criticisms of the engineers, whether justified or not. Bingham's comment on 3 October: 'we have not talent enough amongst our engineers to compensate for the want of means' is harsh but was probably a common view in the army at this time.[51] The decision to make this third breach was not part of the original plan. Whilst the few guns available were attacking this part of the wall, they were not improving the breaches in front of San Pedro. Burgoyne's concern remained that the very scarce resources were being diluted rather than concentrated at the points where they would have the most impact.

Burgoyne's journal of the siege records the constant work that was required to keep the batteries and trenches in a usable condition. The batteries, which were made of earth, reinforced with gabions and sandbags, were damaged every day through the firing of the French. Each night repairs had to be made to keep the guns and the gunners safe. An additional problem was now caused by the incessant rain, which damaged the batteries and trenches. Trenches, particularly, needed draining regularly and this of course was done by hand.

To make matters worse, a second 18-pounder had a trunnion knocked off. Whilst under normal circumstances, the guns damaged in this way would have been discarded, attempts were made to keep using them. The guns were strapped to block carriages, but they became unwieldy, highly inaccurate, and prone to jumping off the carriage when fired, making working the guns even more dangerous than normal. The two 18-pounders mounted in this way were put into the batteries on 8 October and Burgoyne noted 'they were of little or no service'.[52]

During the night of 7/8 October 1812, the French made another sortie and took possession of the parallel being constructed in front of the second line. They remained long enough to again destroy most of the work and carry off the workmen's tools. Following this second attack, Wellington decided that no further work would be carried on between the first and second lines. The French could attack without any warning and, due to the short distances involved, the covering party could not respond quickly enough to stop them.

The following day, the new breach was declared practicable and a 'communication in zig-zags' was completed round the outer wall towards this breach which would give protected access to any assaulting party.

51 Glover (ed.), *Wellington's Lieutenant*, p.153.
52 REM 4601-72, Journal on Siege of Burgos, 8 October 1812.

Two new attacks were started on 9 October. The first was to fire red-hot shot at the church of La Blanca, to try to destroy the supplies of the garrison. Wellington had mentioned as early as 21 September that the French stores were in a place that might be set on fire, but nothing had been done to attempt this for nearly three weeks.[53] This fire was kept up for three days without any noticeable effect on the church. Burgoyne noted on the first day that 'the grate for heating the shot is bad and breaks; the shot is fired exceeding[ly] slow and apparently not red-hot'.[54]

By this time, the 18-pounders were using French 16-pounder roundshot which had been collected for re-use. Whilst the loss of power would not have been an issue when firing red-hot shot, the loss of accuracy would have been. There is no comment on whether the lack of success was caused by the shot missing the church altogether.

The second new attack started from a completely new direction to dig a gallery to the church on St Roman on the southern side of the city. It is not said who proposed this attack, but it appears that it had not been properly considered. Burgoyne noted the following night that the distance for the gallery was over 150 feet, double the distance of the second mine, where he had already reported great difficulty in the oxygen supply at the end of the tunnel.

With operations now being carried out on three sides of the city, the tiny engineer resources must have been stretched to breaking point. From the Cerro de San Miguel to the church of St Roman was over a mile by foot. The various operations seemed to have lost any cohesion with three different attacks being progressed at the same time. Whilst the artillery was firing red-hot shot at the church of La Blanca, Burgoyne noted that 'The earth escarp of the second line, under La Blanca was so much injured by the little firing that had been on it, that if we had more guns and ammunition a perfect and extensive practicable breach would easily have been made in it'.[55]

The French continued to reinforce their defences around the new breach making any assault more challenging and by 13 October, five days after the breach had been declared practical, had cleared the breach leaving an eight-foot step which would now require ladders.

On 15 October 1812, battery No.2 opened directly against the castle. There was three 18-pounders (including the two badly damaged ones) and one 24-pounder howitzer. As predicted by everyone, against seven French 16-pounders and several other smaller guns, the battery was destroyed in 30 minutes.[56] It is very difficult to

53 Gurwood (ed.), *Despatches*, Wellington to Bathurst, 21 September 1812.

54 REM 4201-68, Journal, 9 September 1812.

55 REM 4601-72, f.1812/16, 13 October 1812.

56 See Esdaile, *Burgos*, p.187, note 26, where J.W. Gordon suggested that the guns were not opened on the castle as they would be overwhelmed; also REM 4601-72, f.1812/17, Note 6.

come up with any suggestion on what was hoped to be achieved by this action. The battery was now repaired and turned back on the third breach.

The dreadful weather continued. Burgoyne complained 'the weather, however, is so bad, with so much rain, that the revetment of the batteries have given way'. Three days later, 'the weather worse than ever, high wind and heavy rain.[57]

The gallery under St Roman was completed and 900 pounds of powder was loaded into the chamber on 16 October 1812. Burgoyne's earlier concern about a lack of oxygen proved wrong, which he attributed to the tunnel being very shallow, allowing air to permeate through the earth.[58] The miners were concerned that the French had heard them and, when the mine was ready, two soldiers were left with the mine with orders to report if they heard any French approach to the chamber. Burgoyne had been given authority to explode the mine at any time if they felt it was threatened by the French.

Wellington was now in a position to plan his next assault. On the morning of 17 October, the batteries on the Cerro de San Miguel opened again against the third breach and to enfilade the second line of defences. This fire was continued through the next day to widen the breach and destroy any interior defences that the French made.

At 4:30 p.m., on 18 October, the mine under the church of St Roman was exploded. This was also the signal for two other assaults, one on the third breach opposite the Cerro de San Miguel and the other on the first mine to the north-west of the church of La Blanca.[59] 200 soldiers from the King's German Legion assaulted the third breach; 200 of the Guards attacked from the position of the first breach and a party of Spanish and Portuguese were to make a false attack on the breach at St Roman.

As before, the small numbers used in the assault proved fatal. The King's German Legion soldiers carried the breach and advanced towards the third line but were driven back on the Guards to their right. The Guards also escaladed the second line but were also driven back by superior forces (probably the same force that repulsed the KGL). On the advance of the Spanish and Portuguese troops on the church of St Roman, the French set off their own mine which brought down the church stopping the attack although the attackers then continued to hold the ruins. Burgoyne commented:

> This last attack failed entirely from the small number of the storming parties against a fort having 1,500 men in it. They carried the works easy [sic] but could not hold them … This attack on the second line having failed, nothing was done in the night but carrying a communication to

57 REM 4201-68, Journal, 16 & 19 October 1812.

58 REM 4601-72, f.1812/16, 16 October 1812.

59 See Jones, *Sieges*, Vol.I, pp323-326 for the orders for the attack.

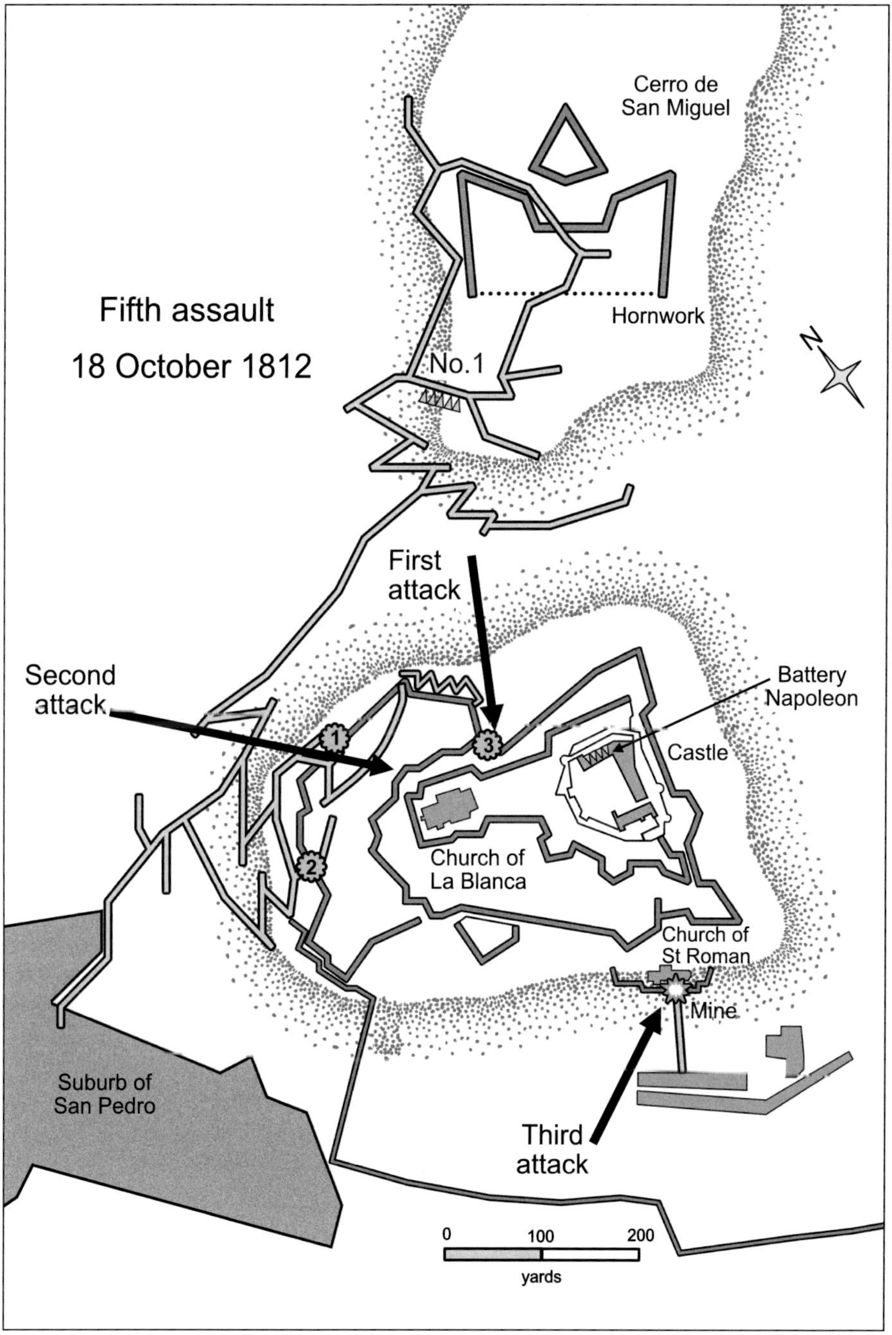

Burgos: Fifth Assault.

> the ruins of the church of St Roman; indeed, it is probable that after this last attempt the determination was already formed of raising the siege.[60]

Burgoyne was correct, the siege was effectively over. Wellington was becoming increasingly concerned about the strength of the French who were concentrating against him. Apart from some minor bickering around the church of St Roman, nothing else occurred until the siege was raised.

Wellington's position was now becoming dangerous. Larger French forces were advancing on Burgos and Hill's forces further south. On the evening of 21 October, Wellington ordered the siege to be raised at 5:00 a.m., the following morning. In the confusion to get everything ready, the powder needed to destroy the hornwork was misplaced and the defences were left intact, 'by the stupidity of an Artificer, the powder, after arriving safe, was sent off, and notwithstanding our endeavours, we could not get it back'.[61] On leaving in the morning, it was discovered that the condition of the roads was too poor to remove some of the guns. The 18-pounders and captured French guns were abandoned. These events were the final blows in the disastrous siege. The dispirited army trudged away; things were only going to get worse.

Wellington reporting the failure, gave credit to the effort of the engineers and artillery and stated that the failures were not their fault. This was a fairer evaluation than he gave after the previous sieges. For Burgoyne however, his failure at Burgos would be remembered 40 years later when he was involved in the siege of Sevastopol in the Crimea.[62]

Observations on the Siege of Burgos

After the siege, Burgoyne prepared three documents. The first was the official report of the siege for his superiors. The second was a critique of the siege, which was clearly not for publication and marked private. The third was a speculative plan for the next attack on Burgos. These documents are all discussed below.

Wellington's intentions on leaving Madrid and before Burgos have confused historians for 200 years. As seen above, he did not bring a suitable siege train forward. In the weeks leading up to the siege, his priority appeared to be the defeat of Soult. His advance on Burgos was initially to push Clausel away from his line of communications and valuable foraging areas; his intention then being to quickly return to Madrid. Writing to Lord Bathurst after only two days of the siege, on 21 September 1812, he reported:

60 REM 4601-72, f.1812/17, Note 16; REM 4601-72, f.1812/16, 18 October 1812.

61 REM 4201-68, Journal, 21 October 1812.

62 Wrottesley, *Burgoyne*, p.237.

> It was impossible to ascertain the exact state of the works of the castle of Burgos till we had obtained possession of the hill of San Miguel; and as far as I can judge of them, I am apprehensive that the means which I have are not sufficient to enable me to take the castle. I am informed, however, that the enemy are ill provided with water; and that their magazines of provisions are in a place exposed to be set on fire. I think it possible therefore, that I may have it in my power to force them to surrender, although I may not be able to lay the place open to assault.[63]

Later in his life he commented to Lord Ellesmere: 'It was not unlike a hill fort in India, and I had got into a good many of them'.[64] In the first days of the siege he launched two costly assaults without making any attempt to weaken the defences. It certainly looked like he believed he could quickly force the French to surrender, in which case a large siege train would not have been required. Wellington's comment about the French stores being vulnerable to destruction is probably correct. Mortars would have been ideal, but there were none. Eventually, he tried to set fire to the church of La Blanca on 5 October, but two weeks had been lost.

Wellington clearly believed that Burgos could be taken without a formal siege, either through a *coup-de-main* or starvation. Like at Ciudad Rodrigo in 1811, Wellington had received information to suggest Burgos was short of supplies. It was late in the siege before he took any action to try and destroy the French supplies, so starvation was not his primary strategy. After it became clear that a *coup-de-main* was not going to succeed, he continued with costly attacks on the walls with little chance of success. His actions became a battle of attrition with better-armed defenders.

A key question is, what was the original plan for the siege? There is lengthy debate in several works about whether the intention was to assault or to mine the defences. These have been discussed above and suggest that his original intention was to take the lines by escalade having softened up the defences.[65] Mining was introduced only after the assault failed on 22 September. Wellington then felt he could not try another escalade on the outer line, as he believed that Lawrie, who led the assault, had his written orders in his pocket when he was killed and the French could have obtained them.[66]

Another common criticism is that the siege train was close to useless with only three effective siege guns, the 18-pounders. There is agreement that with a proper siege train Burgos would have been easily taken. Why did not Wellington take a

63 Gurwood (ed.), *Despatches*, Wellington to Bathurst, 21 September 1812.

64 Ellesmere, *Reminiscences*, p.146.

65 See Fortescue, *British Army*, Vol.VIII, p.584, Jones, *Sieges*, Vol.I, pp.276-7. Oman, *Peninsular War*, Vol. VI, pp.26-9, only talks of taking the hornwork to batter the castle, not to attack the lines in front of the suburb of San Pedro.

66 Esdaile, *Burgos*, p.93.

proper siege train with his army or bring up more guns from Madrid or Ciudad Rodrigo?

In answer to the first point, it should be understood that Wellington did not intend to besiege Burgos when he left Madrid in August 1812. The 24-pounder iron howitzer brigade was conceived as a field brigade, not as part of a battering train. The remaining three 18-pounders were relatively easy to move because there was so few of them and they were each pulled by 20 oxen, more than the normal complement.[67] Again, it seems unlikely that Wellington saw these as a siege train, more likely just some heavy guns for an unexpected need. There was no provision to bring a siege train from the Portuguese border when he started his advance in May 1812. It is likely that Wellington was concerned about the security of such a train, if he had to manoeuvre quickly, either forwards of backwards. The manoeuvring around Salamanca in June and July 1812 could easily have ended with Wellington withdrawing, and against fast-moving French forces a siege train could have been lost.

So, why did he not bring a siege train forward when he arrived at Burgos? This comes back to the question of whether he thought he was going to besiege it or escalade it. As has already been stated, Wellington thought he could take Burgos without a heavy siege train. He expected, not unreasonably, that the assaults on 22 and 29 September and 4 October would succeed. When they did not, he was scrambling for alternative solutions. On 2 October, he asked Rear Admiral Sir Home Popham, who was operating in the Bay of Biscay, for some 24-pounder cannon and these set off on 9 October but had not arrived when the siege was raised. Asking for guns from Madrid or Ciudad Rodrigo on the same date would not have been any quicker, even if the transport could be obtained. Wellington maintained to the end that he could not get transport together to bring other guns forward. Oman believed that 'if he had, on the first day of doubt before Burgos, he had sent urgent orders … they would have been up in time'.[68] Unfortunately, Wellington's first day of doubt did not come until early October. Had it come two weeks earlier, then it would have been possible. Oman also noted that Lieutenant Colonel Howard Douglas offered on 20 September to obtain guns from Popham.[69] Similarly, Major General Edward Pakenham offered to arrange transport of heavy guns from Madrid. Both offers were turned down.[70] All this reinforces the view that Wellington believed he could take Burgos by escalade. Lipscombe is right in calling the decision not to bring more guns forward 'an astonishing oversight'.[71] However, it was the performance of the troops, not the guns, that let him down.

67 Jones, *Sieges*, Vol.I, p.246. The number of draught animals depended on the roads and the weather, but seven or eight pairs was more normal.

68 Oman, *Peninsular War*, Vol.VI, p.26.

69 S. Fullom, *Life of Sir Howard Douglas* (London: John Murray, 1863), pp.208-212.

70 Oman, *Peninsular War*, Vol.VI, p.40.

71 Lipscombe, *Wellington's Guns*, p.249

One final point on the suggestion of bringing up guns. It must be remembered that ammunition must also be sent with the guns. To move twelve 18-pounder cannon with powder and 400 roundshot for each gun would take 600 oxen and 200 carts.[72] Burgoyne in his critique of the siege made a point which was extremely valid in terms of the logistic requirements:

> These carronades [24-pounder iron howitzers] were very bad things; they could not be fired with any accuracy or force; the advantage of their lightness makes only the difference of four or six bullocks per gun while the weight of the main article, the shot, is the same and though they expend but two pounds of powder at each charge, a long 24-Pounder with the same quantity would have at least as good an effect.[73]

Replacing the five howitzers with 18-pounder cannon would probably have taken another 50 oxen rather than the 30 Burgoyne suggested. The three 18-pounders that were travelling with the army had a strong train of 20 oxen, each. This was more than normal, probably to help them keep up with the army.[74] However, 50 extra oxen would have been enough to make the siege train up to eight 18-pounder cannon: whilst still small, would probably have been viable. The howitzers with the field artillery could have been used for area fire instead of the 24-pounder howitzers (in fact, some of the field units were equipped with iron howitzers). The trial of using a brigade of 24-pounder iron howitzers with the army was scrapped at the end of the year.

Burgoyne's other point about the effect was also correct. In terms of accuracy, any cannon would significantly outperform the howitzers. This was demonstrated categorically during the siege, after two days of trying and failing to destroy with 24-pounder howitzers a palisade from which French marksmen were shooting at the working party. Burgoyne complained: 'one 24-pounder carronade from No.1. was opened on the palisade tower which annoyed us so much and fired [for] and hour without once hitting it'. One small French field gun which was captured in the hornwork was brought forward. In three hours, the palisade and the French marksmen were gone.[75] The same improvement in accuracy would have meant the meagre supply of ammunition would have been much better used. As well

72 Guns – eight pairs = 192 oxen; Ammunition – 400 shot per gun – 30 per cart – 13 carts per gun = 156 carts; Powder – 6lb per shot – 4,800 x 6 = 28,800lb = 50 carts. Total 604 oxen and 206 carts. The three 18-pounders with the army had 20 oxen each, to help keep up with army.

73 REM 4601-72, f.1812/17, Note 8.

74 It is based on 20 oxen for an 18-pdr and 10 oxen for a 24-pdr howitzer and adjustments to powder and shot required. NB this is only for 100 rounds which was found insufficient.

75 REM 4601-72, f.1812/16, 25 September 1812; Jones, *Sieges*, Vol.I, pp.289,298. Over the two days, 240 shot and shell were fired from the 24-pounder howitzers and on the second day, 40 shot from the single French 6-pounder. Undoubtedly the latter caused the damage. Porter, *Royal Engineers*, Vol.I, p.324,

as accuracy, the impact of a roundshot fired from a cannon was much greater than from a howitzer. An 18-pounder using the full six-pound powder charge had about three times the energy of a 24-pounder howitzer. Even when using the same charge as the howitzer (2 pounds), it still had a 50 percent greater impact. A 9-pounder field piece had 30 percent more energy than the howitzer and the 6-pounder cannon only slightly less. If Wellington had called in Captain Robert Gardiner's Company of field artillery which was attached to the 1st Division, he would have had five 9-pounder cannon which were more powerful and more accurate than the 24-pounder howitzers. Gardiner's company also had a 5.5-inch iron howitzer, which was very similar to the 24-pounder howitzer. At the ranges at which these guns were firing, the 9-pounder would have made a significant improvement. One wonders why none of the artillery or engineer officers considered this option?[76] It is even more surprising that it was not tried as it appears Gardiner's Company was already in the city. Captain Charles Dansey RA, reported that his company (Gardiner's) was in the city 'being employed to fire on the works'. He also mentioned that during the assault on 4 October, 'field guns [were] placed around the town so as to fire in reverse of the defences'.[77]

Burgoyne was critical of the management of the siege, as was fellow engineer officer John Jones.[78] The three main complaints were, the number of troops used in the assaults; the mixing of men from different units, and the behaviour of the troops. Burgoyne was probably braver than most of the commentators as he 'remarked' directly to Wellington on the size of attacking parties and the relative size of the garrison.[79] It is worth repeating at length Wellington's reply and Burgoyne's view. Wellington said:

> "Why expose more men than can ascend the ladders, or enter the work at one time, when by this mode, the support is ordered to be up in time to follow the tail of the preceding party close"?
>
> My answer is, because a large body encourage one another, and carry with them the confidence of success; because there is more chance of a few very brave men to lead; and because, although we had but ten or twelve ladders to storm the castle of Badajoz, and therefore not more than forty or fifty men could mount at once, I am convinced it was only carried

glosses over this event mentioning the palisade being destroyed in three hours but not mentioning that the howitzers had been trying for two days.

76 See the author's article, 'When is a 24-pounder not a 24-pounder?', *Smoothbore Ordnance Journal*, Vol.11 (2019), pp.9-19.

77 Gareth Glover (ed.), *The Letters of Second Captain Charles Dansey 1806-13* (Cambridge: Trotman, 2006), pp.54, 56.

78 Jones was wounded at the siege and never served in the field again. He did serve under Wellington in Europe during the post-war reconstruction.

79 Wrottesley, *Burgoyne*, p.235.

> by the whole 3rd Division being there, and the emulation between the officers of the different regiments to get their men to mount; and although we lost 600 or 700 men, it caused success, which eventually always saves men.
>
> It was, however, by the faulty mode pointed out, that all our assaults at Burgos were ordered, and with the miserable, doubting, unmilitary policy of small storming parties, because then "if we fail, we can't lose many men," caused us, in my opinion, much mischief throughout, more losses, and gave the enemy great confidence.

Burgoyne and Jones both commented on Wellington's insistence that the assaulting party for the second assault be fed forward in groups of 20 men.[80] This is interesting, as this is not what Wellington's orders stated. His order was for the ladder party of 30 men with five ladders, accompanied by 12 men with axes to advance first. When the ladders were in place, an officer and 20 men would advance to mount the ladders. The next party would be 50 men and then the remainder of the party of 200 (88 soldiers).[81]

One of Burgoyne's comments which Wrottesley did not print in his biography, was 'the last assault failed entirely due to the small number of the storming parties against a fort having 1,500 men in it; they carried the works easy [sic] but could not hold them'. Oman had a similar opinion.[82]

It is difficult to see any reason why Wellington insisted in using such small parties to assault the fortress. With the exception of the first attack, the numbers of attackers were much smaller than the number of defenders. Could the terrible casualties at Badajoz have affected Wellington more than was thought? The first attack was blunt and costly and this may have reminded Wellington of the horrors to follow. However, this seems unlikely. As he said when consoling Beresford after the battle of Albuera, casualties have to be expected if the war is to be won. Wellington had been experimenting with new siege techniques throughout 1812. Perhaps Burgos was a new experiment to see if gradually introducing troops into an assault would work? If so, it did not.

All of the assaults would have succeeded if sufficient troops had been used. In the eyes of the soldiers, the first assault caused unnecessary casualties. With each failed assault, the troops became more disheartened. During the day, they worked in the trenches, in poor weather, and with little defence against the French fire. At night, they were thrown in small groups at the walls. It was clear to all, that the

80 Although it is likely that Jones is repeating Burgoyne's journal of the siege. Burgoyne's diary (and Wrottesley, *Sieges*, p.214) correctly states the distribution of troops.

81 Gurwood (ed.), *Despatches*, Plan for the attack of the exterior line of the castle of Burgos, 22 September 1812.

82 REM 4601-72, f.1812/17, Note 16; Oman, *Peninsular War*, Vol.VI, p.50.

siege train was inadequate. It is not surprising that the troops were despondent. Having said that, one of the traits of the British soldier was his willingness to work under adversity. This was sadly lacking at Burgos.

There are many other commentators at the time making these same complaints,[83] but Burgoyne was probably the most vocal about the behaviour of the troops. We have already seen that the behaviour was so bad that two General Orders were issued by Wellington. Burgoyne got into a furious argument with British officers serving in the Portuguese regiments when he asked for some British soldiers to be included in every working party as the Portuguese were not to be relied on. The argument went all the way up to Wellington who ordered apologies to be made to Burgoyne under the threat of court martial.[84]

Burgoyne was also critical of the behaviour of the British troops, attributing 'our failure to our feeble efforts in the assaults … and to the languor and apparent want of confidence in the troops concerned, whose conduct was very different from what I had been before accustomed to witness'.[85] This is why the siege failed. Neither Wellington nor Burgoyne expected the troops to behave in such a manner. However, Wellington has to take responsibility for assaulting the works with small parties, often from different regiments. This shattered the confidence of the officers and troops.

There is no doubt that the lack of engineering resources was a contributory factor. The engineer officers present had acknowledged this at Ciudad Rodrigo and Badajoz earlier in the year. Burgoyne was no different, saying, 'It is certain that with proper artillery or engineer means we could have reduced this fort in a short time'.[86] Rory Muir, in his recent biography of Wellington, commented that he may have been 'influenced by the enthusiasm and assurance of John Burgoyne … who was confident he could take the place with the means available'.[87]

Like John Jones, Burgoyne believed, both at the time and later, that Burgos could have been taken with the resources available. The key to Burgoyne's assertion was that it could have been taken if the original plan was followed, which it was not. The third breach and the mining of the church of St Roman were not part of the original plan. As each assault failed, the plan was altered and seemed to lose any cohesion. The main reasons for failure were the lack of guns, the behaviour of the troops, and the use of small assault parties.

As on a number of other occasions, Wrottesley adjusted Burgoyne's quotes when they were especially critical of Wellington. In Burgoyne's final paragraph in his private letter to Fletcher, the version published by Wrottesley stated:

83 See, for example, Esdaile, *Burgos*, pp.92-96.
84 Wrottesley, *Burgoyne*, pp.231-2.
85 Wrottesley, *Burgoyne*, p.230.
86 Wrottesley, *Burgoyne*, p.230.
87 Rory Muir, *Wellington; Path to Victory* (New Haven: Yale University Press, 2013), p.485.

> I have heard a hint that Lord Wellington said that the engineers told him "the fort might be taken without guns." This I do not believe; first, because it is not like him to say that he went by other people's advice; but chiefly because I never said any such thing, as I thought that even the little artillery we had might have been of service.
>
> I do not know what his Lordship's opinion may be now; but he certainly appeared, all through the siege, perfectly satisfied with me, and with the exertions of the engineer department; and although he occasionally listened to some project or other, that was put into his head by other people, as an accompaniment to the attack, for a general plan he always declared his approbation of mine.[88]

Burgoyne actually wrote:

> I have heard a hint that Lord Wellington said that the engineers told him "the fort might be taken without guns." This I do not believe because it is not like him, *as I believe he never pays any one the compliment to insinuate that he took their advice, though he may perhaps in a case of failure*, but chiefly because I never said any such thing, as I thought that even the little artillery we had might have been of service.
>
> I do not know what his Lordship's opinion may be now; but he certainly did appear, all through the siege, perfectly satisfied with me, and with the exertions of the engineer department; *unless I may judge the contrary from his constantly [flying?] off to some foolish project or other that was put into his head by other people,* as an accompaniment to the attack, for a general plan he always declared his approbation of ours.[89]

The changes are small but show that Burgoyne was aware of Wellington's insensitive nature and also felt threatened by the alternative advice Wellington listened to as the siege dragged on.

Howard Douglas was clearly one of the officers who was making alternative suggestions on how to attack the fortress. His proposal was for the main attack to be at breach three. Some of his facts are incorrect and he appears to have ignored the presence of the Napoleon battery which would have made an assault on this side very costly. He commented:

> He [Douglas] refrained from pointing out what he considered the insurmountable difficulties in the other [the original] plan in the presence of

88 Wrottesley, *Burgoyne*, p.236.

89 REM 4601-72, f.1812/17, Note 17. Italics added by author.

> the Commanding Engineer and these apparently escaped the notice of the Commander-in-Chief, for he finally gave it the preference.[90]

Officers with egos were in plentiful supply, including in the Royal Engineers. Douglas was commissioned into the Royal Artillery in 1794 and was on the staff at the Royal Military College from 1804. His presence in the Peninsula was as a liaison officer with the Spanish forces. Douglas went on to suggest than when the assaults failed, Wellington came back to him for advice and Douglas advised the artillery and engineer officers on what needed to be done. Douglas then said he kept out of Wellington's way 'that the professional men [i.e. the artillery and engineers] may not accuse me of obtruding an opinion'.[91] This all sounds highly implausible. Douglas' idea of not interfering included raising the matter with the commander of the artillery and the Quartermaster General.

Another officer who was making 'suggestions' was Sturgeon, the commanding officer of the Royal Staff Corps. He had suggested that a gallery was run all the way under the castle from a distance of about 100 yards. He believed the ventilation problem could be solved using a pump from the city fire brigade. Burgoyne thought it was impractical and the idea was dropped.[92] The engineer accounts make no mention of the Royal Staff Corps being involved in the siege, which they clearly were. Sturgeon was ordered to lead one of the parties forward on 18 October.

The result of the siege was 2,000 casualties and nothing to show for it. Burgoyne's summary was:

> Thus ended the siege of the Castle of Burgos, which in my opinion would have succeeded, had the troops on all the various occasions done their duty, had the Engineers had a competent establishment, viz., of stores, sappers and miners, officers, etc., or had a larger force been sent to the attack of the second and third line, on the evening of the 18th instant. The general opinion however was, that our failure was owing to a deficiency in artillery, and some attribute it partly to our attacking the strongest side; but this last, I am prepared to argue with them. [93]

Whilst there are many commentators on this siege, an excellent summary was written by Ensign John Aitchison, who was present at the siege:

90 Fullom, *Douglas*, p.212.

91 Fullom, *Douglas*, pp.208-214. Obtruding – to impose one's ideas on others with undue insistence or without invitation.

92 BL ADD MS41963, Pasley papers, f.87-90, Burgoyne to Pasley, 30 March 1813.

93 REM 4201-68, Journal, 21 October 1812.

> It has undeceived the French of our invincibility; it has dampened the ardour of our men; it has diminished their confidence in our chief; as he betrayed unsteadiness in frequently changing his plan of attack and in resolution of carrying it into execution when fixed upon and lastly, it has excited apprehension in the Spaniards and in some places matured their passivity into indirect hostility.
>
> In short it has blasted our prospects in the present campaign and damaged our plans for the next.[94]

The siege of Burgos was an enormous challenge for an engineer officer. The resources were inadequate; the troops dispirited and underperforming. The same can be said of Wellington. His decision making before and during the siege were often difficult to understand and made the stated aim of capturing the fortress harder. Burgoyne believed the fortress could have been taken but at almost every step, others appeared to obstruct this aim. Looking at the quotes above from Douglas and Aitchison, there is a strong feeling that Wellington was indecisive throughout the siege (and before it), and that the army knew it.

If Burgoyne had had a moment to think about the situation, he would probably have welcomed the arrival of the Commanding Royal Engineer, Fletcher, back to the army on 26 October and the end of his command. Unfortunately, he was too busy trying to slow the French pursuit and then organise emergency repairs at Ciudad Rodrigo.

Retreat from Burgos

The failure at Burgos negated almost all of Wellington's territorial successes during 1812 but the campaign had achieved the primary objective, which was the removal of Soult from southern Spain. This was a setback from which the French in Spain could not recover and sent a message to Europe that all was not well for the French in Iberia.

There now followed a difficult retreat in atrocious winter weather back to the Portuguese border, during which, army discipline and the commissariat almost completely failed. This retreat was probably worse for the army than the retreat to La Coruña in 1808-9. Whilst most accounts focus on the bad weather and bad behaviour, Wellington conducted a difficult retreat skilfully, and there was no let-up for Burgoyne and his small group engineers. As the allied army retreated,

94 W.F.K. Thompson (ed.), *An Ensign in the Peninsula* (London: Michael Joseph, 1981), p.208.

many bridges were mined to delay the chasing French with Wellington using the major rivers as barriers where he attempted to hold the enemy and rest his troops.

The army started its withdrawal in two columns although they were within a few miles of each other. The smaller column with the 5th Division and the bulk of the Spaniards stayed on the northern bank of the Arlanzon and moved towards Tarjados. South of the river the bulk of the allied infantry quietly crossed the bridge at Burgos so as not to alert the garrison, concentrating at Buniel. There was little pursuit on 22 October, but the French pushed very hard the next day, its larger cavalry force overwhelming the allied rearguard made up of Anson's and Bock's cavalry brigades, Colonel Colin Halkett's brigade of KGL Light Infantry, and two horse-artillery brigades. A running battle lasted the whole day with the allies being progressively pushed back to Torquemada having fought the furious cavalry skirmish at Venta del Pozo. Whilst the exhausted rearguard halted just outside the town, much of the rest of the army, which had marched through Celada del Camino and Cordovilla, fell into a drunken rampage in the town many being unable to march in the morning.

On 24 October the army retired to the west bank of the River Carrion around Palencia using the three main bridges in the area at Palencia, Villa Muriel, and Dueñas. Allied headquarters was at Cordovilla on the night of 23 October and Dueñas on 24 October. About 60 miles had been covered in the first three days. The troops were being pushed hard in both armies.

Wellington now tried to make a stand using the River Carrion as a barrier. At 9:00 p.m., Burgoyne was ordered to destroy four bridges in the area at Dueñas, Tariego, Villa Muriel and Palencia. He made no mention of the bridge over the Carrion at San Isidoro which Oman included in the bridges to be destroyed. Having only two engineers with him, Pitts and Reid, Burgoyne also used two Assistant Engineers, Major Thompson and Lieutenant William Barney. Both of these officers had been used as assistants before and had some understanding of the role.

Pitts was immediately sent to Tariego arriving at 11:00 p.m. He was told by the allied outpost that the French already had taken the bridge. He discovered in the morning that this information was wrong and returned to the bridge. Unfortunately, the opportunity had been lost:

> [T]he enemy were very near, and he was consequently hurried; and on the enemy advancing against him, the mine was sprung, and failed, the enemy immediately crossed the bridge, and made most of his working and covering parties, (sixty-two men) prisoners.[95]

95 REM 4201-68, Journal, 25 October 1812.

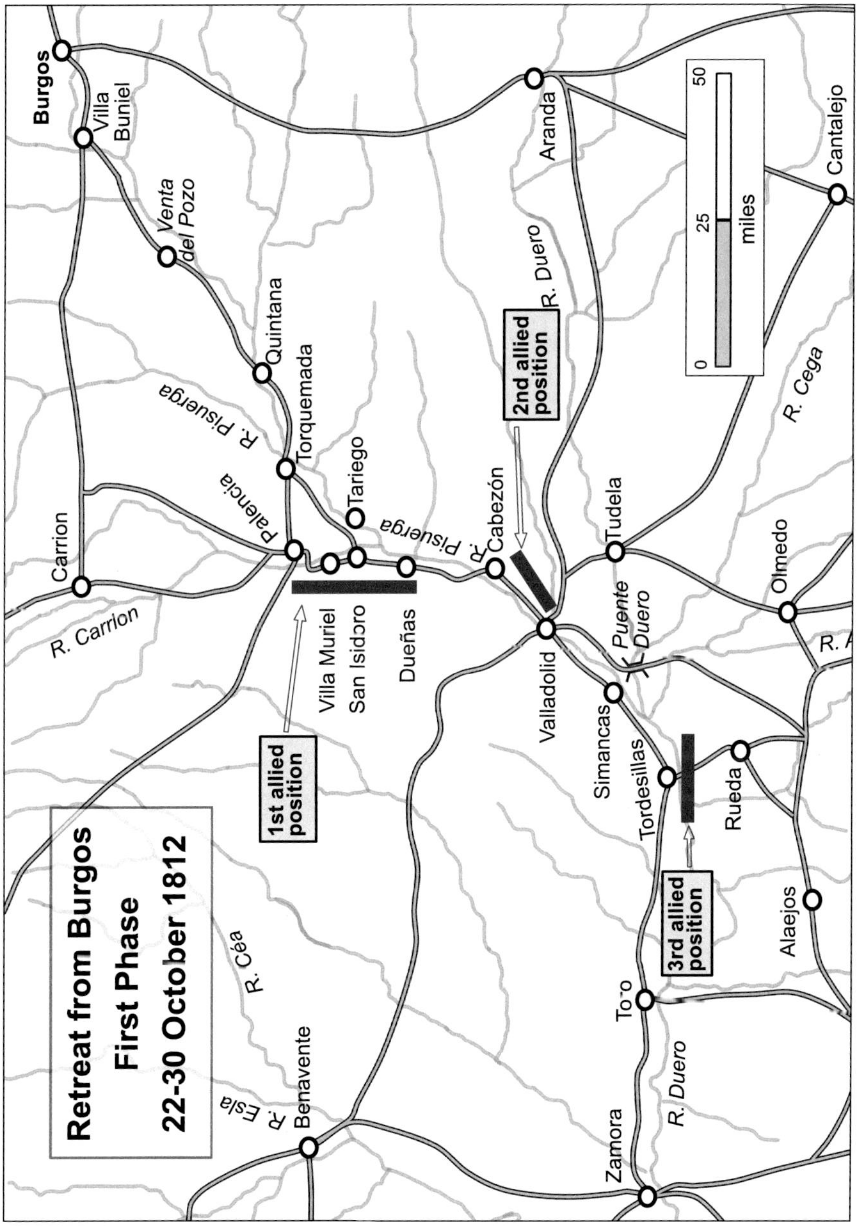

Bridges to be destroyed on first phase of retreat from Burgos.

Oman recorded that the mine did explode, but only destroyed the parapet, leaving the roadway intact.[96]

At Palencia, Reid with a working party from the 3/1st Foot (Royals) was interrupted before the bridge could be mined. Foy's French advanced guard surprised the covering party guarding the main gate and the town had to be quickly evacuated. One account said: 'The engineer officer comes running to Colonel Campbell and says "Colonel Campbell, the bridge is taken. You are at liberty to act as you please with your battalion"'.[97] Palencia was on the left (eastern) bank of the river, so any allied retreat would have to cross the river if the town was attacked. It is difficult to see how the bridge could be taken before the town. The bridge would be the obvious route for a retreat. It is more likely that the rapid assault left no time for the bridge to be blown after the troops withdrew across the bridge.[98]

Thompson succeeded in blowing one arch at Villa Muriel, again under intense pressure from the French. He completed the work under fire from French artillery on the other side of the river. With more time, further damage would have been caused. The French managed to cross the river at fords nearby and took control of the crossing point and the village of Villa Muriel. Wellington could not allow this bridgehead to remain and attacked later in the day, throwing the French back over the river.

Lieutenant George Barney RE succeeded in partially destroying an arch at Dueñas with advice from Burgoyne.[99] As with many of the bridges in Spain, the stone and cement used to build them was extremely hard and trying to quickly make a hole was very difficult, especially when there were no proper tools or experienced sappers available. Two barrels of powder were placed in a shaft and managed to destroy 15 feet of the arch. Unfortunately, this was quickly repaired and allowed the enemy forces across.[100] Burgoyne also noted than a wooden bridge close by was also destroyed.

Wellington's plan to hold the French on the line of the Carrion had failed with the loss of the bridges at Palencia and Tariego. A new plan was required.

On the morning of 26 October 1812, Wellington moved his forces back to a second position on the east bank of the Pisuerga and concentrated them between

96 Oman, *Peninsular War*, Vol.VI, p.79.

97 Stanley Monick (ed.), John Douglas, *Tales from the Peninsula* (London: Leo Cooper, 1997), pp.56-8. Douglas also suggested that the order to destroy the bridge was sent by a dragoon who got lost. This is unlikely as the order was given direct to the engineers and headquarters was less than 10 miles from Palencia.

98 Oman said the fuse failed when the mine was exploded. No source is given. Oman's account says most of the working party from the 3/1st was captured, suggesting they were still working on the mine when the French rushed the bridge.

99 See REM 4601-74, f.80, Blowing of bridges in the Peninsula.

100 See Isaac Landmann, *Treatise on Mines for the Use of the Royal Military Academy* (London: Egerton, 1815), pp.223-4. There is great similarity with Burgoyne's notes on mining, suggesting that experience was being transmitted back to Chatham for the education of other engineers.

Cabezón, and Valladolid. Again, there was still a river between the bulk of the allied and French forces.

There was a significant change in Burgoyne's personal situation on this day. Burgoyne was superseded in command of the engineers with the army. He noted 'Sir Richard Fletcher arrived from Badajoz'.[101] Fletcher had been at Badajoz since April 1812 supervising the repairs and ensuring that it would be capable of defence if the French tried to re-take it. Wellington had been concerned for some months about the slow progress in repairing Ciudad Rodrigo, the responsibility of which had been handed to the Spanish. He could not afford to lose either of these fortresses. A surprise was coming for him.

Burgoyne's six months as Wellington's senior engineer had been very difficult and he had no major operational success. He did however gain the trust of Wellington, something that many officers never managed to do.

On 27 October, the French appeared in front of Cabezón, but when it was clear the allies were there in force, they moved south-west looking for alternative routes across the Pisuerga.[102] Every available engineer was being used to destroy bridges on the retreat to delay the French pursuit. Reid and William Barney were sent to mine the bridges at Simancas and Valladolid over the River Pisuerga, and Pitts was sent to mine the bridge over the Duero at Tordesillas. All were told not to blow these bridges until they received further orders, unless the enemy attacked.[103]

One of the problems faced by the engineers when trying to quickly destroy a bridge was the hardness of the bridges and Pitts realised that he might not have time to prepare the mine in the standard way. The standard way was to sink a shaft near the parapet (the walls) of the bridge and then dig a gallery (tunnel) back to the middle of the bridge (see diagram).[104] The stone and earth nearest the parapet was the hardest. Pitts dug two shafts, the first the standard way and a second shaft straight down at the top of the arch. The earth in the centre of the bridge tended to be easier to work. As he had expected, digging the standard shaft proved too slow, but he was able to blow the arch from his secondary shaft.[105]

On 27 October 1812, another engineer officer joined the army. Lieutenant Harry Jones, the brother of the engineer John Jones, arrived from Madrid and was immediately ordered to Toro to destroy the bridge over the Duero.[106]

Wellington was clearly concerned about the state of the various bridges and on 28 October, Burgoyne was sent from Cabezón to Tordesillas 'to see if the mine was

101 REM 4201-68, Journal, 26 October 1812.

102 Oman, *Peninsular War*, Vol.VI, p.82.

103 REM 4201-68, Journal, 27 October 1812.

104 H. Colburn (ed.), *United Service Journal* (London: Colburn & Bentley, 1831 Part 1), pp.222-3.

105 William Reid, 'Destruction of Stone Bridges', *Royal Engineers, Professional Papers* (Chatham: Royal Engineers, 1837), pp.148-150.

106 C.F.C. Beresford, 'A Diary of Sir Harry Jones', *Royal Engineers Journal* (Chatham: Royal Engineers, January 1890), p.3.

Bridge at Cabezón. (Royal Engineers Museum)

all ready and to get intelligence of the enemy'. He noted the bridge at Simancas had been blown that morning and the bridge at Tordesillas was blown at 7:00 p.m., both on the advance of the enemy. The French were not to be deterred. A daring attack was launched across the Duero at Tordesillas with 50 Frenchmen swimming across the river and surprising the not-very-watchful allied guards. This was quickly turned into a bridgehead over the river and Wellington's second line of defence was breached. The French immediately got to work to repair the bridge, the gap being about 30 feet.[107]

On the morning of 29 October, the bridge at Cabezón was blown up by Burgoyne and the bridge at Valladolid by William Barney.[108] The army started its retreat, crossing the Duero at Puente de Duero and Tudela. Burgoyne recounted a rare difference of opinion between the engineering services after Wellington asked Sturgeon to blow the bridge at Cabezón whilst Burgoyne was at Tordesillas. To Wellington's surprise, Sturgeon reported he needed 36 hours to do it. When Burgoyne was asked for an opinion: he said he could do it much quicker and completed the task in five hours. Three barrels of powder were buried in a shaft five feet deep and then covered with heavy stones and 'succeeded completely' in destroying a 48-foot arch. Burgoyne commented: 'I found his idea was to work into the side of the bridge through the masonry, which would have been quite

107 REM 4201-68, Journal, 29 October 1812.

108 Burgoyne says it was destroyed at 8:00 a.m.; REM 4201-68, Journal, 29 October 1812.

impracticable'. The method proposed by Sturgeon was not really 'impractical'.[109] It was a method recommended by other engineer officers especially when the roadway was very hard.

A number of other orders were given. Reid was ordered to Quintanilla de Onésimo above Tudela, to mine the bridge over the Duero and remain there to destroy it if the French approached. The bridge at Tudela, which had previously been repaired with a wooden arch, was broken in the evening. Pitts was also ordered to mine the bridge at Zamora. The Royal Staff Corps carried out the same task at the Puente de Duero.[110] With these actions, thirteen bridges on the Duero and Pisuerga rivers for a distance of 100 miles were destroyed. Crossing anywhere other than at a bridge was impossible due to the high-water level after the recent rain.

Wellington's made his third line of defence around the French bridgehead at Tordesillas. This was the only place where the French had a foothold on the southern bank of the Duero and Wellington believed he could contain them there. On 30 October, two batteries were started, each for six guns. Burgoyne complained that they intended to start construction of two more redoubts but could only find tools for 100 men. He remarked the following day that work continued on the batteries 'night and day' showing their importance to the army.[111] These defences were Burgoyne's main task for the next few days, they were still being constructed on 2 November 1812. Wellington's army got a week to rest before it became necessary to retire further, which was started on 6 November. Hill's force was approaching, having been ordered from Madrid. Wellington had hoped that he could move south to meet Hill at Arévalo when he retired from the Duero but realised that the French armies were too strong and ordered Hill, who had by this time reached Arévalo, to move direct to Salamanca via Peñaranda.

On 8 November 1812, Wellington arrived at Salamanca, and immediately started construction of redoubts on the heights of San Cristóbal, the position he had occupied in June when facing Marmont. Burgoyne would have been involved in this work. Harry Jones noted in his diary: 'building three breastworks at Aldeaseca and Vilares'.[112] Also on 8 November, Pitts and William Barney (Assistant Engineer) were sent to mine two more bridges over the Tormes at Congosta and Barco de Avila. These bridges controlled the southern approach to Salamanca. The other main bridges at Salamanca and Alba de Tormes were in allied hands and the Tormes formed another river barrier.

Wellington managed to stay there for a week, but superior French forces were concentrating in front of him. Alba de Tormes was approached but held against

109 Wrottesley, *Burgoyne*, p.242.

110 Harry Jones said it was being mined on 26 October. *Royal Engineers Journal*, 1890, p.4.

111 REM 4201-68, Journal, 30 & 31 October 1812.

112 *Royal Engineers Journal*, January 1890, p.3.

the probing attacks. The French were able to ford the Tormes at Galisancho, south of Alba de Tormes, and crossed the river on 14 November 1812, moving north to Mozarbes. Burgoyne commented: 'It is supposed to have been an error, not opposing the passage of the enemy across the Tormes; but [it is] said that General Hill, who was nearest the spot, had no authority to do so'.[113]

It does seem surprising that the French were allowed to cross within 25 miles of Salamanca when Wellington was ordering bridges to be destroyed 50 miles away. Wellington appeared to be convinced that the Tormes was not fordable and maybe this certainty reduced the attention of his subordinates. A few days before the French crossed, he had written: 'All reports agree that the fords are not now practicable. Indeed, there is a considerable increase of water in the river; and the best proof that they are not practicable is, that the people of the country have their cattle grazing on the left [western] bank'.[114]

Wellington in his correspondence with Lieutenant General Hill, who was at Alba de Tormes, did repeat that if any French troops did manage to cross, they 'must be vigorously attacked'.[115] There appears to be a hole in Wellington's despatches around this period which suggests that the crossing was unexpected and that he was very busy making arrangements to counter the threat. When he finally mentioned the circumstances in a letter to Bathurst on 19 November, he gave no details of how the French managed to cross but stated that when he advanced to attack them, they were already too strong.[116] Wellington's actions around 13 and 14 November are confusing. He wanted to hold the line of the Tormes and was sure it was not easily fordable (Hill did not appear to agree). He was warned that the French were looking to cross upstream (south) of Alba de Tormes but did not have any troops nearby. On the morning of the 14 November when the French crossed, by three fords according to Fortescue, Wellington could not bring a force to oppose them before they were over in strength and moving towards Salamanca, necessitating a rapid retreat.[117]

Wellington was left with no choice but to retreat again towards Ciudad Rodrigo as the French were marching westward, south of his position at Salamanca. The bridge at Alba de Tormes was blown when the allies abandoned the town. The weather remained very poor with large amounts of rain making the roads difficult.

On 16 November 1812, Wellington's situation now became much more serious, with news that the repairs to the fortifications at Ciudad Rodrigo, towards which his army was retreating, had collapsed. The responsibility for the repairs had been handed over to the Spanish soon after its capture in January 1812. Burgoyne

113 REM 4201-68, Journal, 15 November 1812; Wrottesley, *Burgoyne*, p.245.

114 Gurwood (ed.), *Despatches*, Wellington to Hill, Salamanca, 9 November 1812.

115 Gurwood (ed.), *Despatches*, Wellington to Hill, Salamanca, 10 November 1812.

116 Gurwood (ed.), *Despatches*, Wellington to Bathurst, Ciudad Rodrigo, 19 November 1812.

117 Fortescue, *British Army*, Vol.VIII, p.614; Andrew Leith-Hay, *A Narrative of the Peninsular War*, 2nd Edition (London: Washbourne, 1834), pp,101-2.

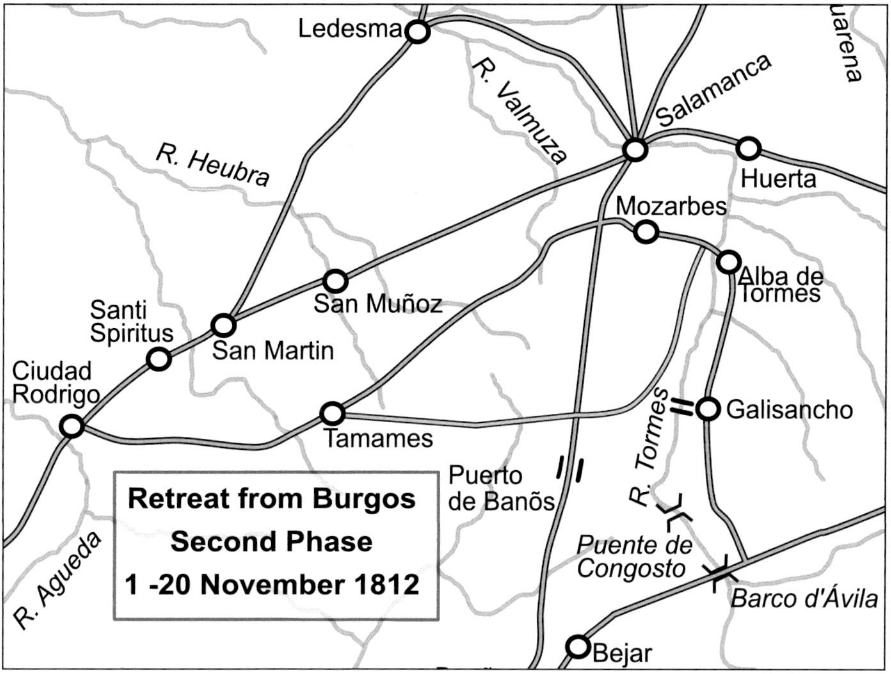

Second phase of retreat from Burgos.

recorded: 'Lord Wellington having information that the new walls to the breaches of Ciudad Rodrigo have fallen in, I am ordered to proceed there immediately, and endeavour to get them put into a state to resist a *coup de main*'.[118]

He was despatched immediately to put temporary repairs in place, arriving on 17 November:

> Found the breaches not fallen in, but menacing it strongly, and propped up with beams. These new walls are five feet thick at bottom, and four at top, twenty-four feet high, without counterforts [buttresses], and apparently without drains, it was to be expected, therefore, that they would fall down. Sir Richard Fletcher, our commanding Engineer, who planned them, declares they were to have been only sixteen feet high; still, however, I should imagine they would.[119]

118 REM 4201-68, Journal, 16 November 1812; Wrottesley, *Burgoyne*, pp.245-6.
119 REM 4201-68, Journal, 17 November 1812; Wrottesley, *Burgoyne*, p.246.

It is difficult to see why Burgoyne now thought 16 feet was too tall. He made no such comment in February when the repairs were planned.[120] Fortress walls were built much higher than this. It is very surprising that, 11 months after the fortress was taken, there was still significant work to be done to repair the main breach. Although the Spanish were given responsibility for the repairs, it is difficult to conceive that no checks on progress had been made and no engineer had been through to comment on the slow progress. This should not have come as a surprise to Wellington. The main issue was not the unstable state of part of the wall, it was the fact that the breach had still not been repaired.

Fortunately for Wellington, the French did not approach close enough to see the damage to the walls. When Wellington started moving west on 15 November 1812, Joseph took a third of the French forces to Salamanca which was thoroughly sacked (again) by his troops. Soult was ordered to follow the allied army but now with an army too small to force a battle. There was no real attempt to interrupt the retreat, the French restricting their efforts to picking up stragglers from the allied army. The pursuit was abandoned at San Muñoz, 40 miles short of Ciudad Rodrigo.

However, the retreat from Burgos had caused significant injury to Wellington's army. The weather was atrocious for much of the period from early October and the troops were suffering even before the retreat started. Even Hill's corps which had come up from Madrid had suffered. The final few days' retreat saw the army, again, fall into disorder, the situation not being helped by a supply failure caused by the new and incompetent Quartermaster General, Colonel James Gordon. In a repeat of both Hill's and Wellington's earlier withdrawals a few weeks earlier, the army behaved very badly and this led to a stinging rebuke to the whole army from Wellington when the retreat had concluded. By the time the regiments arrived near Ciudad Rodrigo they had suffered nearly 5,000 casualties since 23 October without fighting a battle![121] As Wellington remarked, his army had a busy year and needed a rest.

The allied army was kept concentrated for several days until Wellington received confirmation that Soult was retiring eastwards. It then settled into cantonments for the winter and to prepare for the next campaign. Burgoyne was still attached to headquarters and travelled with it to Mealhada Sorda when Wellington returned to the quarters he used the previous winter at Freineda. Work continued to strengthen Ciudad Rodrigo and the engineers were still getting unwanted 'help'. Burgoyne recorded:

> It having been reported to Lord Wellington, that water might be let into the ditch of the fausse-bray at Ciudad Rodrigo, from the aqueduct in

120 In REM 5501-59-3, 3 February 1812, there is a sketch of the proposed wall with dimensions.
121 Oman, *Peninsular War*, Vol.VI, p153.

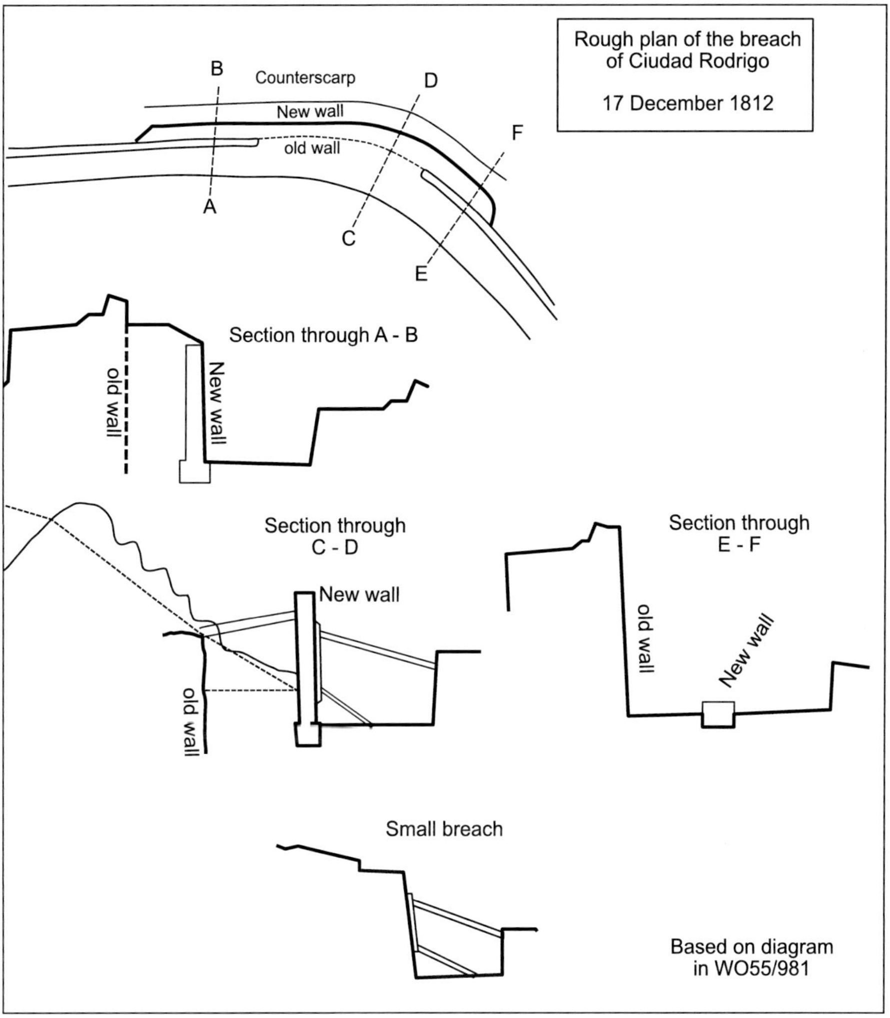

Sketch of Ciudad Rodrigo wall failure, December 1812.

> front of the great breach, with the aqueduct to serve it, Lieutenant Colonel Sir Richard Fletcher, Commanding Engineer, and myself, went over to examine it.

Their conclusion was that without substantial work to line the channel and ditch most of the water would run away; the scarps on each side of the ditch would be weakened and any water that did remain would stand in places that were of no use for defence. He finished with:

> The people who form these projects, very indelicately, take the liberty of interfering and suggesting alterations and improvements in the Engineer department which they would never venture to do to any others and this direct to Lord Wellington.[122]

What is surprising is that even after the fright on hearing the defences were collapsing, there seemed to be little impetus in getting the work completed. Reid, who was working on the repairs complained in mid-December about a month after the army arrived:

> The troops could be employed as labourers, but they have very few masons amongst them … At present the men I employ are paid by the Spaniards, but they are so idle and they are such bad workmen that I do not think I shall have the wall cleared out by the beginning of February.[123]

Whilst there is little further mention of the repairs, it would appear that the work was not finished until May 1813, 16 months after the town was taken![124] About the same date as Reid wrote the letter above, Wellington was travelling to Cadiz and passed through Badajoz. He found the local senior engineer missing; the only other senior engineer present had just arrived at the town and was unable to answer Wellington's questions. Burgoyne's journal noted:

> [Wellington] has ordered Captain [George] Henderson and Captain [William] Slade of the Engineers, who were at Badajoz to complete the repairs of the breaches etc. to be immediately relieved and an officer to be sent there whose judgement and discretion can be relied on.
>
> Captain Henderson, he [Wellington] had not seen, he [Henderson] having gone to Merida without any orders, to destroy the bridge there because he had heard that some French had crossed the Tagus at Arzobispo; and Captain Slade he [Wellington] says "appears to him, to be totally incapable of the charge".[125]

This is the only occasion during the Peninsular War where Wellington demanded the removal of engineer officers. No similar correspondence has been located about Wellington being concerned about the state of the defences at Ciudad Rodrigo.

122 REM 4201-68, Journal, 7 December 1812. Wrottesley 'edited' the published version.

123 TNA WO55/981, Reid to Goldfinch, 17 December 1812.

124 REM 4201-68, Journal, 29 April 1813.

125 REM 4201-68, Journal, 30 December 1812. This is another example of Wrottesley editing his biography. This event was not printed. Burgoyne clearly must have seen Wellington's letter as his journal entry is almost identical to Wellington's letter. Gurwood (ed.), *Despatches*, Wellington to Fletcher, Badajoz, 20 December 1812.

Before Wellington set off for Cadiz, he approved a request for Fletcher to return home during the winter. Fletcher had been in the Peninsula since April 1809 and had to leave his children in the care of relatives when his wife died just before he embarked for the Peninsula. Fletcher appointed the senior engineer, Captain Henry Goldfinch, as commanding engineer in his absence. Fletcher left headquarters on 9 December and Goldfinch arrived from Hill's corps the following day. The timing is interesting in that it looks like Burgoyne waited until Fletcher left and then wrote to Wellington challenging the appointment of Goldfinch. Whilst it is possible that Fletcher had not told Burgoyne until just before he left, this seems very unlikely. Burgoyne's letter to Wellington acknowledged that Goldfinch was the senior Royal Engineer but claimed command of the engineering service with the army, which included King's German Legion and Portuguese engineers as well, due to his superior (brevet) army rank. Burgoyne's argument appeared to be that there were some Portuguese engineer majors 'who report to the commanding engineer' and as Goldfinch was only a captain, this could cause difficulties. Burgoyne's senior army rank would overcome this obstacle.

Wellington's response the following day, confirmed Goldfinch as senior, adding:

> However extensive the command of the senior officers in this country may be, His Lordship cannot but regard it as almost exclusively British; and the fact of reports being sent by Portuguese Majors does not in his opinion materially alter the case; as they are made for the information of the Commander in Chief, and are addressed by persons on distant services to that officer who is in direct communication with His Lordship. In the event however of the British officers meeting either with those belonging to the King's German Legion, or with Portuguese officers, the Marquess of Wellington would then look upon the senior officer of the Corps of Engineers, whether Portuguese, British or German, as the one to have command of the whole.[126]

Wellington was clear that seniority was based on rank in the various engineer corps, not on brevet army ranks. This was certainly the position the Board of Ordnance would have taken and Burgoyne would have known that. Seniority was not a new issue. There were many senior Portuguese engineers up to general rank, but they had specific responsibilities in the management of the Portuguese engineer service and were not employed in the field. This issue could be extended to include the Spanish engineer corps once Wellington was made commander-in-chief of the Spanish army.

126 REM 5501-139, Burgoyne to Fitzroy Somerset, 9 December 1812 and the reply dated 10 December 1812. This event is not mentioned in Burgoyne's journal or Wrottesley's biography.

Burgoyne should not have raised this issue with Wellington. It should have been discussed with Fletcher before he left for England.[127] However, this problem should never have arisen. Captain Howard Elphinstone had been ordered to return to the Peninsula in November 1812 to take command, but took nearly five months to arrive at Wellington's headquarters, only beating Fletcher's return by a couple of weeks! He was promptly sent back to Lisbon.

Burgoyne, writing to his sister in January 1813, commented:

> I am in hopes, however, of having plenty of outdoors work again before long, though I am much haunted with fears of being left on some garrison job. The folks in England do not give us a chance of getting to the top in this country, for as fast as vacancies occur, they send out others over our heads. I have now more senior officers to me belonging to this army than when I had when I came out four years ago. I fancy it is, that now they find something is to be got, they begin to volunteer to come out. I will continue … contented … if I can only contrive to keep with the army in the field … I do not think I have his Lordship's interest since the siege of Burgos, which is, I think rather hard, for he has never, that I can learn, expressed the slightest disapproval on any point.[128]

No evidence has been unearthed to suggest that Wellington was unhappy with Burgoyne's performance, but this did not stop him worrying that he would be left at Ciudad Rodrigo to complete the repairs when the army advanced again. The border fortresses were of critical importance to Wellington, as demonstrated by him leaving Fletcher at Badajoz for several months to complete the repairs. Ciudad Rodrigo was strategically the most important and most vulnerable of the two fortresses.

Burgoyne was constantly concerned about his future and what people thought of him. This was perhaps due to his upbringing where he felt that it was up to him to provide for himself and his sister. He was clearly a proud man and did not want to rely on the generosity of Lord Derby. It is possible that he also felt he had something to prove, to show that he could do better than his father, through his own efforts. Burgoyne's comment about the number of officers' senior to him is wrong. There were at least eight in 1808, whilst there were only three by the start of 1813. His concern was probably due to Elphinstone returning to the Peninsula 'as second in command of the of the Engineers'.[129] Elphinstone originally came out in 1808 and returned home after being wounded at Roliça.

127 Burgoyne was not the only engineer officer who tried to claim engineer seniority based on brevet army rank. Jones did the same when he arrived on the east coast of Spain earlier in 1812 and tried (and failed) to claim command over Captain Frederick Thackeray RE.

128 Wrottesley, *Burgoyne*, pp.250-1, Burgoyne to his sister, 27 January 1813.

129 Wrottesley, *Burgoyne*, p.254.

1812 had been a difficult year for Burgoyne. He was more fortunate than almost any other engineer officer in that he had been able to spend a significant time in 1811 and 1812 with the field army and much of that time as the senior engineer. This would have given him significant experience in the management of engineering services and also exposure to the senior commanders in the army. Burgoyne was well-known and appeared to be well-liked. However, with seniority comes responsibility. The sieges at Salamanca and Burgos were not effective and many will have seen this as the fault of the senior engineer. Burgoyne was certainly frustrated at the limited resources available and at Burgos, by the indecision of the commander-in-chief. Both Wellington and Burgoyne believed that Burgos could have been taken – albeit for different reasons – and neither were happy with the outcome. Having had a taste of command, it is very difficult to accept becoming a subordinate again. The biggest gain for Burgoyne and one that would benefit him for the next 40 years was that Wellington had confidence in his abilities. In the short term, it would see him commanding the engineers in North America and would lead to senior positions in the Ordnance up to and including the Crimean War. In the meantime, Burgoyne enjoyed some well-earned rest.

One thing that had become noticeable by 1812 was that the number of letters Burgoyne sent and received had reduced. The high attrition rate amongst engineer officers was having an effect. Some of Burgoyne's regular engineer correspondents over the years were dead: Edmund Mulcaster, John Squire, Charles Lefebure. Others had been injured and returned home: Charles Pasley, Alexander Thomson, John Jones, Charles Boothby. The pool of officers who he could share his thoughts with was diminishing. Through it all Burgoyne appeared to lead a charmed life and enjoyed good health, something he had in common with Wellington.

13

1813 – Rivers and Castles

Burgoyne's worries about being left at Ciudad Rodrigo were eventually eased when it was agreed that he would be attached to the army when it moved. Initially, with the general shortage of engineers and because Captains Henderson and Slade had upset Wellington at Badajoz, 'it was settled' that Burgoyne would remain at Ciudad Rodrigo. Henderson had been in Ceylon for the last nine years. Slade had only served in the British Isles since being commissioned. Neither had any field experience before they arrived in 1812. Fortunately, Wellington had second thoughts, probably realising that having his best engineers with the army in the coming campaign was better than leaving them hundreds of miles away from the action and taking less experienced engineers with him. Burgoyne also thought that Wellington had been reminded about his usefulness when the subject of El Boden had been raised and 'said they [the engineers] might be very useful in a thousand instances'.[1]

The news of Napoleon's disaster in Russia came through early in the year and Burgoyne noted: 'The very great success of the Russians leads us to expect the French force in Spain will be weakened the next campaign, and that we may be able to act offensively to some effect'.[2]

Wellington planned to move east from the Portuguese border with his forces pushing back the weakened French armies. There were several major rivers to cross and for the first time a large pontoon train was to move with the army as well as a small siege train. Both of these were very unwieldy and slow moving. Another new addition to the army was the attachment of four companies of newly trained Royal Sappers and Miners. There were about 200 men with engineering stores carried on 100 mules.

At the start of 1813, there is another large gap in Burgoyne's diary lasting two months, from February to the end of April. There would have been little engineering work to do apart from the repairs to Ciudad Rodrigo and Burgoyne did not

1 REM 4201-68, Journal, 7 February 1813.
2 REM 4201-68, Journal, 7 February 1813.

appear to be directly involved in it. However, Burgoyne was clearly reflecting on his experiences and considering improvements for future campaigns. In January 1813, he prepared a memorandum with detailed explanations on how to prosecute a siege based on his field experience. The journal ran to 50 pages, with information on the number of troops required, the method of constructing batteries, fascines and gabions, payment schedules for work and many other tasks. It was laid out 'in a manner to be useful to officers in the British service'.[3] The original document was clearly expanded later as it refers to operations in 1813 and 1814 and was published in an updated form after the Crimean War probably to assist officers in any future sieges after the unsatisfactory attempts on Sevastopol.[4] Burgoyne's aim was to produce a practical handbook for use during operations, not a textbook.

In a letter to Pasley, the head of the School of Military Engineering, in March 1813, Burgoyne discussed the issue of ventilation in mine galleries. This had been a significant issue in the first two mines at Burgos but not at the final gallery dug under the church of St Roman, which was the longest of the three. Burgoyne believed that the difference was the depth of the gallery and asked Pasley if he could carry out some experiments at Chatham at different depths and with different types of soil.[5]

Two weeks later, Burgoyne started thinking about a future attack on Burgos. The army was convinced that this would happen again and the soldiers, particularly, were not looking forward to it. Burgoyne prepared a proposal for the next attack on Burgos and there was a change in the plan for the attack.[6] The main difference was the assumption that there would be greater firepower available. A new siege train had been ordered in January 1813 comprising fourteen 24-pounder cannon with 1,500 rounds, six 8-inch howitzers with 1,000 rounds, four 10-inch howitzers with 500 rounds, to which would be added six 18-pounders with 1,000 rounds that were already with the army.[7] Burgoyne's planned point of attack also changed. This could have been because there were more guns available or based on his previous experience. The focus of the attack was now on the castle facing the Cerro de San Miguel. The first step would remain taking the hornwork, then the priority would be destroying the Napoleon battery before concentrating on the defences below the castle.

Although the plan looked similar to that proposed by Douglas and rejected during the previous siege it was different. Douglas' proposal was to attack the wall below the castle without dealing with the Napoleon battery. Experience in 1812

3 REM 4601-72, Memoranda on Some of the Practical Operations of a Siege, January 1813.

4 George Wrottesley, *The Military Opinions of General Sir John Fox Burgoyne* (London: Richard Bentley, 1859), Part III.

5 BL ADD MS41963, f.87-90, Burgoyne to Pasley 20 March 1813.

6 See REM 4601-72, f.1813/5 and f. 1813/6.

7 See REM 4601-74, f.126. The 18-pounders moved with Graham's corps, REM 4201-68, Journal, 21 April 1813.

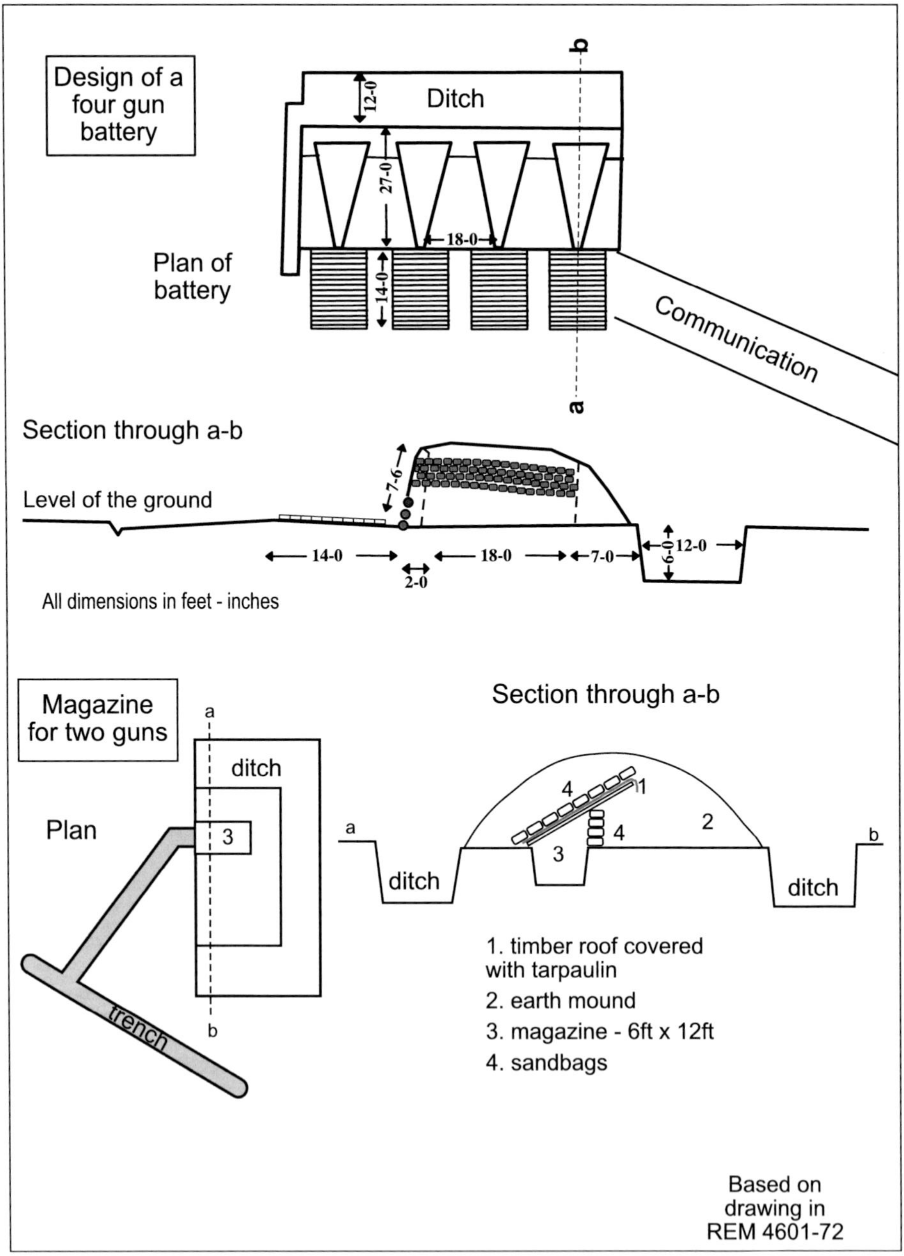

Design of a battery and magazine. (Royal Engineers Museum)

had shown that without dealing with the large French battery any attack exposed to it would be costly. Fortunately for the troops involved, Burgoyne did not get an opportunity to try his new plan.

On 22 April 1813, Burgoyne submitted a proposal for engineer stores to be carried with the army.[8] The stores were to be carried on 110 mules and a full range of tools was proposed; entrenching, mining, carpenters and smiths. The mules were then split across the 1st to 5th Divisions, with half (55), carrying the entrenching tools, allocated to the 1st Division.

On 29 April 1813, Burgoyne speculated on the new campaign. It is clear that Burgoyne did not know Wellington's plan for the coming offensive, although there was no doubt that it would be in northern Spain. He was aware that the army was ready to march:

> [A]nd only wait the arrival of the pontoon establishment from Abrantes. They move very slow, however, are drawn by bullocks, and constantly meet with accidents on the Portuguese roads. They will be up in about ten days.[9]

Wellington's army was never considered swift, always having to drag its supply train with it. It was the main reason it could never outmarch the French, who marched without this tail. Adding siege and pontoon equipment made the situation much worse. The pontoon train that was taken with the army comprised 33 pontoons, one small boat, and 14 other waggons, making 48 in total with 350 men, 310 horses and 520 oxen. The pontoon carriages were best described as brittle and there were, on average, seven breakages a day, each requiring a halt, between leaving Abrantes on 24 April 1813 and arriving on 14 May 1813 – and this was before the actual campaign started![10]

Wellington also expressed frustration about how slowly the pontoon train moved. Apart from the breakages described above, the other likely cause should have come as no surprise to anyone, including Wellington. As early as December 1812. Piper who had command of the pontoon train complained that most of the bullock train drivers had deserted through not being paid and also that the Portuguese seamen attached to the pontoon train were not given rations. The situation did not appear to have improved, with similar complaints in May 1813.[11]

8 REM 4601-74, f.87, 22 April 1813.

9 Wrottesley, *Burgoyne*, p.254.

10 Anon, 'Description of the Pontoon Train in the Peninsula', *Royal Engineer Journal*, 1870, p.14. There were 70 Portuguese sailors attached. In addition, the company of Portuguese pontoniers from the Portuguese engineer corps was assigned in late May 1813; Gurwood (ed.), *Despatches*, Wellington to Beresford, Freineda, 24 April 1813.

11 TNA WO55/981, Piper to Fletcher, 10 December 1812; H.D. Jones Journal, *RE Journal*, 1890, p.6; TNA WO55/981, Piper to Fletcher, 4 December 1812.

Wellington judged the situation so critical that he took the unpopular step of stripping 264 horses from Captain Robert Cairns' field artillery brigade to add to the pontoon train. Cairns was of the opinion that using horses instead of oxen would increase the breakages.[12] It appears that Piper may have agreed with Cairns, with Wellington writing 'The best thing to do would be to leave the train with both the horses and the oxen … the pontoon, should, in general, be drawn by the oxen and the horses should only be used when absolutely necessary'.[13] As Wellington commented to Bathurst a few days earlier, 'I understand that the carriages are shamefully bad … I shall have sad work with this bridge throughout the campaign and yet we can do nothing without it'.[14] The whole of Wellington's strategy for 1813 depended on 33 creaking pontoon carriages! This would not be the last time Wellington's operations were put at risk by pontoons.

Wellington's plan for the campaign was to march in two groups. The southern (smaller) group under Hill, with Wellington present, would march up the main road from Ciudad Rodrigo towards Salamanca, the obvious route for an attacking army. The northern force under Graham would take to the difficult roads in northern Portugal, setting off from Bragança and Miranda, and sweep round the right flank of the French forces. These routes had never been used by such large forces in the past, but Wellington's exploring officers assured him they were passable. As in previous campaigns, the senior engineer officers were assigned to the divisions of the army. Burgoyne noted with satisfaction that he had been reassigned to the 3rd Division and was even happier when it was confirmed that Picton would be returning to command. Burgoyne considered Picton a friend rather than a superior.

Burgoyne started considering the likely routes the army would take without knowing Wellington's plan. Based on his very recent experience, he was concerned about the difficulty of crossing the Douro from the southern side as the 'advantage of ground is entirely on their side'. Later in the same journal entry he noted that the QMG department had been looking north of the river, 'part of the army is certainly to move up that way so as to be on the right bank of the Douro at once'.[15] He also noted:

> The Staff Corps are about to throw a bridge of boats over the Duero [sic] at Pocinho [about ten miles west of the Portuguese border], that is between [Vila] Nova de Foz Côa and Torre de Moncorvo, it is, there, they say 140 yards wide. Another bridge has to be made over the Agueda at its mouth

12 Thompson, *Wellington's Engineers*, p.161.

13 Gurwood (ed.), *Despatches*, Wellington to Fletcher, 14 May 1813.

14 Gurwood (ed.), *Despatches*, Wellington to Bathurst, 11 May 1813.

15 Wrottesley, *Burgoyne*, pp.254-5. The date in the manuscript journal is 29 April and in the published version, 21 April 1813.

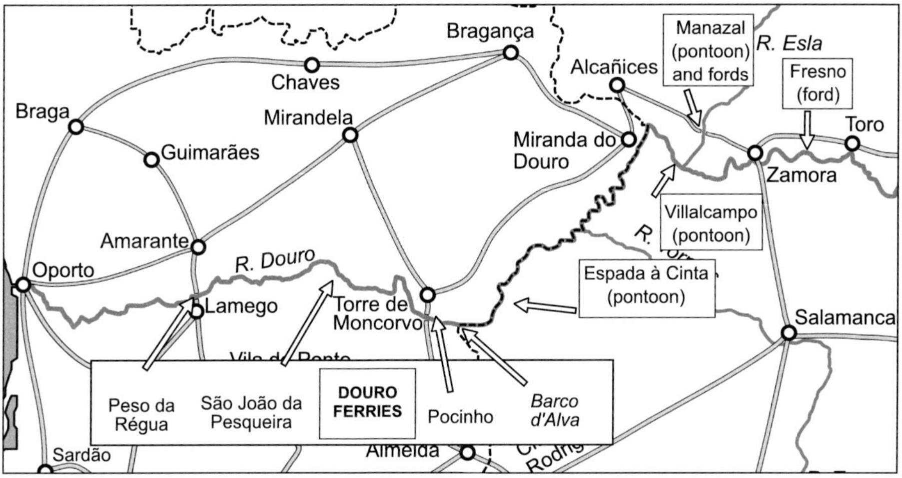

1813 campaign: crossing points on river Douro.

> to communicate from Spain to the temporary hospitals erected at Barca d'Alva from where the sick as required can be sent down the Douro in boats.[16]

These two bridges were almost certainly ferry boats or flying bridges rather than fixed bridges.

The pontoons were not required for the first days of Wellington's advance. The first crossings in Portugal, away from French interference, would use local infrastructure and additional boats, but once in Spain these resources could not be relied on and pontoons would be required. Writing to Beresford, who was still in Lisbon recovering from the wounds he received at the Battle of Salamanca, Wellington explained:

> My intention is to make them [the northern force] cross the Douro … within the Portuguese frontier, covering the movement of the left by the right of the army towards the Tormes, which right shall cross the Douro, over the pontoons … I then propose to seize Zamora and Toro, which will make all our future operations easy.[17]

16 REM 4201-68, Journal, 29 April 1813. Not printed in Wrottesley. Foz Tua, literally means the mouth of the River Tua (at Tua). St Martinho is marked in Burgoyne's journal but not on a modern map. Coleja is more like five miles above St João. It would make no sense if the crossing points were 20 miles apart.

17 Gurwood (ed.), *Despatches*, Wellington to Beresford, 24 May 1813.

Wellington intended to use three crossing points. Pocinho, near Torre de Morcorvo, St João da Pesqueira and Peso da Régua. The Royal Staff Corps was given responsibility for Pocinho and Harry Jones was ordered to Peso da Régua.

On 2 May 1813, Burgoyne received orders to investigate routes across the River Douro for the 3rd Division. He was asked to prepare crossing points at four places which he described as 'the ferries of Foz Tua and St Martinho under St João da Pesqueira and those of Collegio [Coleja] and Villarinho [Vilarinho da Castanheira] about five leagues higher up'.[18] He set off, on 2 May 1813, with Lieutenant John Hulme RE, from his winter quarters at Mealhada Sorda, 40 miles south. He noted that the ferries were good:

> [B]ut it was proposed also to employ boats on the river to pass the troops as quick as possible. The directions, however, are not to interfere with the conveyance of the supplies or stores up the river, though we may apply to the commissaries for boats. The only boats on the upper part of the river are absolutely in the employment of conveying up supplies; the time also is short (the [3rd] Division, we are told will probably cross between the 6th and the 9th inst.) and a great part of the army are to pass by Pocinho ... it is therefore hardly to be expected that we can get any boats at the upper ferries, though we may probably at the two lower ones as at Foz Tua there are usually several ... General Murray promised to endeavour to get two boats ordered down to the upper two ferries.

Burgoyne also noted that it had been very wet for a week which would not be good news when trying to cross rivers.[19] On arriving Burgoyne looked at Coleja and Vilarinho and sent Hulme to look at the other two crossing points.

Burgoyne was very familiar with the River Douro from his detailed examinations in 1809 and 1812. It was only a year since Burgoyne had travelled up this exact stretch of the river. It will have been no coincidence that Burgoyne was ordered to look at the ferries and it does raise the question of whether Wellington had been considering, during the previous year, the potential for a northern advance into Spain.

The normal ferry boats at Coleja and Vilarinho were capable of taking 40 soldiers or eight loaded beasts, but he noted that the roads approaching them were very poor and not suitable for carriages. Burgoyne reported that 360 soldiers and 60 loaded beasts per hour could be transferred at these two crossing points. On 5 May, two other boats were provided. These boats were port barges and were the largest boats that could be used on the river. They had a carrying capacity of 20-25 tons downriver and about half that upriver. Burgoyne estimated that these new boats

18 REM 4201-68, Journal, 2 May 1813. Not printed in Wrottesley.
19 REM 4201-68, Journal, 2 May 1813.

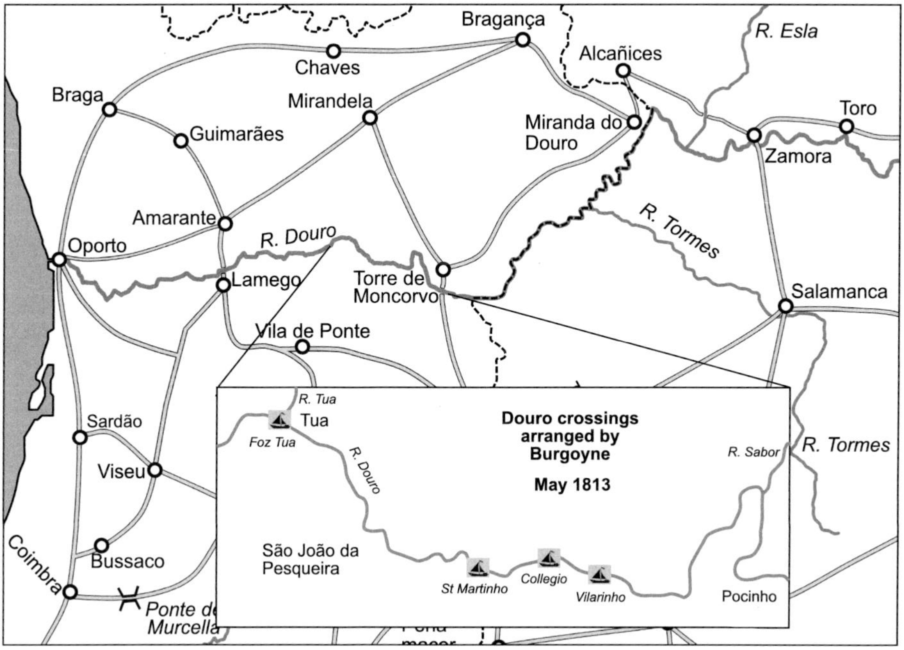

1813 campaign: crossing points established by Burgoyne.

could transfer another 600 troops per hour. Having considered the matter further, Burgoyne wrote to Major General Charles Colville, in temporary command of the 3rd Division, and informed him that 700 men and 60 loaded beasts could be crossed per hour at Coleja and Vilarinha.[20] Hulme has also reported back to Burgoyne that there were no suitable ferry boats at Foz Tua or St Martinho, but he had obtained boats capable of passing 800 troops and 40 loaded beasts per hour.[21] Harry Jones, who had been given the same task at Peso da Rugua, reported that with 11 boats, he estimated 1,300 troops could be crossed hourly.[22]

On 7 May 1813, two companies of Portuguese troops arrived for Burgoyne and Hulme to use to guard the ferries and as working parties for preparing the crossing points. In the coming days Burgoyne travelled the roads in the area familiarising himself with their condition and noting which were capable of taking carriages.

The Quartermaster General, George Murray, issued complex orders to manage the march of the troops to the crossing points, to ensure there was no congestion during the crossing and that the troops marched by different routes to the

20 Wrottesley, *Burgoyne*, p.256.

21 REM 4201-68, Journal, 5-7 May 1813.

22 H.D. Jones Journal, *RE Journal*, 1890, p.6. Also, a brigade of artillery or cavalry regiment in five hours.

concentration point. The first troops crossed over on 18 May 1813. Three columns crossed at Peso da Régua, São João da Pesqueira and Pocinho. The pontoon and most of the artillery crossed at Pocinho as this was both the shortest route and best road to the border at Miranda do Douro.[23] Preceding them at this ferry were the 4th, 6th, and 7th Divisions. The 1st and 5th Divisions crossed at Peso da Régua and marched towards Bragança via Mirandela. The most difficult route was that taken by the 3rd Division which crossed at the ferries organised by Burgoyne. The division then had a difficult march, cross country from Vila Flor to Vimioso through Bornos. The divisional artillery followed the main road from Pocinho to Miranda.[24]

Wellington's advance had been timed so that the major rivers would have settled towards their summer levels and crossing was possible. Whilst he was confident that he could obtain boats to ferry his troops across the Douro within Portugal, he could not risk the same in Spain.[25] This was why he took the trouble of bringing a pontoon train forward. It was possible it would be needed for communication between the two forces advancing on either side of the Douro but the primary requirement was to bridge the Esla, north of the Duero.[26]

The 'instructions for Movement' sent to Graham on 18 May 1813, explained: 'It is intended to lay the bridge of pontoons at the Barca de Villal Campo [Villalcampo], about a mile below the junction of the Esla with the Duero, where it is expected to arrive on the 30th'. Wellington had also identified the ferry at Freixo de Espada á Cinta as a possible communication point between the two corps. The same 'Instructions' had the pontoon train stopping at Villa Velha on the road to Malhadas (i.e. Miranda).[27] He wanted to keep the pontoon train in a position where it could throw a bridge over the Douro north of Torre de Moncorvo (Espada á Cinta) or further north near the junction with the Esla (Villalcampo). Two days later, Wellington received information that there were French forces concentrating around Zamora which could operate on both sides of the Duero using the bridges there and at Toro. He decided to split the pontoon train, sending 14 to Espada á Cinta whilst the remainder moved north with the army.[28]

23 Burgoyne said the siege train of six 18-pounders arrived at Pocinho on 12 May. REM 4201-68, Journal, 12 May 1813.

24 REM 4201-68, Journal, 16 May 1813.

25 Wellington must have been confident as he did not order finding suitable ferry boats until the beginning of May, indicating that the army could be moving within a week. It did not leave the engineer officers long to find boats and build staging points at suitable locations. Burgoyne's notes from his previous survey must have been very useful.

26 The river is called Douro in Portugal and Duero in Spain.

27 Gurwood (ed.), *Despatches*, Wellington to Graham, 18 May 1813. Wellington appeared to use Malhadas and Miranda interchangeably. There is no village called Villa Velha. There is however a village called Villa Delha (marked on the Lopez map and called Villa Della on the Carta Militar) about mid-way between Torre de Moncorvo and Miranda.

28 Gurwood (ed.), *Despatches*, Wellington to Graham, 20 May 1813. Burgoyne noted that they were at Miranda on 27 May 1813. REM 4201-68, Journal, 27 May 1813.

The movement of Graham's troops was planned to have them all arriving at Villalcampo ready for the pontoon train's arrival on 30 May 1813. The right corps under Hill, having reached Salamanca, was then to march north to Villalcampo to join with Graham's force. On the 26 May 1813, the troops which had been hidden behind the Portuguese border and a strong cavalry screen marched into Spain. They moved in three columns; the right towards the ford on Manazal; the centre, including Burgoyne and the 3rd Division, to Losilla two miles north; and the left column to Tabara, three miles further north: all within a few miles of the Esla. Hill, who had arrived in Salamanca on 26 May 1813, was now pushing troops north towards Zamora.

The weather now interfered with the plan and Graham found the River Esla higher than expected and the fords were much higher than expected, Burgoyne commenting that the ford at Almendra was 'the best but now very deep; most of the ferry boats are destroyed'.[29]

Wellington, who had been travelling with Hill's troops, primarily to deceive the French about his main line of attack, now rode quickly north, arriving on the Esla with Graham's force on 30 May 1813. The decision was now made to use the pontoons to cross the Esla rather than cross the Duero at Villalcampo. Wellington's decision would have been easier as there was no evidence of French troops concentrating in the area of Zamora and he would have felt that his split forces were under no immediate danger. Wellington also ordered that the known fords over the Esla should be attempted and that other crossing points should be looked for. On 31 May. the fords at Almendra (south of Manazal) and Montamarta (north of Manazal) were tried and were found passable, with difficulty, by cavalry, although some lives were lost. Others were tried but found impassable. The 3rd Division made an attempt to cross at a previously unknown ford but failed.[30] Eventually, most of the troops passed over the pontoon bridge laid at Manazal, the 3rd Division crossing on 1 June 1813. Burgoyne was not directly involved in constructing the bridge but commented confusingly, 'the bridge being made of four pontoons, 15 feet asunder was not [esteemed?] equal to pass artillery; which therefore forded at the Almendra ford with difficulty'. This appears to be an error. Dickson, wrote that the pontoon bridge laid at Manazal:

> [U]sed 12 pontoons at the widest distance apart, which serves for infantry and horses but not for carriages, the cavalry, artillery and wheel carriages of the army passing at the ford. A flying bridge of pontoons was also constructed for the 18-pounders by which they passed.[31]

29 REM 4201-68, Journal, 29 May 1813.

30 Oman, *Peninsular War*, Vol.VI, p.330; Wrottesley, *Burgoyne*, pp.257-8.

31 REM 4201-68, Journal, 1 June 1813; Leslie (ed.), *Dickson Manuscripts*, Vol.V, p.899.

The rain had increased the height and width of the river and the pontoons available were not enough to bridge it. The siege guns were too heavy for the pontoon bridge and as Wellington wanted to keep the siege guns with the army, compromises had to be made. Having deducted a number of pontoons to make the flying bridge for the siege guns, the remaining pontoons could make a foot bridge and the cavalry and artillery had to use a ford. The 14 pontoons left at Espada á Cinta would have been very useful.[32] As Burgoyne crossed over the bridge, he would have been fully aware of its construction, so him mentioning only four pontoons in his journal must be an error.

A pontoon bridge had not been established at Villalcampo as originally planned. As there was no other crossing point on the Duero until the bridge at Zamora was taken, Wellington was anxious about cutting communications between his forces either side of the Duero. In fact, Wellington had made his position clear, making Hill's priority to ensure 'a junction' with Graham's force. If Hill was attacked and forced to withdraw, it should be towards Villalcampo. Even without the pontoon bridge in place at Villalcampo, Wellington's orders stood, as a bridge could be quickly thrown across the Duero.[33]

Zamora was entered on 31 May 1813, and the advance guard was pushed on towards Toro, occupying the ford at Fresno mid-way between Zamora and Toro.[34] Toro was abandoned by the French on 1 June 1813. Wellington arrived the following day and directed Hill's corps to cross the Duero at Toro. The bridges in both these towns were in allied hands, but both needed repairing. Burgoyne noted that the Spanish repaired the bridge at Zamora on 2 June and at Toro, 'Two pontoons are taken on by relays of horses from the reserve artillery; the whole of the pontoons are ordered up as quick as can be'.[35] These were probably the horses taken from Cairns' Brigade of artillery some weeks earlier and left with the pontoon train. The crossing was restored on 3 June.

Wellington's army continued its advance with the French having to repeatedly withdraw due to the wide flanking movement by the allied army which passed to the north of Tordesillas, Valladolid, Palencia, and then Burgos. Through all this manoeuvring, the pontoon and siege trains were only one march behind.[36] In mid-June, Wellington's army again approached Burgos and, to the relief of the troops, the French destroyed it, leaving no need for a second siege. Burgoyne commented

32 By now, the pontoon at Espada á Cinta was unnecessary and it would appear logical that it would be moved north to join the army, although there is no evidence that this had happened. A second pontoon train had been requested from England to be sent to La Coruña on 19 May 1813; TNA WO55/959, unknown to Mann, 16 June 1813.

33 Gurwood (ed.), *Despatches*, Wellington to Hill, 28 May 1813. 'Orders have been given', not the bridge was in place. On 30 May, Wellington had cancelled the order to have the pontoons available for the Esla.

34 Gurwood (ed.), *Despatches*, Wellington to Hill, Carvajales 31 May 1813.

35 REM 4201-68, Journal, 2 June 1813.

36 REM 4201-68, Journal, 11 June 1813.

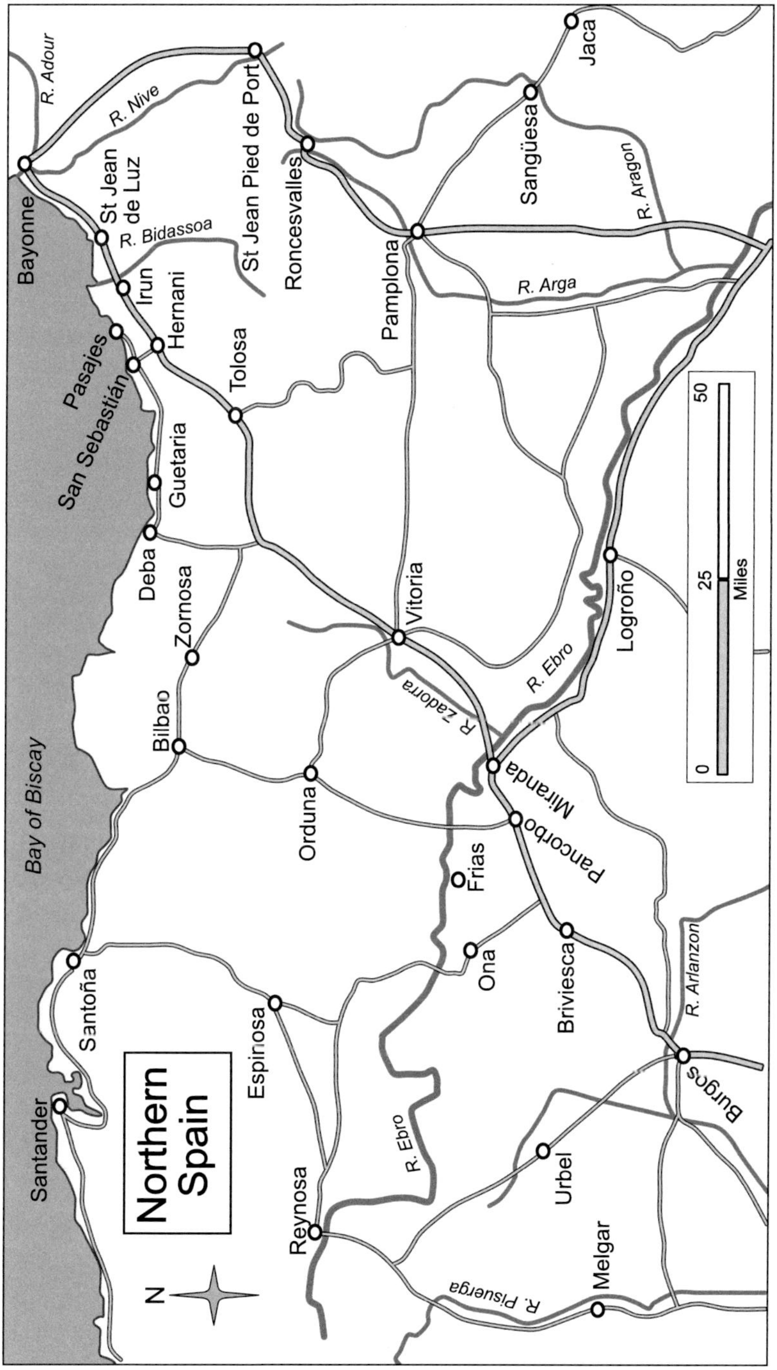

Northern Spain.

about the: 'Foolish dread that has got about our army respecting the difficulty of the enterprise [a second siege], from not properly estimating the cause of our last failure … [and should not be] frightened from a third rate fortress'.[37] Throughout this advance, Burgoyne had little of consequence to do other than to enjoy the hospitality of Lieutenant General Picton.[38]

On 21 June, the French finally stood at Vitoria and were soundly beaten, narrowly escaping being surrounded. Burgoyne was with Picton's headquarters throughout the battle but made no comment on his activities other than reporting that his favourite horse was wounded in three places. He described the role of the 3rd Division:

> The [French] front was attacked chiefly by the 3rd Division and forced repeatedly; and in every part the enemy kept fighting and retiring all day. They showed little confidence in themselves, and seldom allowed our troops to come very near them.[39]

The defeated French army was pursued north and east but were not caught. The 3rd Division had several days hard marching chasing the bulk of the French towards Pamplona and then being diverted to attempt to catch Clausel around Jaca.

Wellington decided that he did not have the resources to besiege Pamplona and San Sebastián at the same time and decided to start with San Sebastián as possession of the harbour there would be very useful. The 3rd, 4th, and 6th Divisions were now sent to blockade the fortress of Pamplona and a ring of redoubts was built around the city to enforce the blockade. Engineers present at Pamplona included Fletcher, Goldfinch, and Burgoyne, the three most senior and experienced engineers with the army. Under the guidance of these engineers, Spanish civilians were employed to build the redoubts and equip with French guns captured at Vitoria. Two weeks later, on 14 July 1813, Fletcher and Burgoyne set off for San Sebastián, Fletcher reporting that the redoubts at Pamplona were not yet finished due to the builders having encountered rock and stone during the construction.

Siege of San Sebastián

Whilst Fletcher was at Pamplona, Major Charles Felix Smith was the senior engineer at San Sebastián, under Graham who had command of the siege. Smith had been at Cadiz for the last three years and had recently arrived on the mainland. He had not been present at any of the previous sieges in 1811 and 1812. There is

37 Wrottesley, *Burgoyne*, p.260.

38 Full details of the movements of the various columns are summarised in the 2nd, New Edition of Gurwood (ed.), *Despatches*, Vol.VI, p.519.

39 Wrottesley, *Burgoyne*, p.263.

no obvious explanation as to why a relatively inexperienced engineer officer was left in charge of making plans for the siege of San Sebastián when three senior and more experienced engineer officers were building earthworks at Pamplona, one day's ride away. Goldfinch and Burgoyne were at Pamplona due to their attachment to the 2nd and 3rd Divisions respectively, but why was Fletcher needed there as well?[40] By the time Fletcher arrived at San Sebastián, the plan of attack had been agreed. Graham was not very familiar with any of the engineer officers and when the siege later ran into problems it cannot have helped his confidence in the ordnance professionals.

The town of San Sebastián lies on the western side of the River Urumea and could only be approach along an isthmus. The isthmus was heavily fortified for this reason. Rising high above the town, on mount Urgull, was the castle, old, but formidable, due to the difficulty of approaching it up the very steep hillside. On the eastern bank of the Urumea were sand hills that overlooked the town. The troops assigned for the siege were the 5th Division and Bradford's Portuguese Brigade, about 9,000 strong. The French defenders, under *Général de Brigade* Louis Rey, amounted to about 3,000 men.

Smith first reviewed the defences of San Sebastián on 1 July 1813. A few days later, Graham wrote to Wellington with Smith's requirements: 'besides the 18-pounder brigade and the field brigades'. He asked for eight 8-inch howitzers, four mortars, and eight 24-pounder cannon, an arsenal entirely inadequate for the task ahead.[41]

The town was invested on 11 July 1813, and a second reconnaissance was carried out by Wellington, Smith, and the artillery commander, Dickson. They concluded that the main attack should be on the eastern wall of the town, on the bank of the River Urumea.[42] As the river was tidal at this point and the water went up to the foot of the wall, the whole of the wall was visible and could be easily breached from the eastern bank. The assault would then be made along the narrow, slippery left bank of the river at low tide. Whilst there was no proposal to assault the hornwork on the isthmus, there were French defences on the isthmus which needed to be taken, to give access to the proposed breaches.

As well as 17 Royal Engineer officers, there was for the first time a significant number of soldiers from the Royal Sappers and Miners; 300, including some recently trained at the new School of Military Engineering at Chatham. Also, for the first time, a company of Portuguese sappers was present with the army.[43] There were at least eight assistant engineers from the line regiments.[44]

40 Wellington had ordered Fletcher to remain at Pamplona to arrange the blockade. This appears unnecessary when two other senior engineer officers were there. Gurwood (ed.), *Despatches*, Wellington to Graham, Lanz, 4 July 1813.

41 Wellington (ed.), *Supplementary Despatches*, Graham to Wellington, 5 July 1813, Vol.VIII, p.61.

42 Jones, *Sieges*, Vol.II, p.17.

43 Thompson, *Wellington's Engineers*, p.167.

44 Jones does not mention assistant engineers in his account of the siege.

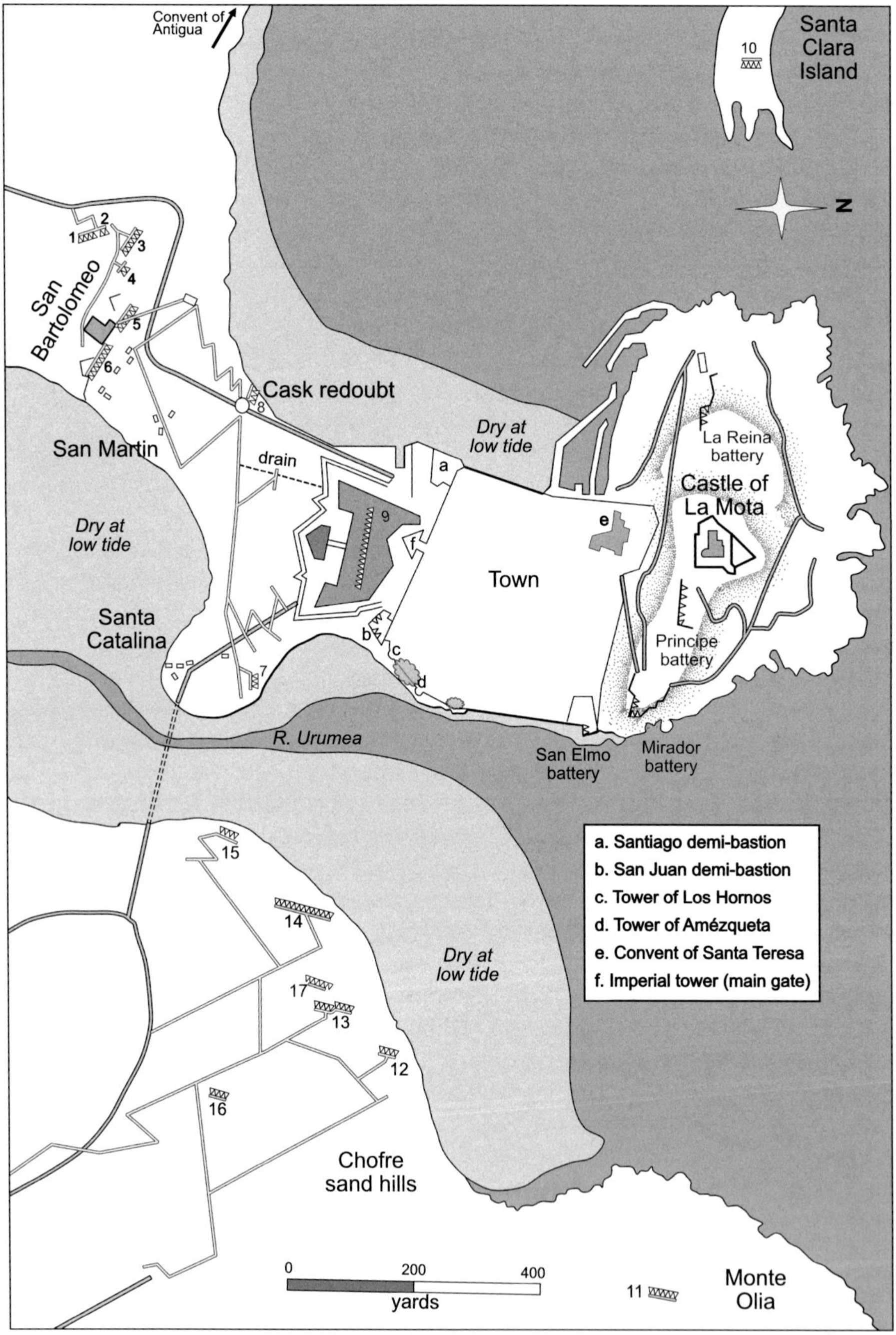

San Sebastián 1813.

The siege train was larger than Smith's initial request, of fourteen 24-pounder cannon, six 8-inch howitzers, four 68-pounder carronades, and four 10-inch mortars. In addition, were the six 18-pounder cannon that had advanced with the army and six, short, 24-pounder cannon borrowed from the Royal Navy. Jones correctly said the 68-pounder carronades were part of the siege train although Burgoyne said they were borrowed from the Royal Navy. The 68-pounder carronade was essentially the same as an 8-inch howitzer apart from the former being iron and the latter, brass.[45]

Work started on the land side on the night of 11/12 July for two batteries against the convent of San Bartolomeo. Two days later, work started on four breaching batteries on the east bank. The timing of the work was to have all elements ready at the same time for the assault. No.1 battery, containing four 18-pounders and No.2, containing two 8-inch howitzers, opened against San Bartolomeo on 14 July and a speculative assault the following day on the convent by Portuguese troops failed.[46]

Arriving on 15 July, Burgoyne was assigned to direct the land attack on the isthmus, Fletcher remained on the Chofre sandhills on the east bank of the Urumea in over-all command. Fletcher expressed concern that the siege train was 'scanty'.[47] Yet another siege was being started with the Ordnance officers concerned about resources.

Burgoyne had few officers to assist him. There were initially two engineer officers, Captain Griffith George Lewis and Lieutenant Stanway. He also had five assistant engineers. Three other engineer officers joined on 18 July.

On 17 July the convent was taken, but the assault suffered significant casualties through a rash advance on the hornwork by the 1/9th Foot. Burgoyne now started work on two new batteries near the convent, battery No.3 for six 18-pounders and No.4 for two 8-inch howitzers. A parallel across the isthmus was also commenced.[48] The plan was to sap forward on the river side of the isthmus, to provide a route for the attacking troops to the breaches that would be made in the town walls.

Like at the sieges in 1812, Burgoyne suffered from difficulty in getting troops to work in the trenches and to prepare siege materials. On the night of 18 July Burgoyne noted that the working party was 300 instead of 500, and on 19 July it did not turn up at all, 'by which we lost an entire six hours work'. On the night of 20 July 1813, Burgoyne noted with frustration that most of the working party of 700 Portuguese troops crept away in the poor weather as did a further 250 men

45 Jones, *Sieges*, Vol.II, p.20; REM 5501-108-4, 14 August 1813; REM 4601-72, f.1813/6, April 1813. The naval cannon were about 10 percent less powerful, and less accurate at long ranges than the longer 24-pounder cannon in the siege train.

46 Battery numbering convention as in Jones' *Sieges* (and also Fortescue). Oman numbers the batteries differently. NB Jones appears to have incorrectly numbered batteries 1 and 2 on his plan.

47 Thompson, *Wellington's Engineers*, p.166. Dickson clearly agreed with Fletcher.

48 Burgoyne's journal described the batteries as one 'sufficient for 8 pieces' and a trench 'which may be converted into a two-gun battery if required'. REM 5501-108-4, night of 17 July 1813.

from the covering party. Out of 950 men assigned, only 150 were present at 11pm! On the night of 22 July, only 400 of 700 were sent.[49] The lack of troops for working parties would remain an issue throughout the siege and showed that Wellington's attempt to impress on the infantry officers their responsibilities during sieges was still ineffective. It would also appear that the hard-learned lesson of 1812, of assigning general officers to the trenches, had been lost already.

Of more significance was the fact that the issues with the working parties delayed completion of the approach trenches and consequently the assault by two days, giving the defenders longer to prepare for the expected assault. The main batteries for breaching opened on the 20 July 1813, and comprised of 39 guns, 25 of which were cannon for breaching. The defenders were now aware of exactly where the breach would be made and the governor immediately ordered retrenchment work behind the breaching points. Attacking two days earlier could have made a significant difference.

On the 21 July 1813, Burgoyne was sent with a summons to the governor. Wellington had written to Graham on 20 July:

> I did not summon Badajoz or Burgos and the reason for not doing so has been confirmed by the King's papers, viz., that French officers are ordered not to surrender a place before it has been stormed. But … I think the place should be summoned. But as it is not desirable that the summons should be given at a period when it will not convey notice to the enemy of our intentions, you had better send it in tomorrow morning.[50]

It is surprising that Burgoyne was used and not an officer on Graham's staff. Although Wellington knew Burgoyne, and clearly trusted him, Graham did not know him. This would indicate that there possibly was another reason to send him: presumably this was so that an engineer officer could get a closer look at the defences. Even more surprisingly, the French, according to Burgoyne, claimed the allies had not stopped work in the trenches and refused to accept the letter.[51]

Whilst digging the parallel across the isthmus on 20 July, a large drain was found which provided the water supply into the town. On 22 July it was explored by Lieutenant Reid and was found to go right to the counterscarp of the hornwork, where it was blocked. It was decided to mine the counterscarp by placing a mine at the end of the drain, although there was no change in the over-all plan of attack.

49 REM 5501-108-4, dates as per text.

50 Wellington to Graham, Lesaca, 20 July 1813 as quoted in Jones, *Sieges*, Vol.II, p.32.

51 Wrottesley, *Burgoyne*, p.267; see also Wellington (ed.), *Supplementary Despatches*, Graham to Wellington, Ernani, 21 July 1813, 4pm, Vol.VIII, p.98; St Sebastián's Road, 21 July 1813, 6:30 and Casa de Ayete, San Sebastián's Road, 21 July 1813 (the summons). Graham in reporting that the French refused to accept the summons, said he had ordered 'firing' to stop, not the 'working' to stop. Could this have been Graham's inexperience in directing sieges?

On 23 July, the main breach was declared practicable and the guns were directed to form a second breach at a point where the French had not made retrenchments. The assault was going to be very difficult and steps were taken to further damage the defences. Mortars and howitzers from two of the batteries on the Chofre sandhills were directed on the breaches causing the buildings in the rear to catch fire. The assault was ordered for the morning of 24 July 1813, but, at the last moment, was postponed for 24 hours because Graham was concerned that the fires raging behind the breach would restrict access into the town.

The assault was made the following morning by Major General Oswald's 5th Division with the blowing of the mine being the signal to attack. The attack failed due to the troops arriving in small numbers: then, when those assigned to the first and second breaches became mixed, the whole attack became confused. There was also a suggestion, which caused much anger, that there had been a lack of willingness amongst the troops of the 5th Division during the assault. Burgoyne commented that the officers said they 'could not get the men to follow them'.[52] Wellington was so concerned about this negativity that he considered using different troops for the second assault.[53]

Gomm's widely quoted criticism of the artillery and engineers is completely unjustified, reflecting badly on his objectivity and was probably caused by his close links to the 5th Division, as an officer in the 1/9th Foot and also being on Oswald's staff. In a letter, he described the behaviour of the 1/9th on 17 July during the attack on San Bartolomeo as, 'in the best style'. Reckless, would have been a better description. His comment that the fortress was being attacked with overwhelming means is clearly wrong. Twenty-four cannon would be better described as scanty rather than 'overwhelming'. Gomm's main criticism was that 'The successes [at previous sieges were] … owing to the almost miraculous efforts of our troops, has checked the progress of science among our engineers [and artillery]'. [54] His point about the miraculous efforts of the troops is valid. His accusation that the failures and casualties were solely the fault of the engineers and artillery officers is not.

Another complaint which has been frequently made about the assault, was about the time of the attack. There is little doubt that the mine was sprung before daylight and consequently the artillery was unable to support the attack.[55] As late as 24 July 1813, Graham, writing to inform Wellington that he had cancelled the attack that morning, commented that if the attack did not go in tomorrow, his options were limited as the ammunition was just about to run out. Reporting the failure of the assault, Graham said it was 'owing to the quantity of musketry

52 Wrottesley, *Burgoyne*, p.268. He makes no mention of soldiers advancing on the hornwork.

53 Oman. *Peninsular War*, Vol.7, pp.16-17.

54 Francis Carr-Gomm (ed.), *Letters and Journals of Field Marshal Sir William Maynard Gomm* (London: John Murray, 1881), pp.308-312.

55 Thompson, *Wellington's Engineers*, pp.171-173 and Wellington (ed.), *Supplementary Despatches*, Vol.VIII, p.131, 'at daylight, the mine having been previously sprung'.

and hand-grenades the enemy brought upon the column in its advance and on its arrival at the breach'.[56] Wellington when informed of the failure, immediately rode to San Sebastián. Due to Fletcher having been wounded during the failed assault, Burgoyne was once again in temporary command, and wrote: 'His Lordship seemed determined to persevere, talked of opening the breach more extensively on the left, said he expected much more heavy artillery and demanded a project attacking the place in front regularly'.[57]

The decision on how to attack the town was made by Graham and Wellington. If Wellington had not accepted the recommendation of the engineers, it would never have been agreed to. The perennial issue of time was the main factor in deciding the point of attack. Wellington wanted the town taken as quickly as possible, due to the threat from Soult, who was now in command of the united French armies. A formal attack, which all agreed should have been against the hornwork, would have taken longer than the time Wellington had allowed. The attack against the eastern wall was the compromise. The assault along the narrow left bank of the Urumea was the consequence. Time constraints driving the decision on the plan of attack was exactly the same issue as occurred at Badajoz in 1811 and 1812. In trying to speed things up, two weeks had been lost in starting a regular attack. Burgoyne's journal infers that a new plan was produced but it appears to have been rejected again in favour of the 'quicker' attack on the eastern side.[58]

Whilst Wellington was engaged at San Sebastián, he received word that Soult had attacked and rushed back to the army. A determined French attack on Wellington's covering positions led to a tense few days of fighting in the Pyrenees before the French were finally repulsed. The siege was suspended due to a lack of ammunition and due to the threatening activity of the nearby French army. The guns were returned to the ships to avoid any risk of damage from a French sortie.[59]

Burgoyne made a number of observations on the first siege. He felt the plan gave the defenders early warning of the point of attack giving them time to prepare. The discovery of the drain should have changed the main point of attack. The eastern batteries would still have breached the wall, but the assaults would have become feints, distracting the defenders away from the hornwork which would then be assaulted when the mine was exploded.

56 Wellington (ed.), *Supplementary Despatches*, Graham to Wellington, 25 August 1813, Vol.8, p.119.

57 Goldfinch, his superior, was at Pamplona.; also, Wrottesley, *Burgoyne*, p.270.

58 Jones, *Sieges*, Vol.II, p.46, 'After some consideration, it was decided to persevere in the same plan of attack'.

59 See the present author's discussion on the criticism of the plan of attack in Thompson, *Wellington's Engineers*, pp.168-173.

Second Siege of San Sebastián

Although it was many days before the siege recommenced, the work in the trenches continued. Burgoyne noted on the night of 25 July that the parallel on the isthmus was extended at the left towards the demi-bastion and the right toward the hornwork. On 26 July after the order to remove the guns had arrived, Graham ordered redoubts to be constructed on the San Bartolomeo heights to enforce a blockade. The French redoubt at San Bartolomeo and the convent of Antigua were repaired for this purpose. On 28 July all the guns and most of the troops were withdrawn from the blockade as Graham became more concerned about a French advance reaching the town, but work continued making gabions and fascines and guarding the trenches.

After Wellington, had pushed Soult back, the troops began returning to San Sebastián, the size of the working parties increased and the guns were landed again at Pasajes. Burgoyne noted on 6 August 'the order now, is continue the works on the besieging principle'.[60] The French however, had made good use of the delay to repair some of the damage.

Although there was some initial consideration of changing the attack to the isthmus, the decision was made to persevere with the same plan of attack against the east wall. It was accepted, again, that an attack across the isthmus would take longer than Wellington was willing to give his engineers. Burgoyne expressed concern about this strategy commenting 'it appears to me [it] cannot succeed … without taking the hornwork and then breaching the main town front'.[61]

Because Wellington was expecting a substantial new siege train to be delivered, he delayed the renewal of the siege until it arrived. Then the plan was to extensively widen the initial breach and destroy the demi-bastion of San Juan at the south-east corner of the town. The new siege guns and ammunition arrived between 19 and 24 August. The siege train now amounted to 63 guns.[62]

On 8 August, following reports that French miners had been heard working under the cask redoubt, Burgoyne requested miners from the line regiments to drive a gallery round the redoubt, 'to quiet our people's minds', not because he believed there was mining activity.[63] This work continued for several days, but no evidence was found that the French were digging mines. For the next week the French continued improving the defences whilst the allies commenced the batteries for the new guns. Burgoyne started batteries No.5 and 6 on 12 August and these were completed on 24 August. On 26 August 1813, they opened with six 18-pounders in No.5 and seven 24-pounders and two 8-inch howitzers in No.6.

60 REM 5501-108-4, 6 August.

61 REM 5501-108-4. 8 August 1813, not 7 August 1813 as printed in Wrottesley.

62 Jones, *Sieges*, Vol.II, p.52, lists 116 guns available.

63 REM 5501-108-4, 8 August 1813.

The main purpose of these batteries was to destroy the San Juan bastion and the curtain wall behind it.[64]

On the right attack, the main breaching guns were moved 60 yards nearer the wall, from battery No.14 to No.15. The primary purpose of the right attack was to widen the breach, destroy the two towers, and connect the breach with the left attack on the San Juan bastion. There were now 15 guns on the left attack and forty-eight on the right attack. Of these, 34 were cannon for breaching the walls. The effects were quickly seen on the eastern wall, but the San Juan bastion proved too distant and it was decided to construct a new battery for four guns (No.7) much closer to the target.[65] Only three guns had been installed when the battery opened on 29 August. The impact of these closer guns was immediately apparent: in order to protect them, the 18-pounders in batteries Nos. 5 and 6 were ordered to supress the defenders' guns.[66]

Burgoyne started another task on 26 August. Two shafts were started at the right end of the advanced parallel to search for any mines prepared by the French which would be exploded when the assault commenced. None were found. On 30 August, three more shafts were dug close to the sea wall to place mines which would be exploded just before the assault, to clear the way for the attacking troops. Exploding these mines would also ensure that there were no French mines on the route of the assault. By 30 August, the main breach was about 300 yards long with a smaller breach further north. Wellington, still concerned about the morale of the 5th Division, asked for volunteers from the 1st, 4th, and Light Divisions and 750 men arrived on the night of 30 August. However, Lieutenant General Leith, who had just returned to take back command on the 5th Division, refused to let the volunteers lead the assault.

Early on the morning of 31 August, the mines were exploded to clear the route for the troops. The assault started around 11:30am and after a serious resistance the walls were taken. Losses in the attacking divisions were terrible due to the constant fire at short range by French artillery.[67] The town then suffered a sacking by the victorious allied troops and, more seriously, was almost completely destroyed by fire.

During the assault, Burgoyne was struck on the head by a musket ball whilst trying to get troops to attack the hornwork and Richard Fletcher was killed, putting Burgoyne back in temporary command.

64 Jones, *Sieges*, Vol.II, p.57.

65 Wellington (ed.), *Supplementary Despatches*, Graham to Wellington, 26 & 28 August 1813.

66 REM 5501-108-4, 28 & 29 August 1813. Not printed in Wrottesley. One of the three 24-pounders in the battery was damaged during the day.

67 Oman, *Peninsular War*, Vol.7, p.36.

Observations on the Second Siege

The increase in the number of guns for the second siege meant for the first time, Wellington had more guns than he could use.

Burgoyne commented on more than one occasion that the French appeared to be setting fires behind the breach to make access more difficult. The claims that the allied army deliberately set fire to the town are still being repeated and investigated today.[68] Whilst the siege was underway and when the assault was due, there was much greater benefit in the French starting fires than the allies. They were of a much greater hindrance to the attacking troops. Burgoyne, like many other officers, accepted that the sack of the town was inevitable, saying 'the plundering and drunkenness were as usual on such occasions'.[69] This is not to say he agreed with the actions of the troops, but this sort of bad behaviour was the same in all armies at this period. It could also be said that such behaviour has been common in war throughout history.

Attack on the Castle

With the capture of the town, Burgoyne immediately commenced a communication from the cask redoubt to the ditch of the hornwork and continued to the Imperial gate. Whilst the loss of San Sebastián was inevitable, Rey obeyed his orders to hold at all costs and continued his determined defence from the castle. On 3 September, the town was still in flames when Burgoyne commenced a battery for 17 guns in the rear of the hornwork to attack the castle. Both Graham and Burgoyne were concerned about the distance from the battery to the castle.

Fire on Monte Urgull from the batteries on the Chofre hills had continued since the town was taken and was causing damage and casualties, but the French refused to surrender.

On 8 September 1813, at 10:00 a.m., 59 guns opened on the castle and the batteries around it.[70] The troops in the castle including about 350 prisoners had nowhere to hide and two hours later hostilities ceased. It had taken nearly 10 weeks to capture San Sebastián, which was now a smoking ruin.

68 There is a good English language summary of the claims in Bruce Collins, *Wellington and the Siege of San Sebastian* (Barnsley: Pen & Sword,2017), pp.172-190.

69 REM 5501-108-4, 31 August 1813.

70 Oman, *Peninsular War*, Vol.7, p.60, says 61 guns, which disagrees with Jones, *Sieges*, Vol.II, p.88. This account follows Jones as Oman appears to have double-counted the guns on Santa Clara.

Observations on the Siege

Debates continue about the best way to have taken San Sebastián. As previously mentioned, Wellington and Graham wanted a quick result and a formal attack on the land side could not be done quick enough. Initially, there was also insufficient siege guns for a land attack. The constant threat of an attack by Soult made Wellington push for a speedy resolution. It is clear that Rey and Soult were in regular communications as it cannot be a coincidence that Soult attacked on the days that the first and second assaults were made. Wellington was clearly concerned that Soult might be able to gather enough troops to raise the siege at San Sebastián or the blockade at Pamplona, so speed was essential.

In hindsight, a formal attack against the land front was probably the best option. Jones believed that the attack should have been against the landward side and would have been quicker than the eventual time taken for the two sieges.[71] It might not have been completed before the end of August, but there would have been significantly fewer allied and civilian casualties. The turning point for Burgoyne was finding the drain leading to the hornwork. He argued, strongly, that the attack should have been changed to an attack across the isthmus. No advantage was taken from the confusion caused by exploding the mine during the first assault.

Burgoyne, as he had done at previous sieges, made a number of observations on the professional conduct of the siege, noting improved methods of constructing batteries, the construction of fascines and gabions and improved ways of encouraging the troops in the trenches. One example was a reflection that more work got done when soldiers were given achievable targets. When completed, the men would be dismissed, even if it was before the end of their shift. There was a clear incentive for them to work hard.[72]

One thing that he did not mention at the siege was the effectiveness of the newly arrived Royal Sappers and Miners. His initial impression was negative based on their attitude rather than their training. Once they had been under the command of an engineer officer for a few weeks, his view was much more positive.[73]

After the Siege

Burgoyne, writing to his sister the day after the successful assault of 31 August, made light of the injury he received, saying his biggest problem was 'with a very

71 Jones, *Sieges*, Vol.II, p.96; Wrottesley, *Burgoyne*, p.271.

72 REM 5501-108-4, Remarks on the siege of San Sebastian, entry for 12 August 1813.

73 Thompson, *Wellington's Engineers*, p.178.

good appetite, I can't eat, except very soft substances'.[74] In the same letter, he also raised the issue of command, describing at length:

> The command, therefore, for the present, devolves upon me; though I don't know how long I shall keep it, as a senior officer to me in the Corps, though not in army rank is before Pamplona [Goldfinch], and another at Lisbon [Elphinstone]. The arrangement will rest entirely with Lord Wellington, as in this mixture of ranks, he can make our situation so as to throw the command into any hands he pleases, and I have no reason to expect he will put it into mine.

The position was the same as when this situation arose before, in December 1812 when Fletcher went home. Goldfinch was still his superior: however, he did not return to headquarters from Pamplona. The siege at San Sebastián was nearly over and the blockade at Pamplona was now the priority task to complete. Elphinstone was at Lisbon and, contrary to what Wrottesley wrote, he sailed from Lisbon as soon as he heard of Fletcher's death and arrived at Wellington's headquarters unannounced and uninvited, before his letter informing Wellington he was coming.[75] By that time, San Sebastián had fallen.

Burgoyne's comment about Wellington 'throwing the command as he pleases' was a reference to the situation in the Royal Artillery where Dickson, a favourite of Wellington, retained command even though there were senior officers available. Wellington certainly 'bent' the rules in making any senior artillery officer so unwelcome that they quickly left, but Dickson retained command based on his rank in the Portuguese artillery and this was not a brevet rank. Elphinstone's arrival at headquarters left Wellington with limited options: he was not willing to break the rules of seniority and he chose not to make Elphinstone unwelcome, although based on his conduct later he probably would have deserved it. Elphinstone told his wife that Burgoyne had written to him saying he would refuse the command if Wellington had offered it to him.[76]

Burgoyne sent the official report of the second siege directly back to the Master General, commenting that he had not sent it by the 'circuitous route to Lisbon' through the senior engineer, Howard Elphinstone.[77] Elphinstone would have been very unhappy at this action but it is understandable that Burgoyne would have wanted recognition for his contribution to the siege.

After San Sebastián surrendered on 9 September 1813, Wellington ordered Graham to give 'the following orders to the officer in charge of the engineer department':

74 Wrottesley, *Burgoyne*, p.281.

75 Wrottesley, *Burgoyne*, p.282 footnote. Elphinstone did not write to Wellington.

76 REM 4201-274, Elphinstone to his wife, Vera, 16 October 1813.

77 TNA WO55/959, Burgoyne to Mann, 10 September 1813.

> The pontoon train must be got together ... and the train should be assembled somewhere near Oyarzun. He must immediately take measures for securing the place [San Sebastián] against a *coup de main*, by clearing the rubbish and blocking the breaches and he must let me have without loss of time, a plan and estimate for the repair of the place.[78]

Burgoyne was now involved in an unpleasant incident which did not make the pages of his son-in-law's biography. A week after the orders were issued, Wellington was furious when he found out that the order to move the pontoon train had not been actioned:

> Lieutenant Colonel Burgoyne is really too bad; this is the eighth day since he received orders to collect the pontoon train ... and he is now not certain that the orders he sent have reached the officer in charge and he has taken no measures to repeat them. He put his letter into the Spanish post office, I conclude, directed in English, and without knowing whether the officer in charge of the pontoons is in communication with that post office and there he left the matter. This is the way in which all our arrangements fail. The officers charged to send an order will not attain to that essential part of their duty, the mode of transmitting it.[79]

Wellington told Bathurst, the Secretary of State, on 19 September 1813, that he had intended to immediately cross the French border (the Bidassoa) and the delay in the 'collection of the pontoon train' had stopped him, blaming 'an officer of engineers'. This of course, is not true. Even in the same letter he continued: 'I have a great disinclination to enter the French territory under the present circumstances ... I should prefer to turn my attention to Catalonia'.[80]

The wording in Wellington's letter to Graham is odd as he knew Burgoyne was the senior engineer officer at San Sebastián. Did Wellington think that Goldfinch would arrive from Pamplona to take command of the engineers at headquarters? It would have been quite reasonable for Goldfinch to do this. Two days before he wrote the blistering complaint about Burgoyne, Wellington had asked Graham to let him know when the pontoon train would be 'on the move'. Graham clearly had not checked either: he wrote to Wellington on 16 September, reporting that the movement order had been lost.[81] Wellington's complaint to Graham was followed by a letter directly to Burgoyne from the Adjutant General asking for details of the transmission of the order, how communications with the pontoon were normally

78 Gurwood (ed.), *Despatches*, Wellington to Graham, Lesaca, 9 September 1813.
79 Gurwood (ed.), *Despatches*, Wellington to Graham, Lesaca, 17 September 1813.
80 Gurwood (ed.), *Despatches*, Wellington to Bathurst, Lesaca, 19 September 1813.
81 Gurwood (ed.), *Despatches*, Wellington to Graham, Lesaca, 17 September 1813.

handled, and how many duplicates of the orders were sent. Somewhat bizarrely, this second letter of 17 September ordered an officer to be sent immediately to convey the order to move the pontoon train. Why had Graham or Burgoyne not done this on the 15 or 16 September? Although Wellington was clearly unhappy about this incident, it did not appear to affect his positive view of Burgoyne, whose previous excellent service would have worked in his favour.

There was no entry in Burgoyne's diary between 9 and 27 September. He would have been fully occupied in making San Sebastián defensible. His entry for 27 September records that he had submitted his report on the repairs and improvements required and Wellington had approved the costs of £10,000. He also noted, probably with some relief, that Stanway had been appointed to carry out the repair work, and he set off immediately for Headquarters.

The next few days were spent reviewing the current situation and familiarising himself with the terrain in which the army was based. He wrote up his observations on the recent campaign in the Pyrenees and the defences that had been prepared around the Bidassoa. He noted that because of the terrain, most of the cavalry was in the rear and that 'the roads are few [sic] practicable for artillery and those very bad'. He continued, the terrain:

> [H]ad not been perfectly understood by all the officers entrusted with the defence of the different passes and positions in the mountains and with the miscalculations of the enemy being enabled to gain the ridge in force in [a] shorter time than our resources could, the troops immediately stationed on the positions being too weak to resist, this alone was the cause of Soult … penetrating … so near Pamplona.[82]

Of the defences constructed by both sides, he made the dubious claim that the designs were adapted to the different modes of fighting, the French preferring star forts to increase firepower and the British preferring straight walls where the bayonet could be used more effectively.

The Pyrenees, October to December 1813

On 7 October 1813, Wellington's forces attacked across the River Bidassoa and having established a bridgehead, Burgoyne now threw a number of bridges 'of trestles, boats and pontoons' across the river and started a number of redoubts to protect the bridgehead.[83] Lieutenant General Hope, had just replaced Graham, forced to return to England for his health, specifically asked for Burgoyne to visit

82 REM 4601-72, Observations on the Position of the Allied Army in the Pyrenees, 1 Oct 1813.
83 Wrottesley, *Burgoyne*, p.286.

and approve the 'considerable works' that were required to defend the bridgehead at Irun.[84] Burgoyne also ordered Lieutenant Hammond Tapp RE to repair the wooden bridge at Irun which in the short term had been replaced by a pontoon bridge.[85] For the next few days, Burgoyne's priorities were consolidating the crossing points over the Bidassoa. There was now a substantial pontoon train attached to the army. It comprised a new 36-pontoon train and an older 13-pontoon set. The older pontoons were called up to Irun and the new train was split, 17 going to Roncesvalles and the remainder in reserve near Irun.

On 12 October 1813, in his typical terse style, Burgoyne noted in his diary that 'Lieut.-Colonel Elphinstone joined from Lisbon, to assume command of the engineers'. Elphinstone's arrival would have been a surprise to both the engineers and Wellington. Burgoyne would have been disappointed as he lost command of the engineers with the army. He prepared a report for Elphinstone detailing the location and responsibilities of engineer, sapper and pontoon resources.[86]

On 17 October 1813, Burgoyne joined the left column under Hope. Whilst there may have been operational reasons for deploying engineers separately to support Hope, there does not seem to be a strong reason. Wellington's headquarters and Hope's headquarters were only a few miles apart. What this move did achieve was to retain Burgoyne in an independent command that attracted command pay.[87] This was possibly Wellington's way of compensating Burgoyne for losing command of the engineers.

The main engineering tasks over the next few weeks were the bridges over the Bidassoa and building defensive positions on both sides of the river as far east as Roncesvalles. Wellington's communications depended on the bridges and the winter weather was approaching. Hope wrote to Wellington on 1 November 1813 reporting that he:

> Had torrents of rain last night and it has just been reported to me that the upper bridge … has been carried away and there is some apprehension the … materials … carried by the river may injure the Spanish bridge. Burgoyne and Tod are however, doing what they can to secure it.[88]

One interesting point in this letter is that Captain Alexander Tod was in the Royal Staff Corps, not the Royal Engineers, and officially they should not have

84 Wellington (ed.), *Supplementary Despatches*, Hope to Wellington, 8 October 1813.

85 REM 4601-72, Statement of the Distribution and Employment of the Royal Engineer Department, 12 October 1813, [at] the period of Lieut.-Col. Elphinstone joining the army, 12 October 1813. The pontoon bridge at Irun was ordered in Wellington's Instructions for the attack, Wellington (ed.), *Supplementary Despatches*, Arrangements connected with the forward movement of the army, 5 October 1813.

86 See previous footnote.

87 TNA WO55/959, Chapman to Mann, 2 March 1814.

88 Wellington (ed.), *Supplementary Despatches*, Hope to Wellington, Andaye, 1 Nov 1813.

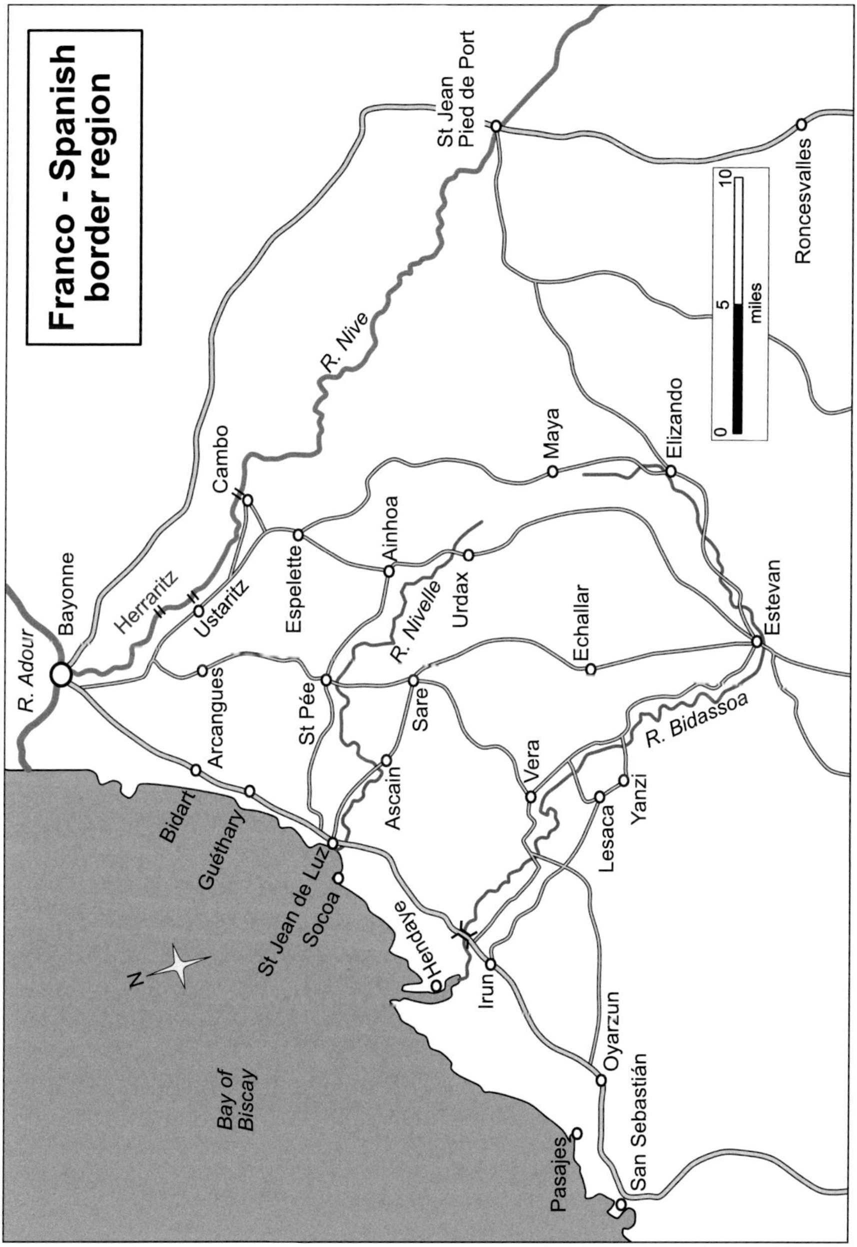

Franco-Spanish border.

been working together. It was encouraging that the officers in the field could make pragmatic decisions to ensure operational requirements were met, even if their superiors could not.

Wellington was unwilling to move further until Pamplona surrendered, which it did on 31 October 1813. He now felt he was ready to cross the next river barrier, the Nivelle. The weather now turned against him and days of driving rain were followed by snow, delaying the advance until 10 November. Burgoyne noted on 7 November that the plan was to attack the French left from Roncesvalles to Sare and Ascain. Burgoyne was with Hope on the allied left which was making demonstrations to stop the French moving troops to meet Wellington's attack. On the 11 November, Wellington advanced to St Jean de Luz where the French had set the wooden bridges on fire, but they were saved. The French also burnt the bridge further north at Bidart. This advance pushed the French back over the Nive and again redoubts were constructed on the southern bank and crossing points on the Nivelle established. The bad weather continued and as much as possible the troops were put under cover to wait for the next attack. As before, the main engineering role was maintaining the bridges and preparing defensive redoubts. Burgoyne provides little detail on what he was doing, his journal concentrating on the manoeuvres of the armies. He did however take time to write to Pasley updating him on the progress of the new sappers, commenting, now: 'they are most active, useful, able and well behaved'.[89] This was a big change from his previous negative comments. Burgoyne wrote again to Pasley a few weeks later updating him on the progress of the new sappers. Clearly Burgoyne was regularly passing information back to England to improve the training being given to engineers and sappers.

Towards the end of November, Burgoyne noted that five pontoons had been ordered up to Ustaritz, commenting that the roads were in terrible condition. Finally, on 9 December, Wellington attacked again, crossing the River Nive near Ustaritz and Cambo, whilst demonstrations were made towards Bayonne to distract the French. The allied army was now split across both sides of the Nive with limited and unreliable communications between them, due to the difficulty in maintaining bridges over the flooded rivers. Soult took the opportunity to attack, first Hope and then the following day, on the other bank, Hill. Both required hard fighting to beat off the attacks. By 12 December there were three bridges across the Nive at Herraritz, Ustaritz, and Cambo.[90] Work now focussed on building defensive positions.

About this time, Burgoyne got his first views of the defences around Bayonne which he described as extensive. He also commented on the River Adour, which for the:

89 BL ADD MS41963, ff.131-2, 24 November 1813.
90 REM 4201-68, Journal, 12 December 1813.

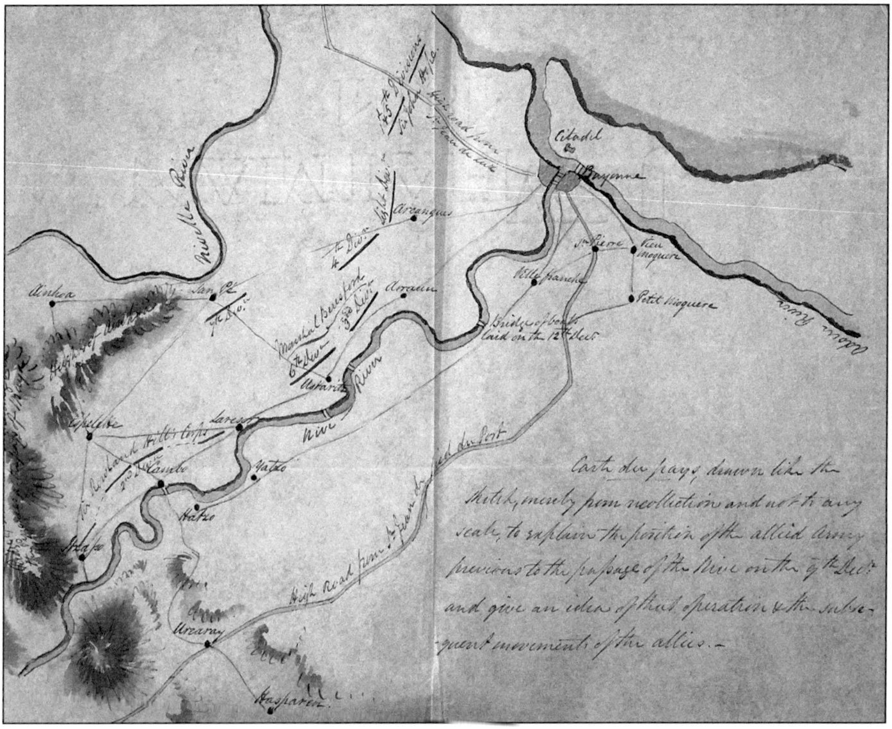

Allied attack on the Nive, December 1813. (Royal Engineers Museum)

> [F]irst two and half miles from the town, … is 800 or 1,000 yards wide; from thence … commence two strong stone walls or dykes, of about fourteen feet high above low-water mark, and fifteen feet thick, which at each bank extend for about a mile, and confine the bed of the river to between 200 and 300 yards wide[91]

Both the city and the river would become challenges in the coming months.

With Wellington having established his army on the right bank of the Nive, both armies went into cantonments for the worst of the Pyrenean winter. The ground was covered in snow, the roads impassable, and the rivers, raging torrents. There would be no more action until February 1814 when Wellington was faced with the largest of the river barriers, the Adour, which runs through Bayonne and on to the sea.

91 REM 4201-68, Journal, 9 December 1813.

14

1814 – Adour and Bayonne

There is a very long gap in Burgoyne's diary over the winter with no entries between 13 December 1813 and 12 February 1814. There was probably little to do other than ensure the bridges across the rivers remained in place, a difficult task through a Pyrenean winter. His opening entry for 1814 begins: 'The weather has hitherto been horrible, constant heavy rain and furious westerly gales. Many ships have been lost on this bad coast'. He also noted that Wellington was 'preparing to move the army'. Planning for crossing the Adour must have been going on some time as Burgoyne noted 'his Lordship's intention [is] to force the passage of the Adour'.[1]

The Adour is a major, fast flowing, tidal river, several hundred yards wide. Towards the mouth, the river had been restricted between large stone walls to about 300 yards wide and this was the point selected to cross the river. Due to the tidal nature and the speed of the current, pontoons would not survive, so 40 large local fishing boats were commandeered to make the bridge. Burgoyne described the boats as about 50 feet in length and 12 to 15 feet across the beam. Elphinstone had over-all control, although the work was managed by Burgoyne and Sturgeon of the Royal Staff Corps. The design almost certainly came from Sturgeon as it was similar to the method he had used to bridge the Tagus at Alcantara and Almaraz.[2] In Burgoyne's journal there is a detailed description of the construction of the bridge but no description of what his role was.

The plan was to moor the boats in line across the river at the narrowest point between the walls. To keep the boats in place, as well as the anchors, five large ropes were stretched across the river and the boats fixed to the ropes. The ropes were tensioned using naval capstans and would both hold the boats in place and allow a roadway to be placed on them. A boom was also placed up-river to intercept any objects the French might send down to damage the bridge.

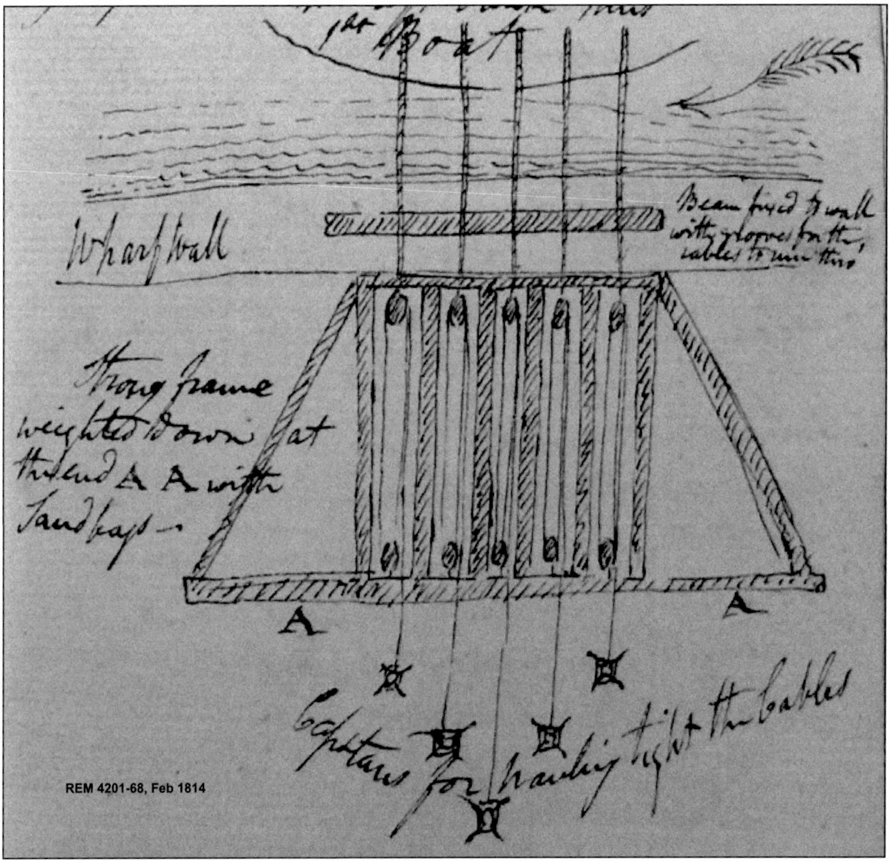

Burgoyne's sketch of capstan on bridge over Adour. (Royal Engineers Museum)

On 18 February 1814, Burgoyne described the plans in detail:

> The whole are collecting in Socoa Harbour; forty *chasse-marées* (large coasting boats, mostly decked) are prepared for the bridge, each with the necessary planks on board for one bay, and two or three with the cables. Five or six officers of Engineers have each a division of the boats of seven or eight, which he is to take care are properly loaded. The boats are numbered with yellow paint on the bow. Each boat will have two sappers on board, with means to cut away the sides above the deck, and a British sailor or two to see them moored in their proper place. To moor them in one line readily, it has been proposed to plant two flagstaffs or poles on our bank, and each boat let go its first anchor when she has them in a line. The ends of the bridge cables are to be fixed on the other bank by six 18-pounders thrown over the wall. Six transports' jolly boats are to be

> carried on six of the old pontoon carriages, and are each to tow over six rafts, made of the eighteen pontoons, to take first possession of the right bank.[3]

It was hoped that the operation could have been carried out as early as 19 February and Wellington had ridden back from the east to oversee it. Unfortunately, the weather was bad and any attempt to cross the dangerous bar of the Adour was impossible. Wellington could not wait and returned to the army.

The first attempt was planned for 23 February, and Hope ordered the pontoon train moved forward. It appears that Elphinstone now told Hope that he did not have the horses to move six of the pontoons because Wellington had ordered six pontoons to join the army. A hurried letter to Dickson obtained a loan of 80 horses from the field artillery brigades.[4] The movement was commenced during the night, but because of the state of the roads and the sandy beaches, the pontoon train did not arrive, causing a 24-hour delay. On the morning of 24 February, the advance party was crossed in jolly boats to dislodge the small French picquet on the far side. This was then followed by rafts made up of three pontoons which made a number of difficult crossings due to the speed of the river. That night, only 600 troops were across but there were a number of artillery pieces on the left bank of the river to support them. A French attack on the bridgehead that night was easily repulsed with the help of rockets, used for the first time in Wellington's army.

Troops continued crossing using the rafts for the next two days and the bridge was started on 25 February 1813 with only 25 of the *chasse-marées* being needed. The loss of boats crossing the dangerous sand bar at the river mouth was less than expected and the remainder returned to Socoa as reserves. The bridge was ready the following morning although by that time all the troops had been ferried across. Surprisingly, the French made almost no attempt to resist the crossing. The bridge would be used as a major crossing point until the end of the war.

Hope in his despatch to Wellington after the successful crossing wrote, 'I am bound to mention to your lordship Lieutenant Colonel Elphinstone for the arrangements he made, and Lieutenant Colonels Burgoyne and Sturgeon, and the officers employed under them, for the zeal with which they executed his orders'.[5] Hope's words are interesting in mentioning Elphinstone. 'Bound' suggests that he had to be mentioned as he was the senior officer present: it is not the word one would choose to express recognition of excellent service. Hope was much warmer in his praise of the other officers involved. Elphinstone had proved difficult with

3 REM 4201-68, Journal, 18 February 1814.

4 Vigors (ed.), *Dickson Manuscripts, 1814,* p.1272. This seems like very bad planning by Elphinstone, along with the inference that the route for the pontoons had not been checked in advance. Wellington surely would have heard about both of these incidents.

5 Wellington (ed.), *Supplementary Despatches,* Vol.VIII, p.595

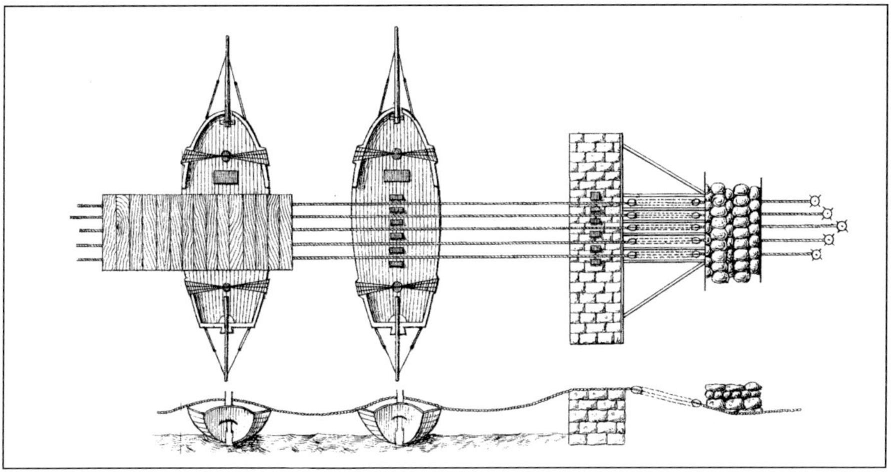

Bridge over the Adour. (Authors collection)

everyone since his arrival at headquarters in October 1813. His letters home to his wife portray him arrogantly arguing with other officers including Wellington. He of course had a different view:

> We have crossed the Adour at its mouth, and I have established a fine bridge of boats. Whether I shall come in for any share of praise I know not, but the whole of what (I have no doubt will be called the greatest attempt Lord Wellington has made) has depended upon my arrangements, and finally succeeded.[6]

It is notable that none of the Royal Engineer or Staff Corps officers were mentioned in Wellington's despatch whereas Royal Navy and army officers were. Even the local Transport Agent got mentioned! Elphinstone was doing no favours to his Corps.[7]

Once the troops were across, the engineers were tasked with the siege of Bayonne, another substantial fortress. Wellington had moved eastwards pushing Soult away from the fortress. He had taken Henry Goldfinch with him as his senior engineer, leaving Elphinstone and Burgoyne to arrange the siege. Elphinstone showed his inexperience and unsuitability when he commented to his wife 'I was not aware at the time that the movement on the right had been of such importance, but I find that Lord Wellington has gained another victory'. No other engineer officer would have been content to remain at a blockade whilst Wellington moved against the

6 REM 4201-274, 27 February 1814.

7 Gurwood (ed.), *Despatches*, Wellington to Bathurst, St. Sever, 1 March 1814.

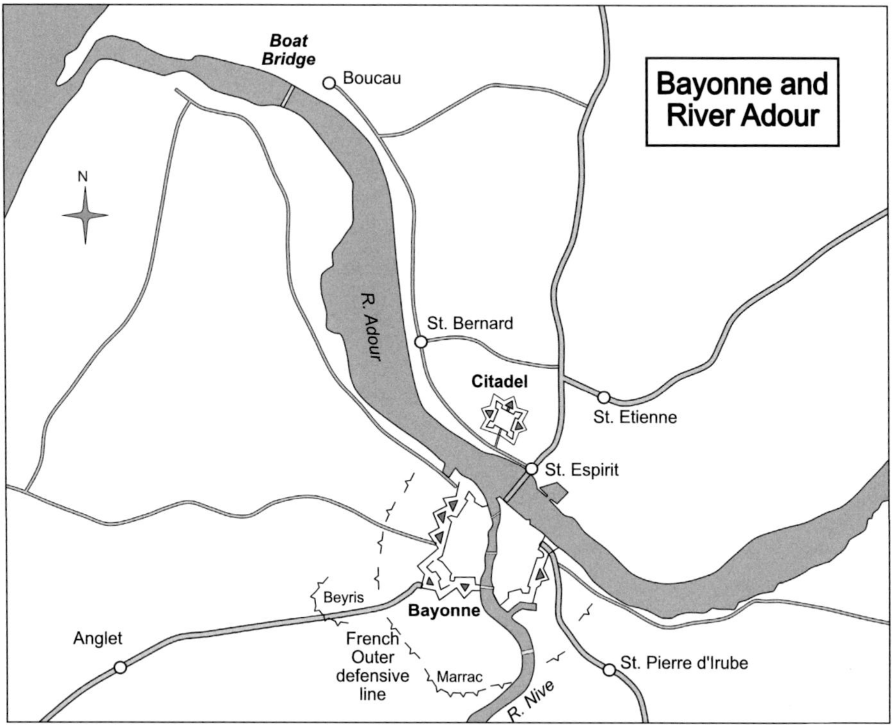

Siege of Bayonne.

main French army.[8] This was Elphinstone's first experience of a siege, as an engineer or as commanding engineer.

Blockade of Bayonne

Bayonne was a substantial fortified place. The main town straddled the junction of the Nive and Adour rivers giving the French access to both sides of both rivers. On the northern bank was a separate fort called the Citadel and this was the direction from which the allied forces approached.

Wellington had asked for a plan to take the Citadel, and Elphinstone's first proposal was rejected as it contained insufficient detail. A revised plan was sent on 4 March 1814 and although accepted, Wellington was unhappy with the number of troops that Elphinstone required for the siege. No-one seemed in a hurry to start the siege, the supplies and guns arrived slowly, and everyone appeared to be

8 REM 4201-274, Boucau, 5 March 1814.

waiting for peace to be declared. It is also likely that, based on the previous behaviour of allied troops, Wellington was keen to avoid the public relations disaster that would follow the sacking of a French town.

Burgoyne was strangely silent through the whole blockade: his last journal entry about the siege was on 8 March 1814. He does not say if he was involved in the planning. Elphinstone makes no mention of him, so it is possible (based on Elphinstone's behaviour) that Burgoyne was not consulted.

Through this period the junior engineer officers continued writing to Burgoyne. There was a stream of reports of the activities of the engineers with the army. There is no evidence that similar letters were being written to Elphinstone. Stanway, who had been left to make the repairs at San Sebastián, wrote, complaining about the problems he was having, being unable to get support from Elphinstone and asking Burgoyne to help. Burgoyne was clearly respected and trusted by the junior officers.

There are some inconsistencies in how the siege was reported. Wrottesley's biography says that Burgoyne was in charge at the siege of Bayonne and Elphinstone was with Wellington. This is clearly an error as all correspondence related to the siege of Bayonne was between Wellington, Hope, and Elphinstone. Elphinstone was based at Boucau, near Bayonne through March and April 1814.[9] There was also a suggestion that Burgoyne was receiving command pay as senior engineer with Sir John Hope.[10] Porter's *History of the Royal Corps of Engineers* does not even mention the blockade and Jones' account of the siege is similarly vague. Jones makes no mention of which engineers were involved, only mentioning Elphinstone although there were about 18 officers present. There is no specific detail on digging approaches. It would seem that the period from 4 March to 14 April was taken up collecting the resources and no work had been started when the French sortied on 14 April and captured Hope. It was another two weeks before the Governor finally accepted that Napoleon had abdicated and no-one was interested in inflicting further casualties.

So ended Burgoyne's involvement in the Peninsular War. He had landed on the Peninsula in August 1808 and apart from two months in England after Moore's campaign had been there the whole of the war. Only one other engineer officer had served longer, Captain Frank Stanway, who remained in Lisbon through the winter of 1808 and therefore served for the whole of the war.

9 Wrottesley, *Burgoyne*, p.297, fn.

10 TNA WO55/959, Mann to Chapman, 2 March 1814. Although, this may be referring to the period from 17 October 1813, when Burgoyne joined Hope until Elphinstone took command of the siege.

15

1815 – America and Missing Waterloo

The end of the Peninsular War did not end Burgoyne's service. The British Government immediately decided to transfer some of the Peninsular army to North America to look to end the conflict with the United States. The intention was to ship Peninsular regiments directly from Bordeaux. As Wellington could not be spared, Hill, one of his most competent subordinates and used to independent command, was selected. The matter of command of the engineers was also raised with Elphinstone, who commented:

> I have this moment heard Lord Hill goes to America, therefore I certainly shall not go ... I have ordered 19 [engineer officers to go to America] which I will think rather astonish them at the office, but I have determined to do what I think right. Goldfinch wishes to go to England and I have not yet Burgoyne's answer. I think he will like it, and the Corps cannot be in better hands.

Elphinstone seemed to think that Wellington not going to America meant there was possibly further campaigning in Europe and he, not unreasonably, wanted to stay with Wellington. A week later, Elphinstone noted that 'Burgoyne goes with the command to America'.[1] Certainly, other engineer officers were being assigned; Harry Jones writing to his brother said 'The American service does not appear to be preferred by anybody. I certainly do not think it a pleasant change, but a soldier must obey'.[2] It is highly likely that Wellington recommended Burgoyne for the position and Hill also knew him well.

Initially the force was to have sailed directly from southern France, but delays in finalising the nature of the expeditionary force and continued uncertainty in Europe meant that it was some months before the troops sailed and Burgoyne

1 REM 4201-274, 14 & 22 May 1814.The original plan was for Hope to command but his injuries during the sortie from Bayonne made that impossible. Wellington (ed.), *Supplementary Despatches,* Vol.IX, p.42.

2 REM 5501-59-7, Biarritz, 13 May 1814.

got an opportunity to briefly return home. Arriving in England on 1 July 1814, Burgoyne had only a few weeks until he was recalled to London to prepare for the expedition. Whilst in London, Burgoyne took the opportunity to write to the Master-General requesting a pension for his services in the Peninsula.[3] In the letter, he stated he was in 'financial difficulties' caused by the expense of the Peninsular campaigns. This is another example of Burgoyne wishing to be independent of the wealth of Lord Derby. There is no doubt that Derby would have covered all his costs, but Burgoyne wanted to be able to pay his own bills.

August was spent making arrangements for the new campaign. Captain Wells and Lieutenant Edward Matson were attached, as was a company of Sappers and Miners; a small battering train of 24 guns was approved. Captain Thomson was appointed to replace Captain Slade who was sick, and Captain C.F. Smith was also assigned.[4] All together, there were 12 engineers attached to the expedition, including Burgoyne.[5]

Considering that Burgoyne had been planning this expedition for months, it is surprising that Dickson, commanding the artillery, was given only three days' notice to embark.[6]

The expedition sailed on 1 November 1814 with the chief command changed from Hill to Edward Pakenham. The size of the army had also been substantially reduced from that first planned due to the uncertainty in Europe.

Although Burgoyne commanded the engineers, it is surprising that he was not told where the expedition was going. Writing to his sister a month after they sailed, when they were near Barbados, he said:

> [W]e are not told on which side we shall direct our course from Jamaica, but I take it for granted that we are going to seize upon Louisiana … Sir Edward Pakenham affects to talk a great deal about Charleston in America, but I can't believe we are going there with such a trifling force and equipment.[7]

It cannot have helped with the planning that the specific needs were unknown.

3 REM 4601-72, f.1814/O, 24 July 1814. He was awarded 10s per diem in February 1817; Wrottesley, *Burgoyne*, p.335.

4 TMA WO55/959, Ouvry to Mann, 2 & 5 Aug 1814. WO55/983, Burgoyne to Mann, 20 Aug 1814; WO55/983, Unknown to Mann, 25 Aug 1814.

5 Porter, *Royal Engineers*, Vol.I, p.359.

6 Vigors (ed.), *Dickson Manuscripts*, 28 October 1814. Dickson suggested that although originally appointed, he believed the command had lapsed after the delay. When Pakenham was appointed, he asked for Dickson.

7 Wrottesley, *Burgoyne*, p.299.

Although Burgoyne would not have found out for some time, he was one of six engineer officers promoted by seniority to lieutenant colonel in the Corps on 20 December 1814.

On the 21 December 1814, Burgoyne first mentioned the mouth of the Mississippi. We also get the first mention of Vice Admiral Alexander Cochrane progressing the attack on New Orleans before Pakenham arrived. Like the attack on Buenos Ayres in 1806-7 this was an expedition proposed by the navy in which the army had little or no input. Cochrane had been raiding the length of the east of America for some time with great success. There are strong suggestions that the attraction of prize money was the reason New Orleans was attacked.[8]

By the time Pakenham and Burgoyne went ashore on Christmas Day 1814, Cochrane had landed troops, who were already in contact with the American defenders. The distance from the navy support to the army was over 70 miles through difficult swampy terrain. The river was passable to small boats but was under the guns of the Americans, as were the roads. Burgoyne's first examination of the defences showed that they were far too strong for a land assault. The American defenders were about as strong as the British force and behind three lines of defences. A risky scheme was proposed, of attacking across the river in boats, combined with a frontal attack on the main defences. The plan required the main American battery to be captured, after which the troops would attack.

The attack was carried out on 30 December 1814, only five days after Pakenham had set foot on American soil. After waiting some time and receiving no word about the capture of the battery, Pakenham could wait no longer and launched the troops. The attack failed disastrously and Pakenham was killed, leading to a council of war in which the decision was made to retreat. Wrottesley wrote that Burgoyne was in favour of continuing the attack, but Burgoyne did not record his opinion at the time.[9] Harry Smith, who was present and argued for the army to retreat, mentioned that Dickson was in the meeting. There is no reason why Burgoyne would not also be present as Commanding Engineer. Fortescue wrote that of the three who were in favour of continuing the attack, 'only one of these, Colonel John Burgoyne, was entitled to be heard with real respect'. Fortescue's evaluation of the plan to take New Orleans was as a mad venture that was little short of criminal.[10] Having said that, Fortescue argued that if the British had pushed on quickly after the first landing on 23 December 1814, they would have taken New Orleans before the defences had been strengthened.

8 Fortescue, *British Army*, Vol.I0, pp.150-1; Wrottesley (ed.), *Burgoyne*, pp.306-8 argues strongly that this was the cause of the failure.

9 Wrottesley, *Burgoyne*, p.306. Fortescue, *British Army*, Vol.I0, p.173. He does not state the source of his opinion.

10 Fortescue, *British Army*, Vol.I0, pp.154.

The army, now under Major General Lambert, remained in America for three more months before it returned to England. During that period, Burgoyne had a minor success, capturing, in a very efficient style, Fort Bowyer at Mobile on 11 February 1815. Three days later, word arrived that a peace accord had been signed on 24 December 1814. This whole expedition, like the end of the Peninsular War at Toulouse and Bayonne, was a waste. Word did not reach America about the armistice until after the Battle of New Orleans. Many thousand more lives had been needlessly lost.

Burgoyne sailed for England on 8 April 1815 and landed at Spithead on 30 May 1815. He arrived home amidst the frantic allied preparations following Napoleon's escape from Elba. The troops from America were directed straight to the Netherlands but Burgoyne was informed by the Board of Ordnance that he would not be joining the allied forces under Wellington. Wrottesley infers that Burgoyne was kept away because he was the senior officer and the current Commanding Royal Engineer with Wellington, James Carmichael-Smyth, would have been superseded. Burgoyne's obituary goes further and says that he was overlooked for political reasons.[11] This however was the same situation as had occurred in December 1812 and October 1813. Burgoyne was senior in brevet army rank but not in Corps rank. The commanding engineer was always selected on rank in the Corps and Carmichael-Smyth was the senior officer.[12] In addition, Carmichael-Smyth had been with the allied forces in the Low Countries through the 1813 and 1814 campaigns. Wrottesley also infers that Burgoyne's request to join Sir Thomas Picton as one of his ADCs was rejected unfairly. This was also wrong, as Ordnance officers were not usually placed on a general's staff as they were not part of the army and were taking opportunities that should be available for army officers.

Burgoyne appealed to Wellington, who supported his application to join the army, and on 27 June 1815, he was ordered to the continent. By then, of course, Waterloo had been fought and the immediate role for the engineers was to support the taking of the many fortresses still in French hands. Burgoyne's role for the next three years would be working with the Duke of Wellington's commission and the allies to audit and take possession of the many fortresses in France and the Low Countries. He remained on this task until the end of 1818 when he returned to England.

Wrottesley continued with the theme that Burgoyne was unfairly treated when honours were bestowed after the war.[13] The first was that Elphinstone was made a Baronet even though Burgoyne had been at almost all the sieges and was

11 'John Fox Burgoyne', *Grace's Guide to British Industrial History*, at <https://www.gracesguide.co.uk/John_Fox_Burgoyne>, accessed 8 May 2019.

12 Wrottesley, *Burgoyne*, p.311. One page later, Wrottesley contradicts himself by saying Burgoyne joined the army under Carmichael-Smyth, the Commanding (i.e. senior) Engineer.

13 Wrottesley, *Burgoyne*, pp.329-334.

senior by brevet rank. Neither of these points were valid. Elphinstone was made a Baronet because he was the commander of the Royal Engineers at the end of the war. Burgoyne was never the Commanding Royal Engineer in the Peninsula although at times he was the senior engineer with the army. Brevet rank was irrelevant. Wrottesley complained 'a worse act of injustice was to follow'. Burgoyne was missed off the list of officers to be awarded the KCB for being awarded five gold Peninsular medals. This was due to an error, and, when this was rectified, the rules had been changed and he was no longer eligible. It was realised too late that the new award would be open to too many officers and the rules were changed to make only general officers eligible. Burgoyne was awarded the lower CB and offered a knighthood, but declined the knighthood as he felt it would condone the lack of recognition being given to Ordnance officers. Whilst in this case, Wrottesley had a point that other officers got the KCB and Burgoyne did not, all officers of his rank were forbidden from wearing the award. This again was not a slight to Burgoyne, but the need to correct the bad decision of awarding KCBs and the potential for making the situation worse by making exceptions. Wrottesley did not dwell on the situation when Burgoyne was awarded two brevet promotions in 1812 much to the concern of officers in both the Ordnance and the army.

Whilst some of his promotions in later life were slow, Burgoyne's rise during the Napoleonic wars was meteoric. He took only 16.5 years to reach lieutenant colonel from being commissioned. Only one other officer was quicker since the formation of the Corps.[14] This timescale was much quicker than could have been achieved in the army.[15] His 'slow' rise through the 19th century took him to the rank of field marshal, something no other engineer officer had ever achieved. There is much to be impressed with, and proud of, in the services of John Fox Burgoyne.

14 This was Charles William Pasley, another officer who complained about his lack of seniority!

15 Average time to reach Lieutenant Colonel in the army in 1791 was 30 years. J.A. Houlding, *Fit for Service. The Training of the British Army* (Oxford: Oxford University Press, 1981), p.109.

16

The Making of a Field Marshal

Returning to England in 1818, Burgoyne was 35 years old. His next active service would be in 1855, when as a 72-year-old, he would go to the Crimea as advisor to Lord Raglan (Fitzroy Somerset).[1] Raglan as Master General of the Ordnance would have known Burgoyne well though the latter's position as Inspector General of Fortifications and also through them both serving in the Peninsular War.

In his 15 years of near constant overseas service during the Napoleonic Wars, Burgoyne had gained invaluable experience of the science of war, the hard way, by doing it. Throughout, he had evaluated events and tried to learn from them. He shared his experiences and thoughts with fellow officers and, more importantly, with the staff at the new School of Military Engineering where the next generation of engineers and sappers would be trained. The last campaigns of the Napoleonic Wars saw the first deployment of trained sappers and after the first few months, once they had gained field experience, they were a welcome and valued addition to the British armed forces.

Burgoyne had been present at most of the British sieges during the Peninsular War, missing only the first siege of Badajoz in May 1811. He had seen at first hand the difficulties caused by not having sufficient trained engineers and sappers with the army. The ability to make, repair, or destroy roads and bridges was absolutely vital for operational mobility and in terrain like the Iberian Peninsula it was a strategic game-changer. Burgoyne was also able to appreciate the value that an engineer officer brought to army headquarters, be it through surveys, reconnaissance, liaison or other roles.

Much of his command experience was negative: Egypt 1807 (illness and expedition failure), Portugal 1807 (abandoned), Sweden 1808 (abandoned); Badajoz 1811 (raised), Salamanca forts 1812 (ill prepared but taken), Siege of Burgos 1812 (failed), end of siege of San Sebastián 1813 (success), New Orleans 1814-15 (failed). However, he was able to look at each event and learn from it. He would have taken

1 Burgoyne was Commanding Royal Engineer for the Clinton Expedition to Portugal in 1827, but no conflict occurred.

these experiences back to the Ordnance where he rose in the ranks to eventually become the senior engineer, the Inspector General of Fortifications, in 1845.

Many of the friends and officers who trained with Burgoyne and gained their operational experience across Europe, Egypt, and America were gone. The peace dividend lost several more.

Burgoyne's relationship with Wellington, not the easiest of commanders, was strong. From their first meeting in 1809, they built an understanding that would be beneficial to both in post-war Europe and peacetime Britain. Burgoyne became a valued advisor to many government officials and would have been a useful asset when Wellington became Master General of the Ordnance in 1819 and later when he was in other roles in the government. After Waterloo, Burgoyne served under Wellington in the Low Countries until 1818 and was then based at Chatham between 1821 and 1827 when Wellington was Master General of the Ordnance. They would have come into regular contact. Burgoyne was not afraid of speaking truth unto power, and his views were listened to, even if they were not accepted.

He would probably have observed with horror the unpicking of the corps and the loss of experience due to peacetime cost cutting. But this was a fact of life for the military both in the past and the present. The arrival of the Crimean War showed how much had been lost. Burgoyne's advice at the siege of Sevastopol was criticised by many and eventually led to his recall, although the present author, for one, remains unconvinced how realistic is was to believe that a *coup-de-main* would have taken the city.

The publication of *The Military Opinions of General Sir John Fox Burgoyne* in 1859 was an attempt to re-introduce the hard-learned lessons of the two previous wars; lessons which seemed to have been lost. Some of the material published was written 40 years earlier, based on his recent experiences in the Peninsula.

In a career that started in 1798 and ended 70 years later, when he retired in 1868, Burgoyne had served his country almost without a break. He served in Europe, the Middle East and America and recorded his experiences, both success and failure, for future generations. Throughout, he comes across as a calm professional who was able to learn and pass his experience on to others. He was willing to criticise the actions of himself and others when there were improvements to be made for the benefit of the service. He served three monarchs and 15 Master Generals. Almost all of the post-war Master Generals, he knew from the Peninsula. Like many post-war engineers he became heavily involved in the introduction of railways in Britain.

John Burgoyne's early years taught him to be independent and he carried this attitude through his life, although the support he received from the Stanley family (Lord Derby) should not be overlooked.

In the end, Burgoyne proved that he could be as good, if not better, than his father as a soldier and had an influence on military and government thinking well into Victorian Britain. It was a legacy he could be proud of.

Appendix I

Note on Documents

The Royal Engineers Museum holds a large archive of primary material and I have used it extensively in writing this book. Of particular importance are the papers of John Burgoyne. One of the main sources is REM 4201-68 where several of Burgoyne's notebooks are stored. They are not always easy to identify, and I have used the following:

- Eight small booklets with journal entries covering period from 25 May 1809 to 21 July 1815. These are cited as 4201-68, Journal, with the date to identify the location in a particular journal.
- REM 4201-68, Siege of Badajoz
- REM 4201-68, Notebook
- REM 4201-68, Bridges
- REM 4201-68, Temporary Mem. Cited as 4201-68, Memorandum

Similarly, there are three sources I have used from John T. Jones.

- The published *Journal of the Sieges*
- The unpublished diaries held in REM 5501-59-1, 2, 3. Cited as Jones' Diary with the date to identify the location in a particular journal.
- The unpublished, autobiography of John T. Jones. Referred to as Jones' Autobiography. Twelve copies were privately printed. The Royal Engineers Museum hold a typewritten copy of the work, Reference 92.1 (Jones): 355.486(RE)

Appendix II

Glossary of Fortification Terms

Auget	A priming tube filled with powder connecting to a mine. The place where the slow match is applied to explode the charge.
Barbette	a battery in which artillery fire over the parapet rather than through an opening (embrasure).
Bastion	Fortification work, usually four-sided (tetrahedral) and situated in the corners of a wall, with a sharp point, making possible defensive and flanking fire.
Bourrage	Tamping
Caponnière	Covered passage across a ditch to an outer fortification structure such as a ravelin
Casemate	Covered chamber for musketry or artillery built into walls of fortification
Cavalier	A fortification built within a larger fortification. It usually consisted of a raised platform within a fort or bastion, so as to be able to fire over the main parapet.
Cavalier de tranchée	Large earth parapet raised by the besiegers near the covered paths of the place, in order to be able to plunge into the defences
Chamber	Open area at end of gallery (tunnel) where power would be placed, as a mine.
Chevaux-de-Frieze	Large pieces of timber studded with blades and spikes, designed to block breaches in walls against attackers
Counterguard	Detached structure protecting a bastion.
Counterscarp	Outer face of a ditch
Covered Way	Passage along the outer edge of a ditch, protected by a rampart forming the glacis;

Crenel	The low part of battlements. The high part is a Merlon and a group of them; Crenellations.
Crownwork	Advanced fortification structure screening the entrance to a bastion fort.
Curtain (wall)	Stretch of wall between two towers.
Embrasure	An opening in a parapet (wall) which guns fire through
Epaulement (French – shoulder)	A barricade of heaped earth for protection from gunfire. Also The angle formed by the face and flank of a bastion; i.e. the shoulder of the bastion.
Fascine	A bundle of sticks bound together, used to strengthen the sides of trenches or earthen work ramparts
Fausse Braye	Low rampart in the ditch, in front of the main fortification.
Fougasse	Improvised mortar constructed by making a hollow in the ground and filling it with explosives and projectiles.
Fraise	Palisades projecting horizontally from the scarp or counterscarp of a fortification's ditch. Designed to inhibit attacking troops entering the ditch or scaling the scarp to reach the parapet
Gabions	Round wicker baskets with open tops and bottoms and filled with earth to protect artillery batteries and troops in trenches
Gallery	Tunnel
Glacis	Rampart of the ditch and Covered Way, sloping away towards the enemy.
Gorge	Rear face of a forward defence (e.g. Ravelin) which faced the main wall.
Hornwork	'Horned' structure, consisting of two demi bastions, one at each end of a curtain.
Keep	Large main building of a medieval castle.
Lunette	Triangular defensive structure, open at the rear, often flanking a ravelin
Merlon	The raised part of battlements. The low part is a Crenel and a group of them are crenellations.
Palisade	A barrier of sharpened logs closely planted in the ground. Can be vertical or horizontally (Fraise)
Parallel	Trenches dug by attacking forces near fortresses to protect themselves from defenders' fire
Pickets	Wooden stakes to hold fascines or gabions in place.

Platform	Wooden flooring within a battery on which the artillery pieces were placed
Postern	Small gateway in a castle from which the besieged could sally forth.
Ravelin	Fortified structure, more or less triangular in plan, sited in the ditch to defend the curtain.
Redan	Is a work in a V-shaped salient angle toward an expected attack. It can be made from earthworks or other material.
Redoubt	Detached, independent outwork.
Retrenchment	Interior defensive work, usually consisting of a trench and parapet.
Revet / revetting / revetement	Retaining wall or face; i.e. a wall supporting a bank of earth or mass of water
Salient angle	The salient was an angle, or sharp point, which faced out towards the enemy
Sally port	A gate (or Postern) through which soldiers could "sally forth" to counterattack. In larger forts may be a tunnel through the walls and earthworks.
Sap	Trenches dug forward from the main parallels to advance nearer the defenders' position
Terrepein	A level space within a fortification. Artillery was typically mounted in the terreplein
Trace	Circuit or fortified perimeter, also known as the enceinte.
Traverse	Small bank or wall that cuts across the line of a covered way. To protect defenders from enfilading fire

Appendix III

Summary of Burgoyne's Ranks and Honours

Commissioned, Second Lieutenant	29 August 1798
Lieutenant	1 July 1800
Second Captain	1 March 1805
Captain	24 June 1809
Major (Brevet)	6 February 1812
Lieutenant Colonel (Brevet)	27 April 1812
Lieutenant Colonel	20 December 1814
Colonel (Brevet)	22 July 1830
Colonel	10 January 1837
Major General	28 June 1838
Inspector General of Fortifications	1845
Lieutenant General	11 November 1851
Colonel Commandant	22 November 1854
General	5 September 1855
Field Marshal	1 January 1868

Companion of the Bath	1814
Knight Commander of the Bath	19 July 1838
Grand Knight Cross of the Bath	31 March 1852
Baronet	18 April 1856
Constable of the Tower	11 April 1865

Bibliography

Archival Sources

National Archives – Public Record Office

MPH 1/1010: Maps & Diagrams.
MPH1/1007: Maps extracted from WO37/10 Scovell papers.
MPH 1/1195/7: RE Maps & Diagrams.
MR1/930: Maps various.
PRO30/35/1: Correspondence and Papers of James Carmichael Smyth 1805-1837.
WO17/2770: Engineers monthly returns August 1813 – Dec 1815.
WO30/35/1: Diary of James Carmichael-Smyth 1808-15.
WO37: Scovell papers.
WO54/251: Returns of Officers 1805-1809.
WO54/252: Returns of Officers 1810-1814.
WO54/253: Returns of Officers 1815-1819.
WO54/727: RMA Embarkation books.
WO55/958: Engineer papers 1798-1811.
WO55/959: Engineer papers 1812-46.
WO55/977: RE Letters 1808.
WO55/978: RE Letters 1809.
WO55/979: RE Letters 1810.
WO55/980: RE Letters 1811.
WO55/981: RE Letters 1812.
WO55/982: RE Letters 1813.
WO55/983: RE Letters 1814.
WO55/984: RE Letters 1815.

Southampton University – Hartley Library – Papers of the Duke of Wellington

WP6/1/10: Index of Letters to the Duke of Wellington Jan-Dec 1811.
WP6/1/12: Index of Letters to the Duke of Wellington Jan-Dec 1812.
WP6/1/14: Index of Letters to the Duke of Wellington Jan-Dec 1813.

National Army Museum

1970-04-16-9: Letters of various Officers including John Birch; C.W. Pasley; J.F. Burgoyne.
1999-06-149: Diaries of Lieut. William Staveley RSC.
2004-05-26: Military Engineering in the Peninsular War 1808-1814. A Digest of References by Maj. J.T. Hancock.
6807/102: Tylden's MS record on Pontoon Train 1814.
7403-147: Oldfield Letters.
8105-46: Copy of Diary of Captain John Williams RE. (Killed at siege of Burgos).

Royal Engineers Museum (REM)

2001.149: Misc RE letters.
2001.150: Ordnance General Orders.
2001.151: Misc RE Letters.
3801.15.3: Letter from Rice Jones, camp before Ciudad Rodrigo 20 Jan 1812.
4201.68: Papers of Sir John Fox Burgoyne (several MS journals).
4201.274: Transcript of letters from Howard Elphinstone to his wife.
4201.305: Peninsular Letters of Captain Landmann and Fanshawe 1808-10.
4501-86/4: Letters from Captain George Ross to Sir Hew Dalrymple.
4601.26: H.D. Jones' Report on New Orleans.
4601.29: Account of throwing bridge across Adour in 1814.
4601.57.1: Emmet's Peninsular Diary 1809-14.
4601.71: Misc letters of Sir Richard Fletcher.
4601.72: Misc letters from Burgoyne.
5501.52: Notebook of Capt West on river crossings in the Peninsula.
5501.59.1,2,3: J T Jones' Diaries from 1810-12 [Cited as Jones Diary].
5501.59.4: Fletcher's Letter book, Nov 1810 – Feb 1811.
5501.59.5: Fletcher's Letter book, Oct 1811 – Oct 1812.
5501.59.6: Reid's notes on the siege of Burgos.
5501.59.7: Letters written to Burgoyne by Squire, Pitts and Wright.
5501.59.8: Letters of Fletcher and Jones related to Torres Vedras.
5501.59.10: Letters written to J T Jones RE, by his brother Harry D Jones RE.
5501.59.18: Book of letters on Torres Vedras.
5501.59.21 to 31: Various letters.
5501.79: Letters of RE officers, Peninsula, Egypt and Crimea.
5501.91.3: Wellington's orders for the attack on Badajoz April 1812.
5501.106: Notebook of Harry D Jones Oct 1812 – Feb 1814.
5501.108.4&5: Burgoyne's diary and sketch on Siege of San Sebastian.
5501.108.6&7: Letters from Moore and Wellington to Burgoyne.
5501.108.8: Instructions on lines of Torres Vedras.

5501.123.1,2,3: Reports written by H.D. Jones.
5501.139: Various letters on Peninsular War.
5501.139.1: Letter from Burgoyne to Pasley with description of siege of Ciudad Rodrigo.
5501.139.3&4: Letters to/from Fitzroy Somerset regarding ranks.
7804.16: Diary of Gustavus Nicholls 1799-1808.
9312.13.2: Letter from A.J. Wortham on Siege of San Sebastian.
9312.13.3: Letter from Goldfinch to Morse on battles around Nive and Bayonne.

John Rylands Library, Manchester

Clinton Papers (unreferenced) (with thanks to Gareth Glover for supplying images).

British Library

ADD MS36306: Letters from Wellington Beresford.
ADD MS41766: Pasley biography by Tyler.
ADD MS41961-5: Pasley Papers 1807-1828.
ADD MS57544: Supplementary Moore Papers.
ADD MS63106: Letters of John Squire RE to Sir Henry Bunbury,1810-12.

Published Primary Sources

Anon, *Personal Narrative of a Private Soldier who Served in the Forty-Second Highlanders for Twelve Years During the Late War* (Cambridge: Trotman, 1996).
Anon. (ed.), *Relations de Sièges en Espagne* (Paris: Tesseidre, 2000).
Blakeney, Robert, *A Boy in the Peninsular War* (London: Greenhill, 1989).
Blakiston, John, *Twelve Years' Military Adventure in Three Quarters of the Globe* (London: Henry Colburn, 1829).
Boothby, C., *A Prisoner of France* (London: A&C Black, 1898).
Boothby, C., *Under England's Flag from 1804-1809* (London: A&C Black, 1900).
Boutflower, Charles, *The Journal of an Army Surgeon during the Peninsular War* (Privately printed, no date).
Bunbury, Henry, *Narratives of Some Passages in the Great War with France from 1799 to 1810. By Lt General Sir Henry Bunbury formerly Quartermaster-General to the Army in the Mediterranean* (London: Richard Bentley, 1854).
Carr-Gomm, F.C. (ed.), *The Letters and Journals of Field-Marshal Sir William Maynard Gomm from 1799 to Waterloo 1815* (London: John Murray, 1881).

Eliot, William Granville, *Treatise on the Defence of Portugal*, 2nd edition (London: Egerton, 1811).

Fletcher, Ian (ed.), *For King and Country. The Letters and Diaries of John Mills, Coldstream Guards, 1811-14* (Staplehurst: Spellmount, 1995).

Gleig, G.R., *The Subaltern* (Edinburgh: Blackwood, 1825).

Gleig, G.R., *The Campaigns of the British Army at Washington and New Orleans* (London: John Murray, 1879).

Glover, Gareth (ed.), *Wellington's Lieutenant, Napoleon's Gaoler* (Barnsley: Pen & Sword, 2005).

Glover, Gareth (ed.), *The Letters of Second Captain Charles Dansey 1806-13* (Cambridge: Trotman, 2006).

Glover, Gareth (ed.), *Eyewitness to the Peninsular War and the Battle of Waterloo. The Letters and Journals of Lieutenant Colonel the Honourable John Stanhope 1803 to 1815* (Barnsley: Pen & Sword, 2010).

Glover, Gareth (ed.), *Wellington's Voice: The Candid Letters of John Freemantle* (London: Frontline, 2012).

Grattan, William, *Adventures with the Connaught Rangers* (London: Greenhill, 1989).

Gurwood, John, *Dispatches of the Duke of Wellington*. 1st edition, 12 volumes (London: John Murray, 1834-38).

Gurwood, John, *Dispatches of the Duke of Wellington*. 2nd New and Enlarged edition, 8 volumes (London: John Murray, 1852). This is the edition cited unless specifically stated otherwise.

Henegan, R.D., *Seven Years Campaigning in the Peninsula and the Netherlands* (Stroud: Nonsuch, 2005).

Horward, Donald (ed.), *The French Campaign in Portugal. An Account by Jean Jaques Pelet* (Minneapolis: University of Minnesota, 1973).

Jones, J.T., *Journals of the sieges undertaken by the Allies in Spain in the years 1811 and 1812 with Notes*, 1st edition (London: Egerton, 1814).

Jones, J.T., *Journal of the Sieges carried on by the army under the Duke of Wellington in Spain Between the Years 1811 to 1814*, 3rd edition (London: John Weale, 1846). This is the edition referenced unless specifically stated otherwise.

Jones, J.T., *The Military Autobiography of Major-General John T. Jones* (London: Privately published, 1853). Twelve copies only, privately published for family use. Cited as Jones' Autobiography.

Landmann, G., *Recollections of Military Life 1806-1808* (London: Hurst & Blackett, 1854).

Landmann, G., *Historical, Military and Picturesque Observations on Portugal* (London: Cadell & Davis, 1818).

Lamare, J.B., *Relation des Sieges et Defences D'Olivenza, de Badajoz et de Campo Mayor en 1811 et 1812*. 1st Edition (Paris: Anselin et Pochard, 1825).

Lamare, J.B., *An account of the second defence of the fortress of Badajoz by the French in 1812. Translated by an Officer of the Royal Engineers* (Chatham: Royal Engineers, 1824).

Leith-Hay, A., *A Narrative of the Peninsular War*, 2nd Edition (London: Washbourne, 1834).

Leslie (ed.), *The Dickson Manuscripts, 1809-13* (Cambridge: Trotman, 1987).

Maurice, J.F. (ed.), *The Diary of Sir John Moore* (London: Arnold, 1904).

May, John, *A Few Observations on the Mode of Attack and Employment of Heavy Artillery at Ciudad Rodrigo and Badajoz, in 1812, and St Sebastian in 1813* (Cambridge: Trotman, 2004).

Monick, S. (ed.), *John Douglas, Tales from the Peninsula* (London: Leo Cooper, 1997).

Muir, R (ed.), *At Wellington's Right Hand. The Letters of Lieutenant-Colonel Sir Alexander Gordon 1808-1815* (Stroud: Army Records Society, 2003).

Neale, Adam, *Letters from Portugal and Spain, Comprising the Account of the Operation of the Armies under their excellencies Sir Arthur Wellesley and Sir John Moore* (London: Richard Phillips, 1809).

Page, Julia V., *Intelligence Officer in the Peninsula. The letters and diaries of Major the Hon. Edward Charles Cocks 1786-1812* (Tunbridge Wells: Spellmount, 1986).

Pasley, C.W., *Course of instruction originally composed for the use of the Royal Engineer Department* (Chatham: Royal Engineers, 1814-17).

Pasley, C.W., *Essay on the Military Policy and institutions of the British Empire, Part 1*, 1st Edition (London: Edmund Lloyd, 1810).

Perret, Bryan (ed.), *A Hawk at War. The Peninsular War Reminiscences of General Sir Thomas Brotherton* (Chippenham: Picton, 1986).

Porter, Robert, *Letters from Portugal and Spain written During the March of the British Troops under Sir John Moore* (Cambridge: Trotman, 1985).

Sabine, Edward (ed.), *Letters of Colonel Sir Augustus Frazer, K.C.B., commanding the Royal Horse Artillery in the army under the Duke of Wellington written during the Peninsular and Waterloo campaigns* (Uckfield: Naval & Military, 2001).

Schauman, Augustus, *On the Road with Wellington* (London: Heinemann, 1924).

Sperling, John, *Letters of an Officer of the Corps of Royal Engineers, from the British Army in Holland, Belgium and France to his Father from the latter end of 1813 to 1816* (London: James Nisbett, 1872).

Thompson, M.S., *The Peninsular War Diary of Edmund Mulcaster* (Sunderland: Amazon, 2015).

Thompson, M.S., *The Peninsular War Letters of Lancelot Machell, 1809-13* (Sunderland: Amazon, 2017).

Vigors, D. (ed.), *The Dickson Manuscripts Series C, 1809-1840, Part 6 (1814), Vol. VIII* (London: Firestep, 2018).

Wellington (ed.), *Supplementary Despatches of the Duke of Wellington* (London: John Murray, 1858-1872).

Whinyates, F.A., *Letters written by Lieut.-General Thomas Dyneley C.B., R.A., While on Active Service Between the years 1806 and 1815* (London: Trotman, 1984).

Published Secondary Sources

Belmas. J., *Journaux des sieges faits ou soutenous par les francais dans la Peninsule, de 1807 a 1814* (Paris: Firmin Didiot, 1836).

Beresford, Marcus de la Poer (ed.), *William Carr Beresford, The Ablest Man I have Seen with the Army* (Newbridge: IAP, 2019).

Collins, Bruce, *Wellington and the Siege of San Sebastian 1813* (Barnsley: Pen & Sword, 2018).

Colville, J. (ed.), *Portrait of a General* (Salisbury: Michael Russell, 1980).

Connolly, T.W.J., *History of the Corps of Royal Sappers and Miners* (London: Longman, Browne, Green & Longmans, 1855).

Connolly, T.W.J & Edwards R.F., *Roll of Officers of the Corps of Royal Engineers From 1660 to 1898* (Chatham: Royal Engineers Institute, 1898).

Divall, Carole, *Wellington's Worst Scrape: The Burgos Campaign 1812* (Barnsley: Pen & Sword, 2012).

Douglas, Howard, *An Essay on the Principles and Construction of Military Bridges.* 3rd Edition (London: John Murray, 1832).

Duncan, Francis, *History of the Royal Regiment of Artillery* (London: John Murray, 1873)

Ellesmere, Francis, *Personal Reminiscences of the Duke of Wellington* (London: John Murray, 1904).

Esdaile, Charles, *The Peninsular War* (London: Penguin, 2002).

Esdaile, Charles & Freeman, Philip, *Burgos in the Peninsular War, 1808-14. Occupation, Siege, Aftermath* (Basingstoke: Palgrave, 2015).

Fletcher, Ian, *In Hell Before Daylight. The Siege and Storming of the Fortress of Badajoz, 16 March to 6 April 1812* (London: Baton Press, 1984).

Fortescue, John, *History of the British Army* (London: Macmillan, 1899-1930).

Franklin, C., *British Napoleonic Field Artillery* (Stroud: Spellmount, 2012).

Fullom, S., *Life of Sir Howard Douglas* (London: John Murray, 1863).

Glover, Michael, *Wellington's Army in the Peninsula 1808-1814* (Newton Abbot: David & Charles, 1977).

Graham, John Murray, *Memoir of General Lord Lynedoch* (London: Blackwood, 1868).

Grehan, John, *The Lines of Torres Vedras* (Staplehurst: Spellmount, 2000).

Griffiths, Paddy (ed.), *A History of the Peninsular War, Volume IX, Modern Studies of the War in Spain and Portugal 1808-1814* (London: Greenhill, 1999).

Hall, John, *The Biographical Dictionary of British Officers killed and wounded, 1808-1814* (London: Greenhill, 1998).
Harding-Edgar, John (ed.), *Next to Wellington: General Sir George Murray* (Warwick: Helion, 2018).
Horward, Donald, *Napoleon and Iberia, The Twin sieges of Ciudad Rodrigo and Almeida, 1810* (London: Greenhill, 1994).
James, Wiliam, *The Naval History of Great Britain, from the Declaration of War by France in 1793 to the Accession of George IV* (London: Richard Bentley, 1886).
Jones, John T., *Account of the War in Spain and Portugal and the South of France from 1808 to 1814 Inclusive*, 2nd edition (London: Egerton, 1821).
Jones, William D., *Records of the Royal Military Academy* (Woolwich: FJ Cattermole, 1851)
Leslie, John, *The Services of the Royal Regiment of Artillery in the Peninsular War* (London: Hugh Rees, 1908).
Lispcombe, Nick, *Wellington's Guns* (Oxford: Osprey, 2013).
Lipscombe, Nick, *Bayonne & Toulouse* (Oxford: Osprey, 2014).
Moore, James, *A Narrative of the Campaign of the British Army in Spain* (London: Johnson, 1809).
Moore, James Carrick, *The Life of Sir John Moore* (London: John Murray, 1834).
Moore-Smith, G.C. (ed.), *Life of John Colborne, Field Marshal Lord Seaton* (London: John Murray, 1903).
Moorsom, W.S. (ed.), *Historical Record of the Fifty-Second (Oxfordshire Light Infantry) from the Year 1755 to the Year 1858* (London: Richard Bentley, 1860).
Muir, Rory, *Wellington: The Path to Victory 1769-1814* (New Haven: Yale University Press, 2013).
Myatt, F., *British Sieges of the Peninsular War* (Tunbridge Wells: Spellmount, 1987).
Myatt, F., *Peninsular General: Sir Thomas Picton 1758-1815* (London: David & Charles, 1980).
Napier, W.F.P., *History of the War in the Peninsula and in the South of France from the Year 1807 to the Year 1814*, 1st edition (London: T&W Boone, 1828-1840).
Nichols, A.S., *Wellington's Mongrel Regiment. A History of the Chasseurs Britanniques, 1801-1814* (Staplehurst: Spellmount, 2005).
Norris, A.H. & Bremner, R.W., *The Lines of Torres Vedras. The First Three Lines and Fortifications South of the Tagus*, 2nd edition (Lisbon: Privately Printed, 1980).
Oman, Carola, *Sir John Moore* (London: Hodder & Stoughton, 1953).
Oman, C.W.C., *A History of the Peninsular War* (Oxford: Clarendon Press, 1902-1930).
Oman, C.W.C., *Wellington's Army 1809-1814* (London: Greenhill, 1986).
Parkinson, Roger, *Moore of Corunna* (Oxford: PBS, 1976).
Porter, Withworth, *History of the Royal Corps of Engineers* (Woolwich: Institute of Royal Engineers, 1889).
Robertson, Ian, *A Commanding Presence: Wellington in the Peninsula 1808-1814: Logistics-Strategy-Survival* (Stroud: Spellmount, 2008).

Shore, H.V. (ed.), *An Engineer Officer under Wellington in the Peninsula* (Huntingdon: Trotman, 2005).
Stanhope, Earl of, *Notes of Conversations with the Duke of Wellington* (Oxford: OUP, 1938).
Thompson, M.S., *Wellington's Engineers* (Barnsley: Pen & Sword, 2015).
Uffindel, A., *The National Army Museum Book of Wellington's Armies. Britain's Campaigns in the Peninsula and at Waterloo 1808-1815* (London: Sidgewick & Jackson, 2003).
Verner, W., *Major George Simmons A British Rifle Man* (London: Greenhill, 1996).
Ward, B.R., *The School of Military Engineering 1812-1909* (Chatham: Cattermole, 1909).
Ward, S.G.P., *Wellington's Headquarters* (Oxford: Oxford University Press, 1957).
White, Kenton, *The Key to Lisbon* (Warwick: Helion, 2019).
Wrottesley, G. (ed.), *Life and Correspondence of Field Marshall Sir John Burgoyne*, (London: Richard Bentley, 1873). All citations are to Vol.I.
Wrottesley, G. (ed.), *The Military Opinions of General Sir John Fox Burgoyne* (London: Richard Bentley, 1859).

Theses

Phillipson, A, 'The Business of Engineers', (PhD Thesis, University of Portsmouth, 2007).
Redgrave, T.M.O., 'Wellington's Logistical Arrangements in the Peninsular war 1809-1814' (PhD Thesis, Kings College London, Not Dated).
Reese, Paul, 'The Ablest Man in the British Army. The Life and Career of General Sir John Hope' (PhD Thesis, Florida State University, 2007).
Thompson, M.S., 'The Rise of the Scientific Soldier' (PhD Thesis, Sunderland, 2009).

Journal Articles

Meyerhof, Max, 'A Short History of Opthalmia during the Egyptian Campaigns of 1799 – 1807', *British Journal of Opthalmology*, (March 1932), pp.129–152.
Reid, W., 'On Intrenchments as support in battle'. *Royal Engineer Professional Papers*, Vol.2 (1838), pp.2-10.
Reid, W., 'On Assaults', *Royal Engineer Professional Papers*, Vol.1 (1837), pp.3-18.
Reid, W., 'On Destruction of Stone Bridges', *Royal Engineer Professional Papers*, Vol.1 (1837), pp.148-150.
Sandham, H., 'Memoir of Lieut.-General Sir Harry D Jones', *Royal Engineer Professional Papers*, Vol.16 (1868), pp.ix-xiv.

Parker, Alice, 'Incorrigible Rogues: The Brutalisation of British Soldiers in the Peninsular War 1808-1814', *British Journal of Military History*, Vol.1, Issue 3, (2015), pp.42-59.

Thompson, Mark S., 'When is a 24-pounder not a 24-pounder', *Smoothbore Ordnance Journal*, Vol.11, (2019), pp.9-19.

Online Resources

Dick Tennant 'Maps in the Peninsular War', *The Napoleon Series*, <https://www.napoleon-series.org/military/organization/Maps/PeninsularWar/c_MapsPeninsularWar.html> (accessed 17 May 2019)

C. San-Antonio-Gómez, C. Velilla & F. Manzano-Agugliaro, 'Tomas Lopez's Geographic Atlas of Spain in the Peninsular War', <http://oa.upm.es/14061/2/INVE_MEM_2011_120868.pdf> (accessed 21 June 2019)

Index

From Reason to Revolution series – Warfare 1721-1815

http://www.helion.co.uk/published-by-helion/reason-to-revolution-1721-1815.html

The 'From Reason to Revolution' series covers the period of military history 1721–1815, an era in which fortress-based strategy and linear battles gave way to the nation-in-arms and the beginnings of total war.

This era saw the evolution and growth of light troops of all arms, and of increasingly flexible command systems to cope with the growing armies fielded by nations able to mobilise far greater proportions of their manpower than ever before. Many of these developments were fired by the great political upheavals of the era, with revolutions in America and France bringing about social change which in turn fed back into the military sphere as whole nations readied themselves for war. Only in the closing years of the period, as the reactionary powers began to regain the upper hand, did a military synthesis of the best of the old and the new become possible.

The series will examine the military and naval history of the period in a greater degree of detail than has hitherto been attempted, and has a very wide brief, with the intention of covering all aspects from the battles, campaigns, logistics, and tactics, to the personalities, armies, uniforms, and equipment.

Submissions

The publishers would be pleased to receive submissions for this series. Please contact series editor Andrew Bamford via email (andrewbamford18@gmail.com), or in writing to Helion & Company Limited, Unit 8 Amherst Business Centre, Budbrooke Road, Warwick, CV34 5WE

Titles

No 1 *Lobositz to Leuthen. Horace St Paul and the Campaigns of the Austrian Army in the Seven Years War 1756-57* Translated with additional materials by Neil Cogswell (ISBN 978-1-911096-67-2)

No 2 *Glories to Useless Heroism. The Seven Years War in North America from the French journals of Comte Maurés de Malartic, 1755-1760* William Raffle (ISBN 978-1-1911512-19-6)

No 3 *Reminiscences 1808-1815 Under Wellington. The Peninsular and Waterloo Memoirs of William Hay* William Hay, with notes and commentary by Andrew Bamford (ISBN 978-1-1911512-32-5)

No 4 *Far Distant Ships. The Royal Navy and the Blockade of Brest 1793-1815* Quintin Barry (ISBN 978-1-1911512-14-1)

No 5 *Godoy's Army. Spanish Regiments and Uniforms from the Estado Militar of 1800* Charles Esdaile and Alan Perry (ISBN 978-1-911512-65-3) (large-format paperback)

No 6 *On Gladsmuir Shall the Battle Be! The Battle of Prestonpans 1745* Arran Johnston (ISBN 978-1-911512-83-7)

No 7 *The French Army of the Orient 1798-1801. Napoleon's Beloved 'Egyptians'* Yves Martin (ISBN 978-1-911512-71-4)*

No 8 *The Autobiography, or Narrative of a Soldier. The Peninsular War Memoirs of William Brown of the 45th Foot* William Brown, with notes and commentary by Steve Brown (ISBN 978-1-911512-94-3)

No 9 *Recollections from the Ranks. Three Russian Soldiers' Autobiographies from the Napoleonic Wars* Translated and annotated by Darrin Boland (ISBN 978-1-912174-18-8)

No 10 *By Fire and Bayonet. Grey's West Indies Campaign of 1794* Steve Brown (ISBN 978-1-911512-60-8)

No 11 *Olmütz to Torgau. Horace St Paul and the Campaigns of the Austrian Army in the Seven Years War 1758-60* Translated with additional materials by Neil Cogswell (ISBN 978-1-911512-72-1)

No 12 *Murat's Army. The Army of the Kingdom of Naples 1806-1815* Digby Smith (ISBN 978-1-912390-09-0)

No 13 *The Veteran or 40 Years' Service in the British Army. The Scurrilous Recollections of Paymaster John Harley 47th Foot – 1798-1838* John Harley, with notes and commentary by Gareth Glover (ISBN 978-1-912390-25-0)

No 14 *Narrative of the Eventful Life of Thomas Jackson. Militiaman and Coldstream Sergeant, 1803-15* Thomas Jackson, with notes and commentary by Eamonn O'Keeffe (ISBN 978-1-912390-12-0)

No 15 *For Orange and the States! The Army of the Dutch Republic 1713-1772. Part I: Infantry* Marc Geerdinck-Schaftenaar (ISBN 978-1-911512-15-8)*

No.16 *'Men who are Determined to be Free': The American Assault on Stony Point 15 July 1779* David Bonk (ISBN 978-1-912174-84-3)*

No 17 *Next to Wellington. General Sir George Murray. The Story of a Scottish Soldier and Statesman, Wellington's Quartermaster General* John Harding-Edgar (ISBN 978-1-912390-13-7)

No 18 *Between Scylla and Charybdis: The Army of Friedrich August II of Saxony, 1733-1763. Part I: Staff and Cavalry* Marco Pagan (ISBN 978-1-912174-89-8)*

No 19 *The Secret Expedition: The Anglo-Russian Invasion of Holland 1799* Geert van Uythoven (ISBN 978-1-912390-20-5)

No 20 *'We Are Accustomed to do our Duty' German Auxiliaries with the British Army 1793-95* Paul Demet (ISBN 978-1-912174-96-6)

No 21 *With the Guards in Flanders. The Diary of Captain Roger Morris 1793-95* Peter Harington (ISBN 978-1-911628-15-6)

No 22 *The British Army in Egypt 1801. An Underrated Army Comes of Age* Carole Divall (ISBN 978-1-911628-17-0)*

No 23 *Better is the Proud Plaid. The Clothing, Weapons, and Accoutrements of the Jacobites in 1745* Jenn Scott (ISBN 978-1-911628-16-3)*

No 24 *The Lilies and the Thistle. French Troops in the Jacobite '45* Andrew Bamford (ISBN 978-1-911628-17-0)*

No 25 *A Light Infantryman With Wellington* Gareth Glover (ed.) (ISBN 978-1-911628-10-1)

No 26 *Swiss Regiments in the Service of France 1798-1815. Uniforms, Organisation, Campaigns* Stephen Ede-Borrett (ISBN 978-1-911628-12-5)*

No 27 *For Orange and the States! The Army of the Dutch Republic 1713-1772. Part II: Cavalry and Specialist Troops* Marc Geerdinck-Schaftenaar (ISBN 978-1-911628-13-2)*

No 28 *Fashioning Regulation, Regulating Fashion. Uniforms and Dress of the British Army 1800-1815 Volume I* Ben Townsend (ISBN 978-1-911628-09-5)

No 29 *Riflemen. The History of the 5th Battalion 60th (Royal American) Regiment, 1797-1818* Robert Griffith (ISBN 978-1-911628-46-0)

No 30 *The Key to Lisbon. The Third French Invasion of Portugal, 1810-11* Kenton White (ISBN 978-1-911628-52-1)

No 31 *Command and Leadership. Proceedings of the 2018 Helion & Company 'From Reason to Revolution' Conference* Andrew Bamford (ed.) (ISBN 978-1-911628-53-8)

No 32 *Waterloo After the Glory. Hospital Sketches and Reports on the Wounded After the Battle* Michael Crumplin and Gareth Glover (ISBN 978-1-911628-48-4)

No 33 *Fluxes, Fevers, and Fighting Men. War and Disease in Ancien Regime Europe 1648-1789* Pádraig Lenihan (ISBN 978-1-911628-51-4)

No 34 *'They Were Good Soldiers'. African-Americans Serving in the Continental Army, 1775-1783* John U. Rees (ISBN 978-1-911628-54-5)*

No 35 *A Redcoat in America. The Diaries of Lieutenant William Bamford, 1757-1765 and 1776* Edited and Annotated by John B. Hattendorf (ISBN 978-1-911628-47-7)

No 36 *Between Scylla and Charybdis: The Army of Friedrich August II of Saxony, 1733-1763. Part II: Infantry and Artillery* Marco Pagan (ISBN 978-1-911628-08-8)*

No 37 *Québec Under Siege: French Eye-Witness Accounts from the Campaign of 1759* Translated and Annotated by Charles A. Mayhood (ISBN 978-1-912866-73-1)

No 38 *King George's Hangman: Henry Hawley and the Battle of Falkirk 1746* Jonathan D. Oates (ISBN 978-1-912866-64-9)

No 39 *Zweybruken in Command: The Reichsarmee in the Campaign of 1758* Translated with additional materials by Neil Cogswell (ISBN 978-1-911628-55-2)*

No 40 *So Bloody a Day: The 16th Light Dragoons in the Waterloo Campaign* David J. Blackmore (ISBN 978-1-912866-66-3)

No 41 *Northern Tars in Southern Waters: The Russian Fleet in the Mediterranean 1806-1810* Vladimir Bogdanovich Bronevskiy, translated and annotated by Darrin Boland (ISBN 978-1-912866-71-7)

No 42 *Royal Navy Officers of the Seven Years War: A Biographical Dictionary of Commissioned Officers 1748-1763* Cy Harrison (ISBN 978-1-912866-68-7)

No 43 *All at Sea. Naval Support for the British Army During the American Revolutionary War* John Dillon (ISBN 978-1-912866-67-0)

No 44 *Glory is Fleeting. New Scholarship on the Napoleonic Wars* Andrew Bamford (ed.) (ISBN 978-1-912866-69-4)

No 45 *Fashioning Regulation, Regulating Fashion. Uniforms and Dress of the British Army 1800-1815 Volume II* Ben Townsend (ISBN 978-1-911628-45-3)

No 46 *Revenge in the Name of Honour. The Royal Navy's Quest for Vengeance in the Single Ship Actions of the War of 1812* Nicholas James Kaizer (ISBN 978-1-912866-72-4)*

No 47 *They Fought With Extraordinary Bravery. The III German (Saxon) Army Corps in the Southern Netherlands 1814* Geert van Uythoven (ISBN 978-1-912866-65-6)*

No 48 *The Danish Army of the Napoleonic Wars 1807-1814, Organisation, Uniforms & Equipment: Volume 1: High Command, Line and Light Infantry* David Wilson (ISBN 978-1-913118-91-4) (large-format paperback)

No 49 *Neither Up Nor Down: The British Army and the Flanders Campaign 1793-1895* Phillip Ball (ISBN 978-1-913118-90-7)

No 50 *Guerra Fantastica: The Portuguese Army and the Seven Years War* António Barrento (ISBN 978-1-911628-11-8)*

No 51 *From Across the Sea: North Americans in Nelson's Navy* Sean M. Heuvel and John A. Rodgaard (eds) (ISBN 978-1-913118-92-1)

No 52 *Rebellious Scots to Crush: The Military Response to the Jacobite '45* Andrew Bamford (ed.) (ISBN 978-1-912866-74-8)

No 53 *The Army of George II 1727-1760: The Soldiers who Forged an Empire* Peter Brown (ISBN 978-1-913118-96-9)*

No 54 *Wellington at Bay: The Battle of Villamuriel, 25 October 1812* Garry David Wills (ISBN 978-1-913118-95-2)*

No 55 *Life in the Red Coat: The British Soldier 1721-1815. Proceedings of the 2019 Helion & Company 'From Reason to Revolution' Conference* Andrew Bamford (ed.) (ISBN 978-1-913118-94-5)

No 56 *Wellington's Favourite Engineer. John Burgoyne: Operations, Engineering, and the Making of a Field Marshal* Mark S. Thompson (ISBN 978-1-913118-93-8)

* indicates 'Falconet' format paperbacks, page size 248mm x 180 mm, with high visual content including colour plates; other titles are monographs unless otherwise noted.